# OUT OF THE
# WILDERNESS

**Escaping My Father's Prison
and My Journey to Forgiveness**

# ELISHABA DOERKSEN
## WITH MIKE YORKEY

**C◯RE**

# PRAISE FOR *OUT OF THE WILDERNESS*

"Back in 2004, I was a cub reporter at *The Reflector* newspaper in southwest Washington State, and Robert Hale and his family came to town from Alaska. Their son, Abraham, needed medical attention at a larger hospital in Portland after nearly losing a finger in an accident. I wrote about a series of bluegrass concerts that Hale and the Pilgrim Minstrels band gave throughout the area to raise money to cover the medical bills.

"When I interviewed 'Papa Pilgrim,' he came across as exactingly polite, but once in a while, he said something to his children that came out quite sharply. Little did I know of the horror and oppressive mandates he had placed on his family. In my article, I quoted one line from Elishaba, who was then twenty-eight, a line that in hindsight is both frightening and heartbreaking—'I can't think of a better life.'

"A courageous, disturbing, and ultimately redemptive book, Elishaba's story will shake you to the core."
**—Marcus Brotherton, bestselling author of *Blaze of Light***

"This may be the most dramatic survival story I've ever read. Yes, there's abuse and pain in these pages, but most of all, *Out of the Wilderness* is an extraordinary portrait of endurance and the power of forgiveness to heal and bring lasting freedom. This is just the story the world needs right now."
**—Leslie Leyland Fields, author of *Your Story Matters* and *Surviving the Island of Grace: Life on the Wild Edge of America***

"Elishaba's story is an extraordinary one of survival, faith, and salvation. It's incredibly captivating and serves as an example of the power of the human spirit to overcome even the most savage of experiences. *Out of the Wilderness* has all the ingredients of a gripping documentary or feature film."
**—Bill Katz, executive producer at Espiritus Productions**

"The Hales became famous as the Pilgrim family during my term as Lieutenant Governor of the State of Alaska. Their fifteen beautiful, talented, and well-behaved children caught our attention and touched our hearts. Patriarch Robert Hale's fight with the federal government over access to their remote

Alaska property, an in-holding in Wrangell-St Elias National Park and Preserve, was inspiring to many freedom-loving Alaskans. Only later did we learn that the wholesome family image promoted by Hale, who fancied himself as Papa Pilgrim, was a façade.

"As the father of two girls (and a boy), I find it hard to understand how a father could be so demented—and downright evil toward his daughter. I found *Out of the Wilderness* hard to put down and stayed up far too late one night to finish it. I compare Elishaba's will to live and survive her torturous prison comparable to stories I have read from survivors of the Holocaust.

"*Out of the Wilderness* is perhaps the most riveting story of human endurance, redemption, and forgiveness I have ever read. There will be many who need to read her story and pursue their own journey toward redemption, forgiveness, and true freedom."

**—Loren Leman, former Alaska legislator and Lieutenant Governor of the State of Alaska from 2002-2006**

"Years ago, after Elishaba's story had been all over the news, I asked her if she would come speak at a women's event. Feeling exposed enough already, she didn't want to come. And then one day, she called back and said she would tell her powerful story, which is told in greater detail in *Out of the Wilderness* and told so well. Elishaba has brought clarity to my own calling to fight trafficking. I cannot think of a better representation of the power of Jesus Christ. Out of utter darkness, Elishaba has emerged as a bright light of hope to everyone around her."

**—Gwen Adams, founder and Executive Director of Priceless, an organization that fights sex trafficking in Alaska**

"As the co-author of a book about a man who harbored a secret that nobody knew—being sexually abused as a child by a Catholic priest—I have a good understanding of the courage it takes to come forward and share your story of trauma and hardship with the world. Elishaba Doerksen is to be saluted for her vulnerability in lifting the veil of what sexual and physical abuse really looks like."

**—Bob Welch, co-author of *Boy in the Mirror: An Athletic Director's Struggle to Survive Sexual Abuse as a Child***

"With *Out of the Wilderness*, we have an incredible story of resiliency. In fact, something far beyond resiliency. Elishaba's years of horrid abuse—and safety lost from the very people who should have been her protectors—would leave common individuals thoroughly broken and faithless. Elishaba, however, is anything but common.

"This book is her stunning journey in overcoming. Psychologists would count her among what are called 'super survivors,' those rare individuals that not only have endured enormous trauma but then go forward to do great things. This compelling story, and the long journey of healing from atrocious wrongs committed against her, required enormous courage and faith to tell. Elishaba has all that, and more."

—**Stuart McDowell, a retired educational psychologist in Pacific Grove, California**

"I speak from the perspective of a father whose eleven-year-old daughter, Mandy Lemaire, was abducted, raped, and murdered in 1991 in our hometown of Tazlina, Alaska. The heartache and suffering that our family has dealt with for three decades can never be described.

"*Out of the Wilderness* will give you a glimpse of what our family went through. I was deeply moved by Elishaba's story—a story of pain and trauma inflicted by a father who should have been her protector. She and I have walked through completely different valleys, but her tale about her journey out of the wilderness of bitterness to healing and faith in God is a place I pray that every victim of a horrible crime can come to."

—**Dave Lemaire, a reader in Tazlina, Alaska**

"*Out of the Wilderness* is easily the most shocking book I have ever read. As a dad of four wonderful daughters, I cannot comprehend the depths of depravity that Robert Hale inflicted on Elishaba and her family for decades. If you're like me, you will wince, shed tears, and want to jump off your couch screaming, 'No!' as you read this horrifying account. Yet in the end, after discovering the miraculous work of redemption that God did in Elishaba's life, you'll also offer a prayer of thanks for this incredibly courageous woman and the transforming peace that is available to us all."

—**Joshua Cooley, *New York Times* bestselling author whose dozen books includes *Creator, Father, King: A One Year Journey With God***

"Sitting across from Elishaba, you would never know the pain, the anguish, and the absolute injustice of her upbringing. Her eyes, body language, tone of voice, and demeanor all communicate true peace and genuine joy.

"Having worked in the field of anti-child sex trafficking for some time, across several continents and with over a dozen different organizations, I can say that I have never seen someone come out the other side of something like this with such a genuine, beautiful faith. Elishaba is not just a survivor. She is truly an inspiration and a reason for all of us to fight injustice with everything we have."

—**Leigh S., member of an anti-child sex trafficking organization**

"I'm amazed at how Elishaba's story is embodied in the photo on the cover. Elishaba has a desperate look on her face, but if you look closer, you will notice the sunlight embraces half of her face and the other half is cast in shadow. As we turn toward the Son, He illuminates and brings healing, reflecting His glory."
**—Laura McHenry, Women's Ministry Leader at Lazy Mountain Bible Church in Palmer, Alaska**

"Over the past few years, I've been privileged to journey alongside Elishaba and hear her story. I was struck by how even as a young girl, Elishaba talked and cried out to God. While Papa Pilgrim used God's Word to justify his purposes, God quietly used His Word to reveal Himself to Elishaba. The Lord also gave her a fantastic ability to remember Scripture. These nuggets helped sustain her until one day she could finally sort out enough truth from the lies and manipulation she had grown up with to realize she couldn't go on living that way.

"God has led Elishaba on a long journey toward healing. We all have our own stories, and I pray that *Out of the Wilderness* challenges you to look at yours."
**—Debbie Kenny, Heart Care Director (retired) with Lazy Mountain Bible Church in Palmer, Alaska**

"*Out of the Wilderness* is a gritty tale of bravery and determination that will haunt readers, as it did for me. Ultimately, this is a true story of one family's battle to escape the evil in their lives while clinging to the binding ties of family loyalty. Elishaba's story—brutally honest in its portrayal—is one that must be told. From the first page, you will be compelled to finish."
**—Brenda Davila, a pediatric nurse at Providence Alaska Medical Center in Anchorage, Alaska**

"Elishaba's horrific account of her growing-up years—years that should have been filled with the joy and laughter of childhood—is tragic and true. I can say that because it's my distinct honor to call Elishaba my niece. She and her siblings did not experience anything close to resembling a normal and loving family. But her faith was so big that it could not be squelched by the evil of a man who was not a 'dad' but a harsh and cruel tyrant. Thank you, Elishaba, for sharing your story with the world."
**—Becky Speckels Hare, a reader from Kansas City, Missouri**

"*Out of the Wilderness* delivers the most intense story of survival and faith I have ever read. The raw, honest telling of physical and emotional abuse sheds a bright light into the darkness, lighting up the path towards healing and thriving. Elishaba, you are an inspiration beyond measure!"
**—Tina M. Hall, a reader from Sterling, Alaska**

"After reading Tom Kizzia's book *Pilgrim's Wilderness*, we were struck by Elishaba's part of the story, so we prayed that we would have a chance to meet her one day. The next thing you know, she was signed up to come to a conference that we were hosting at our ministry. Her family stayed at our house for ten days.

"As we began hearing more of her story and simultaneously watching her pour into the lives of others, we were in awe of how far God had brought her through some very tough times. We've often heard the saying, 'hurt people hurt people,' but Elishaba shows us how 'hurt people can heal people.' Elishaba didn't allow her wounds to dictate her future. Instead, she's a beacon of hope, showing that people don't have to live as victims."

**—Andrew and Megan Rowland, conference coordinators at the Tanalian Leadership Center in Port Alsworth, Alaska**

"*Out of the Wilderness* is difficult to read but clearly shows God's mercy and grace. Elishaba's father was evil and appalling, but her faith kept her alive. She is a testimony to what God can do and should give hope to many."

**—Linda Ross, a leader with Hearts Growing Towards Wellness in Anchorage, Alaska**

"One of the most interesting books I have ever read . . . the huge family, a peculiar lifestyle. Some portions were hard to read, but the suspense and exciting parts made it very hard to put down. Elishaba is a remarkably courageous young lady whose tenacious faith helped her overcome an incredibly abusive environment. Her story will give hope to those in the direst of circumstances."

**—Janice Chiu-Kikta, information management consultant (retired) from Encinitas, California**

"It's rare to find people who have been through the depth of abuse and suffering Elishaba has and use their experience to help others find God. When abused, the normal human experience is to either bury the pain using coping mechanisms, which further destroys a person, or to live in a state of anger, which leads to the abuse of others. My friend Elishaba shows us how to avoid these extremes as she explains how God's truth set her free and ultimately gave her the freedom to forgive. *Out of the Wilderness* will change people's lives."

**—Jason Daughtry, Pastor of Lazy Mountain Bible Church in Palmer, Alaska**

"I first met Elishaba in 2015 when she and her family came to Australia to visit my dad, Geoff, after he'd spent time with them in Alaska. As I got to know her, I quickly realized that one of Elishaba's greatest desires was to be 'real.' When we talked, she didn't try to sanitize the unsanitary or shy away from the hard conversations. Despite everything she'd been through, I could see she was willing to be open and vulnerable.

"In the times Elishaba and I spent together, we didn't actually talk much about her story. The focus was on more immediate issues. She wanted to discuss how to be a godly wife and mother, how to be fully relational, and how to share her heart best to meet others where they were at.

"That said, reading *Out of the Wilderness* was quite an eye opener. But what I really love is how Elishaba refuses to let her past define her—she lets God define her. Throughout her story, God's unwavering love and commitment to the purified and beautiful daughter He has adopted as His own shines through."

**—Fiona Beavan from Nowra, New South Wales, Australia**

"Elishaba's harrowing account of her first thirty years enlightens the reader on the many ways a perpetrator uses manipulation and fear to control a person or an entire family. The damage can often be covered up or underplayed since that is part of how it's all accomplished. I pray that *Out of the Wilderness* brings hope, inspiration, and subsequent healing to those still carrying their silent painful load."

**—Debbie Rowland, a reader in Palmer, Alaska**

"After reading *Out of the Wilderness*, I'm astounded by what Elishaba Doerksen had to endure with a self-serving earthly father, but it's because she kept her eyes on her heavenly Father. Her blunt and plain-spoken portrayal is bound to raise a sensitivity in all of us to prevent other victims from going through what Elishaba experienced. I believe many readers will be hugging their children tighter and appreciating the many small blessings in their lives. I could not come away from her story without prioritizing these choices in my life."

**—Jim Barnes, a part-time schoolteacher from Visalia, California**

"There is an intensity to *Out of the Wilderness* that kept me turning pages. The danger, the set-up for entrapment, the unspeakable evil. I found myself weeping for this battered and lost little girl.

"I'm pleased to call Elishaba a friend and have watched her transform into a godly woman of significance who replaced debilitating fear with God's love, peace, and reason."

**—Lydia Wood, a friend and neighbor from Palmer, Alaska**

"Elishaba's family came to visit our home in Plano, Texas, when I was a college student and she was ten years old. As both families stood around the piano that night singing hymns, I had no idea what she and her siblings were experiencing at the hands of their earthly father behind closed doors. It would be two decades later before the truth of her abuse and suffering was revealed.

"Elishaba's story is difficult to read at times, but God has turned her painful past into a powerful testimony of healing and forgiveness. *Out of the Wilderness* conveys the darkness Elishaba endured but also demonstrates the restoration and beauty possible through God's grace and love."
**—Melissa Hatfield, a cousin of Elishaba Doerksen and second-grade teacher in Fort Worth, Texas**

"When Elishaba and her family visited Australia in 2015, she shared her story with us. But in reading *Out of the Wilderness*, I realized I'd heard maybe only a quarter of it. Her redemption was possible as she traveled the journey of forgiving one who didn't deserve it—as none of us do!"
**—Mary Richards, former missionary with the Indian Missionary Society in India and currently living in Nowra, New South Wales, Australia**

"As a police officer of twenty-nine years who was also a crime scene specialist, I needed no reminder of the evil and depravity that people are capable of, and yet I was still shocked to learn the extent of Robert Hale's controlling influence on Elishaba and her mother and siblings.

"I met Robert several times when he visited family in Texas, and I remember how he wanted to argue with my mother (his cousin) over Scripture verses and their meaning. His very presence unsettled me; there was something 'off' about his eyes and manner.

"*Out of the Wilderness* was difficult to read and difficult to put down to do other things. I respect my second cousin Elishaba more than I did already, both for her willingness to share her story, and for her faith in God's strength to help her survive."
**—Larry Marx, a police officer in Hurst, Texas, and a resident of Fort Worth, Texas**

"Like a classic fairy tale gone wrong, this story has a remote kingdom with a mysterious iconic ruler and lurking evil. A gripping tale of abuse, courage, escape, rescue, and an amazing refuge of healing. A story that could only happen in bush Alaska. It will grip your heart, build your faith, and add a new list of heroes."
**—Fred Dyson, a former Alaska state senator who was instrumental in legislation addressing abuse and protecting the vulnerable**

*Out of the Wilderness: Escaping My Father's Prison and My Journey to Forgiveness*
by Elishaba Doerksen with Mike Yorkey

**For bulk purchases of *Out of the Wilderness*, please call or text Matthew Doerksen at 907-315-1321 or contact him through elishaba.com.**

# TABLE OF CONTENTS

# FOREWORD
## by Tom Kizzia

The first time I met Elishaba Hale, she was up on top of a horse and wouldn't get down. Elishaba and two of her brothers were guiding me and a photographer over a wilderness trail to their family compound in the mountains of Alaska. By lunchtime, I was horseback sore and ready for a break, but Elishaba declared she was most comfortable in a saddle and preferred to eat her sandwich up there. After she was done eating, she smiled and hooked her boots in the stirrups and leaned back for a short nap. I was left to conclude that twenty-seven years of growing up in complete isolation had made her a remarkable cowgirl—and also maybe a bit cuckoo.

Years later, I learned the truth: her father had forbidden his terrorized daughter from getting down off her horse in the presence of the stranger from the city.

I had come to the Wrangell Mountains to write for my newspaper about Papa Pilgrim's war with the federal government, touched off by his decision to run a bulldozer over this fourteen-mile route through Wrangell-St. Elias National Park. After a night at the homestead, however, the land-rights dispute receded into the background. Something strange and deeply troubling was going on at the place they called "Hillbilly Heaven."

It would be another two years before Elishaba and her sister attempted their dramatic escape. Finally, the real story of Papa Pilgrim began to emerge. I wrote about the criminal prosecution of Robert Hale, as I had covered his political battles, and when it was all over, dazzled by the bravery of Elishaba and her siblings, and by the sincerity of their struggle to find grace and forgiveness, I told their story in my book, *Pilgrim's Wilderness*.

I could not have written a bestselling book if Elishaba had not shared with me the nearly unbelievable facts of her upbringing. She impressed me then

13

with her clear-eyed recollection, and even more in the years that followed, as she fought her way to a happy family life, and then as she put the horrors she experienced to use in the service of others, counseling abuse victims and in particular women who had suffered under a despotic patriarchy justified by religion. All while holding on to her own deep Christian faith. I say this as a nonbeliever. Very impressive.

Now, at last, Elishaba has accomplished what to this writer is the most impressive thing of all. The cowgirl who grew up without books and reading has written her own story. This is a terrific act of redemption, but brace yourself: it is an honest, unrelenting book, filled with unflinching scenes of psychological torment—a father's vile but fascinating manipulation of family and outsiders, a child's searing sense of guilt and isolation, and episodes of appalling violence and sexual assault (I may never be able to go into a laundromat again without thinking of these chapters).

Readers new to this story may wonder if this could really be true? I am here to tell you, as the journalist who tracked down many of the witnesses to this or that part of the story, in Alaska and New Mexico and Texas, that yes, this really happened. The most shocking scenes of all, appearing here for the first time, take place between two people alone—the daughter, struggling with her sense of duty to God and family, and the father she was forced to call "lord," a title she renders in print today with a lower-case letter, though clearly capitalized in the roaring hellscape of Papa Pilgrim's mind.

And yet there is a faint sense of wonder and hope that pulls the reader forward. Elishaba's dedicated co-author, the professional writer Mike Yorkey, has worked to keep the narrative flowing without losing her distinctive storytelling twang. Together they bring us into the sunshine of the present, describing Elishaba's complicated feelings about the large Christian family that reached out to save her family, her own efforts to reconcile with her mother, her unexpected courtship and marriage, and her struggle to free herself from the burdens of the past.

Every good memoir takes us on a journey toward understanding, but rarely has a writer led us through a wilderness as dark as Hillbilly Heaven. Hold onto your saddle. She delivers us, at long last, into the light.

*Tom Kizzia is the author of* Pilgrim's Wilderness, The Wake of the Unseen Object, *and his latest book,* Cold Mountain Path: The Ghost Town Decades of McCarthy-Kennecott, Alaska. *He was a reporter for the* Anchorage Daily News *for twenty-five years.*

# A NOTE TO THE READER
## from Elishaba Doerksen

What you are about to read is a true story. *Out of the Wilderness* is based upon my memories, stories my parents and siblings told me, and research. It's real, it's raw, and it's redemptive.

While parts of my story are sexually graphic, it's not my intention to cause offense to anyone. Beyond that, my greater hope is that by being frank with the depths of evil that I grew up with, the reader will see more clearly the tangled mess of relational dynamics surrounding abuse. Furthermore, it's my heartfelt desire that the reader will realize that there is hope, healing, and growth for anyone who has experienced the trauma of sexual and physical abuse.

# PART I

---

# THE ESCAPE

# 1

# A SLICE OF HILLBILLY HEAVEN

Locals say we have five seasons in Alaska: summer, fall, winter, spring, and breakup.

The breakup season is short, usually a few weeks in April. As the days grow longer and the bears come out of hibernation, deep drifts of snowmelt and river ice break up, making crossings treacherous on snow machines or by foot.

It was the snow-shrouded and ice-covered McCarthy Creek near our homestead that gave me worry on an April day in 2005, as I'll explain shortly. I was twenty-nine years old, the oldest of fifteen children born to Papa Pilgrim and Country Rose, living the pioneer life on a private parcel inside mountainous Wrangell-St. Elias National Park and Preserve, set in eastern Alaska and bordering Canada. With 13 million acres of some of the most pristine wilderness on earth, Wrangell-St. Elias was America's largest national park, the size of Yellowstone National Park, Yosemite National Park, and the country of Switzerland combined.

Our property—which had been the site of an old copper ore mine called "The Mother Lode" during its heyday one hundred years earlier—contained several buildings, including the Main House, a twelve-hundred-square-foot home constructed in bits and pieces by the previous owner, Walt Wigger.

Wigger had been an old pioneer with dreams of striking it rich by finding another massive vein of copper ore at the Mother Lode, but that never happened. When he reached his early eighties, he decided it was time to let go of his dream and sell his 420-acre parcel to our family. So, in 2002, we moved into Main House—all seventeen of us—which was primarily unfinished and without electricity or running water.

Our family got to work fixing up the place. A barrel stove in the living area kept us warm, and Mama, my sisters, and I cooked on a wood-fired stove in the kitchen. A gas generator in a nearby shed provided light in the evenings and electrified our kitchen appliances and power tools. For water, one of our daily chores was filling plastic containers with pristine water from nearby Diamond Creek and hauling them into the Main House.

Elsewhere on the property, there was a workshop, a bathhouse, and two small cabins that my siblings and I had fixed up. One was a tiny shack that Papa had us girls fix up, named "Happy Cabin." Miners used to sleep there during Mother Lode's mining days. The other was a cabin that my siblings and I built, called the "Peace Cabin."

Despite its primitive nature, Papa called our property "Hillbilly Heaven." This is how he envisioned life for our family—unencumbered by "stuff" and as far away from godless civilization as possible. "We are in the world but not of the world," he preached a million times. "The world hates us because our deeds are godly, but if you don't stand with me, you'll be just like them, condemned to damnation."

Woe to anyone who didn't stand with Papa—or who crossed him in any way. We weren't allowed to speak up, talk back, or disobey his commands. If we did, we were in rebellion, and he was duty-bound to set us straight. He was the family's patriarch, ordained by God to run our lives and shield us from the world's evil ways.

That's why we lived by ourselves—and under his thumb—in a deserted Alaskan valley, tucked away in the heart of this vast and unpopulated Alaskan national park. Our off-the-beaten-path homestead was fourteen miles from the nearest town, McCarthy, population forty-two—and that count included the seventeen members of my family.

Surviving the elements was a full-time job. For food and fuel, we had to drive a couple of our old trucks—that we kept parked in McCarthy—all the way to Anchorage, a six-hundred-mile round trip. While in Alaska's largest city (population 275,000), we'd storm a Costco and fill a dozen shopping carts with bags of flour, sacks of potatoes, packages of beans, crates of eggs, twenty-five-pound bags of sugar, large boxes of rice and cornmeal, and necessary cooking items—butter, oil, and the like. We couldn't buy much meat or any dairy products since we had no refrigeration at the homestead. For protein, we hunted local game and ate moose, caribou, bear, Dall sheep, and mountain goats. Each fall, we harvested salmon at a fish camp in Chitina, sixty miles away, where we canned our catch for the long winter ahead.

While in Anchorage, we filled several 55-gallon fuel drums with gasoline, which we kept at our storage shed in McCarthy. Then we'd offload fuel into a smaller drum for transport to Hillbilly Heaven via a sled hooked up to one of our snowmobiles—which we call snow machines in Alaska. In the summer, the only way to get fuel and food to the homestead was by horseback or by bush plane, an expensive proposition.

No matter what the season, fuel was vital for our existence. During our long winters, we needed fuel to fire up the generator and keep the snow machines gassed up to maintain our supply route to McCarthy.

My siblings and I had been living this way all our lives. It's all we knew. Whenever we went down the valley to McCarthy or elsewhere in Alaska, Papa forbid us from anything more than superficial contact with outsiders. My sisters and I could not look any males in the eyes nor speak to them, even at Costco. We had to remain mute among strangers.

Or risk a reprimand from Papa Pilgrim.

On this spring morning in April, I was cutting fresh lumber on our portable sawmill, under brilliant sunshine. Several of my siblings helped me get the heavy logs into position, clamp them down, and then steadily push the saw carriage along the length of the log, using a feed bar. We were sawing lumber into 2x4s, 4x6s, and 6x6s to use on the property.

There was talk among the family about building a bed-and-breakfast where tourists could experience the Alaskan wilderness with wagon outings and horseback rides because we could always use the cash. During the summer months, we hustled vacationing families visiting McCarthy for wagon rides (we kept a couple of horses in town). In addition, my brothers were excellent bush guides during the fall hunting and fishing seasons. Truth be known, though, we mainly subsisted on government assistance—welfare, food stamps—and the Alaska Permanent Fund Dividend money that every resident received just for living in the 49th state. The PFD amount was $919 per person the previous year, which added up for a family of seventeen.

On this April morning, Papa left the Main House to inspect our work with a mug of coffee in his right hand. Dressed in blue denim pants smudged with dirt, a button-down western shirt, and bundled up against the chilly spring day with a heavy, fur-lined jacket, my wizened father looked like he could have mined for riches a century earlier. A straggly white beard with streaks of gray hid his wrinkled features and ran down to his chest, and long strands of white hair tumbled to his shoulders from underneath a floppy-brimmed hat. He looked older than his sixty-four years, but I didn't have much experience with people aging since I wasn't around older people very much.

Papa Pilgrim was constantly checking on us, making sure we were productive. But something else was weighing heavily on his mind: the revolt of five brothers a month earlier. Joseph, Joshua, David, Moses, and Israel had all taken off— it's hard to describe them as runaways since they were legally adults—because they couldn't take my father's abuse and autocratic ways any longer. Their last confrontation began when Joseph challenged Papa inside the Main House.

"We all want to hear from you why Elishaba looks so beat-up," Joseph demanded.[1]

My brother, the second oldest after me, wasn't exaggerating. I looked like I had received a thorough thrashing. My face was a mess of purple splotches, and my arms were black and blue from deflecting Papa's blows. I appreciated how Joseph had my back. Beatings were a regular occurrence for me and often for my brothers.

Papa turned and glared at his son. "Elishaba will tell you why she looks the way she does," he replied curtly.

Joseph and I both knew that Papa wouldn't have said this if he wasn't sure that I'd answer favorably, something along the lines of, *I disobeyed Papa and deserved what I got.*

But that wouldn't be the truth, so I hesitated.

"Well, come on, Elishaba," my father urged.

I stayed quiet, still unsure if this was my moment to stand up to him.

Misinterpreting my silence, Papa raised himself from his chair and got in my face. "Oh, so whose side are you on?" he asked sharply. "You're not going to start this up again, are you? Maybe you didn't get enough."

I lowered my eyes and shivered in fear.

Joseph quickly came to my side. "No, I don't want to hear from Elishaba. I'm asking *you* to tell me what happened."

At first, I was relieved not to answer, but now I feared for Joseph's safety.

"Get out, right now!" my father ordered. "Just get out of my sight."

Joseph was used to being banished from my father's sight; he and Papa had been at loggerheads for years. The oldest of my brothers grabbed a jacket and a brown felt hat and was out of the cabin in a flash. He didn't have many options out in the wilderness: I figured he would crash that night in the Peace Cabin, which seemed ironic.

Papa Pilgrim turned to the rest of us and commanded attention. "Just as I've told you before, you're to never listen to Joseph. He is a rebellious son and deserves to be stoned."

I knew my father meant that literally.

Unexpectedly, Joshua spoke up in his brother's defense. "Papa, you're the most deceitful man I know."

This outburst stunned my father, who advanced on my brother. "So, you just called me a liar, huh?"

I knew Papa was getting ready to unload on Joshua, so I jumped in between

---

1. My name is pronounced *eh-LISH-uh-buh.*

them before my father threw the first punch. But Joshua outstretched his right arm to keep me away. "No, Elishaba. I don't need you to defend me."

Too late. In a flash, Papa nailed Joshua with a right hook that landed square on his nose. The reverberation of crunching cartilage sounded horrible. Joshua dropped to the floor like a sack of flour; I could see that his nose was bleeding profusely.

"Get out of my sight!" my father demanded. "You're no better than that rebellious brother of yours!"

After gathering himself, Joshua slunk off and opened the front door, which he slammed upon his departure. He stayed with Joseph in the Peace Cabin.[2]

For several weeks, my brothers talked about how it was apparent that Papa would never change. Finally, they decided to make a run for it. After everyone was asleep one night, Joseph, Joshua, David, and Moses snuck off after pushing a couple of snow machines down the trail until they were far enough away to fire up their machines without being heard. They had told me they were planning an escape, so I slipped Joseph a fresh loaf of bread without Papa catching on. Israel didn't join them that night, but he, too, took off a few days after that. My brothers knew a couple of families down valley where they could crash and decide what to do next.

The absence of five strong adult men—and all the help they were around the homestead—put Papa on edge. Physical outbursts came out of nowhere, and since I was on the receiving end of most of his slaps and punches, I became his whipping boy. He was used to taking out his frustrations on me. Our complicated relationship was a truth he tried to hide from the others, but he wasn't doing a good job of it.

Now my brothers' escape was eating away at my father. Whenever Papa ranted and railed against their betrayal, the little ones whimpered and flocked to Mama and me. We'd gather them close to our pioneer skirts, which ran from our hips to the top of our snow boots. All of Papa Pilgrim's women and girls were ordered to wear full-length prairie skirts in cotton calico for modesty reasons.

As I gathered my sisters to my side, a powerful thought wouldn't leave me: *Could I, like my brothers, escape on a snow machine before Alaska's breakup season was over?*

---

2. Joshua would later learn that his nose had been broken.

# 2
# SLEEPING ARRANGEMENTS

As April turned warm and the reality of losing my brothers "to the world" took hold, my mother and I did our best to stay away from Papa and his black moods.

That wasn't easy living in what was essentially an open-concept cabin with a small office, tiny bedroom, and pantry. In the main room, an assortment of couches and chairs filled the living space, along with a dining room table and long benches that could seat most of the family if we squeezed all together.

Part of the main living space included a large bed frame raised four feet off the ground, where a couple of large foam mattresses were surrounded by curtains that were four feet tall, supposedly for privacy reasons. My parents slept in that bed, but so did I, along with a couple of preschool-age children. My siblings sacked out on couches or the floor in sleeping bags, but there was also a back room where several of my sisters slept.

As our family got ready for bed that night, I dreaded what would happen next. I hated this part. I knew what he wanted. My father wanted me to rub his feet, then his hands, then his legs, and then to pleasure him. Sometimes it was a

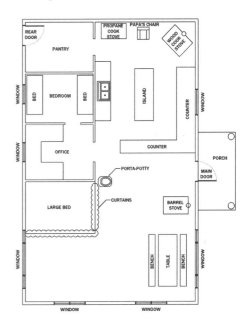

lot more than that if my father thought everyone else was asleep. I'd been doing this since I was nineteen and was sick of it. After seeing my brothers stand up to my father, though, I felt emboldened.

"Papa, I can't go to bed with you. I believe it is wrong for a daughter to sleep with her father."

Now it was my father's turn to be surprised.

"Elishaba, have you become persuaded by the world too? Are you going to throw out all I have ever thought of you? You will destroy this family and lead them all astray. I have told you that you are responsible, and you have been given so much. 'To whom much has been given, much is required.' Likewise, if you don't hold to my teachings, you will be doubly responsible, and God will hold you accountable for not only your actions but all your siblings who will follow you."

If my father wanted me to feel guilty for the thousandth time, he succeeded. When Papa spoke like this, he sounded like an Old Testament prophet. I felt lost for words or a way to describe what my heart was telling me—that it was wrong for me to be in a sexual relationship with my father.

"Papa, I don't know what to say anymore. All I know is that God tells you to be faithful to Mama, and I can't find it in the Bible where Jesus permits you to treat me like a second wife."

My words of desperation felt like they disappeared into the nearby darkness. A couple of low-wattage lamps illuminated the main room.

My father cornered me in the kitchen area. "I've gone through 1 Corinthians 7, verses 36 and 37, a million times with you, where it says a father can 'keep his own virgin,' but your heart is hardened and your neck is as stiff as the people of Israel were toward their God," he said.

It was unbearable to hear these words. I wanted to be found worthy in God's eyes, but Papa made it sound like I was disobeying God's will for my life if I didn't sleep with him. I had been living this way for so long—a good ten years—that I could see no way out.

I braced myself on the wooden island and felt chills ripple through my body. My body physically shook, causing me to lean toward the wood-fired stove to soak up some heat. But I also sensed this was a watershed moment for me. If I didn't fulfill my father's demands this evening, it would be easier to say no to him the following night.

Papa must have sensed the same thing. "Elishaba, tell me this. Do you love me?"

Inside, my thoughts flashed before me. Was my father springing another one of his traps? I knew I had to choose my words carefully.

"Papa, you know that I love you." I figured this was my safest response—or one that wouldn't result in a beatdown.

"Then feed my sheep."

Papa was repeating Jesus' words to the apostle Peter when He appeared to the disciples after the Resurrection, when the Lord asked Peter if he loved Him. To my father, *Feed my sheep* meant that I was to take care of him—one of God's sheep—and, by extension, our family.

"Yes, Papa, I want to do that, but can I move into one of the little cabins and serve the family that way?"

My father and I knew what I was really asking: *Can I sleep in another cabin so I don't have to service your sexual needs?*

My father took a step closer and slapped me across the face. "You fool. Don't mock me. Do you want to keep that up?" He held his right fist tightly against my face.

I didn't care anymore. Even if he killed me, I was so done. But my father wasn't going to let me go without a fight. He was relentless in keeping me to himself.

"You better answer me," he began, "because I believe you are lying. Otherwise, why did you tell me you want me and that you love me? No girl would give the way you have given to me unless she meant it."

"Papa, I've done these things to save the family. You told me you would be happy with us all and that you wouldn't be angry if I did what you wanted."

This time, I never saw the punch that knocked me to the floor. As I struggled to find my feet, I felt the stinging lash of his braided whip against my back. I screamed out in pain. There were more lashes on my back, then my legs. I knew no one would come to my rescue. If my mother or any of my siblings sought to help me, they would have smarted from the lash as well. They were all down for the night, listening to my pleading cries with their eyes shut.

In this moment of desperate pain, I cried out, "Papa! Please! You know that I love you. I will never be able to love anyone else because I have given everything to you."

My answer seemed to mollify him. His anger subsided. Spent, he sat down in the oversized rocking chair that we called "Papa's Chair," located in the kitchen.

"Listen, I'm not going to put up with you talking back to me like that. Do you hear me?"

"Yes, Papa."

I remained on the floor in silence, rubbing my wounds, listening to my father continue justifying his actions.

"You mark my words, Elishaba. You will never find a man to love you as I have. You are not beautiful to the world. And by going against me, you are throwing out the only person who sees your true beauty."

Hearing him say this scared me and confirmed how I felt inside—worthless and unlovable. At the same time, I felt doomed to this existence since I was nearly thirty years old. I would never marry. I would never have a family of my own. I would never hold my own child in my arms.

I pulled myself to my feet and filled a glass with water. It felt good to turn my back on my father, if only for a moment. My head spun with a dark feeling pounding my temples. A piercing headache made it hard for me to take in his hurtful words fully.

"Elishaba, look at me."

My bloodshot eyes dropped to the floor. I couldn't look my controller in the eyes, but I had heard him say this phrase so many times that I knew whatever he said next wouldn't be good for me. Sure enough, he came through.

"Elishaba, take care of my hands."

This time I looked as he held out his battered and bruised hands from Papa's Chair—hands that had clenched into fists and struck my brothers and me.

"I have to suffer from so much rebellion in my family," he said. "Please take care of my hands. You've done such a great job in the past."

I knew this wasn't a request; it was an order. As if flicking on a switch, I turned into the dutiful daughter again. We had some warm water on the stove, so I ladled some into a bowl and found some ointment and bandages in one of the kitchen drawers.

I felt more humiliated as I got down on my knees and placed a bowl of warm water in his lap. Then I took his extended hands into mine and dipped them into the bowl to soak. After a minute or two, I lifted his weathered hands out of the bowl so I could dry them on a ratty old T-shirt—we didn't have much in the way of towels at the homestead. Then I dabbed some ointment on several cuts and wrapped his hands in bandages.

"There, that should do it," I said.

"There's one more thing."

Papa leaned toward me, then reached out with his left hand and cupped my right breast. But he withdrew his hand quickly because family was in the vicinity.

I immediately stiffened, which my father must have sensed.

"Elishaba, your special touch is all I need. I would die without you."

"No, Papa. Don't say this." I tried to hide the tears welling up within me, but they rolled down my puffy cheeks and dropped into his lap.

"Are you ready to go to bed with me?"

Never before had I possessed the courage to tell my father I wouldn't do his bidding. This time I looked him directly in the eye. "I can't," I declared with as much conviction as I could muster.

"Then I will show you who's in charge here."

In a flash, he jumped out of his chair like a raging caribou. Before I could react, he started beating me with his bandaged fists, delivering blow after blow.

I was deflecting each swing as best I could when my mother jumped out of bed.

"Stop it!" she screamed. "Stop hurting my daughter!"

My father grabbed Mama by the arms. "So, are you going to be a hero and take her punishment instead?" he asked.

Country Rose's anger subsided in an instant. She knew all too well that once her husband started beating her, there was no stopping him.

Finally, I gave up. "Okay, I will go to bed with you, but I will not take off my clothes."

I don't know what my father was thinking, but he nodded. I was too tired to fight him any longer and hoped this halfway measure would get me through another torturous night.

I took off my sweater but kept on the rest of my clothes—my long skirt, a long-sleeved button-up shirt, leggings, and woolen socks. Usually, I slept in my leggings, a T-shirt, and no bra.

I looked around the darkened cabin. Noah, Abraham, and Job, in their teens, were snoring. My sisters Jerusalem and Hosanna, ages sixteen and fourteen, respectively, were in the back bedroom. Psalms and Lamb had found spots on couches. The preschoolers, Bethlehem and Jonathan, were cuddling with Mama. My parents had named their children after an interesting assortment of people, places, and things out of the Bible.

Fitting three adults and a couple of kidlets on a pair of big foam mattresses meant tight quarters. What happened was that Mama took the left side of the bed and gathered the younger ones close to her bosom. Papa and I took the other half, with me on the outside.

"My feet," he said as he turned on his side away from me. He was wearing a filthy T-shirt, navy sweatpants, and no underwear.

I knew the drill. Rub his feet. Then his legs. Then his . . .

I scrunched myself lower on the bed to make myself more comfortable to reach his feet. I drew a tattered blanket around me, like a cocoon—as if that would protect me from his prying hands. Then I started rubbing his feet and working my fingers between his toes, taking my time. I kept massaging his feet, over and over, hoping he'd fall asleep and leave me alone.

As I massaged his arches, I remembered a conversation I'd overheard that afternoon. Papa told Noah and Job that the three of them needed to go into McCarthy the next day with an empty fuel barrel and fill it from our stockpile of gasoline. Then they'd put the barrel on a sled and drag it back to the homestead.

I also heard Papa say that one of the snow machines had run out of gas and was abandoned halfway between the homestead and McCarthy, so that was something else my father was eager to remedy. The plan involved Papa, Noah, and Job driving two snow machines to McCarthy for the fuel run, if I overheard correctly.

I was surprised to hear that Papa was planning to leave in the late morning. He rarely let me out of sight because of our "special" relationship. Papa usually dispatched Joseph and Joshua to McCarthy to fetch fuel and bring in provisions that we had stored in our shed. Since they were nowhere to be seen, my father must have figured he needed to supervise the resupply operation.

At that time of year, the only way to McCarthy was by snow machine, and it was only possible if one stayed on a packed-down trail that crossed and recrossed McCarthy Creek at least a dozen times. The crossings were ice bridges that my brothers and I made after the first significant snowfall. During breakup season, though, we lost those ice bridges. When that happened, we would be isolated in Hillbilly Heaven until late May or June when a narrow dirt road reappeared, but that road was only passable on horseback.

Then it hit me: when Papa and my brothers left on their snow machines for the fourteen-mile trip to McCarthy, that would be my chance! I could take one of the extra snow machines—we had a half-dozen—and go partly down the valley and find a place to hide. I'd wait until my father and brothers passed me on their return trip to the homestead. Once they did, I'd hightail it into McCarthy while they were none the wiser. From McCarthy, I'd go up another valley. I knew of an abandoned trapper's cabin that I had found a year earlier. I could stay there, hunkering down with rice, flour, and raisins until I figured out my next move.

I was used to living out in the wild—without electricity, heat, and running water. I'd spent many days and nights—weeks, even—surviving on my own in the wilderness. I had the skills necessary to stay alive. And no one would ever find me in one of Alaska's least-populated valleys.

As I slipped into a deep sleep, exciting thoughts of escaping the monster next to me once and for all consumed me. I was well aware that if I was going to break free from Papa Pilgrim successfully, my best chance to escape was before breakup season took out all the ice bridges between the homestead and McCarthy, where civilization began. The only way out of Hillbilly Heaven—which was a living hell to me—was by snow machine.

Something in my heart told me that it was now or never.

# 3
# ROOM FOR ESCAPE

We had never been a family that got up at the crack of dawn.

There were reasons for this. First of all, it was frightfully cold during the early morning hours inside the Main House, which was as drafty as a miner's shack. We insulated our home with snow that we piled around the wooden building's perimeter to keep the heat in.

Our primary source of warmth was the barrel stove in the main living area, which needed to be stoked with wood around the clock to keep our living space comfortable. In the pre-dawn hours of mid-winter, when temperatures outside dipped to minus sixty degrees Fahrenheit and the stove's fire was down to embers, no one wanted to leave their warm covers and load more split wood into the barrel stove.

Plus, it was dark until mid-morning since sunrise arrived after 9:30 a.m. throughout much of the winter. Sure, there was a little light outside before then, but not much. Since we lived in a valley between snowcapped mountain ridges rising nearly two thousand feet above us, we didn't see the sun until the early afternoon—and then it was gone after an hour. Consequently, bright sunshine never filled the Main House during the winter months.

But the primary reason we slept in until nine or so in the morning was that we were never a family that went to bed early. It wasn't because we stayed up watching television shows or streaming movies—we didn't have a TV or the Internet. Not in the remote Alaskan wilderness, where the nearest neighbor was miles away in McCarthy.

Instead, we stayed up late because we couldn't have dinner until all the chores were done, and sometimes that took a while. Then, after a late evening meal, Papa Pilgrim would gather the smaller children around "Papa's Chair" and plop open his big Bible with its well-worn pages. Sometimes he'd preach, and other times he'd talk about whatever was on his mind. Often, he would return to similar themes over and over: how we were set apart from a wicked world; how we needed to obey him because of the position God put him in; and why we needed to keep our distance from strangers bent on stealing our salvation.

For the last year or two, those sermons happened infrequently because of the turmoil inside our home. Even if Papa didn't hold forth on some topic, we still seemed to stay up late, sometimes past 11 p.m. or midnight, which is the main reason why we slept in each morning.

No matter what time we went to bed, though, I dreaded the moment because sooner or later he would have his way with me—while others were asleep and couldn't hear us, or so he thought.

On this particular morning in April, I crawled out of the covers before Papa stirred, happy to escape the prison-like curtains surrounding our bed. I slipped on a jacket to ward off the cold and walked over to the window facing north, where I gazed at the spectacular McCarthy glacier. Rubbing the dreadful sleepiness from my eyes and feeling faint in my heart, I thought of the words from the psalmist, who wrote in Psalm 55:6–8 (KJV):

> And I said, Oh that I had wings like a dove! for then would I fly away, and be at rest.
> Lo, then would I wander far off, and remain in the wilderness. Selah.
> I would hasten my escape from the windy storm and tempest.

If only I had the wings of a dove. Then I would fly away from my angry father, who undoubtedly was stewing about the moment I stood up for myself and said I was keeping my clothes on when we went to bed, a first for me. I realized, though, that I had crossed a line with Papa, which is why my goal that morning was to stay on his good side. The last thing I wanted was for him to blow up and change his mind about going to McCarthy to bring back fuel with Noah and Job. If he did, my chance to "fly away" by snow machine would have to wait until the following winter. I didn't think I could survive his abuse that long.

As morning light filtered into the house, Mama was in the kitchen, moving pots around. We made eye contact as if to say: *Let's get through another day together.* For years, we had this awkward mother-daughter relationship because of what had evolved between her husband and me. Even though we hadn't fully figured things out between us, our mutual goal was the same: survival. Still, there were moments of closeness, which I treasured. I recalled a wonderful mother-daughter conversation that I had with Mama a few days earlier. When Papa was outside with the boys, she pulled me aside.

"I know I should have said this way sooner, but I want to thank you," my mother said, as if she was confiding in me.

"For what?"

"For taking the blows. For suffering for me. I know what's happening is not easy for you. I wish I could do more, but I think you know why I can't."

At first, I didn't know how to react, but strangely, I took her words as a compliment. I was tough. I was resilient. And I was doing my best to survive the next day, the next hour, and sometimes the next five minutes.

My father was still asleep when I went to the bathroom on the portable camping toilet at the base of our bed.[1] We didn't have indoor plumbing, and the outhouse was fifty yards from the Main House. None of us wanted to bundle up and make the trek to the outdoor privy in sub-freezing temperatures.

After I finished, I joined Mama in the kitchen, where she was crouching in front of the wood stove, laying small sticks of kindling wood on top of a wadded piece of paper. Atop the stove was a pan of water. That could only mean one thing: she was making oatmeal for us. None of us liked boiled oats since we got plain, lumpy oatmeal too many times in our lives, but the porridge-like meal filled our tummies. Papa, who had diabetes, didn't eat oatmeal since it could spike his blood sugar levels.

Papa Pilgrim was up. Out of the corner of my eye, I saw him squatting on the camper toilet in his dirty T-shirt with his navy sweatpants around his knees. I quickly averted my eyes. Like all the boys, my father sat down when he urinated and was big on making sure we never saw one another naked.

When he was finished, he made a beeline to the kitchen. From the way my dad approached me, I knew something else was on his mind. His eyes bore a hole through my forehead.

"Elishaba."

I knew something was coming, but I reminded myself not to make waves today, no matter what he said.

"Your brothers will never be allowed in this home again," he declared solemnly. "They have left us, and now they are polluted by the world. I want to make it clear that you are not allowed ever to see your brothers again. You are my faithful one."

Once again, Papa was playing with my emotions. It was like he *knew* that I was planning to escape. Why else would he tell me not to see my brothers again and that I was his faithful one?

"Yes, Papa. You're right."

I knew I also had to acknowledge the compliment he gave me since they were so few and far between. If I didn't, he might think something was up.

Inwardly though, I was upset any time he spoke like this about my brothers, which gave me more resolve than ever. After Papa left to pick up fuel in

---

1. See the diagram at the start of Chapter 2.

McCarthy, I would make a break for it.

And I didn't care if I died trying.

I didn't eat breakfast very often because my mornings were always spent injecting Papa with insulin, doing his blood sugar test, fixing his coffee, and making his breakfast. Papa ate much better than everyone else. On this particular morning, I made sure he received one of his best breakfasts ever: a couple of scrambled eggs with cheese, two strips of bacon, and toast with sugar-free strawberry jam. I knew his eggs had to have the right amount of salt and pepper. I also added powdered cream to his coffee.

No such mountain breakfast for me. I watched Mama scoop oatmeal into several wooden bowls for my siblings. A bunch of kids came out of the woodwork to snatch a bowl of hot oatmeal from Mama. I could have used something to fuel my day, but that wasn't going to happen because I had been trained to care for my father first, and I wasn't allowed to have any breakfast without his permission. Or any meal.

Then I noticed Jerusalem stepping into the pantry off the kitchen. This was my chance to speak with my oldest sister. Even though she was sixteen years old and thirteen years younger than me, Jerusalem and I were as close as sisters could be. Papa sensed that and didn't like me to be alone with her or any of my siblings unless he was within earshot, probably because he felt we would be talking about him. But when I saw Jerusalem slip into the pantry, I knew I could have a word with her before he would suspect anything was amiss.

"I'm leaving today," I whispered.

Jerusalem's eyes widened. "You're really going to do this?"

"I'm going to a place where Papa won't be able to find me. Please keep my secret. If Papa thinks something is up, he will not leave today, and I will lose my opportunity to escape before breakup, so don't do anything to make him mad."

A look of sympathy came over Jerusalem's face as she leaned closer. "I'm coming with you."

My first thought was to tell her I had to go alone. I didn't want to be responsible for what would happen if we got caught. The worst-case scenario was that we would die—either at Papa's hand or from Alaska's frozen environment. I hoped that wouldn't happen. I planned to make it to a miner's cabin up another valley out of McCarthy and live off the land and the provisions I brought along until I figured out what to do next. The rivers would break up soon, and then Papa couldn't cross them on his snow machine to find me.

My sister was willing to take that risk with me. I had to let her come. "Okay, but be careful how you look at Papa."

Around eleven o'clock, Papa put on his jacket and beckoned Mama and me to come near the front door, along with Jerusalem and a couple of other sisters. Noah and Job were already outside, moving a pair of snow machines into position under a clear sky with little wind. The winter had been an extra cold one: that day, the temperature was crisp and cold in the high teens, which was good for the ice bridges across McCarthy Creek. Breakup season would be late this year.

They were about to leave for McCarthy, but Papa looked like a nervous wreck. I didn't know about what, but seeing him that way made *me* feel skittish as a young colt.

"Country Rose, I want you to keep your hand on your mouth until I get back," he said. "I'm ordering all of you not to talk to each other unless your conversation is related to work. I'll be questioning each of you when I come back, and God will tell me if you're lying to me."

I shivered. Papa was famous for pitting the siblings against each other. The younger ones knew that he kept a few candy bars in his jacket to reward those who squealed on a sister or brother. What made things worse is that Papa always believed the tattletale.

"Elishaba, I don't want you in the house for any reason. I want all these logs sawed up while I'm gone. If you finish before I get back, then you can help the girls get those slabs into the attic."

Papa was referring to the attic in the Main House, where we needed to repair a hole in the ceiling. One of my brothers had been walking around in the attic, where we stored a lot of our supplies, and stepped through the ceiling, so it had to be shored up with planks of wood. Since spring was in the air and we could work outside a lot more, my job was to cut lumber on the long sawmill.

I nodded as if I would do all that he said. I didn't want to do anything to upset him now. He was so close to leaving for McCarthy.

Then he surprised me. "Can you pray for us on this glorious morning that the Lord has given us, that we'll have a safe trip?"

This wasn't the first time Papa asked me to pray out loud. It was his sneaky way of finding out what was on my mind. He had learned that it was hard for me to lie to God, and my real feelings would often be revealed in prayer.

Any fears I had about what would happen that day suddenly vanished. It was like Jesus Himself was standing next to me, holding my hand as I bowed my head and closed my eyes. And then I prayed out loud the words the Lord put into my heart:

"Dear Jesus, teach me what it means to love You more than my father, my mother, my siblings, and even myself. Please give Papa and my brothers a safe trip, and I pray that nothing would go wrong. I pray this in Jesus' name, amen."

There. I had said what was on my heart but in a way that I hoped wouldn't awaken the bear. Still, the test came.

"So tell me this," Papa said harshly. "Explain to your siblings what you mean by that prayer."

I didn't panic. I looked across at my siblings and smiled. "You all understand what I meant, don't you?" I asked.

They all smiled back, their heads bobbing in agreement.

At that, Papa reached for his floppy hat and stormed out of the Main House. Suddenly, the longing of my little girl's heart to be a "daddy's girl" filled my chest. I knew deep down that I would never see him again—at least not like this. Today was a new beginning. If I died trying to escape, then at least I could tell myself that I did all that I could to get away from this manipulative father who had abused me for so many years.

At the same time, I felt conflicted. He was my father. He had spun this protective cocoon around the family and me to protect us from the world, he said—a world I didn't know much about. We had been through a lot together, and I had been taught to respect him.

I watched him swing onto one of the snow machines, which was already warmed up. This would be the last time I'd ever see him. I had to say goodbye.

I ran after him to give him one last hug. "Papa, Papa," I cried out. I wanted my dad to give me one last kiss before he went away. How could I tell him goodbye forever without letting him know about my plan?

I got so close to Papa and the snow machine that I could see myself in his little mirror. I know he saw me, but he ignored me. Instead, he punched the throttle, and the track threw up snow like a rooster tail as he accelerated and took off.

"Papa, good—"

His back was turned to me as he led Noah and Job, sitting together on their snow machine, on the trail to McCarthy. They gunned their engines and left the homestead on a packed path that would lead them to the first crossing of McCarthy Creek via a snow bridge we'd built early in winter.

Hearing the whining engines in the distance, I felt the cold sting of rejection. His empty, miserable heart had blocked me out once again.

*Okay, that's the way it shall be.*

And then the clouds lifted. Papa was really leaving!

And that meant I could follow through on my plan—leave Papa Pilgrim once and for all.

I had no time to waste.

# 4
# GETAWAY TIME

I waited until Papa Pilgrim was gone for good and then sprinted toward the Main House, lifting the bottom of my pioneer skirt so I wouldn't trip over my feet.

Jerusalem was fixing her hair while several young ones were sitting at the table, unenthusiastically working their way through their bowls of bland oatmeal.

"We have to get ready right now," I said to Jerusalem. "We don't know how much time we have until Papa comes back."

One of my younger sisters, Psalms, eight years old, looked up from her oatmeal. "What are you guys talking for?" she asked. "Papa told us to watch you. He said he'd give us a prize or a candy bar if we told him what you talked about."

I played along. "Really? He said that to you?"

Lamb, who was two years younger than Psalms, gave her sister a mischievous look like they knew something we didn't know.

"Well, why don't you two run off to the shed after you finish eating and pretend you didn't see us today," I said.

Psalms and Lamb weren't budging. They sensed something was up.

"Okay," I said, turning to Jerusalem. "Let's start packing."

"You're really leaving?" asked Psalms.

"That's the plan."

Hosanna, who at fourteen was two years younger than Jerusalem, wanted to help out. "Let's call our brothers," she said. "They need to know that you're going."

Mama was watching all this transpire. "You should do that," my mother commanded in a way that made me feel her support.

We had a fixed wireless antenna on top of the Peace Cabin that allowed us to connect a phone like a landline—and this was our only contact with the outside world. Sometimes the phone worked, sometimes it didn't, but Papa had forbidden us to use the phone unless he was standing at our side. If one of us wanted to call someone on the "outside," we had to be sneaky about it.

Because we had a phone, we knew that the five brothers who'd left Hillbilly Heaven a few weeks earlier were safe. They were staying with a Christian family in Glennallen, roughly 120 miles from McCarthy. This family owned a construction company and had hired my brothers to hang drywall and do construction work.

"No, I don't have time for a phone call," I told Hosanna. "Papa's only going to be gone for so long."

I was feeling the pressure. The magnitude of what I was about to attempt nearly crushed me. Jerusalem and I had to get going before I lost my nerve.

The first thing I did was walk into the pantry and get some Ziploc bags, which I started filling with flour, rice, raisins, and some cheese and chocolate chips. After a few minutes of stuffing plastic bags with any nonperishable food I could find, Hosanna joined us in the pantry, her cheeks rosy from being outside in the cold.

"Please, you have to come," she said, panting from the exertion. "I've got Joseph on the phone right now, and he wants to talk to you."

"I told you before. I don't have time to talk with Joseph," I said.

"Please! He really wants to speak with you," she pleaded.

I relented and followed Hosanna out to the Peace Cabin. Jerusalem trailed behind me. When I put the phone to my ear, I heard reassuring words.

"I'm so proud that you're leaving," Joseph said. "This is an answer to prayer. I just really want to encourage you. If you have to go way out into the wilderness, then go. I know you can handle anything, but if you meet up with us, I promise that we'll keep you away from Papa. Let your brothers and me take care of you."

My heart melted. I felt valued and cared for by Joseph and, by extension, all five of my brothers who had left. But I was losing daylight. "I don't have time for this. I really have to—"

In my fragile emotional state, I couldn't envision life with Papa or without Papa. "You don't understand. There's no way I can ever see him again. I'll give in," I mumbled. I didn't know if I was making sense, but those were the conflicting emotions bubbling in my heart. There was no way I could explain to Joseph or any of the others the helpless feeling that gripped me whenever I was in my father's presence.

Joseph would not be deterred. "We already have it figured out. We'll come pick you up in McCarthy. Papa will never find us."

"I don't know . . ." My voice trailed off.

"Then put Jerusalem on the phone. We'll talk to her about what to do. You get ready to go."

"Okay." I passed the handset to my sister. "You guys figure it out," I said to Jerusalem.

I left the Peace Cabin, thinking about the necessities I needed: a pan to cook in, a few lighters, a small ax, two sleeping bags, and a medical kit. Also, a Bible. I'd need my snow pants and the warmest coat I had since I planned to sleep outside, at least for a few nights. I also brought a white bedsheet to hide the snow machine—a Ski-Doo Tundra—when Papa came back up the hill. Our paths would intersect sometime in the mid-afternoon, so we had to hide in the trees while he passed us.

Hosanna came through the front door again, her cheeks still rosy from the noontime cold. "I can't get the snow machine started. It's been sabotaged."

My heart leaped into my throat. *The snow machine won't start? We can't escape?*

I looked to Hosanna for some sort of explanation. "What do you mean, 'sabotaged'?" I asked.

"I mean, it doesn't even have a sparkplug."

All the color drained from my face. "Oh, my word. He knew we were leaving? How did he hear us?"

Before anyone could answer, Hosanna's face brightened. "I have an idea," she said. My younger sister turned on her heels and ran outside.

Hosanna, like most of my brothers, was mechanically gifted. If anyone in our family could figure out what was wrong with the snow machine, it would be her.

I returned to stuffing a duffel bag with food, sleeping bags, a handsaw, a shovel, various tools, and a few kitchen utensils, including a cooking pot, but now I was worried sick that I would be foiled. Snow machines needed three things to run—a spark, air, and fuel. Without a sparkplug, the engine would never fire.

Minutes passed, and then I heard the familiar whine of an engine kicking in. I stepped outside to see what the commotion was all about. Outside the Main House, Hosanna sat on the Tundra, with its yellow hood over the engine, pushing the throttle to a higher pitch before settling on a steady hum in idle. She got it working!

I was super excited that the escape was back on. "How did you get it started?" I asked.

"I found a sparkplug in the shed, but the engine had been messed with," Hosanna explained. "I had to reconnect a couple of hoses and pump primer into the carburetor intake, but I got it going."

Hosanna had always been resourceful. "Good for you!" I exclaimed.

By now, Papa and the boys had been gone for forty-five minutes or so. If they made good time, they could get to the shed in McCarthy in another thirty minutes. It would probably take them a good half hour to load up and get the fuel transportation squared away. The return trip would take at least twice as long since the grade was uphill. They'd be towing sleds filled with a heavy barrel of fuel and provisions from the storage shed.

Our descent would be harrowing because, at some point, our paths would cross. We would have to hide in plain sight, but I knew just the place to go.

The question was whether we could make it in time to the place I had in mind.

Jerusalem, a full-blown teenager, had so much energy. She'd been wanting to flee the homestead ever since the brothers left, but anytime she mentioned it to me, I shrugged her off and said, "You don't understand." That's because of the power and influence Papa held over me.

I noticed that she was stuffing notes into her pockets—messages she had retrieved from the trash and hidden away. Anytime someone from the outside world wrote us personal letters, Papa would throw them in the trash bin to be burned. She had saved a whole packet of them just before they went into the fire, so they meant a lot to her.

Jerusalem didn't pack anything else. She was literally taking the heavy winter clothes on her back. Since we were riding tandem on the Tundra, we could only tie down one duffel bag anyway. We figured there was enough fuel to make it to McCarthy.

There was one more thing I had to do before we could go. I wanted to write a note to Papa. I found a piece of stationery and sat at the table, pen in hand. Then I wrote the following words as legibly as possible, but I was a horrible speller since I had never gone to school and had barely learned to read.

> To my Papa, I am gonna go off in to the montane to fas and pray for a
> long time. plese reed 1 corinthans 7:5 I lov you
>   Yur dauthr
>   Elishaba

Tears formed in my eyes as I folded the letter in half. This was it: I was leaving everything I knew in life, which is why there was an inward war in my soul. Though I was planning never to see my father again and be physically miles away from his grasp, I also knew he needed me and relied on me for so much. He needed to hear from me one more time.

I have to admit, though, that my note was manipulative. The reference to 1 Corinthians 7:5 was a shot across the bow because in it the apostle Paul was writing to *married* couples that celibacy, at times, could be good, especially after giving yourself to "fasting and prayer," as the King James Version said. We were not married, of course, which is why I made sure I signed off as "*Yur dauthr*" ("Your daughter") in the closing—a reminder of our parent/child relationship.

But the real reason I left the note behind is that if he really thought I was going into the mountains to fast and pray, perhaps I could buy myself some more time until he decided that was a ruse and came looking for me. And I knew he'd come searching for me. That's why every hour counted.

Since I didn't want him to find the note right away—but to find it eventually—I hung it from the old gas stove next to Papa's Chair, figuring that he would be too worked up by our escape to sit down and relax. Once he took a load off his feet, he'd see the note, but we would gain valuable time to get further away from him in the meantime.

While affixing the note to the old gas stove, I noticed his leather-bound Bible on Papa's Chair. I involuntarily shuddered—not from the sanctity of God's Word but from what was inside a slip pocket on the inside cover. At one time, Papa had me sew a tiny, hidden spot in the leather case holding the Bible. Inside that concealed pocket was a memory card that belonged to a handheld digital camera that took still pictures and video.

I knew exactly what was on the memory card: hundreds of pictures and long stretches of video of me naked while I performed various sex acts on and with my father. This was a secret I had to hide from humanity; even my mother didn't know about the existence of these sick and vile images.

For a fleeting moment, I felt sick to my stomach when I was reminded of how my father sexually abused me a couple of months earlier in an abandoned cabin near Glennallen, around 125 miles northwest of McCarthy.

I slipped my fingers into the tiny pocket. The memory card was gone! Papa Pilgrim had taken it with him to McCarthy. He felt he couldn't risk me destroying the memory card or bringing it to the police as proof of how he sexually abused me.

I closed the Bible and bowed my head, asking the Lord to rid me of those horrid memories and keep us safe.

When I opened my eyes, I was more determined than ever to close this awful chapter in my life.

It was around one o'clock in the afternoon when we were finally ready to leave the homestead.

Hosanna took my little brothers and sisters—Job, Psalms, Lamb, preschooler Bethlehem, and toddler Jonathan—to the back of the property so they wouldn't see us go. That way, when Papa got home and questioned them, they could honestly say, "We were out back, and when we returned to the house, they were gone."

My dad would never believe that Mama didn't see us leave, but I couldn't tell her where we were going or what our plans were. I knew Papa would beat Mama to give up that information, but if she had no idea, then she couldn't tell him anything. I regretted that she would get assaulted, but there wasn't anything I could do about it.

I hugged Mama, and she had tears in her eyes. We had a moment: we both knew that the two of us had been through so much physical and emotional pain at the hands of my father.

"I really hope this works out and that you won't suffer more," I said.

Mama's voice quivered. "I'm just glad you're getting away," she replied.

She stood in the doorway and waved while we hopped on the Tundra. My mother looked happy that we were leaving. With my right hand on the throttle and my sister sitting behind me with arms wrapped around my waist, we were on our way.

The noisy snow machine, riding a pair of small skis in the front and powered by a belt drive that transferred power from the engine to the rubber track, quickly gained traction. We were just a few minutes from the homestead—probably three hundred yards—when the thin trail opened up onto a frozen riverbed. Suddenly, disaster struck! The snow machine inexplicably stopped dead in its tracks, nearly tossing Jerusalem and me off the Tundra.

*What do we do now?*

Panic rose in my throat. If we couldn't get the snow machine going again, not only would we fail to escape, but there was no way we could push the heavy snow machine back to the homestead. In other words, once Papa found the broken-down snow machine on the trail to McCarthy, no excuse in the world would convince my father that we weren't trying to escape.

My greatest fear was that he would kill me. Ever since my brothers fled the homestead, he'd been keeping his .454 Casull revolver close to his side and acting erratically. I feared that he wouldn't hesitate to put me down.

You see, I knew too much.

# 5
# THE INTERSECTION

I stood next to the hopeless snow machine and looked down the frozen trail toward McCarthy—the path we needed to be riding on at that very moment. This was not looking good.

"Let's see what we got," I said.

Together, Jerusalem and I lifted the yellow hood to peer at the engine. The reason why the snow machine quit running jumped out at both of us: a thick rubber drive belt that turned the track had split into two.

I couldn't believe this was happening. Suddenly, I felt scared of God—really scared. Was I wrong to leave the homestead? Was God angry with me for abandoning Papa?

I was torn but knew I had to dismiss those dark thoughts and return to the task at hand: fixing the Tundra's drive belt. Fortunately, we had a few emergency tools and baling wire in a small box attached under the engine hood. While I thought about how to attack this repair, Jerusalem had an idea. "I'm gonna run back and see if I can get the other snow machine going," she said.

There was another Tundra at the homestead, but it hadn't been working very well. Nevertheless, I wasn't going to stop Jerusalem. "Sure, see what you can do," I said with all the encouragement I could muster.

I messed around with the rubber belt and baling wire. I put holes at each end of the rubber belt and tried desperately to wire them together—an impossible task, I admit—when I lost my balance and stepped into waist-deep snow. I could barely move, which sunk my spirits. After working my legs furiously, I managed to extricate myself. While dusting snow off my pants, I gazed toward the towering mountains on my right and my left.

Could we hike out of here? Maybe—if we had snowshoes. But it would take time to trudge back to the homestead and pick up a couple of pairs, time we didn't have. Furthermore, I was well aware that hiking up the mountains would be dangerous. We were situated in prime avalanche territory, where unstable patches of snow could break free and rush down the mountain at any moment.

What about staying on the trail and walking to McCarthy on our snowshoes? I suppose that was possible, but sooner or later, we'd hear a pair of snow machines being driven by Papa and my brothers. Jerusalem and I would have to take cover behind thick black spruce or the taller white spruce trees, two species widely found in Wrangell-St. Elias National Park. These evergreens had slender trunks that ranged in diameter from twelve to thirty-six inches, but at our high altitude, they didn't get a lot of sun, so many spruce didn't have thick branches that hung down to afford some degree of concealment. The more significant issue was the snowshoe tracks that we'd leave behind. Once Papa spotted our tracks, he'd find us sooner or later.

I scrutinized the heavens, which were a mixture of cloud cover and a bit of sunshine, for answers. "Please show me what to do, Lord. Are You still angry with me? Are we doing the right thing? But how could You want me to stay and do what Papa wants from me? I have no strength on my own to stand against his demands. If this is wrong, please have mercy and forgive me. If this is *really* wrong and Papa is right, then I deserve to die. I'm okay with that, if only I can be in heaven with You."

Desperation clutched my throat. I even considered turning back and returning to Hillbilly Heaven. But when Papa found out that I tried to escape— there was no way my younger siblings could keep that secret—then that would be the end of me. The whole family would also suffer because of my actions. I pictured myself being beaten black and blue and then being locked up and kept away from the world, never to be seen again by anyone else while I endured frightful punishment from his hands.

That's why I knew I couldn't go back.

As I considered my options for escape, I reminded myself that I had to keep trying, that there had to be a way. I'd never been a quitter, and I wasn't about to give up now, but I sensed that whatever happened in the next couple of hours would demand everything I had physically and emotionally.

I was still caught in this push-pull of what to do when I heard the familiar noise of a snow machine—coming from the homestead! Steering another yellow-and-black Tundra was an angel who looked exactly like my sister Jerusalem.

She roared up with a huge smile.

"I thought that one was broken," I said.

"It was. Hosanna and I figured it out: a wire had been snapped in two. We bound it together and found a couple more sparkplugs. We're good to go," Jerusalem said.

Relief flooded my senses as a phrase from the Bible came to mind: *I will put my hand to the plow and not look back.* For me, that meant I would keep my hand on the throttle and not look back.

I renewed my determination to move ahead with no regrets. "Let's go!" I said to Jerusalem. "We have some time to make up."

We strapped the duffel bag onto the second Tundra and were off again. We had lost so much time. As we snow-machined along McCarthy Creek, crossing several ice bridges and veering into wooded areas a couple of times, I mentally calculated when I could expect to run into my father and brothers. I had a specific place in mind around a third of the way to McCarthy that would be a great spot to hide, but I wasn't sure if we could get there in time. All I could do was hope and pray that it would all work out.

After fifteen minutes on the trail, I came to a halt. Even though stopping cost us valuable time, I decided the prudent thing would be to stop and turn off the engine so we could listen for approaching snow machines.

"What are we stopping for?" Jerusalem asked.

"We have to know if he's coming," I explained. "If he sees us, we'll have to make a run for it."

We sat atop the Tundra for a minute, which seemed like an eternity. As I breathed in the crisp and cold April air, the enormity of the situation prompted tears to fall from my eyes. I brushed them away with the back of my glove, along with flakes of frozen white frost around my fur hat.

As Jerusalem and I listened for distinctive engine notes out in the wilderness, all we heard was the sound of our beating hearts.

My sister broke the eerie silence. "Elishaba, we're going to be okay," she declared with a certainty in her attitude. "God is with us. He's not going to abandon us."

How could my sister be so confident? Even though I was plagued with doubts, I knew she was right. God would not let us down if we relied on Him.

I pulled the cord to start the engine. The whining sound of the Tundra gave me strength as we continued following the contours of McCarthy Creek until we came to a crucial ice bridge.

This time, when we crossed the river, we'd have to charge up a steep wooded trail that took us further into the wilderness and away from McCarthy Creek. I worried that our underpowered Tundra wouldn't have the juice to make it up the mountainside.

As our snow machine negotiated the climb, rising a thousand feet in elevation, my heart pounded with fear that we would run into Papa along this old miner's trail etched into the side of the mountain. We didn't have any room to maneuver if we had to make a getaway. We were taking a real chance, but if we got up the ridge and down the other side, I knew of a great place where we could hide when the trail reached McCarthy Creek again.

We were making good time along the ridge when the Tundra coughed and sputtered—and the engine shut off. We skidded to a sudden stop.

"Oh, no!" I cried out. We had come so far, and now this. The Tundra had quit on us.

Jerusalem and I hopped off the snow machine to see what happened. Maybe this was something we could fix.

"Open the gas tank," Jerusalem said.

I spun the gas cap off and peered inside. The fuel tank was dry. Jerusalem took a look as well.

"Yup, it's empty."

A horrible sinking feeling filled my chest. We were doomed; I was sure of it. In the rush to replace the broken-down Tundra, Jerusalem had left the homestead without much fuel in the Tundra's tank.

And then I nearly jumped out of my skin. Up ahead, just twenty yards in front of us was the Polaris!

Of all the places to run out of gas and get stuck, we had come to a complete stop a matter of yards from one of our best snow machines. What were the odds of that?

There were no odds. This was a total God thing. Any doubts about escaping that were still harbored in my heart immediately vanished. God had orchestrated this unbelievable miracle. He was going to save us!

Jerusalem glimpsed the snow machine at the same time I did. She shrieked with joy. "Amazing! Let's see if we can get it started," she exclaimed.

But was there any gas in the Polaris? It was entirely possible that Papa didn't fill it on the way down to McCarthy, as I expected him to do. Something could have happened.

Jerusalem and I practically ran to the Polaris, but under my breath, I was praying, *Lord, please let it have a full tank of gas.*

Jerusalem unscrewed the gas cap and peered inside. "It's gassed up!"

A burst of adrenaline shot through my veins. Now we had a newer, faster, and more powerful snow machine for our escape to McCarthy.

"Let me start it up." I swung my leg onto the black leather seat. With one pull, the engine growled and then idled. A quick transfer of our gear, and we were in business. As we left the Tundra and raced ahead, I thanked God for His provision: a new snow machine at *precisely* the right moment and *precisely* the right place. Jerusalem and I were totally pumped for the rest of our journey.

*God, I know You're there, watching over us*, I prayed. *Now please protect us from Papa.*

Because I knew he was coming in our direction.

We continued along the ridge, traveling as fast as I dared. If I made a colossal mistake and plowed off the side of the ridge, we could tumble down the mountainside to McCarthy Creek, which was a thousand feet below. No one could survive that.

I let up on the throttle when the old mining trail started its descent back to McCarthy Creek. This long, treacherous hill demanded my attention. When we came out of the trees and reached the frozen riverbed, we arrived at the best place to hide from Papa. Instead of continuing on the snow machine trail, which ran along McCarthy Creek, I veered left toward a thicket of trees.

"What are you doing?" Jerusalem yelled in my ear. "This doesn't look like a good place to hide."

"We'll be okay. You'll see."

I steered the Polaris to a spot around twenty or thirty yards down the creek, where we could be hidden from exposure by a grove of trees along the bank.

I turned off the motor. "Shush. He has to be coming any minute, so we have to be ready."

I zipped open the duffel bag, took out the white bedsheet, and gave one end to Jerusalem. "Let's get covered up," I said.

I knew exactly what to do. Papa had taught us to cover our tracks and hide from others since we could walk. Over the years, we'd had run-ins with authorities—Child Protective Services, Forest Service rangers, and local police. If one of those civil authorities came onto our property, we knew where to hide so that they wouldn't readily find us. Or ever find us.

We spread the bedsheet over the snow machine, which camouflaged it completely. When we heard the snow machines coming our way, we got underneath another bedsheet I'd brought along.

I thought we were in a good spot. When Papa was driving past us, I hoped that his eyes would be focusing on the hill ahead of him and not on the tracks leading to our hiding place. On this spring day in the mid-afternoon, there wasn't much light with the sun low in the sky. I knew that was working in our favor.

We settled in, but it wasn't long before we were shivering, praying, and wondering what would happen when Papa and the boys passed through.

Because they were coming.

# 6
# ON THE RUN

Crazy thoughts bounced around my head during our vigil.

*I can't believe I'm doing this. But I have to escape Papa. Then again, what if he catches me? Will he beat me until I'm dead?*

I couldn't escape a feeling of dread in the pit of my stomach that something would go wrong, and that would be the end of me. Jerusalem must have sensed my inner turmoil because she spoke reassuring words.

"Don't worry. Everything's going to work out just fine. I'm happy we're escaping. I can't wait to get out of here," she said.

My sister's upbeat presence and teen optimism picked me up. At an incredibly significant time in my life, when I was waning and feeling very weak, she was hopeful and supportive.

The minutes slowly passed as we waited. Then, within ten to fifteen minutes of bringing the bedsheet out, we heard the unmistakable sound of snow machines coming our way. My heart nearly fell out of my chest. This was it.

I wondered if I had thrown away my whole life. Had I made a huge mistake? If I had, there was no going back now.

Would I ever see my younger siblings again? Would the family suffer more because I had left? Would they be able to take care of themselves without my help?

What about all the promises I made to Papa, saying that I would never leave him and that I'd always be by his side? I could hear him in my head: *You're a liar, Elishaba. I knew I couldn't trust your word.* These thoughts had been dogging me from the moment we left the homestead.

When Jerusalem and I got under our bedsheet, we lay down on our stomachs so we could peek out and see what was happening—through the trees—on the snow-packed trail along the riverbed.

While we waited for their arrival, I paged through the possibilities in my mind. When Papa passed us, would he spot our tracks that led directly to our hiding place? Or would he glance over his shoulder and see the bedsheet covering the snow machine?

If he turned in our direction to investigate, I knew we had seconds to hop on the Polaris, slalom our way through the trees, and try to outrun him to McCarthy. I'd been driving snow machines since we moved to the Wrangells and felt confident in my abilities.

Even if he passed by and didn't spot us, we weren't in the clear, however. Once he reached the ridge, he'd come upon the abandoned Tundra—and no Polaris—and *know* we had switched snow machines. This meant he'd turn around and come after us.

Tucked under the bedsheet, I heard two revved-up engines shattering the stillness of the Alaskan wilderness. *Vroom . . . vroom.*

From our vantage point, looking through the spruce trees, we saw Papa's snow machine first, followed by Noah and Job's, each pulling a sled. Papa was staring straight ahead—a good sign. His snow machine was hauling a 55-gallon barrel full of fuel, and Noah and Job's sled was filled with boxes of food and provisions, covered by a tarp.

I didn't dare breathe as Papa passed by. His concentration was locked on the steep hill ahead of him. His head never swiveled as he steered his snow machine from McCarthy Creek to the miner's trail that led to the ridge we had just come down.

As I saw him pass by, a strange feeling came over me—one of sympathy for my father, despite his cruel behavior toward me. So many times, he'd said, "If you ever leave me, I will die. No one can care for me like you can."

For some reason, I felt like *I* would die if Papa passed away before me. I recalled hearing Papa pray, "Lord, we are a family that will either live together or die together for You." I wondered if trying to escape was going against his prayer. Would I be responsible for causing the death of us all?

*Please, Jesus, forgive Papa,* I silently prayed. *Please keep our family safe when the truth comes out.*

My heart thumped in my chest as I watched my bearded father, followed by the boys, gain elevation.

*He didn't see us!*

The thought which tempered my excitement was that we had ten minutes, maybe fifteen, before Papa discovered the disabled Tundra on top of the ridge and would know something was up. But by then we'd have a half-hour jump on him.

"C'mon, we've got to go right now," I urged Jerusalem.

We stuffed the bedsheets into the duffel bag in seconds and hopped on the

Polaris. The snow machine fired up immediately, and we were off. I continued to cross back and forth over the riverbed and through the trees until I reached the main trail on the frozen creek bed. Then I gunned the Polaris for all she was worth.

"Hang on!" I yelled to Jerusalem.

We zoomed along the frozen trail, keeping our speed high until we turned into a wooded area along McCarthy Creek. We were moving well until I took a corner too fast. In a flash, I saw a tree directly in my path!

I pulled on the handbrake, sending the Polaris into a skid. We struck the base of the tree but with little force. Except for a bit of a dent in the tube bumper, we were okay.

Jerusalem and I jumped off the snow machine and pulled it back onto the trail. Within seconds, we were back up to speed, although I was more careful after that mishap. I was still willing to take risks to stay ahead of my father, though.

For the next hour or so, I made record time on our way to McCarthy, which was a handful of buildings and lightly populated with a couple of dozen year-round residents. We stopped to listen and didn't hear Papa's snow machine chasing us, which gave us some relief.

I planned to stay on the McCarthy Creek riverbed and *not* go into town because I didn't want anyone to see me. Let's just say that our unusual pioneer family was a topic of gossip among the locals. They all knew who we were, which is why I didn't want anyone to see us.

I knew that Papa would be asking anyone he could find in McCarthy if they had seen Jerusalem and me sailing by on our Polaris snow machine.

We continued along McCarthy Creek until it merged with Kennicott River just outside of town. We needed to cross Kennicott River, which was a hundred yards wide, to meet my brothers. Jerusalem had set up a rendezvous with our brothers at a cleared-out area a mile or so west of town, close to the Glacier View Campground.

The set-aside area, which was state property, was adjacent to McCarthy Road, a two-lane dirt-and-gravel road that was the only transportation route to the rest of Alaska. So, this was where our brothers would be coming from.

Just in case Papa was following our tracks, I turned into the public area and proceeded to make a series of random circles around the spruce and alder trees, following other zig-zagging impressions in the snow. Of course, no one could ever decipher my crazy tracks from the others. Then again, I had learned these evasion skills from my father.

After going round and round in the public area, I drove the Polaris into a grove of trees near McCarthy Road, maybe five yards from the snow-covered route. We needed to be close to the road so we could flag down our brothers when they arrived.

We waited and waited, probably for a half hour or forty-five minutes. We didn't see *any* cars or trucks the entire time, so my brothers weren't showing up.

Meanwhile, the sun was getting close to dipping underneath the mountainous horizon to the west. "We can't stay here much longer," I said. "We have to find a place to camp before it gets dark."

Jerusalem begged me to wait a little longer. "We gotta wait for them. I'm sure they'll show up."

Jerusalem and I had gotten along well all day long, but when our brothers didn't meet us like they were supposed to, we were both thrown off. My survival instinct kicked in, and when I got in this mood, you didn't mess with me.

"Listen. You didn't have to come with me," I reminded my sister. "I would have been just fine going into the wilderness and disappearing on my own. But you got our brothers involved, and now look where we are."

"Sorry. I was just trying to help."

Jerusalem's shoulders sagged. She meant well. For some reason, things didn't work out with my brothers. Now it was time to go underground, to become part of the wilderness. Big Sister took control of the situation. "First things first. Let's get the snow machine covered," I said.

We took away the duffel bag and unfurled the bedsheet to cover up the Polaris for the second time that day. Then Jerusalem helped me spread sticks, brush, and limbs from spruce trees onto the bedsheet. This would help camouflage the snow machine.

I told my sister that we couldn't risk camping out *near* the snow machine, but I wanted to be close enough to hear anything that was going on. That's when I decided that we should spend the night *across* McCarthy Road. But we'd have to cover our tracks as best we could.

I grabbed the duffel bag and told her to follow me. When we got to the side of the road, I took out another bedsheet and spread it on the snow. I wanted us to slide onto the road instead of making tracks in the snow. I knew we had to cover our tracks to hide from Papa.

I had Jerusalem slide feet first onto the hard, icy road, and then I tossed down several items from the duffel bag: a small saw, a cooking pot, and a sleeping bag.

Then I slid down with the rest of our belongings in the duffel bag. We gathered our belongings and headed west on McCarthy Road—in the direction of Anchorage. Since the two-lane road was nothing but hardpack snow and ice, we didn't leave any footprints.

We had walked twenty yards or so when I saw an area on the other side of

McCarthy Road that looked like a secluded spot to spend the night. There was a gap through some trees and several logs on the ground that we could hopscotch on so that we wouldn't leave any tracks.

"Let's see if we can find something over there," I said to Jerusalem, pointing to a patch of trees.

We stepped off the road and were careful to smooth out our tracks and step on logs and thick branches until we were about a hundred yards from the road. The spruce trees at this lower elevation had a large circular patch of dry ground around their trunks. Underneath a canopy of branches, we could lay our sleeping bags on dirt instead of the cold snow. I found the perfect tree up on a small hill, which afforded us a view of McCarthy Road. This would be the ideal place to hide in the forest.

We settled ourselves under the branches of a spruce tree and caught our breath. Then, like a wild deer, I looked in every direction and listened for any approaching vehicles. After living for almost thirty years in the woods, I was attuned to every sound.

As dusk neared, there was no traffic on McCarthy Road.

"I think we're going to be okay," I said. "From here, we can keep an eye on who's coming and going. I don't think Papa would think of looking for us here."

Then I felt this sudden attack of extreme fatigue. I think it was because I hadn't eaten anything all day. I wondered if I was about to faint.

"I'm getting dizzy," I said to Jerusalem.

"You need to eat something," she said.

"You're probably right."

My body began shaking uncontrollably as temperatures dipped quickly.

"Here, eat these," Jerusalem said.

She handed me some cheese and raisins. I ate them ravenously because I was so hungry. We were munching on the snacks when Jerusalem stopped eating.

"Elishaba, are you okay? You're not gonna die, are you?"

"I don't know. I need to get my sleeping bag out and go to sleep. I wish we could build a fire, but someone might see us."

As I lay down and crawled inside my sleeping bag, I reminded myself that I'd slept outside many times during an Alaskan winter and survived Arctic temperatures. Unfortunately, it was getting very cold very quickly. I figured that it would get to minus twenty below that night.

I needed some rest after such an intense and nerve-racking day.

I fell asleep, knowing that surviving in the frozen wilderness would be far easier than living another day with Papa Pilgrim, whose real name was Robert Allen Hale.

# PART II

---

# THE RISE OF BOBBY HALE

# 7

# BACK TO THE BEGINNING

I didn't know much about my father growing up. He preferred things that way, but in my later years, after talking to others, plus doing research, I learned more.

I start with my father's birth, which happened on April 7, 1941, a few weeks ahead of schedule. Robert Allen Hale was born seven minutes before his twin brother, William. They were the first children of I.B. Hale and his wife, Virginia. The Hales, married just a couple of years, lived in Fort Worth, Texas.

For some reason, Billy was placed in an incubator for quite a few days while Bobby snuggled up with his mother between breastmilk feedings. My father always felt like he was his mom's favorite child since he got to bond with her during those first few days after birth.

I don't think my father ever bonded that much with his father, known for his gruff, no-nonsense demeanor. I never met I.B. Hale; he died of a heart attack at the age of fifty-four, five years before I was born. I always wondered how anyone could go through life being called "I.B." until I found out that the initials stood for Insall Bailey.

*Insall?* I've never heard of anyone called Insall before—or since.

I.B. was larger than life. He was big and strong for his time—six feet, two inches tall and nearly 250 pounds. At Woodrow Wilson High in Dallas, his football coaches put him on the line of scrimmage as a tackle, where he overpowered linemen fifty to seventy-five pounds lighter than him. He was such a dominating player that he went on to play college football at Texas Christian University in Fort Worth, where he was voted to the All-American team twice during TCU's most triumphant football era. He was also co-captain of the undefeated 1938 team that was voted as the national collegiate football champion.

After his senior year, the Washington Redskins drafted him in the first round of the 1939 NFL Draft. These days, being a first-round pick earns you a multi-million dollar contract, but back in the early days of professional football, players were paid a few hundred dollars a game, if that. Short careers often left the leather-helmeted players badly injured or crippled.

I.B. passed on the NFL. He applied with the FBI and got a job as a special agent, and the story goes that legendary FBI chief J. Edgar Hoover took a liking to him. I.B. was a workaholic, gone for weeks at a time on cases. Climbing the FBI ladder moved the young family into a nice upper-class neighborhood in Fort Worth, but he had also married into wealth. His wife, Virginia, was a fragile woman with beautiful features. She struggled to take care of the twins by herself, who were a handful.

One night, after Bobby and Billy had started primary school, they plotted a plan to go swimming in a nearby mudhole—in the dark.

"We'll wait until Mom is asleep, and then we can sneak out to that mudhole," Bobby said. My father always seemed to be the ringleader in these escapades.

Later that night, his mother heard some severe knocking on the front door. She gathered a robe around her and opened the door.

"Sorry to bother you, ma'am." Standing before her was a Fort Worth Police Department officer with a pair of shivering and muddy youngsters. "But you need to control your kids."

Virginia would find it nearly impossible to tame the wild boys born to her in the years to come. If they weren't bickering or picking on each other, they were arguing about who was Mom's favorite. When Virginia got exasperated, she'd send them off to their room, telling them to keep the door closed and their mouths shut.

One time, they were too quiet—and then she heard the sound of glass breaking. When Virginia went to check on them, she nearly fainted from the sight of blood. The twins had broken the window and cut themselves when they stuck their hands out to wave at their friends walking through the neighborhood.

They got into more mischief when they decided to play "David and Goliath." My father took the role of David with his slingshot. For some reason, Billy grabbed a big stick and agreed to be menacing Goliath. Bobby pulled back on his slingshot—and to his horror, he struck his twin brother in the forehead with a rock, just like a shepherd boy did with a sling three thousand years ago.

His brother slumped to the ground, out cold.

Bobby ran to the house, a jumble of tears. "Mom, I . . . I killed Billy!"

She sprinted past him and out the front door, where she found Billy in the grass, still as can be with a sliver of blood rolling down the side of his face.

Unlike Goliath, Billy survived.

When they were ten years old, a bully in the neighborhood loved harassing kids and taking away their footballs, their basketballs, and their baseballs.

Bobby and Billy decided that they would do something about the giant kid pushing them around one day. They formulated a foolproof plan: Billy would dive for his ankles, and Bobby would wrap his arms around his neck and upper torso. Together, they would wrestle him to the ground and pummel him into submission.

That's precisely what happened. By the time the twins were finished with him, the bully was begging for mercy. He never bothered the Hale boys again, and their friends treated Bobby and Billy like heroes.

This was when my father realized that he could let his fists do the talking. When he grew older, he took up boxing and learned how to punch and flick jabs. Bobby and Billy practiced their fighting skills on each other.

Even though my father didn't like to tell us much about his boyhood, he seemed to enjoy telling us how tough he was. What he didn't mention was that from a young age, he learned that he got what he wanted when he hit people.

My father hit his teenage years in the mid-1950s, a time when kids his age wore white T-shirts, straight-leg dark blue Levi's, and slicked back their hair with Brylcreem and Vaseline. Bobby liked hot rods and speeding. One time, he was driving around with a bunch of other teenagers, goofing off. He spotted a trooper up ahead, parked by the side of the road.

"How much do you want to bet that I can speed past this cop and he won't give me a ticket because I'm I.B. Hale's son?" he asked in a moment of bragging.

His dare was returned with roars of laughter. "Ha! You think you're really that special?" asked one of his buddies.

My father took the challenge. "Who's betting me? Come on, put your money where your mouth is."

"I have a dollar that says you're getting a ticket," said one of his friends. "But you have to get stopped first."

"Me too. I'm in," another said.

Bobby floored the accelerator. The Chevy picked up speed and zoomed past the state trooper, the speedometer pushing seventy-five mph in a fifty mph zone.

A siren split the air, which prompted an uproar in the car.

"Look, he's coming after you!" said someone in the back seat.

Bobby glanced into his rearview mirror. Sure enough, a boxy vehicle lit up like a Christmas tree with flashing red lights was on his tail. Bobby pulled over to the sandy shoulder.

The boys could barely keep from busting out laughing as the trooper, wearing a wide-brim hat, beige uniform, and knee-high black boots, approached the driver's side window.

"Good evening, officer," my father said. His polite tone was so different than his usual smart-alecky manner that his buddies were pinching themselves not to chuckle.

"Do you know why I pulled you over?"

"Ah, no, officer."

"I got you doing seventy-five. Can I see your license?"

Bobby reached into his hip pocket for his wallet and pulled out his Texas driver's license. "I'm Robert Hale. I.B.'s son."

"No kidding." The state trooper took a long look at the driver's license photo of my father. The slicked-back, ducktail hairstyle matched.

"Robert, I'll let you go this time, but you better start being more careful. Say hi to your father. I watched him play in the Cotton Bowl when they beat those Razorbacks."

"Yeah, he was a great football player. Thank you, officer."

As soon as the state trooper was out of earshot, my father had one thing to say to his friends: "Pay up, boys!"

My father attended Arlington Heights High School in Fort Worth, an all-white public high school whose classrooms were filled with the sons and daughters of affluence. A prominent attorney, John Connally, sent his children there.[1]

I don't know how my father met John Connally's daughter, Kathleen, who was two years younger. Bobby was a seventeen-year-old senior with no real goals in life, and Kathleen was a fun-loving fifteen-year-old sophomore that friends called "K.K." The age difference meant quite a maturity gap between the two—something that my father could exploit.

There was a bond of heartfelt love between them, intensified by their young ages. I can imagine that Bobby and K.K. started fooling around since my father viewed "love" as sexual. I know K.K. wasn't Bobby's first girlfriend since he was popular among the girls, but K.K. wasn't just another pretty young thing to chase. Bobby wanted her to be his, and he wanted her in his arms. He wasn't going to lose her.

With teenage hormones near the boiling point, the inevitable happened as

---

1. John Connally would be elected as Texas' governor in 1962 and become famous a year later when he was seated in the same Lincoln Continental as President John F. Kennedy during a motorcade through downtown Dallas on November 22, 1963. Shots rang out in Dealey Plaza, killing the President and seriously wounding Connally, who survived. In a fascinating footnote to history, President Kennedy and Connally were shot by Lee Harvey Oswald, who attended Arlington Heights High School and was a grade ahead of Bobby and Billy Hale.

the two adolescent lovers took chances: K.K. got pregnant.

She had just turned sixteen on February 17, 1959. Her parents were pillars of the community, so news of a pregnancy would be scandalous if word got out. Neighbors and friends would have a field day sharing the titilating morsel of dirt. K.K. was scared and didn't know what to do. Abortion wasn't an option in those days.

Bobby tried to smooth things over, comfort her fears, and remind her everything would be all right. *We can leave Fort Worth and all those gossip hounds. We can get married. Start a life of our own.*

K.K. wasn't so sure, but she listened when Bobby hatched an audacious plan: they would hop in his car and elope in Oklahoma, where she could get married at the age of sixteen without a parent's consent. Then they'd drive on to Tallahassee, Florida, where someone he knew could get him a job with the Lone Star Boat Company, founded in Grand Prairie, Texas, in 1945.

They were married before an Episcopal minister on March 16, 1959, in Ardmore, Oklahoma, a hundred miles north of Fort Worth and just over the state line. Then they drove east to begin married life in the Florida panhandle.

One can only imagine what K.K. was thinking as they sped past the bayous of Louisiana and Mississippi. But, for sure, reality was setting in: she was sixteen years old and pregnant; she had dropped out of school and ran away from the only home she'd ever known; she had left her family with nary a word about her plans; and she was with an older guy adept at manipulating her emotions.

They settled into a threadbare second-story apartment at 223 West St. Augustine Street. Bobby started work at the Lone Star Boat Company, where he was paid seventy dollars a week to put fiberglass into molds.[2] K.K. got a retail job at a five-and-dime store.

It wasn't long before they had visitors: John Connally and I.B. Hale had jumped into a car and driven to Tallahassee as soon as they received a collect phone call from a sobbing K.K., who was feeling buyer's remorse. They tried to tell her that all was forgiven and that she and Bobby could come home, that they'd work things out. Whether she was scared to face her family or afraid of what Bobby would do to her if they returned to Fort Worth, she sucked in her breath and said she was staying.

Just a month into the marriage, though, K.K. became despondent. Feelings of guilt threatened to suffocate her. They fought and got into arguments over matters big and small. They were kids, after all.

One day Bobby came home from work to an empty apartment. He knew K.K. had the day off. He searched everywhere but couldn't find her. Had she

---

2. Seventy dollars a week in 1959 is the equivalent of $785 a week today, but the cost of living was a lot lower then.

taken the Greyhound bus back to Fort Worth? He didn't know.

This was the second time she disappeared: two weeks earlier, she had taken off on a Thursday and checked into a hotel in nearby Thomasville, Georgia, without notifying him. She returned the following Tuesday, after having left Bobby without a car and wondering what was going on with his new bride. And now she had taken off again, throwing him into another emotional tailspin.

At 10:15 p.m., there was a knock on the door. When Bobby opened it, expectantly, he saw Ethel Hawes, the landlady who lived below him.

"Here," she said, handing him an envelope. "Your wife asked if she could spend the night at my place. I said yes."

In her rambling letter, K.K. wrote that she was hurting, felt that he didn't love her anymore, and wondered if she could ever return to him.

The following morning, she refused to leave the landlady's apartment. Bobby left to do some errands. When he returned at noontime, he opened the door to his apartment and saw K.K. before him, sitting on a couch. Across her lap was a 20-gauge shotgun.

"K.K. You're back—"

He watched in horror as she raised the gun and awkwardly placed the barrel against the side of her head, given the length of the shotgun.

"No! Don't shoot! I beg you!"

"It's over, Bobby. This was all a huge mistake." Her voice was dull, lifeless.

"No! We can figure something out. But not this!"

Bobby edged closer to her. "Just hand me the gun. And then we can talk."

"This isn't going to work. I can't go on."

"You don't have to be afraid. I'll make it work. I love you so much." Bobby was pleading, near tears.

"Don't come any closer." K.K. maintained a precarious grip on the shotgun.

"Sweetheart, please put the gun down. We can talk," he pleaded.

Then he saw her right index finger squeeze a bit against the trigger. Fearing that she would do the unthinkable, Bobby lunged for the gun to knock it away from her.

In a microsecond, a shotgun blast exploded behind her right ear, filling the air with the sulfurous smell of gunpowder. Half the shotgun pellets struck K.K. in the back of her skull, the other half of the discharge lodged in the ceiling.

Bobby screamed in terror. His body went into shock as everything slowed down. Then, numbly, he cradled her slumped body in his arms, blood soaking his clothes. Tears streamed down his face.

"Oh, K.K. What have you done?"

Upon hearing the shotgun blast, neighbors called for an ambulance. K.K. died en route to the hospital. The date was April 28, 1959.

Robert and Kathleen Hale had been married only forty-four days.

Whenever my father spoke to me about K.K., he would start crying and become depressed. I could tell that losing K.K. at such a young age had a huge impact on him, which manifest itself throughout his life. Witnessing her death and losing a child in the womb was something he never got over.

When those tragic memories came back, his voice would become winded with deep groans, as if she was right next to him. "Oh, K.K., if only you hadn't done it. I tried to convince you that I could love you. And oh, the baby! The baby!"

Inside the apartment, as sheriff's deputies and homicide detectives took evidence from the crime scene, Bobby was nearly inconsolable as an ambulance crew attempted to keep her alive. Neighbors told police that they had to restrain Bobby from jumping out of the second-story window.

Torn to pieces, Bobby wailed that he wanted to go to the hospital to be with K.K. An Episcopal minister agreed to accompany him, but doctors didn't let him see the body. Instead, they gave him a sedative to deal with his gut-wrenching grief.

Homicide detectives, after a preliminary investigation inside the apartment, determined that K.K. either committed suicide or was killed while Bobby tried to take the gun from her. They decided not to file charges against my father, but they did take him into protective custody at Leon County jail, where he spent the night.

The following day, Bobby appeared at a coroner's inquest. His dazed parents, I.B. and Virginia, along with the grieving Connallys, had flown in from Dallas. While entering the courthouse, Virginia pressed close to Bobby and attempted to shield their faces from photographers with sheets of newspaper. Because K.K. and Bobby were from "prominent" Fort Worth families, the press splashed the story atop the front page of the *Fort Worth Star-Telegram* and *Tallahassee Democrat* newspapers.

The coroner's inquest consisted of a jury of six men who listened to nearly three hours of testimony. Nellie Connally wept openly at times, and I.B. Hale dabbed at tears in his eyes.

The *Tallahassee Democrat* reporter said Bobby was calm and showed little emotion until he took the stand. This is what the reporter wrote:

> At times young Hale was almost incoherent as he told the jury of a stormy honeymoon and then finding his bride of forty-four days seated on a couch in their small apartment with a shotgun in her hands. He knelt at her feet and pleaded with her to put the gun down.

LARGEST CIRCULATION
IN TEXAS—
DAILY AND SUNDAY
OVER
250,000 COMBINED DAILY

# FORT WORTH STAR-TELEGRAM

EVENING
EDITION

A Fort Worth Owned Newspaper

SEVENTY-NINTH YEAR, NO. 88.  FORT WORTH, TEXAS  ★★  Where the West Begins  ★★  WEDNESDAY, APRIL 29, 1959.  FORTY-TWO PAGES  PRICE FIVE CENTS

## House Votes Spending Bill Down

AUSTIN, April 29 (AP).—The House rejected the Senate's $1,100,000,000 general spending bill Wednesday and asked for a conference committee to work out differences.

Then it killed, 117-4, an effort to instruct its conferees to write a one-year appropriations bill if there is not enough money for a two-year measure.

Rep. Ben H. Lewis of Dallas urged the one-year spending plan if the conferees could not agree on a two-year bill that could be ratified by the comptroller.

Rep. W. S. Heatly of Paducah, chairman of the appropriations committee, opposed the one-year idea. He said its effect would be to drain away current operating funds needed for colleges, pensions and other services during the next two months.

### No Tax Bill

"It would close down on," said Heatly. Lewis argued that his plan is necessary to keep the departments operating after about of the new fiscal year that start.

The difficulty is that the Legislature has been unable thus far to approve a tax bill to finance state operations in fiscal 1960-1961. The House and Senate have approved varying versions of how much is owed, but the general fund is already $46,000,000 in the red. No money has been found to erase that. No new revenue is yet in sight.

Heatly's motion to reject the Senate's spending bill, $30,500,000 higher than the House measure, was not opposed. A conference committee is the usual route for working out the spending bill.

### Annual Salary

The Senate expected to set public hearings early next week on the House-passed general tax bill. The estimated $77,000,000 it would raise in 1960-1961 is about than $230,000,000 short of the estimated new money needs.

The House voted 130-27 Tuesday to put legislators on a $4,800 annual salary, plus $12 a day extra for legislative sessions, plus some travel and office expenses.

The salary plan still has to be approved by the Senate and Texas voters. A proposed annual constitutional amendment would raise it to $4,800 — coupled with a provision for normal expenses, was defeated last November. Texas legislators now get only $25 for 120 days of a regular session and 30 days of a special session.

### "Horks Want It."

The House also agreed to Senate changes in a proposed constitutional amendment allowing the Legislature to set interest rates and charges on all loans. The action cleared the way for a popular vote on the issue in November 264.

"This is the anti-loan shark bill that the loan sharks want," said Rep. J. C. Kilpatrick of Liberty.

The loan sharks are going to get hit if this is passed," Kilpatrick wanted to control loans secured by property, such as homes and automobiles.

The Senate approved 29-6 a proposed constitutional change extending the line of succession to the governorship. After the lieutenant

*Turn to House on Page 6.*

INJURED FIREMAN AIDED—Two firemen connect an emergency oxygen supply to aid stricken Fireman George Zauf, left. Zauf later was taken to Harris Hospital from the downtown blaze Tuesday afternoon.

OCCUPANTS WATCH BLAZE—Saul Cohen, left, and L. L. Burchfield, who operated businesses in the building housing Cheney's, women's wear store, watch firemen battle the two-alarm blaze there Tuesday afternoon.

### Couldn't Stand One a Week
## Poisonous Smoke Makes Firemen Earn Their Salary in Short Time

BY PHIL RECORD

Those firemen are earning 10 months' salary on these jobs.

Such were the sentiments of Charles James as he stood watching a late Tuesday afternoon fire eat away at Cheney's women's wear shop at 442 Houston.

And James knew whereof he spoke. He is a former member of the Fort Worth fire department, now serving as fire chief at Corsicana.

"For him it was good to be a spectator Tuesday.

"The public just doesn't realize what a man goes through in a fire like this," James continued. "It takes a lot of skill and guts to go into that smoke."

The smoke was the special characteristic of this two-alarm blaze.

"It was a putrid, yellow-green smoke, low in oxygen and high in poisonous gases."

"It has the worst effect on a man," explained Assistant Fire Marshal Bixon.

"It sets the eyes afire, sears the face fresh red, and makes the lungs feel they will explode from lack of oxygen."

Bixon said the toxic smoke is a product of incomplete combustion.

"There's not enough oxygen for the materials to burn, so they just give off the toxic gases," he said.

Smoldering clothing in the shop combined with other factors, aggravated the situation, Bixon said.

Time and again firemen were forced to a smashed second-story window by the boiling smoke to gasp for fresh air, the several occasions it appeared that one of the exhausted men would collapse and plunge to the street below.

But before he would yield, a comrade would seize him, then lead him outside where other firemen would administer aid.

It is a blaze like this that a fireman earns his salary of "smoke color."

One of those assisted from the smoke-choked structure was 30-year-old George Zauf.

That smoke's the roughest," he said while propped up against the bumper of a fire truck. "It gives off gas that will kill you."

"A man can't fight those kind of fires every week—he'd die."

Tears streamed from Zauf's eyes as he fought for relief giving fresh air. Finally, one of his superiors ordered him to Harris Hospital for additional treatment. Zauf was in good condition Wednesday.

"We'll have men with sore lungs and eyes for days after this one," said a fire official.

There are soldiers and miners. It wouldn't be the thing to do—they just didn't fight shading all them. He ran up and grabbed her arm away, I started shooting at him. The two up and grabbed her away. That's when I shot her.

"I didn't mean to, I worshiped the ground she walked on," he said.

*Turn to Firemen on Page 6.*

## Severe Weather Due in W. Texas

A severe thunderstorm forecast for a large portion of West Texas was issued by the U. S. Weather Bureau Wednesday afternoon.

It said portions of the South Plains and country east of the Pecos, the southwestern portion of North Central Texas and the Panhandle would have thunderstorm activity throughout Wednesday afternoon in the Pre-Panhandle and moving southward, some of the storms producing large hail and damaging surface winds.

The forecast was for an area along and 125 miles to the north-west of a line from Alpine northwest of Big Spring to Junction from 3 to 9 p. m.

## No Mutiny in Bounty When Policeman Plays

BY EDDY GILMORE

ALDERNEY, Channel Islands, April 29.—You British know timely and are Tuesday night at Bligh's Beauty Bar, it being the 170th year to the day since the crew of the Bounty got rid of the hard-voiced Capt. William Bligh.

The bar's proprietor, Jack Bligh, is one of Captain Bligh's descendants and a tolerant man. I've had that the mutiny on the bounty took place thousands of miles away in the Pacific in a time the ships he's relieved of.

"Alley, don't matter," he said. "The anniversary does. This is the best excuse for a celebration in years."

But the Alderney—a British possession situated in the chan-

At the same relaxing atmosphere only eight miles off the coast of France—an excuse in good for a celebration.

"How long," asked a visitor from England where the public can usually drink to later than 10 p. m. or night, "is the Beauty Bar open?"

"As long as you want to drink," answered Bligh. "We'll stay open until a o'clock never run warning if you want it and if that isn't long enough, we'll stay open until 6 o'clock the next day."

"Don't you have any drinking laws?"

"Oh, yes, we've got some laws."

"Do policemen he enforce them?"

BY DON WILLIAMS

A little upstairs tiff with "little upstairs tiff with hair" Tuesday afternoon caused the shooting death of a 10-year-old Fort Worth bride, Mrs. Robert Allen Hale, according to a Tallahassee, Fla. detective.

The detective, Capt. Bob Maige, said of the shooting, which occurred in the presence of the 20-year-old husband:

"It looked like it was very possible that it was accidental."

Young Hale, who spent the night in jail at Tallahassee, was to appear at 1:30 p. m. Fort Worth time Wednesday at an inquest before County Judge James C. Gwynn.

The husband is the son of Mr. and Mrs. J. P. Hale of 4472 Portland Rd. He and Miss Kathleen Connally, daughter of Mr. and Mrs. John R. Connally of 4610 West

### Fire's Cost May Reach $100,000

Houston St. Store's Damage Toll Revised Upward by Marshal

A revised estimate of loss starting upward from $75,000" was set Wednesday morning by Fire Marshal Killion after the two-alarm fire which Tuesday swept the upper floor at Cheney's women's wear store at 442 Houston.

Total damage could easily reach $100,000, Killion said.

An all-night vigil by an solid ladder company of firemen was Wednesday morning as the crew prepared to return to station.

Barricades placed in front of the damaged stores were removed about 7 a. m.

Undetermined smoke and water damage to Shaw's Jewelers and Dolafey Shoe store on either side of the burned building as firemen confined the blaze to the second (floor) and attic of Cheney's.

First alarm on the fire was rushed in by a police car at 3:45 p. m. with a second alarm sounded at 3:53 p. m. Firemen

*Turn to Fire Cost on Page 6.*

### Today's CHUCKLE

The only people who can live like millionaires these days are millionaires.
(©1959 General Features Corp.)

## Three-Way Tightening of Labor Bill Urged on Congress by Eisenhower

WASHINGTON, April 29 (AP). President Eisenhower called on Congress Wednesday for tightening of the Senate's labor control bill at three points.

Eisenhower told his news conference that the measure passed by the Senate has very definite weaknesses.

He said he is very disappointed with it.

The President said he believes the House should write in amendments to (1) curb secondary boycotts, (2) outlaw blackmail picketing and (3) clarify the no-man's-land area where the authority of the National Labor Relations Board and that of the states is cloudy.

Eisenhower was asked if he feels it necessary to have such amendments in light of the fact of rights' for rank and file that some voted into the Senate measure.

Eisenhower replied that as a first was offered by Senator Mc-Clellan of Arkansas, he thought the bill of rights proposal was a fine thing.

But he said a compromise much finally was adopted was

but a real substitute for the kind of thing that should have been put in.

The substitute was opposed by senator Thomas Kuchel of California, the assistant Republican leader, and backed by a group of Republicans who have been regarded as friendly to organized labor.

That was Eisenhower's first Washington news conference since March 25, he dealt with these other topics:

Berlin—Eisenhower said from the outset of John Foster Dulles illness that Christian A. Herter would be a first-rate secretary of state if it became necessary for Dulles to resign.

When Dulles was forced to resign earlier this month because of cancer, Herter, who had been serving as acting secretary, was his immediate choice for the job. As the President said, preceded his readiness to go to the border.

The situation is tying to the most dangerous in the world, but he added it certainly is not an easy situation.

Nixon-Kuntsel — At the Vice President Nixon never would attend any summit conference with the Russians simultaneously. Eisenhower said. That would be feasible because of the nature of the American governmental and the necessity for the President to remain here at the country for any length of time.

A bit later, in reply to another question, Eisenhower said he had not meant to imply any probability that Nixon might next star her him during part of any summit meeting. There are no summit plans for that, he said.

*Turn to Eisenhower on Page 6.*

## Murder Charge Filed In Arlington Killings

Charges of murder were on Wednesday in Peace Justice Ray's court at Arlington against J. N. McMurtrey for the Tuesday night slaying of his 21-year-old wife, Virginia, and James L. Mitchell, 36, of Bill Greenway of Arlington, a man described by McMurtrey as his wife's boyfriend.

McMurtrey, a Grand Prairie butcher, was brought to the Tarrant County Jail at 12:18 a. m. Wednesday.

Marshall, spoken at Morgan's Mortuary, M. L., was a butcher at a supermarket in the Park Plaza shopping Center where Mrs. McMurtrey worked as a meat wrapper.

The shooting occurred shortly after 8 p. m. at Mrs. McMurtrey's residence in the Silver Sail Apartments at 3332 E. Abram in Arlington. Earlier it was reported that the apartment was above a tavern.

Mrs. McMurtrey worked the apartment a week ago, and said Tuesday filed divorce papers against her husband.

McMurtrey, who is the father of three children, said that yesterday evening right lower she, high Thursday upper No, Wind southerly 10 to 20 m.p.h.

North Central Texas—Partly cloudy through Thursday.

West Texas—Partly cloudy and warm through Thursday. Sentered thundershowers lower Pecos Valley, eastward. Warmer.

East Texas — Partly cloudy through Thursday. Warmer north and central portions.

South Central Texas—Considerable cloudiness and warm through Thursday. Widely scattered showers Wednesday afternoon and night.

Weather map on Page 26.

THE WEATHER

Rain to date 3:39, normal accumulation 11.21.
Sun sets 7:35 Wednesday, rises 6:43 Thursday.
High temperature Carter Field Tuesday 81, minimum 58.

THINK IT OVER
BY H. W. STEINBERG

The best way to repent is to repair.

## IKE SURE MRS. LUCE'S SENATE ROW NOT DAMAGING IN BRAZIL

WASHINGTON, April 29 (AP). President Eisenhower said Wednesday that the Clare Boothe Luce's resignation as ambassador to Brazil will cause no loss of standing as an ambassador to any major way by her row with Senator Wayne of Oregon.

The President told a news conference that he had a telephone talk with Mrs. Luce and received Thursday from Valley road to Waitsel.

Eisenhower said he asked what kind of thing that should have been put in.

Some Democratic senators who had voted for confirmation of the nomination said that if they had to do it over again they would vote against her.

And Mrs. Luce's husband, Henry R. Luce of the Time-Life-Fortune publishing empire, said in New York he had asked his wife to resign the ambassador-ship because of the criticism of her.

Then Eisenhower said he feels there has been no major punishment of Mrs. Luce's usefulness.

He also said that she had on the world-wide tour her husband and after in reign.

Eisenhower hesitated a moment and then joined in a roast of laughter touched off by the question was put — whether the Senate was just unusual about stability" on Mrs. Luce's part.

THE INDEX

## Golfing for Cash Gets Under Way

Regular play in Colonial Country Club's National Invitation Tournament will start Thursday, but the entry field is frying for spoils and take in any cash today. Page 39.

(Index section listings — page numbers)

"She was telling me she was going to kill herself," he said, "She said, 'Bobby, I'm sick in my mind, and I need help. I know now that no one can help me.'"

She brought the gun up to her head, Hale said. Then—

"At the last desperate moment, I lunged at the gun and hit it. I hit it as hard as I could. It hit the wall, and she was still . . ."

His voice died away, and he sat mute and wide-eyed for several moments.

"Did the gun go off before you hit it?" asked County Judge James Gywnn, conducting the inquest.

"I don't know. She opened her eyes and fell back, and I caught her and said, 'K.K..'"

A fingerprint expert and a lie detector operator both testified they could find nothing to implicate Hale in the shooting.

After forty minutes of deliberation, the jury ruled that the death of K.K. Connally Hale was accidental.

Whatever happened that day, I truly believe from my heart that an emotional battle went on between the two of them that drove her to her death.

There was something else that caught my eye when I read the newspaper clippings about the tragedy. In a story about the coroner's inquest, the *Tallahassee Democrat* reporter wrote this:

A juror asked Hale if he and his wife had made a suicide pact. The question seemed to startle the youth.

"No," he answered. A long pause. Then another, "No." Connally and the elder Hale [the fathers] both testified letters from the young couple indicated they were happy and getting along well.

However, Deputy Sheriff Jack Dawkins said he found correspondence in the apartment indicating Kathleen "was very much disturbed and emotional—apparently having trouble with her husband."

It doesn't surprise me that K.K. and my father were having significant issues in their marriage, just weeks old. But a murder-suicide pact?

Years later, when the law was closing in on us, my father would tell us, "My number one prayer is that we either live together or we die together."

At the time, I knew he really meant it.

# 8
# SWEPT UP BY THE SIXTIES

There was no way Bobby was going to finish his senior year at Arlington High. It seemed like everyone in Fort Worth had heard about K.K.'s tragic death—and suspected there was more to the story than the accidental discharge of a shotgun.

From the corner of his eye, Bobby noticed the sideways glances and overheard the furtive asides. He holed up inside his parents' home, his only company being his twin brother, Billy. Eventually, Bobby got out of the house and enrolled at Polytechnic High School to earn his secondary education diploma. Two times during the spring of 1959, he drove to Tallahassee to speak with the ambulance driver who raced to the hospital to save K.K.'s life. Bobby was having a hard time putting the tragedy behind him.

His mother, Virginia, generally let him do whatever he wanted because she felt sorry for him following K.K.'s death. She tried to protect him from life's realities, like when she escorted him into the coroner's inquest, using a newspaper to shield themselves from the photographers.

Bobby eventually came around and enrolled at Texas Christian University, his father's alma mater, in the fall of 1959. He had a drinking buddy named Dick, and they raised some hell and landed in jail a couple of times. One night they were out partying when their car veered off the road. Luckily, Dick's car got caught up in some fencing, or they would have tumbled over a cliff and into a lake, suffering serious injury or death.

Bobby shook off the crash and dove back into the dating game. Whenever he met a pretty coed and she agreed to go out with him, he'd sit across the restaurant table and—with all the sincerity he could muster—solemnly tell her that this was his "first date" since the death of his young wife. The disclosure, of course, elicited all sorts of sympathy, but there was an ulterior motive: his emotional revelation softened up her defenses. Bobby used the "this is my first date" line often during his freshman year.

Bobby cruised through his college years in a fancy blue Corvette sports car from money his grandmother had left him. He also earned a pilot's license one summer, which he treated as a lark. One time, he was flying with his brother, Billy, and my father suddenly shut off the engine and allowed the single-engine plane to go into a nosedive. Naturally, Billy freaked out and screamed that they were going to die, which is the reaction Bobby wanted. Just when Billy thought they were going to crash, Bobby switched on the engine and leveled the plane out, laughing the entire time.

While attending TCU, my father became serious with a woman named Linda. This would have been two or three years after K.K.'s death. They married while he was still in school, and she quickly bore him a son named Alan. Bobby hustled for jobs in between his schoolwork and proved to be a hard worker in whatever he did, usually in the construction industry. As far as I can determine, Bobby spent the better parts of seven years at TCU before earning a master's degree in business finance.[1]

Not much is known about Linda because she left him early on, but what's evident is that my father was swept along by the cultural turbulence that produced great upheaval during the 1960s. This dramatic decade was marked by assassinations, urban rioting, campus buildings under siege from Vietnam protesters, and masses of young people at rock concerts. The Sixties were a rebellious era when young people took to heart a saying from a psychologist named Timothy Leary who famously said, "Turn on, tune in, drop out."

By the mid-1960s—an era of free love, mind-altering drugs, flower power, love-ins, and acid rock—my father was ready to join the parade of those wanting to "drop out" of society. He didn't care about material things anymore and certainly believed that he wasn't suited for the nine-to-five world. Sometime around 1966 or 1967, he chucked all his belongings, including the Corvette sports car, and decided that he wanted to live a life free of things. Bobby grew out his black hair down to his shoulders and allowed a full beard to cover his face.[2]

He traveled wherever the wind took him on his Triumph motorcycle, his only mode of transportation. He was one of the original hippies, content to

---

1. Details about my father's life in the early 1960s are murky at best. Several writers—journalist Seymour Hersh, Mark Kirby with *Outside* magazine, and Tom Kizzia, author of *Pilgrim's Wilderness*—did some investigation and discovered that the FBI spotted my father and his brother, Billy, breaking into the Los Angeles apartment of Judith Campbell Exner, who was purported to be one of President John Kennedy's mistresses. This happened in 1962. My father never spoke of this incident to me.

2. Billy took a more conventional career path. He graduated from North Texas State University and went on to veterinary school. He married Patsy Dorris and established a successful veterinary business in Fort Worth.

wear rags and not worry about where his next meal was coming from or where he was sleeping that night. He became adept at hopping from one crash pad to another. His drugs of choice were marijuana and LSD, the latter a potent mind-altering hallucinogenic drug that produced psychedelic "trips" that altered his consciousness and awareness of his surroundings.

You can imagine how the transformation into an acid-taking, long-haired hippie went over with someone as straitlaced and clean-cut as I.B. Hale, who never passed up the chance to express his disgust with his oldest child. When Bobby was back in Fort Worth for some reason one time, I.B. called his prodigal son into his den and sat him down.

I.B. reviewed what a messed-up person Bobby had been, airing every misstep, recounting every mistake, and recalling every grievance he had against his son. Then, in his gravelly voice, he announced his verdict: "Son, you are the biggest disappointment to me. I don't ever want to see your face again."

My father pursed his lips. He didn't say a thing, but he was wounded to the core. Not only had he never heard his father express his love for him throughout his childhood, but he would be burdened for the rest of his life with the knowledge that he had failed the great I.B. Hale. No matter what my father did in life, he would never be good enough, never measure up.

That day, Bobby was determined to get as far away as possible from Fort Worth.

And he would never see his father alive again.

Bobby hit the open highway and traveled the back roads to out-of-the-way places where hippies congregated in Oregon and California. He liked the kindred nonconformists he found in communes. These free-spirited hippies listened to his ideas on what they should do—from sharing food to how chores should be divvied up to the commune's casual sexual relationships that were part of everyday life.

My father saw a power vacuum in the communes that he could exploit through his considerable charm when it suited his purposes, and his ability to argue for his way of thinking. He had a way of winning people over to his side because they were smitten—even mesmerized—by his mystic personality. Having the hippies value his point of view allowed him to be in charge, and when he was in charge, he could control people. In the years to come, he would develop an incredible talent for manipulating others to do what he wanted. My father was a natural-born leader who wanted others to follow him, and follow him they did.

Some of the stories my father told me sounded bizarre, like the time when multicolored trees surrounding their encampment started bowing down to him. Then he spoke to everyone in the commune with a voice that sounded like thunder—majestic and amplified. The hippies who witnessed these weird happenings were scared by this mystical event. They viewed my father as some sort of spiritual guru with higher consciousness than them—a notion he didn't discourage.

Now, whether the trees actually bowed down to him or were some type of LSD flashback, I don't know, but he insisted the story was true. He also claimed to have seen UFOs—unidentified flying objects—on three different occasions. Another time he sought out a fortune-teller, who said he would be a great leader one day.

With my father, it was always something.

It was in the communes that my father found another calling: as a midwife. At the time, he may have been one of the first men to take on this traditional role, but that only made him feel more special. My father told me stories about the entire commune gathering around him to watch him deliver a woman's baby. He never had any specialized training, but in the freethinking hippie world of love and acceptance, he took great pride in developing a needed skill that he taught himself. He believed he was someone special when he brought a new life into the world.

My father always had a soft spot in his heart for babies. I think it had something to do with K.K.'s death and how that meant he would never see the child that was growing within her. Whenever he was asked to assist in the birth of babies, he jumped at the chance. He loved it when everyone looked at him to manage one of the building blocks of life.

At Sunnyridge, a commune near the southern Oregon town of Holland and located in the Siskiyou National Forest, Bobby took up with a woman named Christine, who had a little girl named Alia from a previous relationship.[3] Together, my father had two children with Chris: Micah and Shawn. Micah was born on September 9, 1971.[4]

This was a time when my father got into Transcendental Meditation, which was sweeping through the counterculture in the late '60s and early '70s. Developed by Maharishi Mahesh Yogi with acolytes like the Beatles, TM, as it was called, was a type of meditation in which each participant closed his or her

---

3. Alia's hippie name was Singing Waters.
4. In the last few years, I've gotten to know Alia and Micah, but Shawn has disappeared from the face of the earth.

eyes and whispered their personal "mantra" for twenty bliss-filled minutes twice a day. Once they did this, they were well on the road to experiencing nirvana.

My father was trying to fill a spiritual hole in his heart and find meaning in life, so the mysticism of this spiritual discipline was right up his alley. Soon, he led TM sessions in the commune, which gave him another audience to play to.

One time, my father sat in on a TM session led by the Maharishi himself. Bobby was the kind of man who wanted to know everything and would do what it took to make it to the top of the course. The Maharishi took notice of this fervent disciple and was impressed with his desire to spread the TM gospel. Eventually, Bobby was asked to accompany the Maharishi on a lecture tour throughout Europe to work the merchandise table and help out as a roadie.

After several months traveling with Maharishi Mahesh Yogi, my father discovered that the Maharishi and his handlers were more bent on fleecing the sheep than delivering on the promise of inner harmony and world peace. It all came to a head in a Spanish hotel. My father was standing in an elevator when two of the Yogi's top people stepped on, unaware that Bobby was standing in the back of the crowded elevator.

The two men joked and laughed about TM and how they knew it didn't work, but it didn't matter because the Yogi's fans were clueless about how much money they were raking in.

Overhearing their cynical dialogue sickened my father. Instead of joining the TM presentation that night, Bobby checked out and headed for the airport. He made his way back to Sunnyridge, where he reunited with Chris and their children.

I have no idea how my father supported himself or his family during his hippie commune years. They had to be poor and must have done their best to live off the land.

One day, my father was bathing in an outdoor bathtub with little Alia when Chris walked up and announced she was done with him and that he could keep the girl, who was three years old at the time. That day, Chris took off with Micah and Shawn for parts unknown. Why she left stepdaughter Alia in my father's custody is a mystery to me.

Her departure prompted my father to travel to South America with Alia and another woman and her daughter. I'm not sure what the woman's name was, but he called her Cow. She had one of her legs amputated for some reason and got around on a wooden prosthesis. When they traveled together, she kept my father's money inside her wooden leg to foil would-be robbers.

How they got to the Andes Mountains of Chile is yet another puzzle. My father told me stories of wearing flour sacks he'd sewn together and traveling through the high-elevation mountain passes with a couple of thin blankets to shield them from the mind-numbing cold.

"Alia and I used to cuddle up to the belly of a horse to stay warm," he told me one time. To feed themselves, he had Alia stand at street corners and beg for food and money to keep them going.[5] Another way to get passersby to drop a few coins in a hat occurred when my father would sit in a public plaza and play his flute while allowing kids to pet his coatimundi—a type of South American raccoon with a long snout—perched across his broad and tan shoulders.

They had many fun adventures and met up with an old friend from the commune named Ray, but my father and Alia were deported when their tourist visas ran out. They eventually ended up in a different commune outside of Apple Valley, midway between downtown Los Angeles and Las Vegas in the Mojave Desert.

By his early thirties, my father had been in probably a half-dozen serious relationships, fathered three children who were no longer living with him, and was feeling restless. He had a sense that life was passing him by.

One day at the commune in the Mojave Desert, Bob decided to go for a soak in a nearby hot spring. When he arrived, he saw the gorgeous figure of a naked teen girl standing next to the riverbank.

He would tell this story to me and my brothers and sisters many times in the years to come: on that day, when he saw her standing there without a stitch of clothing, a cosmic voice from heaven spoke to him.

*This woman will be your wife, and she will bear you many children.*

Her name was Kurina Rose Bresler, the daughter of Dan and Betty Bresler. During this time, Betty was an actress with several film credits, including roles in the action films *Shaft* and *Trouble Man*. Kurina's parents separated when she was three, and her father gained custody. Since Dan had a busy career as a photographer, Kurina was basically raised by her grandmother. As she reached her teen years, she lived with her mom, who had married a Hollywood producer named Joel Freeman. Lonely, without many friends, and not fitting in with her Beverly Hills classmates, she ran away and ended up in a hippie commune outside Apple Valley.

My father approached her at the hot springs that day and introduced himself as "Ram," short for Ramachandra, a principal deity in Hinduism. He was enthralled with Kurina, no doubt fueled by the cosmic message he heard. Finding out she was sixteen years old was a good omen, my father decided.

*Sixteen . . . the love of my life, K.K., was sixteen . . .*

The fact that my father was more than twice Kurina's age wasn't a stumbling

---

5. Alia came to Alaska to meet me a few years ago, and I believe her absolutely horrendous and sad stories.

block to him nor her. I suppose therapists could have a field day figuring out why sparks flew between a thirty-three-old man who'd been around the block and a naïve sixteen-year-old teen, but they did.

One time, she was getting a ride into the nearby town of Hesperia when the hippie behind the wheel of the truck started calling her "Sun Blossom."

Hippies, wanting to rid themselves of the past, couldn't wait to scrap their Christian first names and last names. When Bob heard that, he thought "Sunlight" would be a better name for her, but they couldn't think of the right name for him.

They eventually landed on "Firefly" for Bob. As for the last name, Sunlight had a brainstorm after Firefly purchased a '41 Ford flatbed truck. She was looking at the hood one day and noticed faded stars. Initially, there had been red-and-white stripes too, but the previous owner had painted over the stripes with yellow paint. To Sunlight's eyes, that looked like a sunstar, so they adopted that as their last name. Their new names grew on them so much that they eventually went through the hassle of legally changing their names·to Firefly Sunstar and Sunlight Sunstar.

They didn't marry, however, even though they started living together in 1975. Alia, five years old, was part of the package. The three of them moved to a commune in Hawaii, where Alia—who ran around naked most of the time—eventually caught the attention of the local Child Protective Services. They took custody of Alia and eventually returned her to Chris on the mainland.

Meanwhile, Firefly and Sunlight carried on. She had learned that Firefly liked to be in charge, which she accepted early on since he was more of a father figure. But as they became lovers, Sunlight began to realize that Firefly treated her like everyone else in his orbit—as a subject in his kingdom. If she spoke her mind, she steeled herself for another tongue-lashing. Sunlight quickly learned that she had to fall in with his moods, which changed direction as often as the trade winds that lashed the Hawaiian Islands.

Sunlight was overwhelmed at times, unsure of how to react to his pot-smoking daze or alcohol-fueled outbursts. But she came under his spell because Firefly could dominate a conversation like no other. She found it easier to keep her head down and let him be the king because he would argue with her until he got his way anyway.

As they lived the vagabond life, Sunlight knew she had to be available to meet his sexual needs, which were enormous, and his sexual proclivities, which meant sharing her bed with other women.

When Firefly and Sunlight's union produced a pregnancy, they decided to move back to Apple Valley in California's high desert.

On January 23, 1976, with Firefly acting as the midwife, a daughter was born.

They named her Butterfly Sunstar because she was fully intact in her amniotic sac and looked like she was in a cocoon when she exited the birth canal.

That baby girl was me.

# 9

# AN EARLY ARRIVAL

I came into this world a good month premature because the day before my birth, my mother went horseback riding amid the junipers, Joshua trees, and sagebrush found in the high desert, something she shouldn't have done so late in her pregnancy. All that bouncing up and down—she rode bareback—produced labor contractions.

When she talked to my father about what to do, he assured my mother that she'd be okay because he'd delivered many babies in the different communes he'd lived in.[1]

"Don't worry," he said. "I had to deliver twins who were premature one time. I'm the first midwife who's ever done that." Self-confidence was his strong suit.

My father coached her through the contractions. When I came out of the birth canal, he chewed off the end of the umbilical cord, figuring that was more hygienic than using his trusty pocketknife.

They didn't have a weight scale, so after a couple of days, they took me to a grocery store in Hesperia, a small town of five thousand located in California's high desert near Apple Valley. Mama set me on a scale in the produce department and discovered that I weighed five pounds.

I was a healthy baby, although Mama told me, with regrets, that I weaned myself at twelve months.[2] As I grew older, Papa would boast to anyone within earshot that I was a Daddy's girl. He loved taking me into the shower with him and gloating over my shiny naked body.

---

1. My mother didn't have a family physician, nor did she see a pediatrician or any medical expert throughout her pregnancy.
2. Mama was planning on nursing me for a couple of years, but I wanted to be with my daddy, who held me most of the time. I wonder now if that partially explains how I became so attached to my father early in life.

We slept in the attic of a building in the commune, which was accessed by a rope ladder through an opening. During my toddler years, my parents would let me nap there with a net fastened underneath the access hole for safety. When I awoke, I would cry out to be picked up.

When no one came, I would crawl toward the interesting-looking opening and tumble into the protective net, where I would cry loudly to be released. This tendency irritated my impatient father so much that he refused to come or allow Mama to rescue me because he wanted to break my will.

All I was seeking was a tender touch from one of my parents. When I wouldn't stop crying and my father reached his boiling point, he would flick me with a fly swatter to stop the flow of tears.

Consequently, I grew up knowing it wasn't safe to cry.

As I was learning to walk, my father received some inheritance money from my grandma—his mother—and used it to purchase an old Chevy '41 flatbed truck. The cost was $350. My father, handy with a hammer and saw, built a structure on the back that he called "The Barn." My mother called it home sweet home as we started traveling around with no real destination in mind. We bounced around different communes scattered throughout the Southwest until we ended up in Colorado, where my brother Joseph was born eighteen months after me on July 25, 1977, also in the back of that old truck. I reveled in my new role as big sister.

Around this time, my father bought a beautiful red Arabian horse that he called Shema. She was full of fire and relatively untrained until my father cleverly broke her. He did this by running up from behind and mounting her bareback, which caused her to take off like the wind. He managed to cling to her mane, guiding her with his knees. She became a great horse.

Shema was the first of the many animals I truly loved. She brought me friendship and security over the years, even a deep sense of self-worth. I felt like she *knew* me at a time when I often felt my parents did not.

Neither owning horses nor parenthood changed the hippie lifestyle that my parents embraced. One warm evening in the desert, we were sitting naked around a campfire in a primitive fashion while my mother nursed my baby brother. My parents, as happened often, were arguing furiously about something.

Without warning and high on drugs, my naked father jumped into the fire, where he picked up hot coals and tossed them in all directions. I cried out in fear, which infuriated him even more. Then a lump of red-hot coal landed on my upper left thigh. I screamed in pain, feeling as though I was on fire.

In the confusion, my mother scooped me up, brushed off the coal, and ran with baby Joseph and me in her arms to a nearby barn where the three of us spent the night. She desperately tried to soothe the pain of my third-degree burns, though nothing could relieve the pain or the uncertainty I was feeling about my father. I was learning early on that my daddy's anger was erratic, even dangerous.

The following day, Mama heard my father calling. When she left the barn to meet him, he apologized profusely. We went back with him, but cautiously.

I was left with a scar,[3] but what I could not foresee was how my father would disfigure me far more deeply in ways invisible to the naked eye.

I was three years old when my daddy suddenly felt a growing compulsion to see his twin brother Billy in Fort Worth. He'd married Patsy, started a veterinarian practice, and was raising two boys and two girls older than me. We all piled into The Barn atop the '41 Chevy flatbed. A ramp allowed Shema and her colt to join us.

We began from the hippie commune outside Apple Valley. I don't know how long the 1,300-mile journey took, but I do know that our old Chevy truck labored to reach speeds of forty mph on the interstates and back-road highways. While my father drove, the rest of us rode in The Barn, where my little brother and I crawled around the horses' hooves and dirty hay on our long drive to the Lone Star State.

Along the way, we stopped at a little town with a laundromat. My daddy lowered the ramp to allow Shema and her foal to be led out onto the road. While the horses nibbled on some grass in a nearby empty lot, Joseph and I crawled down. Daddy swept out the horse manure from my bed while Mama cooked us lunch on a tiny gas stove in the corner.

I felt exceptional when my father let me go with him into the laundromat to wash our filthy old blankets smeared with stinky horse manure. A sweet lady waiting for her clothes to dry looked up.

"Well, look who we have here," she said to me. "You're a really pretty young girl. I love your blonde hair and blue eyes."

I had never been complimented in that way. When she offered me some candy, I shyly accepted because I hadn't been around many strangers. We were either by ourselves or around hippies who didn't pay much attention to small kids underfoot.

While the blankets were getting washed, my father spread fresh hay on the dirty floor of the flatbed truck. When it got dark, Mama set a kerosene lamp on

---

3. The scar is still visible today.

a corner shelf to give us light. Each night, we piled into the single bed together while the horses grazed and slept outside.

As we traveled, my father would look for grocery stores and pull around to the back of the building. Then he and Mama would rummage through the dumpsters for tossed-out food. If there were trash cans, I joined in the treasure hunt. We were always on the lookout for milk, bread, crackers, snacks, perishable fruit, and any sort of expired meat. I'm sure we were quite a spectacle—barefoot and wearing tattered, colorful clothes, with hair unkempt and not too clean, but pawing through trash cans for food seemed normal to me.

After a long time on the road, we finally pulled into Fort Worth and parked in front of Uncle Billy's home, situated in a manicured suburb. His wife, Aunt Patsy, was cautious around us, sensing rightly that their lives were about to be turned upside down by our arrival. I'm sure the sight of a rusty forty-year-old flatbed truck with a homemade "camper" housing a pair of horses had the neighbors talking. Shema and her foal made their home in Uncle Billy's front yard during their stay.

The time in Texas became a life-changing experience for my parents. As Daddy told the story every year on the anniversary of a specific Sunday in January, we were sitting in the back of a prominent Baptist church wearing our torn, worn-out clothes. I don't know why we were in church that morning, but my father was in a restless mood on the drive over. "Family, I'm going to die," he announced. "Satan is going to kill me. I want to say goodbye to each one of you."

I had no idea what he was talking about, but what he said sounded scary and made me want to stay close to my father. I couldn't imagine losing him.

My parents escorted us into the stately church, where our motley group took up an entire pew. At some point, while the preacher was teaching about how the wages of sin is death but the free gift of God is eternal life, my father decided to take me to the nursery, glad for the opportunity to escape the conviction gripping his heart.

Once we arrived at the nursery, I begged for him to take me back because I was afraid to leave my father. I sensed something was wrong and that my father wanted to escape the church and go outside.

"Don't leave, Daddy!" I cried out. "Don't leave me!"

My father was flustered. "Okay," he said, picking me up off the nursery floor and returning to the sanctuary.

The timing turned out to be providential because we sat down just as the preacher was making his altar call.

"John 3:16 tells us that 'God so loved the world, that He gave His only begotten Son, that whoever believes in Him should not perish,'" the preacher said as he looked out at the congregation. "So there are only two choices: Will you choose to follow Jesus, or will you reject Him? Look how plainly Moses made the choices clear when he said in Deuteronomy 30:19, 'I have set before you life and death, blessing and cursing; therefore choose life.' So today, you can choose life. I know God is tugging at your heart. You may be asking yourself, 'What do I have to do to receive eternal life?' All you have to do is say yes to Jesus. If you want to join the family of God, please walk to the front right now and receive Him."

The preacher had everyone stand to sing a song, but my father remained seated while paging through a Bible. Then the church began singing "Have Thine Own Way, Lord."

> Have Thine own way, Lord,
>   Have Thine own way;
> Thou art the Potter,
>   I am the clay.
> Mold me and make me
>   After Thy will,
> While I am waiting,
>   Yielded and still.

Something clicked. Something removed the scales off my father's eyes. He began wiping away tears. He stood up and worked his way out of the pew. My mother reached out and grabbed him, begging him not to go.

"I need to get right with God," he said. "Will you join me?"

"No, and don't do it. I don't want you to change," she pleaded. She hadn't liked what she saw in the fancy world of straitlaced Christians. She preferred the feeling of freedom and doing whatever she wished.

I sat there, holding onto Mama's frayed dress while she clutched Joseph close to her breast. My father looked at my mother. "I have to go," he said, and with that, he strode up the aisle toward the preacher.

The pastor, holding a Bible, smiled as my father knelt in front of him. He leaned over and said, "Welcome to the family of God, young man."

My father was overcome with emotion. With his head bowed, my father poured his heart out to the Lord.

"Oh, God, save me. I am a wretched lost sinner. I repent from all my evil ways. I will put away all my sins to follow You all the way. Make me a perfect Christian, and no matter what the sacrifice, I will follow You. Have Your own way with me. Make me to be Your servant now. You paid the price for me. I am willing now to live for You whatever the cost."

That day, my father felt he had made himself right with God.

His life—and ours—would never be the same.

# 10
# A TOTAL CHANGE

Over the years, my dad would get a twinkle in his eye and say, "Daughter, it's all your fault. You were the one who made me go back into that church and get saved."

I always smiled, but each time he credited me with his spiritual turnaround, a strange underlying feeling always came along with it. He acted as though this was another sign of my God-ordained closeness to him.

His first convert was my mother, who had a change of heart and decided to follow in his footsteps three days after he went forward in the Baptist church. They were out in a field when he proselytized to her, and she made a commitment to Jesus and became a Christian.

My father had never done anything halfway in life, and "getting religion" was no different. Overnight, he cut his hair, trimmed his beard, quit smoking pot, stopped taking drugs, burned his tarot cards, and used every spare moment to read from a King James Bible. He devoured God's Word and felt like he'd been given some sort of special revelation on what the Bible was trying to teach every believer. He decided that he was going all the way to the top of the spiritual heap and would be closer to God than anyone else.

He didn't want to go through the rest of his life with a hippie name like Firefly Sunstar. My father legally chucked the Sunstar last name and identified himself again as Robert Allen Hale. He also changed my name from Butterfly to Elizabeth, which was an adjustment as a three-year-old. I couldn't be expected to understand why people were suddenly calling me by a new name.

My mother went back to being Kurina Bresler since my parents were not legally married, although she liked being called Rose Hale. They both concluded that they were married in God's heart since they made that commitment to each other.[1]

---

1. My parents legally married a year later when I was five.

After sorting out things in Fort Worth, my father sold everything—the Chevy truck, the horses, and all of his belongings—and used the money to buy a blue compact car. We drove out to Southern California, where we moved in with Nana, my name for my grandmother.

She lived in a luxurious Beverly Hills home that was unbelievable to me. Being with Betty Freeman was the total opposite of what life was like in the communes, where running water was considered a luxury and electricity wasn't available unless it came from a generator.

Then, for some reason, my father left us and drove back to Fort Worth to stay with his twin brother and his family. While my parents were separated, they agreed that they would each read Psalm 91 every day. My father chose Psalm 91 because that particular Scripture brimmed with declarations and promises of God's protection.

I was only three at the time, so I didn't know a lot of what was going on—just that my father was no longer around, which grieved me. While my father was in Texas, my mother decided that she hated city life, dealing with so many people and all the traffic, and wearing shoes with heels. She had gotten used to the vagabond lifestyle found in the communes. She couldn't wait for my father to come back for her and us kids.

In Fort Worth, my father made deep dives into his Bible, seeking more revelations, verse by verse. His new and emerging worldview was that "religious" people were all fakes—his experience with Transcendental Meditation was still fresh in his mind—but he would be different. My father would be the one to live a life pleasing to God and stand up for righteousness in a fallen world.

My father became very good at nitpicking Scripture verses every day of the week and twice on Sunday. It didn't take long for my argumentative father to raise all sorts of doctrinal disputes with church pastors and elders he ran into in Fort Worth. My father reserved his most condemning language for those he judged to be lukewarm or misinterpreting Scripture. He didn't shy away from giving his opinions or telling people they were going straight to hell unless they repented from their evil ways.

Naturally, the people he ran into often saw things differently and didn't want anything to do with such a judgmental person. He replied that they were sinners and that he'd been given a special insight into God's truth through visions and signs that came straight from Jesus.

One of those revelations came when he heard God telling him that he needed to marry my mother and he would become the father of many more children.

Like twenty-one children.

Confident that God had given him a clear path to follow, my father left Fort Worth and returned to Los Angeles in the blue car to make things right with my mother and become the father Joseph and I needed.

When my father pulled into the driveway of Nana's Beverly Hills home one evening, my grandmother wasn't exactly thrilled to see him again. I was excited, though, since I'd always been a Daddy's girl and missed him.

My father did his best to make amends with Mama. First, they agreed that they had been faithful to carrying out their promise to each other to read Psalm 91 daily while they were separated. Then my father said something interesting.

"Did you know it's been exactly ninety-one days since we last saw each other?" he asked her.

My mother was astounded by the coincidence with Psalm 91, but Nana rolled her eyes.

We found out that my father had returned with a plan: he wanted to bring everyone back to Fort Worth because he was sure he could get back their old '41 Chevy and their animals. We could get a fresh start again, he said.

Against Nana's objections, we crammed into the small blue car for the return trip to Fort Worth, where my father miraculously repurchased his '41 Chevy truck with The Barn as well as our two horses. This felt like a modern-day miracle of the loaves and fishes to my father.

"Hallelujah!" he exclaimed. "Praise Jesus!"

He strongly felt the Lord was leading him to evangelize those he knew best—hippies. For someone who thought of himself as a hippie prophet to the hippie world at one time, he now assumed a similar Christian mantle.

From Fort Worth, my father decided to drive us to Reserve, a tiny town in New Mexico's Gila National Forest and home to a hippie encampment. Some of them were refugees from the commune outside Apple Valley who knew my father, like a bearded man who called himself "Buffalo."

My father was on a mission to share the gospel with Buffalo and other "lost" hippies. Along the way to Reserve, the '41 Chevy broke down, and a generous couple brought our family into their house. Mama was pregnant with her third child. Unfortunately, while we were there, she ran into difficulties and suffered a miscarriage.

My father showed compassion toward Mama. "Kurina, my rose, how do you feel?" he asked her after the miscarriage.

"I'm set free in Jesus," she replied. "But it was so painful, just like labor."[2]

Hearing her say that made my father feel that his wife was more like Abraham's Sarah than ever because of her willingness to follow him. After the truck was fixed, we packed up and continued on to the hippie commune in Reserve, where Daddy enthusiastically preached, won some converts, and gained a following, which energized him.

One day, he visited the commune's outhouse and spotted a three-by-five-inch card tacked on the side. "Caretaker Wanted," said the top line.

My father was intrigued. Upon reading further, a land manager was looking for someone to live on their acreage west of Mora, New Mexico, in the Sangre de Cristo Mountains northeast of Albuquerque. The card contained a map, directions to get there, and a note explaining that the property was at the nine-thousand-foot level and was often snowed in during the winter.

A shiver shook through my father's body but for a different reason. Ever since he picked us up in Los Angeles, my father had been saying that we had to set ourselves apart from a wicked world bent on destruction. "We need to isolate ourselves and get ready for Jesus," he kept saying to Mama.

And now this—someone was looking for a caretaker to manage his land high up in the mountains, away from civilization and all its evil and sinful behavior. This had to be a sign from God!

My father *knew* he was being called, like the patriarch Abraham, to move to a new land, a place where he could lead his people—his family and his converts—into a closer relationship with God and live how Christ wanted us to live, unencumbered by the world.

Several of his long-haired disciples said they would follow him, which only stoked my father's emerging view that he was destined to lead others to a Promised Land where they could prepare themselves for the Lord's Second Coming.

My father packed up the '41 Chevy with our family, two horses, a large St. Bernard dog we called "Mountain," a cat that gave birth to many kittens along the way, and all kinds of stuff, from bongo drums to pots and pans. Several hippie families caravanned with us in their cars.

We pulled into Mora, where my father met the man managing the mountain property. He gave us exact directions to the two-hundred-acre property, which was at the end of a steep, rutted dirt path that snaked up the foothills and mountains jutting above the valley floor. When we arrived in a grassy meadow, we didn't find much—just a rundown shack that looked like it was going to fall over.

---

2. In years to come, my father would claim that it was a girl and named her Hope, even though they didn't know if the unborn baby was a boy or a girl. I grew up always counting this child as part of the family. I remember feelings of real disappointment, and there were times when I even resented God for not letting me have a sister during the first fourteen years of my life.

There wasn't a source of water either, which was a big problem too.

My father placed his hands on his hips, surveying the situation. "Here's what we're going to do," he said to my mother and his disciples. "We're going to dig ourselves a well, and if God fills it with water by the morning, then that's a sign from Him that we should stay."

Daddy had been putting out "fleeces" before the Lord whenever he had to make a big decision, and this was one of those moments. The following day, the hole was brimming with water, which pleased my father to no end. He announced we had heard a direct answer from God Himself: we were to stay.

My father worked out some sort of arrangement with the land manager. He decided that we would live in The Barn until he built something more permanent. As for the disciples, my father helped them erect a temporary dome-shaped wooden structure that they covered with a tarp and dirt. Daddy called it the Earth Lodge.

Meanwhile, I loved my new surroundings. After the desolate landscape of the Mojave Desert and the flatness of Fort Worth, the majestic mountains and the scent of tall pine trees seemed like a treat to me. There was so much to explore!

At the bottom of the mountain, seven miles down the road near the small village of Ledoux, was a set of squatters named Tin Man and Papa Bear. They were chopping down massively tall old-growth trees and using a white workhorse to haul them to a flatbed truck. There was a lot of money made in rustling lumber, so they didn't cotton to newcomers or interference.

After our arrival, they came onto our property and fired warning shots in our direction from a distance, which scared me. I immediately panicked and ran into the arms of my protective daddy and then grabbed onto the long skirt of my mother, who was holding Joseph on her hip.

I shivered in fear, unaware that over the next twenty-one years, there would be many more moments when I would be terrorized in the mountains of New Mexico.

# PART III

---

# LIFE IN THE
# SANGRE DE CRISTO
# MOUNTAINS

# 11
# SETTING UP CAMP

The Earth Lodge, situated on the south face of a mountain ridge, became our gathering place. One time, a bearded man who called himself "Buffalo" was sitting cross-legged in the circle. He waved me over, saying, "Butterfly, come sit with me!"

Being a preschooler, I naturally obeyed and plopped down on Buffalo's lap, as innocent as could be. I reveled in the attention he gave me.

I noticed my father glaring at the bearded man. I figured it was for using my old hippie name—which reminded my father of the past he'd left behind in California—but I was wrong.

Back in The Barn, my father set me straight.

"Elizabeth, I do not want you sitting on anyone else's lap besides mine from now on. I don't appreciate you sitting on other people's laps. I want you close by me all the time, okay? That's where God wants you to be. You're *my* little girl, and you belong with me."

Somehow, from the tone of his voice, I felt I had done something horribly wrong. Even though I'd acted in complete innocence, it turned out I'd been displeasing my daddy the whole time.

The next time we gathered in the Earth Lodge with Buffalo, Moon Stone, and Bear, I walked with a determination to please my daddy with all my heart. Then, right in front of everyone, Buffalo called me over again. "Hey, honey, give me a hug and sit with me," he said, tapping his legs. "I want to hear about your day."

I frowned. Eager to please the one man in my life, I said plainly, "No, I'm not allowed to sit on your lap anymore. I can only sit on my daddy's lap from now on."

My matter-of-fact reply stunned Buffalo *and* Daddy. My father had no idea that I would be so bold.

"Now that's my girl!" he said, opening his arms for me to come to him.

I fell onto his lap, sure that my loyalty was a sign of my closeness to him. His embracing response made me feel like it was worth sacrificing the attention I would receive from others.

There was nothing I wanted more in life than to be special to my daddy.

As the first cool bite of wind swirled through our encampment just after Labor Day, my father's disciples decided that sticking around the Sangre de Cristo mountains during the snowy winter months—and living in such primitive conditions without running water or electricity—was foolhardy at best and a surefire way to freeze to death at worst. One day, Buffalo and his friends packed up and left.

That was fine with my father, who liked our living situation more and more with each passing day. "Family," he said to Mama and me, "we're going to live out an old-fashioned lifestyle in these rugged mountains, just like in the olden days when they traveled west across the country. We're going to do something no one else does these days. When those pastors in Fort Worth told me I needed to find a mountain, they were right. They were just trying to get rid of me, but little did they know they were speaking a word from God."

Papa had wanted us to live a simple pioneer life without the distractions of television or a ringing telephone—and now he got it. If living by ourselves high in the mountains meant he couldn't drive to a convenience store when we were low on milk, then that was okay with him. Then again, we didn't have a refrigerator anyway. Daddy told Mama that once we got settled, we would get our own cow and goats for milk.

Getting settled was taking some time. Even though my parents were living on the property with permission, nothing was in writing. One day, my father drove down the mountain to Mora, also the county seat, to check into who owned the property. That's when he learned that Hollywood actor Jack Nicholson had purchased the land a couple of years earlier.

Now that was interesting. Hollywood . . . Kurina's parents belonged to the entertainment industry. Her stepfather, Joel Freeman, had worked with Nicholson on a picture one time. Mama wrote her mother and asked if she could help them contact Jack Nicholson. Betty Freeman asked around and found out who Nicholson's business manager was and his address. She made an appointment and explained to the business manager how her daughter was trying to raise a family away from the hustle and bustle of the city and live a simple life apart from civilization. They would be the perfect caretakers for the property, she said.

Touched by her story, the business manager agreed to put a lease agreement in writing. Betty, noting all the work needed to maintain and safeguard the property, suggested a ten-dollar-a-month payment. The business manager readily agreed to the token amount.[1]

My father was up to the challenge of being a caretaker of a property in such a remote locale and wasted no time preparing a more permanent shelter. He managed to build a log cabin—through his brute strength and by using Gypsy, his black horse, to haul felled trees—around a lean-to shack left behind by the previous caretaker.

My father drove long spikes into the trunks of trees that he chopped down, each with a diameter of between two and three feet. He hitched them to Gypsy and found a way to get the walls up and a roof on all by himself. My father furnished the inside of the structure with a small table and an oil lamp and installed a wood-fired stove used for heating and cooking. We moved from The Barn into the log cabin as winter set in.

Each evening, we snuggled up close together to stay warm in our simple abode,[2] which was lit with kerosene lamps. I looked forward to cuddling with my daddy each night; he felt so big and safe and secure.

We had the basics—barely. My father said we needed a more dependable water source, so he dug in several areas, hoping every moment that water would spring up, but it didn't happen. He persevered, though, until one of his holes about seventy-five feet from the cabin produced a steady source of water. He had to dig down ten feet to reach that spring. He carried water into the house in five-gallon buckets, which were heavy, again without complaint.

Our food came from big bags

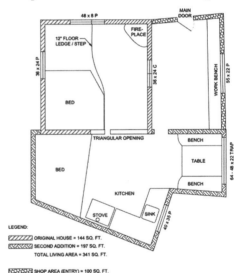

This is a floor plan of our home in the New Mexico mountains. There was 341 square feet of living space.

---

1. You'd think that Jack Nicholson, who was at the height of his film career following the release of *Easy Rider*, *Five Easy Pieces*, and *Chinatown*, was too busy to be apprised of the caretaking request, but Joel Freeman happened to be sitting in a first-class seat next to Nicholson during a flight one time. They spoke about the Hale family living on his property in New Mexico, and it was clear that Nicholson had been informed.

2. Over time, there would be ten of us crammed into this small living space.

of flour, cornmeal, and rice, along with jars of tomato sauce and canned meat stored in our cabin's attic, which became our pantry until my father built a storage shed in coming years. Mama prepared fantastic meals from a small wood-burning stove that sat in the corner of the cabin. The stove was also our heat source.

Going to the bathroom? My father placed a portable camper toilet on the floor in the main room, right next to his chair. Next to the toilet was an old T-shirt that we used to wipe ourselves. Trying to find a clean spot was difficult since everyone used the same shirt.

Every few hours, that portable toilet would be full of brown poo and yellow pee. My father didn't complain each time he had to carry that gross plastic bucket out to the latrine pit and dump the contents.[3] He had the attitude of a hard worker, and if that's what needed to be done, then by golly, he did it.

It wasn't long before the first snowstorm of the season hurled giant snowflakes on top of us. I'd never seen snow before, so I loved playing outdoors and exploring what was around me.

About four hundred yards from our tiny house, out in the woods, was a small but sturdy hundred-year-old cabin with a fireplace. Back in the day, local Spanish-speaking people had built a shepherd's hut for the herdsmen to stay in while they cared for their goats in the mountains.

As winter took hold, there were times we moved into that cozy hut to be warmer.

I turned four years old that first winter, in early 1980, but there was no birthday party. My father decided that birthdays were a pagan custom and not worthy of celebration. One evening, though, Daddy told Joseph and me that something extraordinary was going to happen.

"As soon as we begin to see flowers blooming, you're going to have another little brother or sister!" he said.

This announcement excited us because that meant we would have a little brother or sister to play with.

At last, the snow melted, and springtime arrived. One morning, I wandered through the grass, eagerly searching for that one little flower that would be the

---

3. The camper toilet was an upgrade from the "honey bucket" we used in The Barn. As soon as I was old enough—around age six—dumping the camp toilet became my chore.

fulfillment of the promise my parents had given me. I knew . . . just knew that as soon as that one flower popped up its pretty little head, we would have a new little brother or sister. And suddenly, there it was!

Never was a flower so beautiful to the eyes of a little girl. I knelt with utter joy to pick the dandelion, and with great enthusiasm, I ran, hooting and yelling, "We're going to have a baby! We're going to have a baby!"

In my excitement, I ran right to Mama, holding out the flower of promise to her. She smiled and looked over at my daddy with a look that disconcerted me.

"What is it?" I asked. "Isn't it exciting?"

My daddy looked down at me. "I'm sorry, Elizabeth, but it will be a long time before the baby will actually be born. There will be lots and lots of flowers, and the leaves will begin to change colors first."

I bowed in tears and walked away, feeling I had been lied to. *How can I wait that long?* All of my hopes and expectations disappeared.

One morning, I woke up in our shepherd's cabin to the sound of people screaming, yelling, and pounding on our door. I didn't understand what they were so upset about.[4]

My brother and I huddled close to Mama as Daddy stepped outside and confronted the intruders. It was the timber rustlers again—Tin Man and Papa Bear. I heard awful threats that they would kill us if we didn't leave, but when Daddy returned, his defiant, confident look was an unspoken promise that he would win this battle.

Another time, my daddy asked me to come with him to get some mustard for Mama. My parents had already begun to store supplies in the attic of our new log cabin. When he asked me to accompany him, though, I withdrew in fear.

"Oh, no, Daddy, you can't go out there! Those people will kill us."

"No, they won't. I'm stronger than them, so they can't hurt us."

While walking through the hilly meadow, holding my daddy's hand, I was convinced that my father and I were walking straight to our death. I held his hand so tight, hoping that he would be strong enough to keep me alive. We made it back safely, but the squatters' animosity against our family continued to run deep.

That fear was justified the day when we heard rifles being shot and bullets striking our new cabin. We immediately hit the dirt floor, and I huddled close to Mama. Meanwhile, Daddy, our fierce defender, rose with fire in his eyes as he

---

4. Most likely, the neighbors shooting at us felt aggrieved that newcomers had been granted a caretaker's lease that they believed belonged to a local.

held his rifle, waiting for the charge that never came.

He never fired back, but he sure looked like he wanted to.

Later, I would learn that the rustlers left the property. I never found out how or why that happened, but I was happy that no one would be shooting at us anymore.

Our "family" began to grow as we accumulated more animals to join our two horses. My father had an uncanny way with animals and possessed a particular ability to control horses with only his eyes. He would get Gypsy to kneel or lie down and allow us children to walk all over him. If we were sitting, Gypsy would place his head on our laps. When my father would shout, "Gypsy for Jesus!" the horse would stand.[5]

I was so excited the day we acquired a pregnant Jersey milking cow that we promptly named Rosie. That spring, my father built a small barn to house her and the animals to come. Rosie's warm milk was a welcome addition to the family diet. When Daddy was ready to milk her, he would sing a song that sounded something like, "Country Rose, take me home," and she would stop chewing grass and come to the barn to be milked.

Soon several rabbits and a few bantam chickens joined the menagerie, giving us the promise of a more reliable food supply. In due time, Rosie gave birth to Jonah, a pretty bull calf that would become my special responsibility in coming months. We trained him to let me ride on his back, and it was an enormous sadness when, as a yearling, he was stolen by our unhappy neighbors.

The rabbits and chickens needed their own home, so Joseph and I eagerly "helped" our daddy build a rough shed that was more of a dugout. He made the walls out of thin aspen poles and covered the roof with a tarp and buckets of dirt to protect the shed from the severe winter weather to come. After the shed was finished, the dugout became a favorite spot for Joseph and me to play.

The rabbits soon made holes in which to disappear and have their young. Joseph and I learned that if we waited quietly, we could grab the rabbits as they emerged from their burrows. One glorious day, several baby rabbits appeared from one of the rabbit holes, which felt like heaven to us.

When the day's work was done, I felt so pleased and proud when my daddy praised us for working hard. As a reward, he created the "grab jar"—an old clay

---

5. Sadly, his use of this mysterious gift was not confined to animals. Years later, Aunt Patsy, who knew him well, told me, "I've never seen a three-year-old and a one-year-old baby be so controlled by their father's eyes. He would line you kids up on my couch and make you sit there for hours—just to prove he had control over you." That gift would be a tool of control he used on us throughout his life.

cookie jar filled with all sorts of candies. After Mama got it all ready, he called Joseph and me. I will never forget putting my hand into that jar and getting to grab as much candy as I could. I learned that day that working hard pleased my daddy.

About this time, Daddy rode Gypsy down the rough trail to Ledoux, a village of six hundred located underneath our high mountain home, a half-dozen miles or so down the dirt road. Ledoux is where my father picked up our mail.

Waiting eagerly for his return, I heard him call out loudly with his special call, "HOOOO, JEEESUS!" that rang across the mountains. Daddy was home!

One time, he leaped off his horse and said, "I have a special surprise for the two of you, but you must first turn around and close your eyes." How we waited with anticipation!

"All right, now turn around and pick a hand," he ordered as he smiled.

After we had chosen, he pulled two teeny kittens from his back pockets and gave one to each of us. Typically, he gave us the names for them both. Mine was to be called "Praise the Lord," and Joseph's would be called "Hallelujah."

Meanwhile, Mama was getting larger with the child growing inside of her. I was allowed to press on her swollen tummy through her rough dress. When I felt the baby move against my hand, I thought the baby wanted to come out. My imagination went wild trying to figure out how that would happen.

The big day came during August in 1980. When my mother went into labor, I couldn't understand why she was crying so much. I thought this was supposed to be a happy occasion.

My father seemed to be orchestrating everything as he allowed us to observe the delivery, which was pretty traumatic for a four-year-old. As I watched my new little brother enter the world on August 10, 1980, I couldn't believe how tiny he was. My daddy held him up in the air declaring, "His name is Joshua, and he will be a prophet." I was allowed to hold Joshua for a moment before we crawled into our communal bed to rejoice together.

I will never forget the following day when the sun came out and the birds were peeping outside. I woke up first and crawled up close to my new baby brother to look at him. He was so perfect, nestled against my mother.

Just then, I noticed my daddy's eyes peeking at me. He quietly got up, gently lifted the baby from Mama's arms, and whispered, "Come outside with me."

We sat together near the giant pumpkins growing in our garden, where he let me hold my tiny brother, smaller than the pumpkins.

That was a moment that I wanted to continue forever.

# 12
# GRAVEN IMAGES

Before Joshua was born, Daddy took me with him to find a special oak branch. "We need to find a limb and turn it into a Native American-style cradleboard. It will fit snug to our backs when we carry the baby," he explained.

I enjoyed this fun project. We found a curved oak limb, peeled it, and sanded the branch until it was smooth. Then I watched Mama sew leather strips onto it to make comfortable padding for the baby. I was allowed to sew squirrel hides on the top of the cradleboard to shade Joshua's eyes.

As my little brother grew, resentment grew in my heart. My father held my baby brother most of the time, so there was seldom any time for me to snuggle in his lap. On these occasions, I would cuddle with my little dolly and play mommy and baby with her instead.

Every morning Daddy would sit us down and read to us at length from the Bible before we started our chores. Many times I got tired of sitting for so long.

"Quit moving around and listen," he'd growl if I got antsy. His authoritative voice pushed me to tears.

If Joseph or I didn't buckle down, he would clench his fist and rap us on top of our heads with his knuckles. I found paying attention for so long challenging, mainly because I wasn't allowed to glance elsewhere. Sometimes I could avoid my father's condemnation by crawling into his lap, which he seemed to like well enough. Then he would treat me nicer.

My energetic, four-year-old body looked forward to going outside and helping with the chores. One of my favorite things to do was ride in the open drag sleigh behind our handsome horse when we gathered adobe for the inside of our cabin. My creative father took an old Chevy car hood, turned it upside down, and fashioned a sled. I loved the familiar rattling of the harness as Gypsy strained tall and proud, pulling with a strong will.

The horse would patiently stand while we dug down into the earth for red clay, slowly filling the improvised sled. When mixed with water and hay, the adobe was excellent insulation for the inside of our cabin walls as well as our floor. Daddy also used the clay to build a fireplace inside the cabin and a Dutch oven outside, where Mama would bake bread.

For all of the growing "normalcy" of our mountain life, my daddy's behavior and sudden mood changes often disturbed me. I wanted to please him, but he rarely seemed satisfied with me. The exception was when he drew me close in our family bed or placed me between his legs when he sat in his chair and studied his Bible for hours at a time. Sometimes he would not release me, and I felt as though I was in a trap. I even invented the need to go to the bathroom to get away from him for a few minutes. He would sharply call me back if I took too long.

My father was spending more and more time reading his Bible. When I asked why he read so much, he said he was looking for new revelations. Several of those revelations devastated my young heart, especially when Daddy announced that God had revealed to him that dolls were evil and had to be cast out.

I had only one dolly, which I loved very much, so I found this sudden pronouncement disheartening. My young mind ran through a series of questions:
- *If my dolly is evil, then how dare I love her?*
- *If I love my so-called evil dolly, will Daddy still love me?*
- *If I continue loving my dolly, will I be cast out too?*

I fearfully listened as he sat us down and opened his fat Bible.

"Here is what the Bible says in Exodus 20:4-5," he began. "'Thou shalt not make unto thee any graven image, or any likeness of any thing that is in heaven above, or that is in the earth beneath, or that is in the water under the earth. Thou shalt not bow down thyself to them, nor serve them: for I the Lord thy God am a jealous God, visiting the iniquity of the fathers upon the children unto the third and fourth generation of them that hate me.'"

Of course, I had no idea what he was talking about, so Daddy put things into his own words.

"You see, Elizabeth, God says that graven images are very wicked, and toys are graven images. They're foolish, worldly, and a waste of time, so God wants you to get rid of them."

"You mean I can't have any more toys?" I only had a couple of things to play with: a doll I'd named Betty and a stuffed rabbit.

"That's what God says."

The next morning, my father handed me a white feed sack. "Let's go find your toys," he said.

Tears came to my eyes. "Do we really have to do this, Daddy?"

"Yes, we do." His stern answer told me that his mind was made up.

My father walked over to my doll and held open his feed sack. I clutched Betty to my chest one more time and then dropped her in. The same went for my stuffed rabbit and Joseph's toy trucks and teddy bear.

The next day, we drove to the local dump down in the valley. My father backed up the '41 Chevy to offload some other trash.

"Now it's your turn," he said.

"Do I have to?" Near tears, I clutched the feed sack to my chest with both arms.

"Yes. God wants you to do this."

I knew I had to obey my father and God. I stood a long time at the edge of the dump, wondering what we had done wrong and why Daddy was acting so excited. This was so sad.

"God's waiting," my father said.

I could tell Daddy was getting impatient.

With a flick of the wrist, I tossed the sack with my doll and toys and watched it roll all the way down to the other rubbish.

For days, I cried for my lost dolly, wondering why I had to do that.

A week later, Daddy said he had another revelation. "If the sack is still there at the dump, that means God is allowing you to have your toys and dolly after all," he stated.

"Really?" Hope filled my heart.

The next day, we drove to the dump again and parked in the same exact spot. "Look, Daddy! I see it!"

Sure enough, the feed sack—a bit more worse for the wear—was clearly visible below us.

"I guess God wanted you to have your dolly back. I'll go get it," my father volunteered.

I watched as he walked into the dump and scooped up the sack, wondering the entire time if Daddy felt bad for taking my dolly away. I also wondered what I did that was good enough to let me have my doll back. My little girl's heart weighed everything on a scale of whether I'd done something good or something bad to merit the way my father treated me.

When he returned, though, I was overjoyed. The cloth had a particular overripe smell, but Betty was in my clutches again.

My joy didn't last long, however. My father became upset that I loved my dolly so much. His anger burned fiercely, and his eyes narrowed. "That doll has become an idol for you. It needs to go."

This time he got rid of Betty by himself, and I never saw her again. Without any toys to play with, no television, no radio, and no children's books to read (and not being taught to read anyway), Joseph and I had to rely on our imaginations to have any fun. Sticks and stones were our toys, and the woods were our playground.

Each day, Joseph and I would enter a make-believe world. I would gallop furiously astride a stick for my horse, with an imaginary mane and tail blowing in the wind. We would make a "fort" in a nearby meadow where we would play church.

Since Joseph was a boy, he was the pastor, of course. He would take a little Bible from our cabin and emulate our father as he preached fiery, convincing sermons about the reality of hell for sinners whose hearts had never been made right with God. He was merely repeating what he'd heard my father say a zillion times.

I would have loved to add my two cents, but I was just a girl, and girls did not preach, my father solemnly told me. After Joseph finished delivering his message at our fort, we would pretend to have communion, passing make-believe bread and wine reverently to each other.

One day, Daddy sneaked through the woods and caught us playing church.

"What are you doing?" he bellowed.

"Playing church," I answered. "See? We're having communion."

I then pantomimed the consumption of the elements.

"That's blasphemous!" he roared.

I had no idea what that big word meant, but it sounded pretty serious.

He roughly grabbed us, sat us down on a tree stump, admonished us again, and then told us to get a switch from the aspen trees. Then he whipped our wrists and hands, causing huge welts and bruises on our skin. But that blistering pain was nothing compared to the growing fear I felt for my father and for God. I was terrified.

"Elizabeth, I hold you accountable because you are the oldest," my father solemnly said as I rubbed my hurting wrists. "You have spit on God and made a mockery of what is holy. I hope this correction I gave you will be enough to please God because I'm ultimately responsible for your well-being and making sure you get to heaven."

I whimpered, doing my best not to cry because I didn't want to make my father any angrier with me.

Daddy never used the word "spanking" with my siblings or me. Daddy said the word spanking wasn't in the Bible, so we shouldn't use that word. He called the whippings "corrections," which became a greatly feared word in my mind.

"Oh, and one more thing," he said. "I never want to see you playing church again."

On that, I heard my father loud and clear.

When Joshua reached toddler age, I now had two little brothers to romp around with outside. We were playing hide-and-seek one day when my father's voice rang out.

"Children! Come now!"

We all knew we better not hesitate if we didn't want a "correction." As we sprinted back to the cabin, my heart beat fast with fear.

*What have we . . . I . . . done wrong?*

I was so careful with our baby brother. Maybe Daddy had been watching us from behind the trees as we'd seen him do other times.

"We're coming," I cried.

As we panted up to the door of our one-room log cabin, with the adobe floor, our father was standing there looking grave, yet excited. We stood anxiously in front of him and waited. When he spoke, his voice was clear but demanding.

"Come inside," he commanded us. "I have something I need to talk to you about."

My six-year-old mind raced with apprehension as we gathered around him, sitting on the dirt floor in front of the fireplace.

"You are no longer to call me Daddy," he announced. "From now on, I'm to be called Papa. Do you understand?"

"Y-y-yes," I choked out, hiding the tears that were about to overflow. "Papa" sounded wrong to me—even scary somehow.

My mind churned with different thoughts.

*Why can't I call him Daddy anymore?*

*What if I mess up? He is my daddy, the daddy I love to cuddle up to.*

*And what did I do wrong that he can't be a daddy for me?*

I knew better than to ask questions about why this was happening. I decided that it would be best just to call him Papa and not get into trouble.

He sent us back outside after this declaration, and I watched him read his Bible again. I heard him say to Mama, "Isn't this amazing? I'm now Papa—no longer like everyone else in the world. And look here, the Bible says that even Jesus called His Father *Abba*, which means Papa."

Once again, I had no idea what he was talking about.

One day, my brothers and I played our favorite game with our big St. Bernard dog named Mountain. We pretended that Mountain was a donkey, my brother Joseph was Joseph, I was Mary, and my little brother was baby Jesus!

Something was wrong with Mountain, though. I looked closely and found big open wounds on his belly, hidden under his thick fur. A few days earlier, he'd been trampled by a mule.

I sprinted and told Papa, who inspected the wounds and decided they needed to be sewn up. I really wanted to assist my father, but he gruffly told me to take care of my little brother Joshua, who wasn't very happy at the time.

A few days later, I was with Papa at the old shepherd's cabin, helping him take care of some chickens we kept there. Upon our return, Mama and Joseph met us on the hill. With a sad look on her face, Mama exclaimed, "Mountain has died!" Joseph broke out into tears.

"Dead? What do you mean dead?" I asked.

When they showed me his still body, a feeling of deep shock rippled through me. Mountain was part of the family, and now he was gone. I began to cry with Joseph and my mama.

Papa was unmoved. He picked up the dead dog, flung him over his shoulder, and said, "Come on, Elizabeth."

Brushing back tears, I followed him down a path that opened up to a clearing. I trudged numbly behind my papa with tormenting, confused thoughts, wondering what he would do with Mountain.

He led us to a tree with branches that he could reach. He dropped Mountain to the ground and reached for a knife inside a leather sheath attached to his belt. "Here, hold this," he said gruffly.

I gripped the knife and trembled with fear as he used a piece of rope to string my dead friend to a branch. Then he roughly took the knife from my hand and started to expertly skin dear old Mountain.

Aghast, I couldn't believe my eyes. In a few minutes, Mountain was no longer covered with his beautiful furry clothes but was pink and white and desecrated. With bloody hands, my papa tossed the hide over his shoulder.

"Okay, let's go!" he said.

In shock, I followed him back to the cabin but not before looking back to where my beloved dog's carcass swung from a tree branch.

That night, I snuggled ever so closely to my faithful kitty, crying quietly until her purring sent me to sleep.

But the haunting image of Mountain's carcass wouldn't leave my mind.

# 13
# OFF TO CHURCH

"C'mon everybody, time for church!"

It was early on a Sunday morning, and Papa had already saddled up our two horses. My father loved going to church, although our isolation limited how often we could attend Sunday services. He watched as Mama bundled three kids into hats, scarves, and ponchos against the chill of the autumn day.

Going to church meant a long ninety-minute ride over the mountain into Gascon, a tiny settlement where we would hitchhike seventeen miles to Mora, a town of four thousand residents. Usually, someone with a big truck took pity on the hippie-looking family of five sticking their thumbs out for a ride.

We attended a Baptist church, where Papa played guitar. That morning, Papa strummed the simple chords for "For Those Tears He Died" as Joseph and I acted out the song's words—something he had us practice—in front of the church congregation. Papa seemed to like deliberately making us the center of attention wherever we went.

Whenever my father engaged in a conversation with a stranger—be it in a church foyer, at a truck stop, inside a market, or on a street corner—it wouldn't take him long to reach for a pocket Bible he always kept tucked between his Levi's jeans and his shirt, right next to his back right pocket.

"You need to get right with God right now," he'd say. "This is a matter of life and death because God hates sin, and you're a sinner. So what are you going to do about it? Are you going to repent right now?"

My father reveled in putting people on the spot and had a way of dominating conversations with his over-the-top enthusiasm for the Lord. His presence certainly created a buzz in valley towns like Mora, where the locals took to calling him "Preacher Bob." He was zealous, unyielding in his faith, and tried his best to win converts.

One time after returning home from church, Papa discovered that his rifle was missing from underneath his pillow. The single door leading into our cabin didn't have a lock.

Papa was processing what this meant when he heard shouting from the direction of the south ridge. Papa stepped out with his binoculars to check out the commotion. The next thing he knew, the sound of gunfire disturbed the mountain silence. Someone had taken a shot at my father. The bullet hit the ground a few feet from him.

Papa ducked back into the cabin, panting from the quick exertion.

"What is it?" Mama asked.

My father exhaled. "Someone took a shot at me," he said.

That didn't sound good. He let some time pass and gingerly stepped outside again. There was no more gunfire. Papa found the bullet in the ground and realized the shot came from his rifle.

Energized by the discovery, Papa returned and gathered us around him.

"Family," he began dramatically, "it's time for us to rejoice over persecution! The Scriptures tell us to leap for joy when people hate us and persecute us for our righteousness."

I was happy Papa wasn't upset about being shot at, but then I got scared when he added, "The Bible says we are to put God's Word into action, so I want everybody to come outside with me. We're all going to leap up and down and praise God because whoever is shooting is persecuting us."

*But what if he takes another potshot at us?*

I didn't ask the question because I realized that Papa would be happy if we died for Jesus.

Mama knew better than to tell him that didn't sound like a good idea, so we fell in and complied.

"This is a test from God to see if we are ready to die for him," my father announced outside our ramshackle cabin. I stood next to my mother and two brothers, silently praying to Jesus that He would keep us safe and help me rejoice in persecution.

When no gunfire erupted after a few minutes, we all leaped and danced for joy. If the person who stole Papa's rifle did see us, perhaps he was too amazed to fire again!

Nearly every morning, as I woke up, I would hear loud, excited hoots from Papa. He did this whenever he found another revelation while reading the Bible.

One day he was out in the front of our cabin, studying God's Word while Mama perked coffee and cooked breakfast on an open campfire. I always loved the early morning birdsong and the fresh smell of Mama's cooking. After waking up, the first thing I did was run into my papa's arms and give him a big kiss on the lips.

"That's my girl," he said. "You know those kisses make me happy."

I also knew that if I failed to kiss him, I would be questioned why and get off on the wrong foot with him, which was never a good way to start my day.

"Go wake up your brothers," he said on this particular morning. "I have something God has revealed to me from the Holy Scriptures. I'm overjoyed to share this with everyone. We are really going to be a peculiar people separated in this world to obey God."

I did as he asked. As we gathered around him, sitting on a large throw rug on the adobe floor, he declared, "In the days of Noah, God looked upon the earth and destroyed it with the flood because of the imagination of man's heart. Do you know what imagination means?"

I looked at my younger brothers, and they had no clue either. I was scared to death to give the wrong answer.

My father broke the silence. "That's what I thought. None of you knows what that means. Well, imagination is when you pretend."

This time I didn't hesitate to speak up. "Pretend—as in playing?"

To me, playing and pretending were the same thing. This is how I enjoyed my time since I didn't have any toys. Pretending was everything to me.

"You are no longer to pretend," he said. "If I catch you pretending, then I will be forced to discipline you."

I struggled to hear that. This didn't make any sense to me.

"Does that mean that we'll never be allowed to play again?" I asked.

Papa's reaction was swift and sharp. "Get me a switch—and run!"

Bitter resentment accompanied me as I sprinted to a nearby sapling tree. While I broke off a small limb that would serve to administer the punishment, my tears were mixed with confusion.

When I returned, I asked Papa why I had to be punished. "I'm not saying that I want to play anymore," I said. "I'll do what you want. I just don't know what you mean."

My father was unmoved. He grabbed the switch from my hand and said, "Put your hands out."

I screamed out in pain from the scorching slashes across my hands and wrists, but I was still quite confused because I was pretending that I didn't want to play anymore. I still didn't understand what was wrong with pretending.

A few days later, Papa was sitting and reading his Bible in front of the cabin while my brothers and I played in the yard. Without thinking, I filled my shirt up with egg-size rocks and started hopping around, squawking like a chicken. Then I squatted and lay all my "eggs" in a nest not too far from where Papa was sitting.

In other words, I was pretending to be a chicken.

I turned cold with fear when he jumped up and yelled at me for disobeying him. "I made it clear that you were never to pretend again," he growled.

Once again, I had to fetch a switch and receive more painful lashes on my hands and wrists.

I honestly couldn't understand the difference between playing and pretending. We always pretended when we played; there wasn't anything else to do since we didn't have any toys or dolls to speak of. We *had* to make up everything in our minds, which is why I developed a strong imagination. Even a stick could become my baby doll when I wrapped that stick in a blanket and cuddled beside my kitty. That was a form of pretending, right?

I was devastated the day when I finally understood what Papa's edict *really* meant: we were not supposed to have fun anymore. I was too scared to ask any more questions, so I took great pains *not* to pretend and reminded my brothers to do the same—though we still did from time to time. In other words, I took it upon myself to protect my brothers from the switch by constantly telling them what to do.

I had no way of knowing how much grief my controlling attitude would bring to my brothers in the coming years. Nor did I know how my father would manipulate that nature in me to his own ends.

One day my grandpa, Mama's papa, came from California to visit us. Dan Bresler had to be quite the adventurer to come up our mountain to see us. I liked his infectious attitude and how he loved to make little jokes.

We were standing outside one evening when my grandfather looked toward the dark heavens. Then, with his arm around Joseph, he asked. "Do you know where the North Star is?"

Joseph would have been starting grade school at the time, but we weren't going to school. We hadn't been taught anything about the stars. My brother got scared and didn't know what to say.

Grandpa chuckled as he pointed. "It's in the north, young man," which he thought was funny.

Joseph began to cry. My grandfather didn't realize that our inability to answer a simple question usually meant condemnation from my father.

Right on cue, Papa's pride was hurt by Joseph's ignorance in front of his father-in-law, so my father took Joseph inside the cabin, where he scolded him and whipped him, calling him a "foolish boy" with each blow.

Papa made sure that my grandfather didn't know about my brother's punishment. "Go to the barn and clean out the milk stall, and don't come back until you've washed away all those tears and the way you look," my father said. "And don't you say a thing to Grandpa about this. We wouldn't want him to take you away and raise you in a God-awful world. He doesn't even believe in God."

The next day, my grandfather announced that he brought a special present for me.

"What is it, Grandpa?" I was excited because I never got presents.

My grandfather reached into a tote bag and pulled out a small guitar that looked to be exactly the right size for me. I couldn't believe my eyes. I had often tried unsuccessfully to play Papa's big guitar when he wasn't around, but this was perfect. Now I had my own instrument and something to play with.

"Thank you, Grandpa!" I shouted as I ran into his arms and hugged him as tightly as I could.

I wasted no time in learning some chords that I enthusiastically strummed over and over. Grandpa was impressed by my enthusiasm as well as by my improvement.

"I promise to practice hard," I told him just before he left.

Once Grandpa departed, though, Papa called me over.

"You can't have the guitar, so give it to me," he said.

I started crying. "Why, Papa? Why can't I have it?"

"I only let you have it while Grandpa was here because I didn't want to disappoint him. But you are a girl, and it is wrong for girls to lead out with anything, even music. The guitar is something only a man should play as he leads his family in singing. I want you to give your guitar to Joseph. Because he's a boy, he can have it. But I don't want you ever to tell Grandpa, and if he ever asks you how playing the guitar is going, you are to tell him that you are learning well."

When Papa said I had to give Joseph the guitar, it was almost more than I could bear. I started crying really hard, trying to convince him to change his mind.

"Please, Papa, please don't take it away! Oh, Papa, please . . . ."

My pleading only came to an end when I was told to fetch a switch. Then Papa ordered me to write a letter to Grandpa, thanking him for the guitar and lying to him about how much fun I was having playing it.[1]

Because I was almost illiterate, Papa wrote out a letter first and then had me copy what he'd done to make it look like I was schooled and could write well. That's how I would learn how to write—and read—a little bit.

For some reason, I had a feeling that Papa didn't want me to learn to read and write too well.

---

1. Turns out Joseph wasn't interested in learning to play the guitar, so I had to watch that little guitar sit in a corner and slowly rot away for years.

# 14
# RAINBOW CROSS

A t our homestead one day, Papa decided that we needed to erect a large cross in our mountain meadow that would stand as a gateway between us and the world below.

He started by taking two logs cut to the proper length. After carving notches with an ax, he then fastened them together with spikes. I sat on one of the logs, holding on tight and keeping it steady as Papa pounded on those nails with a sledgehammer. I pictured Jesus lying there—all bloody and torn as angry men nailed His hands and His feet.

When Papa was done, he dug a hole in the ground, and we helped him lift the six-foot cross into the air and place the base deep in the earth. Papa then tamped stones and dirt in the hole to secure the cross. When he was finished, he had the entire family kneel at the foot of the cross. Then he opened up his Bible and read a verse from Galatians 2:20 (KJV) that he had burned into the cross:

> I am crucified with Christ: nevertheless I live; yet not I, but Christ liveth in me: and the life which I now live in the flesh I live by the faith of the Son of God, who loved me, and gave himself for me.

My heart was caught up with emotion. *I want Jesus to live in me. Does this mean I have to die on a cross too?* I wondered.

My thoughts were interrupted by my father's words. "We must be reminded to carry our cross daily," he said. "This means we must die to ourselves and the pleasures of this world. We must fear God and His wrath, which is going to come upon this evil world. Being like Jesus is what separates us from others. This cross will stand and be an open sign between us and the world. Whenever we pass by this cross, let us stop and pray and give glory to God for choosing us to be His people."

I could tell that Papa believed this with all his heart. My five-year-old heart was mixed, holding feelings of awesomeness, fear of God, and a willingness to stand for Jesus whatever the cost.

From that day on, if I happened to walk by the cross without praying, I would feel so guilty that I had to go back and make it right. I would kneel and beg for God's forgiveness, hoping the entire time that He wouldn't hold it against me.

In the summer of 1982, when I was six years old, I was doing my chores, which included taking care of the chickens, watering them, and gathering the eggs. Suddenly, I heard Papa's excited voice say, "Everyone, come here! See this rainbow. It's a sign from heaven!"

Hurrying, I put the eggs down in the house and ran outside to see this natural phenomenon. I arrived last, but I couldn't see anything above the trees. Mama was trying to show me where the rainbow was touching the cross, but by the time I figured out where to look, the rainbow was gone. Black clouds rolled back in and darkened the sky once again.

My father, though, was ecstatic about seeing a rainbow touch the top of the cross. I was afraid to tell him I hadn't seen the rainbow since I longed to please my father.

Fortunately, my father was thinking about something else. "That's it," he said. "We'll call this place Rainbow Cross."

I shrugged my shoulders. Over the next few days, I wondered, *How does a rainbow land on a cross?* The multicolored meteorological event mystified me.

Since I didn't see the rainbow, I felt that perhaps God wasn't happy with me. That explained why I had missed out on seeing this great sign from heaven. Papa had always made it clear that our sins were sure to find us out and that God saw every little thing we did and knew our every thought. There had to be some sort of unconfessed sin in my life, but I didn't know what that was.

I found it frightening to live with the thought that God was Someone who would throw me into hell if I didn't live a perfect life pleasing to Him. Papa told me that the only way I could receive God's mercy and forgiveness was to accept his discipline with a willing, thankful heart. In essence, I had to allow Papa to beat the devil out of me. Only then could I be found worthy of going to heaven to live with Jesus.

The way my little mind saw things, I decided that if Papa were happy with me, God would be pleased. Keeping Papa happy was a problem, though. I knew that one way to get him on my side was to kiss him each time he came into the cabin.

One time Mama had just finished bathing us children in an old metal washtub. Papa had filled the tub with water from the well while Mama added hot water from the kettles heated outside on the campfire. We only bathed once a week, so I always loved the feeling of being clean and putting on fresh, clean clothes. After this bath, I put on the only special clothes I had—a pretty little red skirt and blouse. Feeling quite festive, I hopped and skipped toward Papa like a little lady to seek his expression of approval.

I did not doubt that my father would be pleased because, in the past, he had always expressed great delight anytime I went out of my way to kiss him or do something special for him. Papa also really liked it when I cuddled close to him at night, and he would tell me how special I was to him. I was sure he would think I was pretty now. I had heard him talk about things and animals being pretty, but I had never heard him tell me that I was pretty. I felt the need to listen to him tell me that.

Instead, Papa turned to me with a look that sent chills down my spine.

"Elizabeth, you are a proud little girl. It is wicked for you even to think thoughts about being pretty. That is a vain thing to do."

I gave my father a puzzled look. The rejection I felt was worse than the desire I had for Papa to see me as beautiful.

"Do you know what *vain* means?" he asked.

"No," I managed, trying to hold back tears.

"Well, being vain is thinking more highly of yourself than you ought to. I call this a 'Jezebel.'"

I couldn't hold back the flood of tears another moment. Relenting, he beckoned me to sit in his lap. "Don't cry, my girl. As long as you do what's right and obey me, you are beautiful to me. Don't forget that, okay?"

Just a moment before, I had longed to hear the words, "Come to me." Now those words made me shake in fear.

"I am a Jezebel?" I asked. I knew Papa well enough to know that this was something bad.

"When you're vain, the answer is yes. But if you hear my voice and listen to me, then you're my special girl."

He drew me closer, but the entire time, I felt totally mixed up and confused.

As the days passed, I was determined to please Papa because his rejection was too painful to bear. I always knew when he wasn't happy with me because he would immediately not want my kisses and treat me roughly. Then an admonishment from his lips: "You need to confess your sins to me to get right with God."

*Confess what?*

To get back into his favor, I began confessing all kinds of wrongdoing—hitting Joseph, loafing when carrying water into the cabin, or not getting up right away, hoping my confession would include something he wanted to hear. But he was never satisfied.

My young conscience was being scrambled and profoundly shaped by my father, and I didn't even know it.

One early winter morning at our homestead, I woke up feeling chilled because of the inadequate scratchy wool blankets we slept with. The smell of Mama's strong coffee filled our little cabin as I disentangled myself from a litter of sleeping brothers[1] and watched as my heavily pregnant mother served Papa his coffee, which he called "mud," and only drank with cream and sugar.

As always, I hastened to him to kiss him on the lips, my first sacred act of the day—a habit he had insisted on from my infancy.

Papa had his own sacred morning ritual in those early mountain years. He saw himself as a kind of apostolic figure, like Paul of Tarsus, who had spent years studying the Scriptures before beginning his ministry or embarking on his missionary trips.

I heard him say, "Paul had an evil past, so he studied the Scriptures for three years before he started preaching. Like Paul, I too have an uneven past, and God has called me to study the Scriptures so that I can preach the Word."

On this particular morning, I crawled out of bed with my blonde hair flying and my stomach growling. I found Papa sitting, cross-legged, in front of our rock-studded, adobe fireplace, where a roaring fire blazed. He was wearing his usual velour pullover and blue jeans. His long hair and flowing beard had been trimmed a bit by Mama.

While Mama fixed oatmeal for breakfast, I crawled into his lap as he made a place for me by moving his Bible aside. I curled up there, sleepy-eyed. I craved affection from him, but the little I got was never enough, which is why I often felt the need to reassure myself that Papa still loved me.

I lay against my father's breast as his chest vibrated with excitement. Soon, my brothers stirred. They knew that after they woke up, they were to sit at my father's feet and listen to him talk about whatever was on his mind.

Time was of no consequence as Papa wielded his Bible and lambasted "hypocritical preachers" who were "out to destroy the innocent, like our family, with their hypocrisy and distortion of the Scripture." They were "wolves in sheep clothing" who would be "judged greatly and held accountable by God

---

1. My two oldest brothers and I all slept in the same bed.

with great suffering."

Whenever he spoke with great intensity like this, which happened nearly every day, my heart would beat fast, and my muscles would tense.

At my age, I didn't know why I felt that way, just that I did.

Woe to us if we did not pay attention during Papa's daily mini-sermons, which was difficult because we weren't allowed to eat any breakfast beforehand.

When he was finished preaching, he would send us off to do our chores instead of allowing us to eat something. The reason we couldn't have breakfast before we finished our morning chores was because Papa had found a Bible verse that said people were to look after the welfare of their beasts, which Papa interpreted to mean that our animals should eat before we did. Consequently, we were always famished while we performed our morning chores.

Papa, however, stayed behind and always enjoyed a hot mountain breakfast prepared by Mama. I never could understand why Papa got to stay back to eat. The only thing I could figure was that my father had done the chores God had called him to do, like the apostle Paul.

There was one chore that I detested—and it always fell to me because I was the oldest and strong enough. This was the task of emptying the camp toilet, called the "poo bucket" by us, that occupied space in our main room. The plastic tub in the camp toilet was usually filled to the brim by the time I got up, so that was my first duty. My brothers and I had other chores, like bringing in more firewood or milking Rosie, our cow.

One bone-chilling wintry morning, Joseph and I left the cabin and hustled down a cleared path to the barn, where Rosie would be waiting for us. This time, however, she was not there. High snowdrifts had built up over the fence, and she had calmly walked over them and out of the pasture.

We knew there was no way we could return to the cabin and tell our papa. He would simply blame us and send us out again to find the cow while he continued to seek Scripture for more "revelations."

Hungry and worried, Joseph and I climbed the drifts and headed through the fields and woods toward the frozen creek. I was trudging my way through the snow when I noticed that Joseph was no longer next to me. When I looked around, he was ten yards behind me. Joseph cried out, "Elizabeth, my boot is stuck."

Frustrated, I hollered at him, "Then get it out!"

"I can't," his voice called back at me.

"Come on!" I yelled. "We have to find Rosie and milk her, or Papa will be mad."

I watched him struggle to pull his right foot out of the deep snow. After a minute, he said, "I got my foot out, but I can't get my boot."

I sighed. That meant Joseph needed help. After trudging back to him, I must have tried for twenty minutes to get his boot out of the deep snow while poor Joseph hopped up and down on one leg, shivering and trying to keep warm.

Finally, it dawned on me that I would never free the boot, so with great reluctance, I told Joseph to lean on me as a crutch so he could hop and hobble back home. I hoped that Papa would overlook our failure to find Rosie, much less milk her, in the joy of having his son return alive.

With no sock, Joseph's right foot became very red with cold. I had to stop every few yards to warm his exposed foot with my own hands, but I didn't have gloves myself, so my hands were cold.

We were a pair of miserable children when we finally burst through the door into the warm cabin. Both of us began speaking at once, trying to placate Papa.

He would not accept any of our explanations or pleas. "You were goofing off, so get out there and don't come back until you've found Rosie and milked her. Understand? I don't want to see you until you've done those things."

We approached the fire to warm up, but Papa wasn't having any of that. "I want you to go—now!" he thundered. He did, however, permit Joseph to dig through our boot bin to find one that would cover his frozen foot. As soon we were outside again, our tears froze on our cheeks as we headed once more for the barn.

This time we were rewarded with the most welcome sight—a docile Rosie chewing her cud and waiting to be milked as though nothing untoward had happened.

"Oh, thank you, Jesus, thank you!" I cried out. What a relief to milk her as quickly as my frozen hands would allow and return to the cabin with a pail full of milk, which was always part of our breakfast.

In the spring, when the snow disappeared, I pleaded with Papa to help us look for the missing boot, but he refused. I don't think he ever believed our story, and my little girl's heart hurt to think that he did not trust my word.

One morning, I was sitting with my papa as he read and studied the Bible. His cup of coffee was sitting close by when my kitty, named Praise the Lord, approached me, purring loudly, and crawled into my lap.

"Watch my coffee!" warned Papa. He tried to push the kitty off my lap, but a struggle began as she hung on with her claws—as kittens often do. Amid all of the commotion, Papa's coffee cup was knocked over, spilling onto his Bible. Immediately, he grabbed my kitty and walked outside, where he furiously threw her against our earthen chicken coop about thirty feet away.

Shaken and scared, I watched as my dear little companion lay flat and limp on the ground. "Papa, she's dead! You killed her!" I cried out, grief-stricken.

"Good, she deserves it," he replied heartlessly. "Now get back over here and sit down."

I heard nothing of Papa's morning preaching session that day; I couldn't pay attention to anything he said because I was worried about my little companion. I didn't know what I would do without my kitty. She was often my greatest comfort—especially when Papa was upset with me for some reason.

For once, he didn't rap me on the head for not being locked into every word he said. I almost felt that Papa seemed a bit remorseful for what he had done.

After Bible time, I quickly went outside with a faint hope that my kitty would still be alive, but she was nowhere to be found. After many weeks passed without seeing Praise the Lord, I imagined that she had crawled off in the woods and died somewhere.

At least her suffering was over.

# 15
# TAKING JESUS' HAND

I didn't even know what I had done wrong.

But there I was, banished to the attic of our little cabin by Papa for some transgression. I had to lie down and not move from that position.

*Papa must be right,* I reasoned dismally. *Papa is always right. After all, he has often said so. Therefore, whatever happened must be my fault.*

I'd been staying in the attic for more than a week, lying on Mountain's dusty, dried-up dog hide morning, noon, and night.

One afternoon, I reached my limit. "Jesus, help me. Please help me!" I cried out. I was feeling desperate.

Papa said I had lied about something. I didn't know what he was referring to, but truth be told, I was far more afraid of my father than of going to hell—the place, he said, where all liars go. After whipping me with a willow switch and sending me off to the attic, he declared, "You'll be blessed to get even leftovers to eat." I subsisted on scraps from breakfast and dinner and glasses of water that my mother brought to me.

Papa made it clear that I could not move for any reason. He gave me a bucket to use with the terse instruction that I could not go to the bathroom unless I called him and asked if I could use the bucket.

This was a double-edged sword because every time I needed to relieve myself also provided him with an opportunity to give me another whipping, so I would try to hold it as long as possible until I could bear the pain no longer. In addition, the smell inside the attic was atrocious because Papa didn't allow me to empty the bucket.

I was cold and hungry with nothing to do. I was not even allowed to get up from a lying position. All I could do was toss and turn from one side to the other. Other times, I froze into a fetal position with no life left in me. I figured this is what prison had to feel like.

All I could think about was when Papa would forgive me. I had always thought I was his little girl. Did he have a merciful bone in his body? Would he ever forgive me and let me come down from the attic?

And then my thoughts turned to the Lord. *Does He even know I'm here? Does He know I'm lonely and feeling abandoned? Does He see my broken heart? Oh Jesus, where are You?*

I lay alone, suffering from the stinging pain of Papa's repeated whippings. My arms and wrists were black and blue from his willow switch. The worst lashes were on my legs and the back of my head, and those were on top of the old bruises he'd administered to me from previous punishments. Then the miracle—a small but undeniable one—happened.

During one of the many dark, scary nights, as I lay there crying out for Jesus, I was startled by the sound of my precious kitty, Praise the Lord, purring close to me. Then I felt a familiar furry body lie down next to mine. I hugged her close. Somehow, Praise the Lord had survived her brutal handling by my father.

I spent most of my days wondering what I could say to my father so I could be released from this prison. If I confessed to what he wanted me to admit— whatever that was—then I would be in trouble for changing my mind. But if I held to what I said—that I didn't know what he was talking about—then I would continue to receive the daily punishment until I would confess the truth.

I couldn't win!

Then one day, while still in the attic, I heard a four-wheeler coming up the mountain. Suddenly, Mama appeared, holding a hairbrush. If Papa had arrived with a hairbrush, I knew to brace myself for another whipping. But Mama?

"Come on out," she said. "Hurry."

I didn't have to be asked twice. I stepped out into the bright sunshine, shielding my eyes since I hadn't seen the sun in a long time. Mama brought me close and started running her brush through my hair.

"I think CPS is here," she said, referring to Child Protective Services. "Someone must have reported us."

My father often talked about the "authorities" coming and taking us kids away because he followed God's direction to discipline children. He loved reading Proverbs 13:24 to us from his King James Bible: "He that spareth his rod hateth his son, but he that loveth him chasteneth him betimes."

All the *-eth* words sounded foreign to me, but Papa's explanation was crystal clear: if he didn't punish us with a rod or stick, then he hated us. He further explained that Proverbs 29:17 directed him to discipline his children so that we would give him peace of mind and make his heart glad. That's why he wasn't going to spare the rod with us.

"The law will not agree with what the Bible says," Papa declared, adding that the police would take us away forever if they found out about his "corrections." Not only that, he said, but my brothers and I would be scattered throughout the world once that happened.

I could not bear the thought of being separated from my family or never seeing my siblings again. Even worse, we would all go to hell because they would make us watch television—that monstrous agent of evil!

Mama made me look presentable just in time. But then a stroke of luck: the man on the four-wheeler happened to be a local looking for several of his cows. False alarm.

One good result came out of the unexpected visit: I was released from the attic.

"Elizabeth, are you ready to be forgiven?" my father asked.

"Yes, Papa."

My lips quivered, and then I broke out into a loud cry as Papa hugged me. I was once again back into his good graces, so quickly that my heart blocked out those painful dark days as my pale, frail body shook from hunger.

As life returned to the "old normal," it became pretty apparent that Papa's way of punishing my siblings and me was a matter to be hidden from anyone in the valley.

When I was seven years old, Papa's teachings began to become well-grounded in my heart. He often spoke of being "born again" so that we could be sure that we were going to heaven. Since I longed to please my father to the uttermost, I asked him, "What do I have to do to be born again, Papa?"

From his chair, my father looked up from his big Bible.

"Well, if you get on your knees and confess all of your sins, asking God to forgive you, then you will be born again. But I want you to be careful because you're making a lifetime commitment with no second chances. So you better be very careful not to sin anymore!" he said.

That sounded scary to me because I knew that was not possible. Besides, if I confessed all of my sins, then Papa would punish me all over again, and I'd be right back in the attic. I wasn't so sure I wanted to be "born again."

As I thought this through, my guilty conscience reminded me of the many times I'd been a sinner. Like the time when I was out in the woods playing with my brothers instead of gathering sticks and bringing in armloads of twigs and small branches to pile up for the campfire. Like the time when I'd gotten angry with my brothers and been a tattletale to make myself look better to Papa. Like all those times when I got away with doing things behind Papa's back, acting like I was doing what he wanted when he wasn't looking.

But I knew I wanted to be born again, so I told Papa I wanted to make a confession. While kneeling, however, I began to wonder what kind of commitment I was making.

"Forgive me, God, for all the times I've lied," I prayed, figuring a blanket prayer would cover me.

My all-encompassing prayer seemed to appease my father. When Papa shared another verse from Proverbs about the consequences of sin—"As a dog returneth to his vomit, so a fool returneth to his folly" from Proverbs 26:11 (KJV)—I nodded my head to make it look like I understood. The trouble was my young mind wasn't capable of taking all this in. What did a dog returning to his vomit have to do with sinning?

Still, I did my best to become a "born again" Christian. As weeks and months passed, however, I felt disappointed because I could never measure up to being the super Christian that Papa was.

One thing I did do was make Jesus my friend and truly accept Him into my heart. That part was genuine to me.

There was still plenty of confusion in my mind, however.

My lack of joy must have been noticeable because Papa questioned me one time to see if I had really confessed everything. I thought of an answer that would mollify him: "I need to be baptized," I said. *Perhaps that will cleanse me from all my sins.*

According to Papa, being baptized was the second step I had to take to become a Christian. He appeared to be pleased with my request.

"Sure, Elizabeth. I can baptize you," he said.

A couple of days later, Papa wanted to make my baptism an experience I would never forget. Mama let me wear my best dress for the occasion, and I felt very important as we all walked together to a little creek that trickled down our mountain about half a mile from our cabin. Though we called it "our river," the flowing water was shallow. We took shovels and dug a hole in the riverbed big enough for our washtub to fit, allowing the creek water to overflow into it. This was during the summer.

It was late in the day as our family sat beside the creek listening to Papa speak about baptism and how important it was toward completing our salvation.

Hearing him say that caused me to tremble with all sorts of doubts and fears. *What if I wasn't saved in the first place?*

Standing in the chilly water and looking up at Papa, I felt I was trusting him for my soul. His fervent, firm words sounded loud above the gentle rustle of the trickling stream. Even the birds were quiet.

"This is a big decision that Elizabeth is making today," he began. "She is professing to be born again—a brand new person. She is taking the next step in her salvation, and once she takes the third step by receiving the Holy Ghost, she will be a perfect Christian. She will no longer sin. If she does, she will go to hell."

At the sound of those words, I trembled all the more. Then my father placed me in his arms and lowered me into the cold water. When I came up, I cried out, "Thank You, Jesus!"

I was sure my life would be different.

But nothing seemed to change.

As I grew older, I started acting out everything I saw my papa do. That included lying about things to make me look like a good Christian and lying to impress others, including him.

Here's an example: one time, we returned from a horseback trip after visiting a Christian Bible camp ten or fifteen miles away. I proceeded to tell my papa a made-up story about leading some girls to the Lord.

"That's great, Elizabeth! The next time we visit this camp, you can give each of these girls a Bible."

"Ah, yeah," I replied. "I'm sure they'd love that." But, inside my heart, I hoped that we would never see them again since I had fibbed.

On another occasion, Joseph and I happened to see unusually magnificent clouds in the sky. To impress our papa, we told him that we saw this cloud formation that looked like Jesus riding on a chariot. In other words, we let our imaginations roam wild in describing this supernatural event.

Papa was impressed, which pleased us greatly. Then we were horrified when he started writing letters to various people about our "vision" and turning our fanciful description into some sort of a prophecy about how we were the only true Christians left in a world of growing darkness.

Things got so out of hand that Joseph and I had to confess that we made it all up. What a dreadful day that was! Not only did he start calling me a "pretend hotdog Christian," which sounded awful to me, but he punished my brother and me for an entire year!

Each morning, we had to wake up and meet him with a whip in our hands. After getting whipped on the back of our hands and wrists—or the back of our legs if we didn't hold still—we were not allowed to smile or laugh for the rest of the morning. What was worse was the feeling of being rejected by my father. I missed Papa's arms around me and his early morning kisses. I wasn't allowed to play with my baby brothers or even cuddle with Papa at night. Joseph and

I were now the family's servants. Furthermore, Papa was openly uneasy about whether we would make it to heaven and told us so.

The following 365 days seemed endless. Papa never forgave us until we had received our full punishment.

Papa liked to sleep with his big Bible under his pillow, which meant there was often a race among us kids to be first to find the Bible and put it under his pillow before he went to bed. Then in the morning, as he sat in his chair drinking his coffee, he would ask one of us to fetch his Bible and bring it to him. The bearer of the Bible was to hold it against his or her heart and then lean into Papa's chest as he sat in his chair—all the while pressing the Bible against Papa's heart while he prayed for us.

Needless to say, if we were in trouble, we were not allowed to put his Bible under his pillow at night. We would also miss out on his blessing the next day.

The only thing I was allowed to do with Papa while I was in trouble for that entire year was rub his feet at night. This task was always tricky for me. He seemed demanding and unsatisfied with my care, but I was performing the task half asleep from weariness since the long, full days of work had already made me so tired. If I didn't rub his toes and feet just right, he would get angry at me and tell me I was a lousy foot-rubber.

It turned out that rubbing his feet would eventually lead to other things when the lights went out.

# 16
# A LIGHTNING STRIKE

O ne cold, rainy day, as we huddled inside our cabin, Papa left to gather more wood for the fire. We could hear the thunder rumbling, and occasional lightning flashes lit up the little room as we waited for him to return. The incredible and scary thunder always sounded like the voice of God to me.

A stranger happened to be staying with us at the time of this storm. A pastor had sent him to Rainbow Cross to be ministered to by my papa.

Lightning suddenly struck our house, arcing straight through a spike that held a small cross on the ridge of the roof. Mama screamed and fell to the floor—she had been struck a glancing blow from that bolt of lightning.

Terrified, I grabbed my little brother David from her lap. Joseph and Joshua were screaming as well. For one awful moment, I thought my baby brother and I were the only two left alive. Right then, Papa burst through the door. He grabbed some anointing oil from the mantelpiece above the fireplace, poured it on Mama's head, and begged God that she would live.

I honestly thought Papa had performed a miracle as Mama came to her senses. My poor brothers were crying and scared because they had been struck as well, though not quite as severely as Mama.

Our visitor sat on the bunk bed, looking petrified and confused. He turned to my father and said in a shaky voice, "What does this mean?"

Papa told him, in no uncertain terms, "Your sinful life is the cause of the lightning strike. This is God's judgment on us for having you here."

The man was horrified to hear himself called out like that. As soon as the rain stopped, he packed up and left, and we never saw him again.

Forever after, Papa decided that the lightning strike was the hand of God, telling us that we were never to have another unbeliever in our house. In reality, this meant that we were never allowed to have anyone visit us in our home again since no one ever met Papa's criteria of what a true believer was. Anyone who wandered onto our land or drove up to visit had to remain outside, which made for some awkward conversations, but Papa didn't care. His goal was to keep us pure from the world.

Every once in a while, though, a lost hiker would find his way to our homestead. I remember the time when a Dutch man walked onto our meadow. He was amiable and spoke English with an interesting accent. My parents were friendly with him, and we children were all over him, showing him around and having fun with him. We were probably even a little out of control.

In the late afternoon, the Dutch visitor got the message that he needed to say goodbye and move on. As soon as he was out of sight, Papa came down on me like I had committed the worst sin ever.

"Why were you nice to that pagan unbeliever?" he demanded.

I didn't have a good answer. "I don't know. Because he wasn't from here?" I felt stupid and bad, like I had committed some evil act.

"You foolish little girl. Have I not taught you anything? Why are you unfaithful to me? You know what is right, but the way you acted was evil. You are a girl, so you shouldn't be talking to another man, much less be crawling all over him. That is how foolish women act."

I was in shock as well as confused. "Papa, I didn't know!"

"Don't you even try to give me excuses, or I will send you to the woods for a switch."

With that, my father left in a huff. As I watched him walk away, I felt embarrassed, betrayed, and shamed by his anger. I didn't understand what I had done wrong, especially the unfaithful part.

In the coming years, I would understand exactly what he meant.

As our family grew, so did the size of our cabin. Soon, Papa built an addition to the back of our home and a small entry with a place to hang our coats. The roof of the addition was about six feet tall, and a narrow twenty-inch-wide doorway became the main entry into the cabin. Beneath the floor, we dug a deep root cellar for food storage.

I remember gathering around the potbelly stove we would start up in the evenings after a long day's work. Mama taught me how to make tortillas, the first thing I learned how to cook on my own. I had been taught to go all out with anything I did, so once I learned how to make tortillas, I would make stacks of them for the family each night. It felt good to be a lady like Mama and cook food for the family.

At other times, Joseph and I took turns shaking a quart jar of cream to turn it into butter. We also loved to wind a little crank machine that provided the power to listen to Scripture tapes and praise music. I loved the hymn "What a Friend We Have in Jesus." The lyric, "Oh, what needless pain we bear," puzzled me, but I could well understand what it meant to "take it to the Lord in prayer." This I did countless times, begging for the help of the God who "knew my every weakness."

In the spring of 1984, when I was eight years old, Grandpa Bresler brought a fancy metal bathtub for Mama's birthday present. It was quite a sight to see a brand-new bathtub strapped to the top of his station wagon at the bottom of the mountain. He couldn't bring the tub up the rugged trail, so Papa fired up the '41 Chevy to complete the delivery.

We gathered rock and adobe to build a suitable place for the bathtub, which sat adjacent to the cabin, outside in the elements. Papa designed things so we could make a fire underneath the metal tub to heat the water, which we carried in five-gallon buckets from the well.

We quickly discovered that the bottom of the tub would get quite hot, so Papa found a suitable board to keep us from being scalded. Extra buckets of cold water were kept on hand in case the water got too hot.

During the winter, cooling down the water was simpler. We would ring a bell for someone to come running and throw a shovelful of snow into the steaming water.

We soon found that Papa *loved* to soak in hot water. His time in the tub became such a sacred ritual that he regularly told us that he heard from God and received many visions while letting the hot water seep into his pores.

Eventually, the bathtub became a second "throne" for him, from which he ruled his family.[1] Often, we children would line up beside the tub while he interrogated us about things we had supposedly done wrong.

On one occasion, Papa became completely sad while he was taking his usual bath. He called for us children, and we dutifully lined up alongside the bathtub in fearful anticipation. As usual, he let us know his feelings at full volume.

"What do I do with you guys?" he began. "Punishment doesn't work. You are a bunch of rebellious vagabonds who have never learned a thing. I give up. You torment me with your lies and hypocrisy. I can do no more. You are a bunch of worthless children. You shame me. It's obvious to me you don't even want to be disciplined because you never learn."

I had no idea what we had done to deserve this tongue-lashing. Naturally, we

---

1. His first throne was his big chair inside the cabin that seemed to fill almost all of the living space.

were all weeping because it hurt to hear Papa give up on us. I did not know how I could try harder to do right. Seeing God as I did through Papa, I greatly feared that if Papa gave up on me, then God would as well.

My distraction ended as Papa's following words were the final blow to his weeping children: "You are a bunch of wimps and cowards. Now, get out of my sight. I don't want to see your faces again."

Scarcely believing what we had heard, my brothers and I all turned and walked off, crying profusely. On the one hand, we heard him telling us to leave, but on the other, we had endured enough of his rages to know this was simply another one of his threatening tactics to scare us—and abuse us.

We all began walking away, down toward the meadow as if to leave the mountain. We came to the Rainbow Cross and stopped to pray as always. As I looked up at the cross, I pictured Jesus there, crying out to *His* Papa—His Abba Father. Jesus had also been willing to follow His Father's will—even if it hurt and was hard.

*Could God truly be like my papa?* I asked myself at the foot of the Rainbow Cross. *Surely not. Hadn't He welcomed Jesus back home when He had finished paying for my sins? So what do we do now, God?*

We decided that we would go back to beg Papa not to forsake us. We knew down deep that he wanted us to choose to receive his punishment.

We also understood that we would be disobeying him by going back when he had told us never to let him see us again. We all felt, however, his correction would be worth the sacrifice. It even felt good for us to walk back together as one and tell Papa that we wanted him to punish us and help us make it to heaven.

When we returned, Papa was still in the bathtub. He seemed to be so touched and blessed by our words of repentance—even to the point of tears. He wanted to celebrate like the prodigal son's father had when his wayward boy returned home. He told us we were free for the rest of the day to play and have fun—an announcement that struck us dumb with astonishment. Playing was a special privilege.

We gasped and turned to run off to play, but my father stopped me dead in my tracks. "Elizabeth, why don't you get in the tub with me, and we will celebrate this day of repentance together. Wouldn't that be special?"

Inwardly I groaned. I knew that Papa liked to stay in the bathtub for hours, sometimes up to half the day. I wanted to play with my siblings and not do chores. For a moment, I stood in silent disappointment.

"Elizabeth, did you hear me?" he asked roughly. The invitation was no longer a request but a command. I knew I could not decline, or everyone's whole day would be ruined.

"Right, Papa," I replied with the best grace I could muster, but apparently, I wasn't successful.

"What's this attitude I see, Elizabeth? You act as if you would rather be with your brothers than me."

"Oh, no, Papa," I lied. "I would rather be with you than with anyone in the whole wide world."

He softened at my words. "Okay, that's my girl. That's what I wanted to hear," he said more kindly.

I wanted to take my time, but I knew I had better hurry and change into my bathing suit: a long T-shirt and white cotton underwear.

I returned and jumped into the tub with Papa. Sitting at his feet while he tucked himself in, I tried to look the other way since he bathed in his underwear as well.

"Come on, Elizabeth. Come, get closer to me."

I had grown to hate lying against his bosom while he was in the bathtub. He made me feel so trapped.

Then he reached into his underwear and started touching himself. I tried to pretend that I didn't notice, but lying on his torso made that impossible.

I was confused about why this was happening. But I also felt guilty for the way Papa was allowing me to see him in his underwear.

I was really getting mixed up.

# 17
# ON THE ROAD AGAIN

By the time I was nine, I had four younger brothers: Joseph, Joshua, David, and Moses, who was just starting to walk. Many of the motherly duties fell on my young shoulders: cooking, cleaning, and doing the laundry.

Cleaning clothes meant scrubbing diapers, underwear, socks, shirts, and the stinky T-shirt used to wipe our bottoms following a bowel movement. There were also muddy pants and soiled waist-to-ankle skirts to scrub by hand in a galvanized tub, followed by hanging everything up to dry.

The long skirts belonged to Mama and me, of course. Papa said women were not allowed to wear pants because of what God's Word said in Deuteronomy 22:5 (KJV): "The woman shall not wear that which pertaineth unto a man, neither shall a man put on a woman's garment: for all that do so are abomination unto the Lord thy God."

One morning, Joseph and I happened to walk down to the meadow where the Rainbow Cross stood sentry. That's when we saw that something terrible had happened: a lightning strike had smashed the wooden cross into pieces during the night!

Papa said there was only one way to interpret this catastrophe: God was telling us to leave the homestead and confront the wicked world. He said people in the valley had been challenging him to come off his mountaintop and live out his convictions among them; well, here was Preacher Bob's chance.

His decision devastated me. Rainbow Cross was the only home I'd known. What would happen to all our animals? What would we do?

Papa wasn't sharing his thoughts, which further disturbed me. I couldn't imagine being around all those wicked people that my father constantly railed against, but when Papa purchased a well-used school bus that would serve as our motor home—once he finished fixing it up—I knew we were leaving New Mexico.

For where I did not know.

Before we departed, my father constructed a new cross, which we planted into the same hole in the ground. My siblings and I joined my parents in dropping to our knees and praying that God would bless our trip and keep our family safe. Saying goodbye to our mountain home was sad.

We first drove to Texas to see relatives and then motored throughout the western half of the United States, parking in church parking lots and trying to spend as little money as possible by visiting local food banks or pawing through dumpsters behind grocery supermarkets. One of our first stops was in Colorado Springs, Colorado, home to various Christian ministries that included Youth With a Mission (YWAM), a missionary and outreach group that sends young people worldwide to evangelize.

The YWAM folks opened up their parking lot (and restrooms) to us and even seemed comfortable with our unorthodox lifestyle. After a while, though, Papa's determination to "correct" both the YWAM leadership and the teaching curriculum prompted the leaders to kindly ask us to leave, so that's what we had to do.

Despite embarrassing episodes like that, I found out that I liked traveling because Papa was careful to treat us nicely when we were around other people. I also loved the feeling of washing every day and wearing nice, clean clothes.

Best of all, I was mercifully spared from bathing with him.

We met many Christian people who would take us in, but their hospitality rarely lasted long as Papa's theological hostility caused inevitable doctrinal conflicts, like what happened at the YWAM headquarters. Sooner or later—usually sooner—we would be encouraged to leave. On one notable occasion, members of a local church we were attending even locked the doors while meeting to discuss what to do about us!

Each time we were told to hit the road, Papa insisted that we were suffering for the Gospel's sake. His explanation was supposed to make our sudden departure easier, but my brothers and I missed the childish friendships we had made whenever we stopped in one place for more than a few days.

But even making friends came with risks. We'd play in a campground or church playground, and that evening back in the bus, Papa would demand to know whether we stood up for Jesus that day.

"Did you preach to the children about how evil dolls are?" he'd ask. "Did you tell them how unrighteous it is to wear pants and not dresses?" Papa had a long list of evils we could bully others with.

We learned that we'd better have a good story for Papa, or we'd get whipped and even banned from playing with other children. I took my role as a little soldier for Jesus seriously and did my best to convince my peers that their ways were ungodly and that they needed to change so we could be friends.

One time during our year on the road, we visited Grandma Betty in Los Angeles. One afternoon, she asked my parents if she could take the children to the park to play. My parents never allowed us to be alone with any other people, but they relented and made an exception for Grandma this time.

Before we left, Papa took us aside for a moment. "Now, don't forget what I've taught you about your grandmother. She disagrees with our lifestyle. She's evil and not going to heaven."

I kept his conversation in mind as we walked alongside Grandma to a nearby park. When we arrived, I saw a yellow school bus drive up with a bunch of children on board. I knew this was a *real* school bus—which Papa called a "devil donkey" because the yellow buses took children straight to hell, he said. For the first time, we all stood with our mouths agape as we watched children pile out of this so-called "devil donkey."

"See those kids," Grandma said, after noticing our fascination. "They go to school, but now they're coming to the park to play. It's good for children to be in school, where they can learn how to read and write well, be taught history and math and geography."

Grandma let the thought hang for a moment, the implication being that we needed to be in school. Like me, Joseph figured out what Grandma was really saying and started crying. "Papa says we don't need to go to the 'devil school.' He says he can teach us everything."

"I'm sure he does," Grandma allowed.

I knew this was my moment to be strong for righteousness's sake. I turned to my grandmother and said, "Grandma, I love you, but I hate what's inside of you."

My poor grandmother almost turned white hearing this judgment by her ten-year-old granddaughter. In due course, she took us back to our parents and reported how disrespectful we had been to her. Papa would have none of it, and they got into a nasty argument. Sadly, we had worn out our welcome and were back on the road again.

Later, Papa expressed how proud he was of us for being strong and standing up for the truth. What he didn't know was how torn up I felt inside. To be honest, when we had to leave, my brothers and I felt like we had lost our grandma, and it was all my fault.

I firmly believed that Grandma didn't like us anymore because we had taken a stand against her.

Our excursion into the "Wilderness of Sin" came to an end after a year of wandering through the Western states like gypsies. What a disaster.

Somehow, Papa constantly alienated people and kids we longed to befriend in every town or city we visited. We were ejected from churches and rejected by friends and family everywhere.

*I will never have any friends,* I thought. *I am doomed to a life of loneliness because our family is weird, strange, and unusual.*

Our return to the mountains was dramatic. The new cross that Papa had erected had been struck by lightning again and was chopped to pieces! My heart sank because that was a clear sign from God that we were not to return. After all, we had left after the first cross was knocked down by lightning, right?

Papa saw things differently. "See, God striking this cross is a sign from heaven that we are to return to the mountains. It's His sign to us that He wants us back here."

Which was the total opposite of what he said a year earlier. Even at eleven years old, I could see how he was manipulating this story for his own purposes. Even so, I was glad to be back at the old homestead and even happier when we found Shema, our horse, and Ruth, my dear lamb, in good condition after being on their own for so long.

However, our familiar mountain cottage seemed quite run down, especially after we had been in and out of a few fancy homes and nice churches the previous twelve months.

Being back on the mountain had a strange effect on Papa. For some unknown reason, he quickly became as ornery as he was before, his wrath oozing out of the grass he walked on.

One afternoon he gathered us all together, sat us down at his feet, and pulled out his Bible. He gave us a vivid picture of our mountain home being a light while darkness was moving in all around us.

"We stand alone," he said solemnly. "I know of no one who truly believes in God's Word. The end times have come, and we will have to prepare for them as Noah did in the Bible. Like the faithful patriarch, we will be righteous and build an ark."

I had no idea what building an ark meant, but I could also tell he was a bit angry with us.

"I'm a bit disappointed in my children," he said, frowning. "You have all proven to be very worldly and man-pleasers. It is my God-given duty to wash the evil brainwashing you have picked up from the world out of your system. I will do whatever it takes to beat it out of you. Remember, I wouldn't love you if I didn't correct you."

This sounded serious. Then my father startled everyone when he said, "Joseph, stand up."

My oldest brother, ten years old at the time, complied.

"You are a rebellious one," Papa maintained sternly. "Joseph, I'm going to make you an example to the rest of the family so that none of you will ever say a curse word again."

*A curse word? What is a curse word?* I wondered.

Joseph looked at me blankly, and I realized he had no idea what Papa's accusation meant either. Then in a flash, my father reached for a braided whip at his feet and quickly snapped the lash across the back of my brother, who instinctively shielded his head with his arms and hands. Joseph screamed in pain as another lash of the whip arrived.

I immediately shivered, wondering if I would be next. Instead, my father surprised me when he said we could go.

Later that day, I waited for my chance to whisper secretly to Joseph as he passed me with a load of wood.

"What is Papa talking about?" I asked. "What does he mean by curse words?"

Joseph looked disgusted. "I didn't say any curse words. Papa doesn't even know what he's talking about. He's just trying to find something wrong with me again."

I was shocked at his words and attitude. "Joseph, you mustn't talk like that about Papa. That's not right. He's our father."

My father himself couldn't have said it any better.

"The last days are coming!" Papa would thunder. "They are nearly here, so we better make preparations now that the Lord has brought us back to this mountain, where we will be saved." Accordingly, Papa had us dig caves and stock them with food so we could be ready for the end times, a period when great destruction and turmoil would come upon the world.

I noticed that my father didn't constantly work like he once had. He preferred to sit in his big chair or bathtub filled with hot water and act imperiously like a lord of the manor while we did our chores, hauled wood, and fetched buckets of water from our well.

I knew that helping my father draw his bath kept me on his good side. I had grown to be quite a strong little girl, even at eleven years of age, and I could carry two five-gallon buckets from our well to the bathtub. I saw how this pleased Papa very much.

The more my father encouraged me, the more I noticed Mama growing resentful toward me. We even seemed to compete to see who could serve him his morning coffee first. Papa liked it when I would go get him a cup of coffee without being asked, followed by handing him the mug and kissing him.

Mama's eyes would shoot daggers at me, but all I was doing was trying to stay on his good side. Then I noticed how Papa started getting on Mama's case by praising me for working hard around the cabin or filling his bathtub. He even preferred my homemade tortillas to hers.

"Country Rose, your daughter's much better at doing things around here than you are," he said one time.

That was a surefire way to launch an argument between the two.

My mother would fight back, prompting my father to retaliate by saying to Mama, "You don't give me enough attention."

I thought that meant she wasn't nice to Papa. I also naively believed that I could make up for Mama's neglect by giving him some attention, which would make him happy.

My father further cemented her status when he gathered my brothers and me around him one time. "You're not to take into account anything Mama has to say if she's going against me," he stated. "I forbid you from standing up for Mama or even obeying her if she is going against my will."

We heard him loud and clear.

Over the next few weeks, whenever Papa would send the children out of the house to do our work and not come back in until he said so, I knew that this meant my parents were addressing a serious issue. This would be confirmed when we heard Papa yelling at her and Mama screaming angry words back at him, often for hours at a time.

These shouting matches were enough to give me horribly vivid nightmares of Papa killing our mama. Once I even tried to tell Papa about my dream, hoping that he would change his mind about being so mean to her.

Nothing ever really helped, and my relationship with Mama would grow more and more distant as I went through adolescence.

# 18
# CAST OUT

O ur "Wilderness in Sin" tour opened my eyes when I saw all the toys and books other children had. Toys were forbidden by Papa, who called them "tools of the devil." Other than the Bible and *The Pilgrim's Progress*, we didn't have any other books lying around the cabin.

As far as Papa was concerned, those were the only two books worthy of reading. The Bible, of course, contained God's Word and teaching for our lives. *Pilgrim's Progress*, a Christian book written hundreds of years ago by some guy named John Bunyan, told the story of an everyman figure named Christian and his journey from the City of Destruction, representing earth, to the Celestial City, representing heaven. Papa said it was an allegory, but I didn't know what that meant since I'd never had formal schooling.

My papa had a memorable way of reading, and it was pretty amusing to listen to his dramatizations. He would add to or take away from what he was reading without our knowledge. Sometimes he even did this with the Bible, simply to test us to see if we were listening. But he loved "acting out" *Pilgrim's Progress*, especially the part in which Christian seeks to rid himself of a terrible burden—the weight of his sins.

One time, though, my parents surprised us by going to the library and borrowing several books, including a couple of the *Little House on the Prairie* books by Laura Ingalls Wilder.[1] The idea that my father would check out *any* books was totally out of character for him, but he must have been drawn to the series since the storyline revolved around a pioneer family living on a Kansas farm in the late 1800s.

One evening, Papa was reading from one of the books about Nellie Oleson,

---

1. There were originally eight books in the *Little House on the Prairie* series.

a spoiled girl and daughter of a wealthy general store owner. She got everything she wanted, and as a result, became rather bratty.

Reading about a rebellious character was like waving a red cape in front of a charging bull. "That's enough of that book," Papa said, firmly clasping it together.

Fortunately, we could still hear about Christian's journey to the Celestial City atop Mount Zion.

Whether it was his choice of reading or how he led our family, the only predictable thing about my father's behavior was its unpredictability, like when he returned from town one day with a special present: a soccer ball.

I couldn't believe my eyes. Now my brothers and I had something to play with. And then Papa did something else that was totally out of character: he put the ball on a grass patch not far from the cabin and started kicking it around to my brothers and me. He even called for Mama to join us, and the next thing I knew, the entire family was laughing and having fun as we kicked the ball back and forth between us.

The green grass, the birds singing, the bright sunshine, my happy brothers, a smiling Mama, and a cheerful Papa—this felt like heaven on earth. We must have kicked that ball around for hours. Then, as the sun started to set, one of the boys kicked the ball very close to the front door of our tiny cabin.

I sprinted after the ball, scooped it up, and quickly ran into the cabin to use the porta-potty, holding on tight to that ball as if it were my life. I couldn't let go because I would be out if I did, and I certainly didn't want that to happen. I figured I would go to the bathroom and be back before anyone would miss me.

I looked up. It was Mama, thrusting her arms out.

"Give me the ball," she demanded.

"No. I just need to finish. I'll be coming soon."

I could tell that Mama was shocked to hear me say no to her. I was surprised myself because I knew better, but it had slipped out. She quickly turned and left the cabin, clearly disgusted with me. Then a sense of dread came over me: she was going to tell Papa.

When I stepped out of the cabin, cradling the ball, I saw Papa listening intently to my mother. That's when I knew this heavenly day was about to turn to hell.

Papa charged in my direction, loaded for bear. "Get me a switch—now! No daughter of mine says no to her mother."

He severely beat me and announced I was "cast out" of the family, which meant that I was effectively banned from being with the family until Papa decided to allow me back in. I could not smile or come inside the cabin unless it was to receive further punishments or do kitchen chores. I was always the last to eat, which meant I might be scraping the bottom of the serving bowl or chewing on scraps of bread or bits of tortillas.

I never knew when I would be called in for another whipping to make sure I learned my lesson. I heard my father say this each time he punished me: "No one has ever said no to their mother or their father before, and this will be the last time."

Then another *smack* on my arms, on my fingers, or on my legs.

For the rest of my life, Papa would boast to the world that his kids never said no except the one time when his daughter Elishaba said no to her mother.

I felt like I carried a family curse.

In the future, I could go from being Papa's favorite to being "cast out"—even on the same day.

"You good-for-nothing daughter who fails to obey me at every turn—I hereby declare that you are cast out of the family," he would thunder if I failed to perform a chore correctly or fast enough for his pleasure. Questioning anything also earned banishment.

To mentally get through these difficult times, I told myself that it was my job to slave away to make everyone else happy. *They will be happy as long as I'm suffering.*

At such isolated times, I felt very alone—even forsaken—as I spent long hours washing our clothes by hand and hanging them on fences to dry. I worked hard scrubbing dirty diapers, trying to make them clean while I fought off hordes of flies. There were no Pampers at nine thousand feet. Since Mama gave birth every two years, there was always a brother wearing—and soiling—plenty of cloth diapers.

At the age of twelve, with four younger brothers, I longed for a sister—someone just like me who would understand how I felt. Each time I picked up the dry laundry from the fences, folded it, and put everything away in the dark pit beneath our bunk bed, I felt like I was all alone. At times like these, I would cry and beg God to hear me. "Please, Jesus, send me a sister who I can talk to, someone who will understand me."

I loved my brothers, but Papa treated them differently from how he treated me, which made me conscious of a growing gap between my father and me. Having a sister, I was sure, would change all that.

Then, good fortune came my way: when Mama was getting ready to have her sixth child, Papa was certain that the baby would be a girl.

"I have heard from the Lord, and He told me that Mama will have a baby girl," he announced with excitement in his voice. I always believed Papa, especially when he said he heard from the Lord. What Papa said had to be true. As Mama's pregnancy progressed, I eagerly waited to hold that precious sister in my arms.

When Mama went into labor, Papa wanted a picture taken of him hugging me to commemorate his "last only-girl hug." After all, I would no longer be the "only girl" after the new baby's arrival.

As he put his arm around my shoulder and we faced the camera held by my mother, I felt strangely lost inside. *Does this mean I won't be his special girl anymore?*

By now, I was allowed to participate in the birth process, which was overseen by the midwife—my father. We watched intensely as the baby presented and then came out . . .

*It's a boy!*

Instead of childbirth being a time of celebration, a considerable pall descended upon our cabin as my father solemnly cut the umbilical cord and handed his fifth son, whom they named Israel, to Mama to suckle at her breast.

Papa, for once, was speechless. He was *sure* that the Lord told him we were having a girl. As for me, my emotions were overtaken by bitter and hurtful feelings toward my father. He was wrong! How could he do that to me?[2]

As the oldest of six, I was proud of being the biggest and strongest child since my younger brothers hadn't reached adolescence yet.

High in the mountains, I had little opportunity to develop girlish behavior. Papa even called me his "right-hand man." Sharing an openly communal life in a cramped cabin and using a portable toilet in the middle of the living area meant that I couldn't be too particular about feminine modesty, which wasn't modeled for me anyway.

Working hard to please Papa was all I lived for, which was why I helped out around the kitchen, did laundry, cared for the animals, and cleaned up. Mama was too busy breastfeeding and caring for my youngest brothers to cook a whole lot for everyone, so I taught myself how to prepare a nice meal like Mama could.

When it came to sustenance, Papa made sure he controlled how much we ate, starting with breakfast. We were not allowed to eat until we'd listened to Papa's preaching *and* done our morning chores. While we milked Rosie, chopped and gathered wood, brought in water, dumped the poo bucket, and washed clothes,

---

2. In many ways, my father resented Israel. In the future, Papa Pilgrim would make life very difficult for him because he wasn't the girl he was expecting.

Papa stayed in the cabin and feasted like a king, sitting in his chair enjoying a big breakfast with eggs, toast, and even bacon sometimes, prepared by Mama.

We children weren't allowed to take a break until noontime, when we would be ravenous with hunger since we didn't have breakfast. Since Mama was often busy with the young ones underfoot, I would fetch a three-pound can of corn from the barn to make what we called "barn patties."

Inside the cabin, I would grind the corn in a small hand grinder, mix in some flour, and then drop the dough into a frying pan. My brothers would gather around the skillet, watching me fry up the barn patties. When they were golden and crispy, I'd set them on a plate to cool down. Then we'd eat with our hands, saving on dishes.

As for something to drink, I would add sugar or molasses to soured milk and make a kind of nutritious drink. Even if what I concocted tasted strange, we could not afford to be particular. The milk jug served as our common cup as we took turns drinking one long sip after the other.

I received mixed messages from my father on what it meant to be a girl. On the one hand, I was expected to be tough and physical and perform manual tasks without complaint. On the other hand, from Papa's preaching, he made it quite clear that a girl's job was to personally serve the master of the house. He talked about a Bible verse that said the woman was the weaker vessel,[3] which I thought meant that a woman couldn't pull her weight like a man and had to remain quiet.

One day, from his throne-like chair, he gave me a new directive: "I want you to start being a real woman. You need to start cleaning and caring for our home," he said.

I'd already been doing those sorts of things for years, so I was puzzled by his statement. Nonetheless, I knew better than to say anything.

Keeping the cabin clean wasn't easy. All the floors were dirt, except for the living room, where we had a throw rug on top of a wooden floor. We had no electricity and hence no vacuum cleaner, so I had to carry the rug outside, drape it over a fence, and beat it with a broom. Then I used a broom to sweep the living room and the dirt floors.

I constantly struggled, not having any explicit instructions regarding what was expected of me. Somehow I was supposed to know what it meant to "clean

---

3. 1 Peter 3:7 (KJV) says: "Likewise, ye husbands, dwell with them according to knowledge, giving honor unto the wife, as unto the weaker vessel, and as being heirs together of the grace of life, that your prayers be not hindered."

house." If I took too long about a task, I would get a whipping. It didn't help that Mama was always busy taking care of the babies while Papa sat in his armchair and yelled at both of us for being lazy.

I was becoming quite confused as I lived a life condemned to dreary days. I longed to get away and work outside in the woods and take care of the animals with my brothers. But since Papa always stayed inside the house and only went outside to bathe in the bathtub, I was trapped. Some days I would spend half my morning at his feet, listening to him pontificate while I rubbed his feet, and half my late afternoon in the bathtub with him—longing to be free to go elsewhere.

But freedom never came.

Not only did we all live on top of one another in unsanitary conditions, but our house also served as a barn, especially during the long and cold winter months when the baby animals would live with us to stay warm.

In the summer, they did fine in the barn. Summertime was also when we would erect an Indian-style teepee to camp out. This was a way to get some fresh air and get away from the flies that filled our cabin.

Sleeping in sleeping bags like my brothers was also a welcome change from the way I usually slept. Ever since I could remember, I had slept in the same king-sized bed as my parents, although there were times when I slept with all my brothers, who shared a big bed.

But for the most part, I slept next to my parents in general and my father in particular. While Mama tucked the latest baby close to her, I lay next to my father and slept in his arms, curled up in a fetal position and pressed against his bosom.

Before I fell asleep, though, Papa often asked me to rub his feet and toes. Of course, I did what he asked. From the moment I woke up until the moment I couldn't keep my eyes open any longer, pleasing my demanding papa was what I did every day.

# 19
# SISTER ACT

On a crisp, chilly October morning in 1988, the orange-hued colors of fall enveloped us in the Pecos Wilderness. Papa sat peacefully in his chair while we all gathered around him. Resting inside his arms was my first baby sister, Jerusalem. I was so happy that I could have turned cartwheels!

*God, You heard me after all! You did hear my cries. You gave me a sister! I'm sure we'll be the best of friends.*

We all sat around, waiting our turn to hold the seventh child of Papa and Country Rose. When I was allowed to take that little, sweet baby girl into my arms, I felt like heaven had come down to earth for a moment.

Papa reached for his Bible and flipped to a specific page of Scripture. "This morning, I want to talk about what the Bible has to say about jealousy." Then, turning in my direction, he asked politely, "Elizabeth, do you feel jealous now that you have a baby sister?"

I was astonished, even offended, that he would raise such a question. I felt as though a horse had trampled my heart.

"No, of course not!" I quickly replied.

Seemingly, Papa set out to prove to me that I *was* jealous. In the coming days, then months, he doted on Jerusalem and made sure I saw him doing it. The way my little sister bonded so closely to Papa caused me to wonder if I was no longer daddy's girl. He even changed our sleeping arrangement together. Now it was Jerusalem who got to sleep in the crook of his arm while I was relegated to the foot of the bed and expected to rub his feet as we both nodded off.

This was the start of a rivalry that Papa would encourage in the future. He did this by pitting Jerusalem against me, and he found pleasure in our quarrels.

Not only did we have to listen to Papa preach before he sent us off to do our morning chores, but we also had to listen to him expound upon Scripture when we came in from our chores every night.

And it was night. There were never enough hours in the day to milk the cows and goats, tend to the lambs, haul water and hay, feed the dogs, rabbits, and chickens, rake out the corral, and chop wood. We rarely finished our daily chores before eight or nine o'clock in the evening.

My brothers and I would enter the cabin, bushed and hungry, but we couldn't eat anything until we listened to Papa preach his evening sermon to us. We had to gather around his big rocking chair, sitting cross-legged on the dirty carpet with a lamb or two, or find a spot on a bench in our dining table nook. Papa, ensconced in his chair like King Solomon, held his thick, well-thumbed Bible in his lap.

He often began by questioning us about our day, which opened the door to him rebuking us for something we had done wrong or done poorly. We never heard the words "well done" or a simple "thank you." Papa told us that praise could make us proud, and pride was a sin. Praise and compliments were as rare as having an ice cream treat in town.

One evening, he turned to Proverbs 3:11-12, which he read to us:

> My son, despise not chastening of the Lord;
> neither be weary of his correction:
> For whom the Lord loveth he correcteth;
> even as a father the son in whom he delighteth.

My father looked around at each of his children, his piercing eyes looking into every soul. "Why do you despise my chastening?" he asked.

Several of my brothers became animated. Joseph, the eldest son, spoke up. "We don't, Papa. We want to do what's right."

"Don't lie to me," my father replied. "Every time you leave the gate open to the barn, you are disobeying me. You could kill all the animals. You are such careless children. When you despise my correction, you despise God. You want me to delight in you? Ha!"

Papa saw this as another opportunity to pit us against each other. "Elizabeth, I don't want you to feed Joseph and Joshua breakfast tomorrow morning because they didn't obey. You can feed the rest. I want to point out to the rest of you rebellious boys that Elizabeth always closes the barn door because she does not despise my words."

This comment was like a double-edged sword. On the one hand, I was happy to be on Papa's good side, which gave me hope that God loved me. On the other hand, I worried that my oldest brothers would resent me.

It was routine interactions like this that gave Papa golden opportunities to remind us that we needed to be accountable to him because God placed him as the head of the family, just like He did with Abraham and Moses.

One time, Papa pointed to a homemade calendar hanging on the wall next to the kitchen table. Every winter, he drew up a calendar for the coming year. Each of the twelve months contained a picture of prophecy or something Christian-related, like his vision of hell with fire coming up and consuming men in chains. My father was a good artist and liked to draw with a set of colored pencils.

His calendar didn't contain the traditional months of the year like January and February, however. "Those are pagan names," he explained. "The days of the week are pagan, too, so we're not going to use them either."

Papa's solution was to refer to the months of the year as "First Month," "Second Month," and "Third Month." For the days of the week, Monday became the "First Day," Tuesday was the "Second Day," and so forth. Keeping track of what day of the week it was got confusing.

It was easy to be puzzled because we were hungry and not allowed to eat dinner until he was finished preaching.

We never knew how long he'd talk. Sometimes he'd preach way past nine, ten, or even eleven at night, even though my bone-tired brothers and I were nearly delirious with hunger. However, we had to show that we were listening because if we didn't, Papa would either preach longer or tell us we weren't getting dinner that night. No one wanted that to happen, so we pinched ourselves to stay awake.

Finally, just when we couldn't keep our eyes open any longer, Papa would close his Bible and pronounce a blessing over us. Only then could Mama serve dinner, which was usually pieces of fried mutton with rice and beans. We scarfed our food like it was our last meal, but there was never enough. Or so it seemed.

After dinner, many of us had to use the poo bucket right next to Papa's chair. The awful smells inside the cabin were sometimes overwhelming. When the last of us had done our business for the evening, one of my brothers or I had to pick up the camp toilet and go outside with a flashlight and dump it.

That was the worst chore of the day.

Only then were we allowed to fall asleep, which was usually sometime around eleven, although there were many evenings where we didn't lay our heads down until midnight.

When my eyelids opened in the morning, I always woke up with one goal: staying on Papa's good side. I did this by snuggling up with him before Jerusalem was born and then nestling close to him before my sister woke up, which he loved. He told everyone how much he liked his "good morning cuddles."

This was far from easy because his moods changed as quickly as the wind-driven weather swirling around Hermit Peak west of our cabin. I couldn't look to Mama for help because she was under his thumb as much as I was. Everyone tiptoed around Papa because we weren't allowed to talk back to him. If we did speak up or make the mistake of challenging him, he'd announce that we were in rebellion and needed to be disciplined.

The punishment was swift. I had grown up with Papa beating me with a switch from a willow tree, but when we were older and getting bigger, his favorite instrument of discipline became the braided whip. He didn't hesitate to use it on me or my younger brothers.

Experience taught me that it didn't take much to get a whipping, so I made sure I paid attention to what Papa expected from me.

Failure to do so had painful repercussions.

Another unpleasant experience happened as I was approaching my twelfth birthday. That's when I noticed two lumps growing on the front of my chest. They HURT!

Now I knew God was angry with me, and I was sure I would die of cancer just like my grandma did. After weeks of hiding this fear, I decided I better tell Mama. There was no way I'd say anything to Papa. This was too personal, too scary. But I worried that she would make me tell Papa.

When I couldn't hold it in any longer, I gathered my courage and told my mother that my chest was hurting.

A sly smile crept across her face. Immediately I felt silly for making a big deal out of this, but why was she so happy? Then she quickly reached under my shirt and felt my nipples. A feeling of shame covered me like a blanket as she fondled them. "Those are breasts," she said. "You're going to be like me now."

I didn't know anyone got breasts unless she had a baby. I was so confused and felt trapped and violated. At the same time, I felt relieved to learn that I wasn't going to die from cancer.

The summer after I turned thirteen, as I was on the cusp of adolescence, a burning question haunted me: *What is life really about?*

If life was about getting to heaven, then I hoped against hope that I would get there. What made me feel uneasy was that I didn't know if I was heaven-bound because of my sin. Papa reminded me time and again that I was a sinner going straight to hell when I didn't obey him. Every time he said I disobeyed him, I worried that I wasn't getting to heaven.

As for life in general, I knew there was a big world out there, but my parents never explained anything to me. I didn't go to school, nor did my parents homeschool me. I received no education at all. I could barely read or write.

As I approached thirteen, I was becoming aware of my sexuality while struggling with terribly conflicting thoughts. For instance, how were babies made? I often saw animals mating, but I didn't see how something like that could happen between a husband and wife. Was it because they slept in the same bed? But I slept in the same bed as Papa. How come I didn't have any babies? I was pretty mixed up.

So I'd go out into the forest, where no one could see and I'd have some privacy, and look at myself. As my fingers explored, I experienced these strange feelings. I didn't know what to make of it.[1]

I felt so guilty that I had to talk to someone about it, and the only person available was Mama. I felt so much shame as I mustered the courage to approach her one time when we were in the cabin alone, preparing dinner.

"Mama, I need to make a confession," I said haltingly. "I'm scared to talk about this with Papa."

"What is it, Elizabeth? You know you can tell me anything."

I kept my eyes down and spoke in a monotone. "I just wanted to tell you that I've been looking at myself and playing around and having strange feelings. I don't know what's going on."

Mama's lips tightened. "You said playing around."

"Yes, Mama."

"You're going to have to tell Papa about that."

I groaned. "Oh, Mama, do I have to?"

"Yes, you have to."

I knew then there was no way out, especially after he came into the cabin around ten minutes later. We were all alone.

"Elizabeth has something to tell you," my mother announced.

My father's eyebrows arched—a look that I had come to dread.

"Okay, let's hear it," he said, taking a seat on the edge of the bed while Mama joined him.

I took my seat on a wooden stool and repeated what I'd told Mama.

His response was a series of interrogating questions:

*"How many times have you done this?"*

*"When did you do this?"*

*"Where were you?"*

*"What kind of thoughts did you have in your mind?"*

---

1. I really believe these uneasy feelings happened when I was thirteen because my father was putting his hands into my underwear when I slept next to him, prompting feelings in me that were inappropriate to our relationship.

I gave him short answers, but I could tell he was *enjoying* the conversation. Even more, I saw a different look in him—a look of delight, which unsettled me.

When I was done, he adopted a conciliatory tone. "You don't need to worry about this. What happened to you has a purpose. Someday, I'll explain that purpose to you, but what you need to know is that people are different from animals. You've seen animals breed, and then they have babies. Well, we're not like animals. That's not how it works for people."

The way he said this told me that we were talking about something special to him. Then he furrowed his brow in such a way that my heart felt like a powerful punishment was on its way.

"Elizabeth, this is very serious," he began, his voice dropping an octave. "You have become a strange woman and a harlot before God. You are walking in disobedience and deceit. This makes you a 'strange woman,' as Solomon talked about in Proverbs. You can't be trusted, even around your brothers. You must be separated and banished from the family. There's no way you can be a Christian and be bound up in fornication like you are. I'm going to have to ask God to give me wisdom on dealing with this. I've made it very clear that you were not to look at or touch yourself, and if you did such things, you were defiling the temple of the Holy Spirit. When you're sinning against your body, you're sinning against God."

I had no idea what the word "fornication" meant, but it sounded like something terrible. My heart was ridden with guilt and hatred for myself as my father pressed on.

"What a disappointment you've become to me. You must know that it's God's command that I have to punish you for this. And I will pray to God in tears that He will forgive you for this evil you've committed. I want to see you four times a day with the leather whip."

I shook with fear. Papa was referring to a thick five-foot-long braided whip. I knew his whippings would really hurt.

Papa continued. "You are not to smile or talk to anyone unless it has to do with chores. I have no idea how long it'll be before God reveals to me that you are forgiven. You've broken my heart, Elizabeth. You are a disgrace to our family. As a punishment, you will sleep in the shed tonight. If you are not up early in the morning, I will send someone out to pour water on your head."

My heart nearly broke at the thought of being banished from the family. Even more, I wondered if God had rejected me as well.

Several weeks passed. Then Papa decided I could be forgiven.

"We will celebrate," he said, "by bathing together. Let this be a symbol of a new start."

For once, I looked forward to this ordeal because I hadn't bathed in a long time and felt as filthy as a sheep pen. I hastened to fill the tub with five-gallon buckets of water and start a fire beneath it.

While soaking, he mentioned that we would be taking a little trip together.

"Where are we going, Papa?"

My father was circumspect. "All I can tell you is it's going to be a special time just for you and me," he said.

I noticed a strange look in his eyes but kept that observation to myself. I had learned that he would question me if I showed any resistance toward him. Questioning often led to a "correction."

"Thank you, Papa. A trip with you would be very exciting," I said. "When are we going?"

"Tomorrow."

The following morning, Papa and I walked past the woodpile next to the "slaughtering tree," where we killed and dressed the sheep we raised. Parked there was a maroon Jeep with a roll bar that Papa had inherited from his mother when she died. The two-door SUV was the latest addition to our fleet of vehicles that included the Army-surplus '41 Chevy truck and the school-bus-turned-RV.

Apprehension filled the air as I hopped in the passenger side. There was something very strange about the way Papa was acting. I felt like it had something to do with my admission to him about playing with myself.

"Scoot over," he said, patting the middle of the bench seat.

I wanted to ask why but thought better of it. When I complied, the manual transmission gear stick was right between my legs.

"From now on, this is where you belong, Elizabeth."

We started down the mountain, following a bumpy, rut-covered dirt road that winded back and forth. In between shifting gears, Papa set his right hand on my left leg. I felt uncomfortable and embarrassed. I'd seen cowgirls sitting next to their boyfriends behind the wheel, but never fathers and daughters.

"Where are we going?" Maybe I would receive an answer this time.

"Ledoux. I need to pick up the mail and drop by a couple of ranchers and ask them about getting some hay. Winter's coming up."

This *was* a special day. Papa didn't like taking me into the valley because he didn't want me talking to boys my age.

As we pulled into Ledoux, Papa spoke up. "Duck under the dash and stay there," he ordered. "Keep your head down."

It was evident that he didn't want anyone in tiny Ledoux, population 550, to see me. After a minute, Papa slowed to a stop and parked.

I knew where we were—the Village Store. The Ledoux Post Office was located in the back. The postmaster, Mr. Garcia, stashed our mail in an extra-large box. Papa would often go for weeks without picking up our mail.

I stayed low as my father exited the vehicle. While I waited for his return, the words Papa told me after I confessed haunted my mind: *Someday, I'll explain it to you.* That's what today had to be all about.

After collecting the mail, we visited two ranchers. I stayed in the truck and listened to Papa bargain for bales of hay. No deals were struck, so it was time to head back up the mountain. Halfway there, Papa startled me when he pulled over and parked the Jeep in a meadow filled with willow trees. After turning off the motor, he folded his hands and turned toward me. I felt uneasy and scooted as far away from him as I could.

"Well, Elizabeth," he said, "are you ready for me to tell you a few things?"

I was definitely *not* ready, especially after seeing the weird look on his face. I sensed what he wanted to talk about had something to do with the strange activity I'd seen between my parents in the middle of the night when they thought I was dead asleep. They were both naked, and Papa was lying on top of Mama and grunting.

Fear rose within me like vomit. My spine tingled with nerves because I felt vulnerable sitting off to the side of a road with my father—a man I feared for multiple reasons. Then I had an idea. Since I knew my father enjoyed my worldly ignorance, I could play to that.

"You know, Papa, I think I would rather not even know about these kinds of things," I responded. "They seem so worldly."

That was a lie. After the last couple of months, I did want to know what happened between a man and a woman. I just didn't want to hear about it from him. Being alone with him in the Jeep, I felt trapped and vulnerable.

Papa shot me an angry look because he never expected to be rebuffed.

"You really feel that way?"

"Yeah."

He started up the Jeep and roughly slammed it into gear.

"All right then," he retorted, and then he drove up the road in silence.

As always, my feelings were mixed. On the one hand, as I leaned against the passenger door and looked at the passing forest, I felt a wave of relief, even pride, that I had outwitted him. But I also felt devastated because I knew I had disappointed Papa.

Even though I felt victorious at the moment, I wondered when he would have his revenge.

Knowing my father, it wouldn't be long.

# 20
# TENDING THE FLOCK

The spring of 1990, when I was fourteen years old, was an uncertain time in my life. I was growing taller with wider hips and hair in places I'd never seen it before. I was acutely aware that I was becoming a teenager.

Mom, sensing that the time was right, told me all about periods. Everything she said, though, made it sound like an awful experience, especially the part about them lasting a week, which sounded like an eternity. I dreaded that this bad thing was going to happen to me any day.

Sure enough, a month later, I suddenly realized that my pants were full of blood. In a moment of desperation, I approached Mama and whispered to her what had happened. We were inside our tiny cabin, filled with my siblings and Papa.

Upon hearing the news, I saw the same slight smile on her face as when I told her that my budding breasts hurt.

"Follow me," she said.

Mama grabbed a flashlight and beckoned me to come with her. Pregnant with her eighth child, my mother was waddling a bit as I followed in her footsteps. I was pleading with the Lord for another sister after Jerusalem arrived a year and a half earlier.[1]

We found a dark corner in the front part of the cabin, behind a door.

"Let me see." Mama shined the flashlight toward my nether region. I froze—I didn't know what to do. Then she pulled down my pants, leaving me feeling exposed, ugly, and dirty.

"Yup, that's a period all right," she remarked. "Okay, here's what you do."

She told me to take an old T-shirt and cut it into strips. Then I was to tuck

---

1. On June 21, 1990, I was excited to assist in the delivery of my second sister, Hosanna.

one or two into my underwear. "Be sure to change them every day. Hide the strips, and then we'll wash them later."

Mama also said a few things that gave me pause, like telling me to make sure I never touched the blood and that I was very unclean when it was my "time of the month."

She also said to make sure that the boys never saw me changing the T-shirt strips or knew about my periods; they were a big, big secret. Since we didn't have a bathroom, this wasn't easy to do. I had to go outside to the barn or behind some tree to perform this unpleasant task.

How embarrassing, wondering if one of my brothers would catch a glimpse of me in this way.

Mom told me that starting my menstrual cycle was a sign that I was becoming a young woman, but if I had to define who I was at the age of fourteen, I would say I was a shepherdess.

After listening to Papa preach in the morning, bringing in more firewood, stoking the fire in the woodstove, chopping more firewood, feeding the animals, and dumping the poo bucket, I could start doing something I enjoyed: taking care of our flock of sheep, which fluctuated between fifty and one hundred lambs and ewes. I had a name for nearly every one of them.

Sheep brought me comfort and companionship. There would be nights when I'd snuggle in bales of hay with my baby lambs, watching over them. Pregnant ewes would give birth in the winter, so we had to be particularly careful when they were about to lamb. The sub-freezing cold could easily prove to be too much for some of them.

During lambing season, Papa instigated what we called a "lamb watch." Every two hours during the night, we older children had to take turns waking up and going out to the barn to check for more lambs being born. We would slip on our big boots and a thick coat and walk out into the sharp cold, half asleep and carrying a big flashlight.

Rousing ourselves awake in the middle of the night was hard since Papa made us stay up late listening to him preach. Since I slept in the same big bed with him and Mama, he'd shake me pretty good until I came out of my stupor.

"Wake up. It's lamb watch!"

"Uhhh . . ."

"Hurry and turn on the radio for some inspiration," he'd say.

We had a tiny radio that ran on a 12-volt battery. We couldn't bring in very many stations, but the country music station out of Albuquerque came in loud and clear at night. I loved it when Willie Nelson and Emmylou Harris sang their country songs. I'd carry the tunes with me to the barn while I checked on the lambs.

Most of the time, though, Papa woke me up to have *me* wake up Joseph and Joshua when it was their turn. I hated doing his dirty work because it was nearly impossible to wake up my younger brothers. They were such incredible hard workers, which is why waking them up out of their deep slumber was almost impossible.

"Joseph, wake up before Papa makes me pour water on your head."

No response. I'd give Joseph a good shake and repeat what I said. He'd stir a bit, but he was out cold.

After the second time, Papa, from his bed, would have enough. "Get a pail of water and pour it on his head."

And that's what I did on many nights. Each time I roused Joseph or Joshua from a deep sleep—startled by the sudden shower, their hair soaked—they looked at me in shock. My heart nearly burst in pain.

I also knew they would try to get back at me when they could.

I started shepherding when I was six years old, but we started adding to our flock when I turned twelve. Each time I left the cabin, I wore a long buckskin leather dress that we tanned with sheep brains.

Papa made sure I always took one or two of my younger brothers with me. That was for our safety, he said, to protect us from other wild animals as well as other humans we might encounter.

"I want you always to have someone with you if you talk to other people," he said. "Be aware. They will try to deceive you and tell you lies, but when two or more of you are together, you will be able to withstand evil temptations."

I knew the other reason why Papa wanted us traveling together: that way, he could ask one of us to report what the other said. Papa's words about avoiding conversations with outsiders were so firm and clear that I was scared to death to talk to someone outside our family when I was all alone.

Papa noticed how good I was with our flock; his approval gave me a sense of worth. I was eager to please Papa because he said, "Elizabeth, my maiden, you are obedient and willing to do all that it takes to please me. When you please me, you are pleasing God. You will inherit the kingdom of God and build your reward in heaven."

I wanted so much to go to heaven, so I did everything I could to earn my way there.

Helping me out was my faithful dog, a Great Pyrenees named Journey. She was a loyal shepherd dog willing to protect our sheep from wild beasts day and night. Even though she wasn't a people dog, we could communicate silently.

One day, a whole herd of older lambs escaped the pen, but Journey stayed with them until she heard us in the distance, ran in our direction, and then brought us to the lambs. Another time, early one morning, I realized we were missing a ewe. I looked down into a meadow, and there was Journey following close behind her with a newborn black lamb in her mouth. When she saw me, she dropped the newborn and turned toward the woods—she wanted me to follow her. That's where I found the other newborn lamb.

That day, Journey was a true hero.

Each time I led our sheep into the forest to search for mountain grass, I brought my shepherd's crook that I made myself by soaking an oak branch in water. Once the wood was waterlogged, I would bend it a bit daily, soak it again overnight, and bend the wood a little more until I had a complete crook that I used to bring wayward sheep back into the fold.

When I left in the morning, I'd take along a compass, a knife, a flashlight, my Bible, and a bean tortilla wrap in a small leather pouch. The tortilla wrap was my breakfast and lunch, so I ate it sparingly to make it last. I also brought along a Bible, which helped me get through the long days that passed slowly. I couldn't read very well, and I certainly didn't understand every word, but I'd study every verse that Papa had us underline.

I also carried a .50-caliber muzzleloader—an old-school rifle that I loaded with gunpowder and bullets through the muzzle. I carried a powder horn over my shoulder and extra bullets in my leather pouch.

Shepherds needed rifles in this part of the world. Mountain lions, coyotes, and bears loved snatching wandering sheep, which were defenseless. My job was to protect our growing flock while guiding them to fresh patches of green grass to eat.

The biggest problem was finding suitable grass at our high elevation. There was a mountain stream about a mile away that was my usual go-to spot, but when there wasn't enough grass to munch on, I knew what to do—trespass onto a neighbor's property. Papa said it was okay to graze on other people's land because they were sinners and God wanted to provide for us. Something about opening a gate and trespassing on other people's land—or sometimes cutting through barbed wire fences—didn't sit well with me, but I knew I had to accept him at his word; I always had.

Sheep were a big deal to us because of the wool they provided (which we could sell), but more importantly, they were our primary source of protein. Since we didn't have a refrigerator or a freezer, we stored our butchered lamb meat inside a small wooden structure that we called an "icehouse" during the winter months.

In March, my brothers and I would build wooden troughs and line them with plastic. Then we filled the troughs with buckets of water. The water would freeze overnight, and the next night we would add more water. Then we took a chainsaw, cut the ice into giant chunks, and packed them into the icehouse that we'd lined with thick Styrofoam. This worked as a cooler to keep the meat throughout the summer.

One time in June, I left the cabin with a pair of tongs and approached the icehouse. The smell of rotting meat nearly caused me to faint and abandon my quest. I poked around and grabbed a leg of lamb. When I lifted the chunk of meat out, the flesh was lime green and rotting.

I stifled a gag. Suddenly, a swarm of flies appeared out of nowhere and followed me while I carried the meat into the cabin and the main room, where our kitchen was. I kept my free hand over my mouth because the stench of rotting flesh was so putrid.

Papa looked up from his chair and set his Bible down on his lap. I knew I couldn't tell him how gross the leg of lamb was. As if reading my mind, he spoke up. "There's nothing wrong with that meat. It's good for you. It's just aged a bit, that's all. Some countries use that green stuff as a natural antibiotic."

I knew what an antibiotic was since we used penicillin on the animals, but we also consumed the vile stuff if any of us got sick or had a badly infected cut. On this occasion, though, the chunk of lamb wasn't aged—it was spoiled. But I couldn't tell Papa that. This was our dinner, and food wasn't plentiful in the cabin.

There were two five-gallon buckets of water on the floor, next to the counter. One bucket contained our drinking water. If we were thirsty, we reached for a small scooper hanging on the wall. We would grab the scooper, dip it into the water, and take a sip. What we didn't drink was poured back into the bucket. Water was way too valuable to be wasted.

The other water bucket was known as our "slop bucket." We dumped all our "gray water"—water used to wash the dishes—into the slop bucket, along with any food scraps, bits of fat off the meat, and rotting fruit. The slop bucket was our version of a garbage disposal.

If we wanted to wash our hands or face, we would pour some hot water from the stove and cooler water from our drinking water bucket into a porcelain bowl. Then that water—which turned black from dirt—was tossed into the slop bucket. When we were done washing up, we cleaned up with an old towel used communally.

I washed my hands before working on the leg of lamb, chopping out green and pinkish chunks until I had all the meat off the bone, stifling my gag reflex the entire time. When the pieces were small enough, I tossed them into a frying pan set on the wood-heated stove. I scooped out a dollop of homemade lard from a container and added that to the frying pan, along with salt and paprika. Then I got a big pot of rice going, filled with water from the five-gallon bucket.

While I waited for the water to come to a boil, I ran out to the barn with a large wooden bowl. We had several big bins filled with grain, wheat berries, and whole corn. I filled a bowl with whole corn and hustled back to the kitchen to stir the meat and check on the water. Satisfied that I was on top of everything, I took a handful of kernels and filled a hand grinder to start making homemade tortillas, which were our daily bread. My biggest goal was to make sure everybody felt full because there was never an abundance to eat. Tortillas helped.

Filling hungry tummies was tough because Papa always got the best portion of everything—and the biggest share—so I made sure that I made enough food for everyone when I cooked.

When the lamb meat was cooked and the rice was ready, I poured everything into a large wooden bowl and mixed everything together. I scooped a small mountain of juicy lamb and rice onto a plate for Papa and served him. My younger brothers and sisters lined up, each with a bowl in their hands.

I ladled out portions, trying to be fair. My older brothers, growing like weeds, needed more food than my younger sisters Jerusalem and Hosanna, but would my sisters' hungry stomachs tell them that? However, tonight was a good night: there was enough for everybody, and my homemade tortillas helped fill them up. They ate everything with their hands since utensils were scarce items in the cabin. We didn't have many forks and knives.

Before I could take a bite, though, I had to show Papa my bowl of food.

He was sitting in his chair, still working on his lamb and rice with his fork and knife. I extended my bowl to him. I was shaking and afraid to say anything because he'd been telling me that I had a weight problem for the last few months and had to do something about it.

Papa shook his head. "No, that's too much," he said.

I sighed. I knew where this was going. I would have to take food off my plate and show him my plate again. But then he surprised me.

"In fact, no. You can't have any of your dinner."

*I can't eat? When I'm so hungry?*

I wanted to object, to express how I was starving, talk about how hard I'd worked, but I couldn't because I knew what would happen next: Papa would say that I was in rebellion and needed to find a willow branch for another "correction."

Stopping me from eating when I was so hungry caused me to shut down emotionally. I turned away as warm tears rolled down my cheeks. Then I gathered myself and took a knife to my plate. I slid all of my dinner back into the large bowl.

That evening, my stunned brothers didn't ask for seconds. Maybe that was their way of showing me that they were on my side.

That didn't lessen the pang of hunger in the pit of my stomach, however.

The summer I was fourteen, I noticed that Papa was becoming more and more subdued, content to sit in his chair and rock for hours at a time, doing nothing. Oh, his temper was still quite volatile, and he would blow up when we made a mistake or did something he didn't like, but he seemed much more depressed as his end-times convictions took hold of him. Personally, I struggled in my relationship with him, torn between love and fear. The angry look on his face could devastate me.

Being a shepherdess was the only thing that kept me strong as I grew to maturity. Something about leaving in the morning with my father smoldering like an angry volcano and trekking out to mountain pastures with placid sheep calmed my heart. Along the way, I'd repeat Psalm 23—"The Lord is my shepherd; I shall not want"—as I accompanied my sheep to still waters and green pastures. There were times when I felt I was walking them through the valley of the shadow of death with my staff, ready to lay down my life for my sheep. Treasuring Psalm 23 in my heart—with its reminder that Jesus loved me as much as I loved my flock—gave me a bit of hope.

Since we lived off of our sheep, caring for them ensured our survival. Uncle Billy, a veterinarian, had generously provided us with a good stock of ointments and medicines, including sutures, Novocaine, etc. Over the years, he had taught Papa and my older brothers and me how to sew up a wounded animal, deliver their babies if trouble came, and do C-sections on our sheep when required.

Since we were on our own, Papa became our family's medical caregiver, including dentistry. One time, a growing cavity in one of my permanent molars was causing me a lot of distress. When I apprised Papa of how much pain I was in, he offered a solution: "Then I'll have to pull it out," he announced.

My parents took me to the dentist a couple of times during my childhood, but Papa said we didn't have the money this time.[2] I nearly fainted when I saw my father return from the shed with a pair of pliers in one hand and a syringe filled with a shot of Novocaine in the other.

"Are you really—"

---

2. The last time I saw the dentist, Papa told the dental practitioner that he knew better what I needed than he did. The dentist became livid, so Papa yanked me out of the dental chair. "We're leaving now!" my father exclaimed. I could tell the dentist felt sorry for me, giving me a pat on the shoulder as we exited his office.

"Sit down," he ordered.

I knew better than to argue. I took a spot on a bench outside the house.

"Now open up," he said.

I opened my mouth and waited as he jabbed the needle to numb me. The medication seemed to work, so Papa started going after the hurting tooth with his pliers. I screamed from the shocking pain as he broke my tooth in half and bits of tooth fell on my tongue.

"I didn't get it all," he said. Pieces of my white tooth remained in my jawbone. The next thing I knew, he inserted the pliers in my mouth and dug out the rest of my molar, but it felt like a hot knife was digging into my jawbone. I don't remember much more; I passed out from the pain as my world turned into a huge blur.

Somehow I survived the ordeal, but the searing agony in my jaw would stay with me for weeks.

Around this time, Papa decided to call me by a Hebrew name he found in the Bible—Elishaba. Even though this was my *third* name after answering to Butterfly and Elizabeth, I liked my new name because Papa would call me Elishaba when I was in his favor. However, if he said, "Elizabeth, come here," then I knew I was in big trouble. That was Papa's signal that he was angry with me.

Meanwhile, in our isolation high in the mountains, I believed we were the only true Christians on the face of the earth. Everyone we met or tried to convert would eventually walk away from us, however. As sure as a sunrise, Papa would end up arguing with them, calling them sinners, and before long, they simply couldn't handle us anymore.

Oh, the tears I cried when a particular family we had grown to love turned away from us. I never thought it was our fault for being so contentious and condemning; I was simply hurt when we were ripped away from hopeful relationships.

I think Papa also felt the loneliness. He would talk hopefully of finding a family just like us with whom we could walk in unbroken fellowship. In my adolescent state, I fantasized about this "dream family." I pictured meeting them somewhere as they wandered around the wilderness waiting for the Lord's promised destruction of the earth. I also imagined this family having a boy my age with whom I could fall in love and marry.

I would discover that my father had other plans for me.

# 21
# THE EYES OF TEXAS

Sometime in the fall of 1993, Uncle Billy drove out from Texas to visit us at the mountain cabin in New Mexico. It seems that God had gotten a hold of my uncle's life. Uncle Billy had a major conversion experience, so much so that he neglected his veterinary practice and came to our homestead wearing a black cowboy hat and dressing like a fancy mountain man. He had also brought along two young men from Texas. I wasn't sure what that was about, but I overheard Uncle Billy telling my father that they were his "disciples."

My father wasn't impressed, saying that even though my uncle was a church-going Baptist, he was a proud man, evidenced by how he walked around with a feather in his cowboy hat. "You are full of the world, and you have been deceived by wolves in sheep's clothing," my father asserted. "You're not even a Christian. You need to be born-again and baptized."

Confusion and despair filled my uncle's face. This was a look I often saw in adults who spent any amount of time in my father's presence. Sooner or later—usually sooner—my father would tell his audience that they were going straight to hell unless they repented and became born-again, no matter what their spiritual heritage was.

Uncle Billy, to his credit, didn't get into his truck and take the two young men with him back to Texas. He seemed especially interested in how Rainbow Cross Ranch operated and how we survived such deprivation without any creature comforts.

One special thing about having Uncle Billy around was how amazed he was regarding what my siblings and I could do around the cabin.

"You've got some phenomenal kids here," Uncle Billy would say to his brother as they stood outside and watched us do our chores. "Look at them. They're making this place a go."

He was particularly impressed with how we handled our flock of sheep and how we trained and managed our herd. My older brothers and I could do everything: take them out to forage all day long, shear the sheep for their wool, and slaughter the rams and ewes for our meat. Uncle Billy even commended my cooking skills.

Since praise rarely left Papa's lips, my heart was filled with joy to hear something positive about my work and effort. My self-respect rose several notches. I wanted to hear more praise, so I worked for Uncle Billy's attention. I even went as far as rubbing his feet like I did for Papa.

That didn't go over well with my father, who was suddenly jealous of his twin brother.

One time, when we were outside and out of earshot, Papa took me aside. I could tell he was ticked about something.

"Elizabeth, the way you are acting around my brother shows me that you are full of pride and have no understanding of what is right. You are never to be alone with Billy. Do you understand?"

Chastened, I nodded my comprehension. "Yes, Papa," I mumbled.

Hearing him say that about Uncle Billy killed a part of my tender heart. Deflated and confused, I suffered one more dent in my self-esteem. I felt like I had no reason on earth to be alive. I even contemplated what it would be like to take my own life. Why go on?

But I had heard Papa say many times that people who committed suicide were doomed to hell. "No one who murders himself or others, no one who is a liar, will be found in heaven. Of that, you can be assured."

I didn't want to end up in hell. I wanted to go to heaven, so I stuffed my hurt feelings deep within me.

On the positive side, it was clear that Papa and his twin brother were kindred spirits. Uncle Billy couldn't get over our homestead life and how we were in the world but not of the world. He said he brought along his two "disciples" to see for themselves how Papa was raising a family high up in the mountains, away from ungodly influences. "They want to change their worldly ways and live like you do," Uncle Billy said.

Hearing that excited Papa. "That's great, but what about you?"

"What do you mean, what about me?" Uncle Billy asked.

"Brother, it's time for you to know that God is calling you away from the City of Destruction. It's time for you to get your Christian walk in order and go on a pilgrimage to the Celestial City. You need to go back and get your wife and four kids and save them from God's wrath that's sure to come."

My father's words shocked my uncle. "Bobby, you don't know my family. The fancies of life, their sports, schooling, their careers—it's all too important to them. They would never come."

"'Love not the world, neither the things that are in the world,'" my father replied, quoting Scripture from 1 John 2:15. "You have to pull up stakes in Fort Worth. God will judge you if you don't. Come live simply like we do. I can help you build a cabin, and we can live off the land. You'd be perfect because you know so much about animals."

My uncle remained unconvinced. "I don't see Patsy leaving the comforts of home for this," he said, waving an arm at our crude cabin with walls that leaned and no running water or electricity.

"Then she's in rebellion, and you need to set her straight."

That was Papa's standard response whenever others weren't doing what he thought they should do. *They are in rebellion.*

Papa and Uncle Billy were at an impasse. As the two brothers sat in our cabin, they rocked back and forth in unison, clearly identical twins. Not only was there a strong facial resemblance, but each had shoulder-length salt-and-pepper hair and whiskers. The difference was that Papa's beard was long, unruly, and always unkempt, while Uncle Billy's goatee was neatly trimmed.

"You need to be strong because Patsy's going to put up a big fight," my father explained. "But you have to get your family out of Sodom before its destruction by fire. If Patsy and the kids won't come, then you have to be willing to lose your family for the sake of the Lord if that's what it comes down to. But let me help you with Patsy. I'll come to Fort Worth to help you save your family before it's too late."

Uncle Billy didn't say he'd accept my father's help right away, but Papa could be quite persuasive if given enough time. I don't know how he did it, but he convinced Uncle Billy that they needed to go back and get his wife and four children out of Fort Worth—the place my father called the "City of Destruction"—and bring them to the homestead.

Until they departed for Texas, my father put Uncle Billy's two "disciples" to work around the homestead—knocking down trees, chopping firewood, and hauling water. They slept in a dug-out area under the other loft, in the dirt. For a couple of city boys, they didn't complain much.

The two young men were a few years older than me—and pretty good-looking. I'd been around a few young boys around my age before, but Papa would inevitably come across as judgmental to them and their parents, and that would be that: we'd never see them again. Several adults, when my father wasn't around, would pull me close and whisper, "Your father has a horrible past. Ask him about it some time. He's a dangerous man." Others told me that I was part of some weird cult, which always hurt to hear.

I hoped that Papa would not turn these two young men from Texas away from me. I kind of liked having them around. When I was out shepherding and had tons of time to think, I would fantasize about what it would be like to marry one of them and have my own family.

In the past, if I ever mentioned that I'd like to have my own family someday, Papa told me that marriage was off-limits. "The world is an evil, wicked place. There's no one for you in this life," Papa proclaimed. "You will have to wait for the kingdom of God to come, and then you can get married."

Waiting that long seemed like an eternity. A deep part of me resisted this comfortless future, which is why I imagined what it would be like to go back to Texas with one of those young guys and start a new life and a new family. Inside my tender heart, I couldn't help dreaming about being stolen away—just like Mama had been when she met my father out in the California desert at the hippie commune.

But that seemed impossible. I could never find a husband since no one would ever match up to Papa's high standards. Even if a godly young man somehow did measure up, he wouldn't want me. I was an unkempt teenager, rough around the edges, and unsure of myself. Papa said that any attempt to make myself attractive and beautiful was simply pride on my part.

That didn't stop me from daydreaming about being swept off my feet, saying my wedding vows, and bringing children into this world. But since there was no one for me in this fallen world, I was doomed to a life of servitude.

One afternoon, while Uncle Billy and his disciples were still with us, Papa and I were chopping wood together when he said out of the blue, "Elishaba, I would like you to come with me to Texas with Uncle Billy when he goes home. I would like this to be an opportunity for me to get to know you better. Would you like to come?"

*Get to know me better? What does he mean by that?*

Papa's question was unsettling. Certainly, a trip to Texas to see Aunt Patsy and my cousins would be enjoyable. Visiting a big city like Fort Worth would be exciting—even if it was marked for destruction. Furthermore, taking a break from all my hard work on the homestead and experiencing new things would be a rare change from my current lifestyle. Even though it meant going with Papa, it sounded fun. Also, I knew that there was only one answer I could give when he asked me to do something.

"Sure, I'd love to come," I said.

My father was pleased and added that he wanted my six-year-old sister, Jerusalem, to join us as well. "Call it a sister trip," he said.

The following day, I walked into the cabin and found him sitting on the poo bucket in the middle of our living space. I was about to turn around and give him his privacy when he called me over. "Mama is not so happy about our going," he said, nodding toward my mother, who was a few steps away cutting up potatoes. "But I know this is what God wants us to do. I want to take you with me because I will need your help and encouragement."

I was used to this line of argument—and when Papa said he knew the mind of the Lord, that always precluded any further discussion.

Meanwhile, Mama's eyes narrowed when I looked her way. What I saw was a dark look that sent chills into my heart. *Oh, no. Mama is not at all happy about this,* I thought.

Then she spoke out in a way I had never heard from her before. "No, you will not take Elishaba and Jerusalem with you. I do not give you permission."

I was stunned. I couldn't believe that Mama had stood up against Papa. *Why did she do that? Why wouldn't she want me to go with Papa?*

"Are you disobeying me?" Papa asked from the camper toilet, still not done with doing his business. "Because if you are, we have a big problem."

"I don't think it's appropriate for my daughters to go so far from home without me," she retorted. "If you don't see that, then I don't know—"

My father cut her off as he wiped himself with the communal T-shirt and zipped up. "This discussion is over. We're leaving tomorrow."

Uncle Billy and his two disciples rode in the front of his pickup truck while Papa, Jerusalem, and I shivered underneath a blanket in the back, sharing the open air on the long drive to Fort Worth.

As we got deeper into the great state of Texas, Papa made it clear that I was to keep my eyes focused on him the entire time. "You will not be the 'strange woman' of Proverbs around those two young men traveling with us," he said, referring to the woman who practiced and encouraged idolatrous promiscuity. "If you need something from either of them, then you go through me. Do you understand?"

"Yes, Papa," I dutifully answered. I didn't engage them in conversation during the entire drive, knowing that my father could hear anything I said.

When we arrived in Texas, we drove straight to Uncle Billy's nice suburban home. Instead of going inside and greeting our relatives, as most families would do, we set up a campsite in their expansive and landscaped front yard. I'm sure we looked like hillbillies to everyone in the neighborhood.

At one point, one of the young men asked me for some help with his tent. After assisting him for a brief moment, my heart sank. I felt utterly covered with shame because I had disobeyed Papa.

The time we spent in Texas became a long-lasting, grueling, and painful episode. I felt like some biblical maidservant as I labored away each day around a campfire in the middle of the front yard, preparing delicious meals for my father, uncle, and two male disciples that I was forbidden to notice. They requested fried chicken and fries each day, which I cooked in a grease-filled skillet over the campfire. I hadn't eaten so much greasy food in my life and could feel the added inches around my waistline.

Papa and Uncle Billy spent hours around the campfire fighting against each other and fighting alongside each other. When they weren't at odds, I was under Papa's constant condemnation as he drilled me about my thoughts and feelings toward the young men when they weren't around. My only relief came from spending quality time with Jerusalem. Despite the twelve-year age gap, we were forming a unique bond of companionship.

All this time, a quiet battle was raging between Uncle Billy and Aunt Patsy. Under no circumstances, my aunt forcefully declared, would she submit to her husband's demand to give up their suburban life in Texas to homestead with us in the New Mexico mountains under such primitive conditions.

Uncle Billy, egged on by my father, was equally committed to having her submit to his authority. The price of battle was obvious as Aunt Patsy's formerly immaculate house was slowly trashed, a little more each day, as we helped ourselves to their pantry, emptied the refrigerator, and raided the freezer with its half-gallons of delicious ice cream. We also used their bathrooms, which meant tramping more dirt into the house.

One time, Papa sent Jerusalem and me into the house to talk some sense into Aunt Patsy. She politely invited us to sit down and have a chat.

"What's on your mind?" she asked as she offered us a glass of homemade lemonade.

"We think it would be great if you would come live with us," I said. "You need to follow your husband and leave the world behind. That's God's will for you."

Aunt Patsy leaned over to refill our glasses. "I'm glad we can have this little talk," she said. "I remember when you came here years ago, and your father got saved. You were called Butterfly back then, so cute, so trusting. I didn't know your father would take this religious thing to this level. Lord knows he's always been a hellion. No one can tame him."

I must have looked confused because my aunt amplified what she meant. "What I want to say is that your father can be as stiff-necked as a mule if you disagree with him. If you don't believe exactly as he does, then he wants nothing to do with you. I'm afraid I'm not moving our family to New Mexico. That's not what I want to do with my life, nor do I want my children raised in that environment, so far from civilization."

"But you'll go to hell if you don't come with us!" I exclaimed. I needed Aunt Patsy to see the light, which is why I repeated a statement I heard my father say a zillion times to people who failed to see things his way.

"I beg to differ," Aunt Patsy replied smoothly. "I guess we'll have to agree to disagree."

I felt embarrassed as I thanked Aunt Patsy for listening. When we left her living room, I was upset that she didn't understand God like our family did.

It wasn't long afterward that Aunt Patsy and her four children, unable to bear the pressure longer, disappeared while we were out one morning. We later learned they went to stay with some of her relatives and wanted nothing to do with the disruptive holy prophets in her front yard.

Uncle Billy was disappointed by this turn of events, but Papa wasn't going to let this opportunity go by. One evening, while they gathered around the campfire, my father got into his brother's face.

"You need to stand up and be a man of God, and you can do that by throwing out every wicked and vain thing your family owns," Papa declared.

"What are you talking about?" Uncle Billy asked.

"I'm talking about taking your house captive and doing the righteous thing by getting rid of everything that is an idol or leading your family into an idolatrous lifestyle."

It took a while for my father to convince Uncle Billy that this was the right thing to do. With great reluctance, my uncle followed us as we walked through the front door and into their home, armed with cardboard boxes and plastic bags.

We walked through the house, trying to figure out what was evil and what was not. For sure, any toys, cuddly animals, and worldly books got trashed. My father's philosophy was that anything evil must be tossed out because that's what God would have us do. We even picked up their television—which Papa called "Goliath"—and carried it out to the driveway, where we smashed the screen with rocks and gave it a few good kicks. Then Papa attached a homemade sign to it that read, "Standing Against Evil."

We filled Uncle Billy's pickup with a massive load of their belongings and took everything to the dump, saying we were saving his family. What we were really doing was destroying Aunt Patsy's beautiful home. I felt awful about doing that, but I did my best to disregard those feelings, knowing that God would reward me for being so obedient.

Papa and Uncle Billy were *sure* they would convert anyone who crossed their paths into believing as they did. Many nights around the campfire, the two would rejoice over the rejections they received while street preaching in downtown Fort Worth during the day.

On one occasion, they decided to confront the preacher at the big Baptist church where Papa had been saved. They wanted Jerusalem and me to accompany them. In the past, I felt embarrassed when I witnessed my father confront people because things got ugly in a hurry. Name-calling ensued. As I walked behind my father and uncle into the church building, I hung my head, wondering what embarrassing episode would be next.

Papa and Uncle Billy soon found the pastor and began battering him with different Scriptures, telling him what an evil, wicked, and unfaithful shepherd he was. As the back-and-forth became more heated, someone called the police. Within minutes, a squad car arrived with two cops brandishing billy clubs. They recognized my father and uncle.

"Oh, it's you two again," the lead cop said. "Okay, Bobby and Billy, enough! It's time for you to leave."

Papa and Uncle Billy departed with precisely what they wanted—another occasion in which they were persecuted for righteousness's sake.

And then it was bound to happen: Papa and Uncle Billy turned on each other one night around the campfire. I forget what caused the argument, but they got into a huge fight.

The next day, we packed our belongings in the back of Uncle Billy's truck. My uncle must have wanted to get rid of us because he readily agreed to allow the two disciples to drive us back to the mountains of New Mexico.

After our return to the Sangre de Cristo mountains, Papa called me into the barn one day. He was standing next to a weight scale with a meat hook. We used that scale whenever Papa wanted to weigh a deer or lamb carcass.

"On the scale," he ordered.

"Why?" I asked, knowing that I was risking his wrath just for asking a simple question.

"You gained weight in Texas. I want to see how much."

*Yeah, from eating all that fried chicken and ice cream.* But I knew I could never say that.

I felt so embarrassed when he hooked the meat scale to the back of my skirt and hoisted me into the air to see how much I weighed. To be honest, I didn't know how much I weighed or *should* weigh. All I knew was that I had put on some pounds, which angered Papa and displeased him.

Completely humiliated, I went off to cry alone. I could not believe he had done this to me, and I felt bitter toward Papa.

We weren't one big happy family around the homestead either. My brothers were resentful toward Papa for choosing to take my sister and me instead of them to Texas. Mama was bitter toward me for reasons I didn't understand. Any relationship we had shared seemed to have evaporated while we were away.

Things were a mess, and they were about to get a lot messier.

# 22
# A TIME FOR THANKSGIVING

Besides Easter, Thanksgiving was the only holiday we celebrated—Papa deemed Christmas a pagan festival. In stark contrast to our usual slovenly meals, on Thanksgiving Day we would always pull out the old china, crystal, and pure silver sets passed down from our grandma, Virginia Hale. The only other day that came close to Thanksgiving's party atmosphere was our yearly celebration of my parents' conversion in January.

Thanksgiving spoke powerfully to the need for beauty in my young heart. When I unpacked those special dishes carefully wrapped in newspaper and pressed an old flatiron off the wood-fired stove onto the tablecloth handmade by Great-Grandma, I felt a reverence for the traditional day we thanked God for all our blessings. Feeling the cloth with my freshly washed hands seemed to connect me to my extended family somehow—it reminded me that I had a history.

After the ironing was done, we would add an extra cut-out board to the little table in the corner of our enlarged cabin so that our growing family could sit together.

Oh, the excitement I felt when I would dip wicks in and out of the melted wax to form such straight white candles in all of their beauty. Once lit, they would illuminate the table with a soft brightness that transformed our dark and dungeon-like cabin into something homier. How their light spoke to my young woman's heart, which beat in the breast of the uncouth tomboy that I appeared to be.

Thanksgiving was the one time of the year we enjoyed special foods such as turkey, dressing, mashed potatoes and gravy, baked egg boats, and fudge and fruit cake for dessert. We had so much fun on Thanksgiving Day that we would celebrate for at least a week, though I cannot recall how Mama made the food last so long.

Turkey was always the central part of the Thanksgiving feast, but instead of buying one as we usually did, this year Papa decided we would hunt for a turkey. His old regard for the rule of law had nearly evaporated, overtaken by his reasoning that since we were God's chosen people, we should be free to help ourselves from His table. This logic justified poaching all sorts of deer, elk, or anything else we could shoot and eat. Turkey hunting was part of the mix.

Turkeys were intelligent wild birds, so we had to take great pains to outsmart them. Our papa's pride was on the line during our hunt because the wild turkeys seemed to always be a step ahead of him. Papa could become so angry when he failed to bag one. He was quick to blame us children for making noise or scaring off the wild creature.

Anything that went wrong was always our fault, which is why during this particular Thanksgiving in the fall of 1994, I had an unusual sense of foreboding—of darkness closing in.

I tried to ignore the weird feeling, but it wouldn't go away.

After I turned nineteen in January 1995, life took a painful turn.

Brought under conviction in some way, my two oldest brothers, Joseph and Joshua, confessed to Papa that they bitterly resented him because of the harsh way he treated them. They expressed these thoughts even though they were aware they would be on the receiving end of Papa's cruel discipline that was sure to follow.

My father was predictably outraged that his sons would even consider going against him, so he quickly looked for a ready scapegoat. He blamed his sons' rebellious spirit on Mama for saying no to him when he had decided to take me to Texas. After coming to this conclusion, he sent my brothers and even Mama out of the house to work and do chores but told me to stay. From his chair, he looked straight at me.

"Elishaba, I've decided to make you my new queen. You are to take Mama's place. I want you to sit right beside me on the stool and serve me. She has said no to me like Queen Vashti in the Bible. She is no longer worthy."

I couldn't entirely take in what I had heard. Lightheaded with apprehension about his announcement, I listened to Papa further state, "You will sit here beside me as I judge my people. Now go call Joseph and Joshua inside."

I paused, fearing for my two brothers. Upon seeing my hesitation, he turned on me with instant anger. "Go quickly now, or I will give you what they have coming."

I followed orders and stood by while Papa individually interrogated them about their rebellious spirits, which I expected. But then my father started a new line of questioning.

"Do you think about women and seeing them naked?" he asked.

"Ah, no," one of my brothers mumbled.

"Do you think about what it would be like to be with a woman?" my father followed up.

My brothers cast their eyes down and didn't reply.

I realized that they were in the same ignorant state I was. Papa told us to look away whenever one of the rams mounted our ewes or when our dogs mated. Anytime I looked a little longer, I felt guilty. I wasn't sure why, but perhaps it was because I didn't know how things worked between a man and a woman.

Papa decided that now was a good time to explain a few things. "Marriage is from God only, so when I married Mama, I was ordained by God to go into her so she would bear me many children. When a man enters into a woman, he is having union with her."

Why was I being forced to listen to this? My young girl's heart felt stained and filled with shame. But then my father decided to interrogate them by asking a series of personal questions.

Once more, I had to listen to some very stark conversation about a topic I knew very little about. I was embarrassed and uneasy by everything I heard, but there was no place to go. I could feel my brothers' shame as well, and I felt sorry for them. I loved my brothers dearly, but I had a feeling that our days as naïve, innocent children doing chores around the farm would never be the same after hearing what Papa made them talk about.

Now it was time for Papa to pronounce judgment for speaking out against him. After stroking his beard a couple of times, he declared, "Since you have cast a spirit of rebellion over this family, I have a new punishment for you. Now go to the barn and get the bullwhip."

My brothers looked at each other like they had seen a ghost.

"You know the oak barrel we have in front of the cabin?" my father asked. "I want you to take your shirts off and lie across the barrel. Then I will administer what you deserve."

His choice of punishment sounded like a fate worse than death. I knew that being lashed with a bullwhip was an awful punishment. I grieved for my brothers because of the agonizing pain they would have to endure from lashes inflicting red-and-purple welts on their skin.

Papa then looked toward me, his face etched in granite. "I want you to stay in here with the children and keep the door closed," he ordered.

*Keep the door closed?* My fear rose several notches. This was worse than I thought. My younger brothers and two younger sisters, frightened as much as I was, gathered around my mother and me like chicks. I could feel my knees knocking together, and I shivered with fright.

*What is Papa going to do to Joseph and Joshua?*

I watched my two older brothers march out of the cabin, hanging their heads like condemned men. Papa trailed them by a couple of steps, his eyes narrowed. A scowl filled his facial features.

Once they were beyond the front door, I looked at Mama, also paralyzed at this turn of events. "Can't you stop this?" I asked her.

"You know what your father is capable of. If I interfere, he'll say that I'm in rebellion to him and whip me on that barrel."

My father's voice interrupted our conversation. "Mama? Come out here! I need your help."

My mother briefly squeezed my hand. "I better go," she said.

As I watched her leave the cabin, I hustled to the front door and put my ear up against the wood.

"Papa, please," I heard one of my brothers plead.

"Don't *Papa* me," he replied with a heart of stone. "You and your brother were the ones with the wicked heart. Bend over that barrel. Mama, put this rag into his mouth."

"No, I won't do it."

Mama was standing up to him!

The next thing I heard was my mother screaming at my father because he must have tried to give her a lash. They yelled at each other, and then there was silence.

"Papa, please don't," Joseph pleaded. I'd never heard him so desperate, but my father was unmoved.

*Thwack!*

With the snap of the bullwhip, I heard Joseph's instantaneous cries, which pierced my soul. He must have spit out the rag.

As lash after lash split the air, followed by yowls of pain—first Joseph and then Joshua—I wondered, *How can they survive such punishment? Oh, God, it has to be inhumane to whip someone like this!*

With tears streaking down my face, I hustled back into the main room, picking up my brother, Noah, who was still a toddler. I did my best to comfort the other children. When the whipping was over, Papa returned to the cabin and settled back in his chair, clearly bushed from the effort.

"Elishaba, my queen, rub my hands. They hurt."

I knew I had no choice but to comply. I set Noah on the ground and knelt beside the man I detested for his lack of mercy. As I took his hands into mine and started rubbing them, what he said next totally disgusted me.

"I couldn't do it without you. It has taken me this long to realize who in this family is faithful."

"Yes, Papa," I mumbled. I had learned over the years that when I made Papa happy, he wouldn't punish me as severely as when I displeased him or was "in rebellion."

I continued kneading the skin and muscles around his fingers, even though I was still in shock at how my father used a bullwhip to provide "correction."

This was the first time he used the whipping barrel, and I figured it wouldn't be the last.

Barred from the family, my dethroned mama and dishonored brothers slept in the shop. Papa made sure my brothers worked late into the night; there were more lashes to endure in the morning. My father made them straddle the oak barrel and whipped them *every day* for the next few weeks. With each lash against their backs, I felt the stings in my heart and guilt for the punishments they received.

I never sought such preferential treatment from my father, yet it was happening. I was also aware that I was being elevated to Mama's place. The unnaturalness of my new role felt completely strange. I did not know how to act appropriately, my siblings thoroughly resented me, and I felt trapped in a life not of my making. Papa seemed to swoon with pride over me, never ceasing to tell me how faithful a daughter I was to him.

"That's why marriage is not for you," he said. "I need you by my side. You are to be a virgin for Jesus. God's heart is for you to serve me in this family."

I would find out what he really meant by that in the coming days.

# PART IV

---

# CROSSING A LINE

# 23
# A BATH IN THE WILDERNESS

For days, Papa was beside himself while I tended to him as his "queen."

One time, when we were alone in the cabin, he called me over. "I'm thinking about leaving your mom and taking you and your sisters and living in the wilderness for the rest of our lives," he said.

My mind automatically zoomed to high alert. I was terrified because Papa was capable of doing something that crazy. "You can't leave Mama," I pleaded. "You can't do that."

My family was all I knew. I had spent all my life isolated in the woods, surviving in the mountains. My brothers and my sisters were my only friends.

"Oh, Papa, please don't give up on Mama. We all love you. We want to stay together."

His reply was cautious. "Well, if you do what I want and continue to fulfill my heart's needs, then I won't leave your mother," he said.

*What does he mean by fulfilling his heart's needs?* I was still processing what he'd said when he rocked back in his chair and looked to the heavens. In a brokenhearted yet whiny voice, he called out: "Why, oh why did I lose her? Oh, K.K.!"

"Oh, Papa." I kneeled in front of him and took his bony hands into mine. He was having a flashback, the tragedy of losing his first wife to a gunshot wound still fresh on his mind.

Papa looked at me with droopy eyes. "You're the best I got!" he cried out, which pulled my heart apart.

Even while my heart broke for him, it was clear that my father was playing with my emotions. But what I couldn't see was that he was also chipping away at my defenses.

In the spring of 1995, Uncle Billy came to live with us, which surprised me because he and Papa left on angry terms when we parted ways in Texas.

I didn't know why Uncle Billy left his family in Fort Worth. I knew better than to ask why. I heard him tell Papa that he had closed down his veterinary practice and prayed and fasted that Aunt Patsy would change her mind about moving to New Mexico with him, but she dug in her heels. Uncle Billy said he got tired of waiting and packed up and left. Now here he was, part of the homestead, at least for the moment.

One day in early summer, Papa announced that he was taking me and my two younger sisters, Jerusalem and Hosanna, on a camping trip accompanied by Uncle Billy. This was out of the ordinary, but once again, I didn't ask any questions.

Papa had me pack food, bedding, and clothes onto a five-ton, six-wheel, 6x6 Army truck that we had at the time, a vehicle similar to our '41 Chevy flatbed truck. The heavy-duty military surplus truck came with wooden sidewalls on the cargo bed, covered with an olive drab Army tarp, solid and sturdy. Papa used plywood sheets to construct a raised platform behind the cab, big enough for a mattress with storage room underneath.

I was planning to sit in the back with my sisters and two baby lambs until I heard Papa say, "Elishaba, I want you to ride up front beside me." That meant sitting between him and his brother.

I had no idea where he was planning to take us, but after we arrived on the valley floor, he followed a route that took us to the other side of the Sangre de Cristo range. My father loved finding old backroads into the national forest with our 6x6 Army truck, which could go anywhere.

Along the way, he spotted a rectangular water trough about ten feet long on the side of the road, obviously used to water cattle. The trough was made of thick steel and painted green on the outside.

"This will make a perfect bathtub," he said. "Let's get it."

I thought the watering trough belonged to someone else, but I wasn't going to voice that opinion. After loading the faded-green trough onto the back of the cargo bed, Papa kept driving deeper and deeper into the forest until we stopped near a meandering creek and set up camp.

Jerusalem and Hosanna, six and five years old, were happy to stretch their legs and explore their new surroundings while the lambs nibbled on the grass alongside the creek. Papa, Uncle Billy, and I lifted the trough off the back of the truck. What I saw as a watering trough, Papa viewed as an outdoor bathtub.

"I feel like a good soak in hot water," he said.

My heart shook at the thought of what this was going to mean. Why did I hate bathing with my father so much? I knew it was wrong to feel this way toward Papa, but sitting next to my father in our wet underwear made me uncomfortable. I wondered if there was a way that I could get out of bathing with my father.

I helped Papa and Uncle Billy carry the grungy cattle trough closer to the creek. Since it was made of heavy-duty steel, we could build a wood fire underneath it and heat the water. Papa ringed the tub with rocks, and I carried over armfuls of firewood that we brought with us. We also collected more firewood from the forest, which seemed to enthrall Uncle Billy—he loved living out the wilderness experience.

But we didn't bathe that night because we didn't have a wooden plank to sit on and the steel bottom would be too hot to the touch. Instead, Papa, my sisters, and I slept together on the cargo bed while Uncle Billy pitched a tent.

The following day, Papa drove us back to the homestead to pick up a wooden plank and a few other things. He left Uncle Billy at the campsite with the two lambs and a promise to be back in the late afternoon.

When we returned, we found Uncle Billy wearing a sad face.

"What happened?" I asked my uncle.

Uncle Billy nearly broke down in tears. "A pack of wild animals attacked the baby lambs. I couldn't save them."

My sisters and I were horrified. Jerusalem and Hosanna became extremely upset at losing their "babies" in such a violent manner. The pair of young lambs were like their baby dolls because my sisters bottle-fed them. I comforted them as best I could.

Papa was displeased. Actually, he was way beyond displeased; he was downright angry with his brother.

"How could you be so stupid?" he demanded. "We leave you here for a few hours only to learn that you lost two of our baby lambs? You are a bad shepherd. Truth be told, you're not a shepherd. You're a hireling who does not care about your sheep. This is a sign from God about who you really are. God will judge you for what you've done and for breaking my little girls' hearts."

Papa wasn't finished ripping his twin brother. For the next five minutes, he continued to tear into Uncle Billy, airing grievances, petty and significant, that went back fifty years, to when the pair were growing up in the home of I.B. and Virginia Hale.

Finally, Uncle Billy had enough. "Okay, I messed up. How about showing a little grace? Isn't that what Jesus preached? I'll make it up to you, do anything you ask. I'll even be your servant."

My father stroked his long beard. "Here's what you can do," he said. "Help us fill that trough with water and fetch us some more firewood."

After I cooked up some dinner, Papa had me put Jerusalem and Hosanna to bed in the back of the Army truck while Uncle Billy threw bucket after bucket of cold creek water into the cattle trough. A fire was lit, and the water started heating up. Papa set the wooden plank inside the watering trough so that we could sit in the tub without being scalded. By now, it was getting dark.

When the water was warm enough, my father stripped down to his underwear and hopped in. I watched alongside Uncle Billy.

"What are you waiting for?" Papa said to me.

Even though I'd been bathing with my father all my life and should have been used to it, I bristled with resentment. Maybe it was my age; I was nineteen and feeling like I wasn't a kid any longer. Perhaps it was because I thought it was immodest to soak next to him in a braless T-shirt and panties that became see-through when wet. But I didn't know what to do about the situation. I felt trapped but also realized that my father *wanted* me to feel trapped. I had to do what he said. To not carry out his wishes was to risk his wrath.

I was wearing a tattered skirt that went down to my ankles, an old beige T-shirt, a light jacket to ward off the evening chill, panties, and socks and boots. I knew the long skirt and jacket had to go. I had never worn a bra because I had never been given one by Mama, who didn't believe in wearing one.

Uncle Billy took his cue and started to leave. "When the water cools off, just holler, and I'll add more wood," he said, still in the servant mode. My sisters were in their sleeping bags in the back of the 6x6 truck.

I watched my uncle retreat to his tent. I removed my coat, took off my boots and socks, stepped out of my skirt, and immersed myself into the trough, where the water was soothingly hot. I had brought along my bathrobe, which I set on top of my clothes.

That was another ritual: Papa and I always donned bathrobes when we were finished bathing. In the past, I'd gather my robe around me and get out of my wet underwear so I could maintain some privacy, but Papa insisted on me holding his robe while he took off his underwear. I always kept the robe above my face so I wouldn't see his naked body, which I didn't want to see anyway.

Our conversation turned to our family because I could sense that's what he wanted to discuss.

"Your mom and your brothers have done the unforgivable sin," he said, clearly aggrieved. "They have gone against me when I speak from the Holy Spirit. I'm not going back to them."

"But Papa, you have to show mercy. Isn't the Bible full of references to God being merciful to His people? You need to be compassionate to Mama and my brothers."

He barely listened to me. Papa never cared to understand another point of view. He kept repeating how rebellious his family was, how they had to get in line behind him, and how they had to obey him because that's what God wanted them to do.

Meanwhile, I noticed that Papa was scooting closer and closer to me. He did this back at the homestead, especially in the evening when he felt assured that no one was watching, especially my mother.

His voice turned seductive.

"Elishaba, you are special to me. God has made you just for me. If it weren't for you, I don't know where I'd be today. You're my only hope. You have remained faithful, and you have such devotion. Your affection is the very thing that softens my heart. You always know exactly what I need, and what I need at this moment is you."

Papa said this a lot to me, but his words carried a new edge this time around.

"You were always my little girl," he continued. "So happy, so trusting. I remember when we put you up in the attic of The Barn. You were fine taking a nap, but when you started crawling, you'd wake up and crawl to the edge of the opening. I told you not to get too close, but you wouldn't listen, even when I'd hit you with a flyswatter to move you back. That's because you wanted to be with me. Finally, I came up with the idea of putting a fishnet across the opening in case you crawled to the edge, and I wasn't there.

"Well, there were times when you'd keep crawling. When that happened, you'd fall right into that net and scream your head off. I'd push you back into the attic, still crying, but that didn't stop you from coming to me."

I'd heard this story dozens of times, but I reacted like this was his first telling. "You've always looked out for me," I ventured. "You're my papa."

"That's why I've known you've been pursuing me for years," he said. "You've done it since you were a baby. You're finally waking up to God's call on your life. I'm sorry it has taken this long, but I know that God has predestined you for such a time as this."

Whenever I heard Papa use the word "predestined" coupled with the phrase "for such a time as this," he put the fear of God into me. He was big on predestination, the idea that God freely chooses certain people to be special objects of His grace and thus are "destined" to receive eternal salvation. He often preached that our family was predestined to be among God's elect.

Suddenly, my father scooted close enough to me to put his right arm around my shoulders. A shiver of shock ran up my spine. He'd never done this with me before.

"There's another memory I have," he continued. "I would pick up my crying girl and go into the shower with you. Ah, you would lay on my shoulder and cling to me. This might surprise you, but your little belly button was so adorable and always stuck out. I remember looking at your little hole where you go pee-pee as I held you under the hot, running water. You loved it when I put my hand on you and gently washed it. I'd hold you close, knowing God had created you for me."

A strange sensation churned deep in my gut. I had never heard my papa speak like this before. Where was he going with this?

Then my father reached down with his right hand and started gently stroking my legs, moving closer and closer to my private areas with each caress. His left hand went inside his underwear. I was very much aware that I was uncomfortable.

My heart spun around with so many confusing thoughts. *Is this right? How can it be okay for a young girl like me to be touched like this by her father? Does every girl have to do this?*

My thoughts were interrupted by Papa's words. "Elishaba, I have some things I need to tell you, and I have been waiting all these years to share them with you. God has revealed to me that now is the time. Some things I will not share just yet, but in time, He will make it clear when you hear them."

When Papa spoke like this, I knew something big was going to happen. As his hand caressed my skin, I was so scared that my whole body froze. The stiffness of my muscles caused him to question me.

"What's wrong? Are you already beginning to doubt me?"

I knew he was verbally cornering me, so I sought words to manipulate him into believing everything was okay.

"No, Papa. I don't doubt you at all. You're always right."

My father blew out a sigh of relief. "O, my daughter, my virgin. Your words affirm God's message to me. He has even given me dreams and visions about us."

Hearing that freaked me out. Where in creation was Papa going with this? I wanted to say something but knew I couldn't. Once again, I attempted to tell him what I thought he wanted to hear.

"You know, Papa, that I love you and always want to be faithful to you. I have decided that I will spend the rest of my life being a virgin, serving the Lord."

My words placated him, at least momentarily, but his face turned dark.

"I strongly feel that I need to put your mother away for rebelling against me. You are to be my Queen Esther and fill that place of making me happy."

*Making him happy?* What exactly did that mean?

I soon found out.

Papa's right hand had been on top of my left thigh, but now that hand moved in between my legs. His fingers kept progressing closer to my private area—

—when his fingers touched the outside of my panties and caressed my privates. His fingers were probing, exploring . . .

I froze. I knew I couldn't say anything about what he was doing. He was Papa. But he was crossing a line that he had never crossed before.

Instinctively, I pulled away, which displeased him.

"Go to the other end of the tub," he ordered.

I scooted away, feeling shame for irritating him.

"The water's getting cool," he said, as if nothing had happened the previous minute. Papa let out a shrill whistle, and I saw Uncle Billy come out of his tent.

"Need more wood?" my uncle called out.

"Yup. The water's cooled off."

Uncle Billy threw a couple more split logs into the fire underneath the cattle trough. I wanted my uncle to look at me . . . have him read the fear in my eyes . . . to come to my rescue. Instead, he dropped the pieces of wood onto the embers and walked back to his tent without so much as a glance at me.

Once again, I was alone with Papa, wondering what would happen next. He adopted a forlorn look.

"Come beside me, my Esther. This is where you belong," he said.

I hesitated, wondering how I could get out of this. An idea popped into my head.

"Here, let me rub your feet," I said.

Papa turned and extended his legs toward me, and I started massaging the balls of his feet.

"You don't know how all the loss in my life has been such a cross to bear," he said. "How my father said I would never amount to anything."

"Papa, everything that has happened is not your fault. You didn't know the Lord back then like you do now. But now He's given you this family to lead, and that's a great calling."

I was parroting what he always told us from his chair when he preached late into the night. He nodded because he agreed with himself.

This type of conversation went back and forth between us for a while as I continued to rub his feet. Papa would say something about how the wicked world was against him, making fun of him for living off the land high in the mountains, and I'd tell him he was merely following God's leading on his life and being obedient to the Lord. I felt like I needed to comfort him with words and bring him back so he could be happy again.

He sharply interrupted me one time. "Are you asking that I forget all the wickedness that your mother and brothers have put our family through? Do you want to take their side? I'm not even sure if there's any hope left for them. God must deal with them very severely if there's any hope for them to make it to heaven."

I searched for the right words. "Please, Papa. Doesn't God say to forgive?"

He looked off in the distance, no doubt thinking about how his family was such a disappointment to him. He needed more sympathy and reassurance.

"Papa, can't you see? You are saying that I am your Esther. Esther, in the Bible, pleaded the cause of her people and saved them from the wrath of the king. Maybe this is my destiny because you've said if I can make you happy, then you can forgive the family."

"That's my daughter," he said, his tone conciliatory. "I understand how much you love your family. Queen Esther was willing to sacrifice her life for her people, and I know you feel the same way, even if it means your life. But what I want you to understand is this: your calling in life is to be here for me in everything I do. It's your God-given gift to serve me emotionally, physically, medically, and in every way. No one else on earth can do this for me but you. If you do these things, I *will* forgive the family. You can be the savior of the family."

What was my father saying? Did he mean I had to let him do things like this so he wouldn't whip my brothers on the whipping barrel? That he wouldn't verbally abuse Mama like he always did? That he would accept the family and keep us together?

My heart was sick with pain because I had witnessed my brothers and my mother suffering great torment at the hands of my angry father for months. I cringed at how he ordered my brothers to lie on top of the whipping barrel and treated them like the slaves of Egypt because they had spoken against Papa, and that was a forbidden sin.

Images of bandaging up the wounds on the back of his bruised and bloody knuckles from beating my brothers came to mind.

My mind raced, searching for answers. While I would've love to be an Esther and save my people, I wondered if he would change and become a loving Papa if I showed complete devotion and gave him the type of attention usually reserved for a husband and wife.

"Is this why, Papa, you have taken me here tonight?"

He didn't hear my question. Instead, he was leaning forward, hands around his head.

"I have lost everyone in my life who I love." His voice sounded like a moan in the wilderness. "Oh, K.K. Oh, my sweet K.K. I will never get over losing you! No one has loved me like you did. Why, oh why, did you have to go?"

Hearing him say this scared me, but he wasn't finished lamenting.

"Oh, Alia, my daughter. I'm so sorry I left you. If only I could find you again. I am so alone. Only my mother, K.K., and Alia have loved me. I have lost my only true loves." At that, Papa gave out a terrible cry.

I felt lost and stuck and obligated. It was my job to comfort Papa, and I wondered how I could do this. I moved toward my weeping father to be closer to him.

At that, he reached out and firmly pulled me in. "Come, my daughter, my virgin. You are the one. You are the only one who truly loves me. You are my K.K., as if she has been resurrected. Yet you are even better. I have always known that God created you just for me. Oh, Elishaba, when you were a baby, I held you in my arms. I saw you there and knew you were for me. I have waited this long to know and to hear you want to be that for me."

I didn't know what to say as he wrapped his right arm around my shoulders and drew me close. Why couldn't my father feel the sound of my heart beating like a drum against his chest? Fear swept over me because I sensed where this was going.

He spoke softly. "God has given me visions and dreams, you know. He has told me that you will set His people free and that you will soften the heart of the king."

I knew the king he was referring to—him.

"Being my queen is your job, your duty, and your life. Everything that you're supposed to do in this life is happening right now. Come to me, my dove."

That's when his right hand settled between my thighs and inched closer and closer to my private area. This time, his fingers reached *under* the side of my panties and touched me where he never should.

The way Papa was caressing me and speaking seductively made me feel like my brains were being sucked out. I thought I was losing control of my mind and all my thought processes. I felt powerless to do anything to stop this.

Because I felt powerless, I suddenly got scared, really scared. Papa had never taken liberties like this before. Shame filled my heart. What we were doing didn't feel right between a father and a daughter.

As his fingers continued to caress my private area, I felt something, and I began to shiver with a peculiar feeling. Then he spoke, his voice sure.

"Elishaba, if it weren't for you, I wouldn't be here today. You alone are faithful to your Lord. Even Jesus turned to His disciples after many of them had walked away and asked if they, too, would walk away. Their reply to Jesus was, 'No, Lord, You have the word of eternal life.' Will you walk away too?"

The question froze me. I was terrified to answer the truth and too terrified to lie. I knew the answer my father wanted me to give, though. He had prepared me well.

I decided to wait him out, hoping this awkward moment would pass and I wouldn't have to answer. When I didn't say anything, my father's fingers resumed exploring, getting faster and faster.

The explosions in my body felt like an atomic bomb had detonated, so great that they could have blown off the top of a mountain. The release of this eruption brought a curious relief. Part of my body came alive with excitement, but I also felt like something happened that shouldn't be happening.

When the moment passed, my father removed his hand from my private area.

"It's okay, Elishaba. You don't have to answer. Go on—get out of the bathtub and go to bed. Don't get dressed. Just leave your robe on."

I was so traumatized that I didn't know what to say—just that I had to comply.

As I started to get out, Papa stopped me. "Go ahead and step out of your wet clothes here. I'll close my eyes."

My heart started pounding faster because deep down, I knew he was lying to me. Nonetheless, I whipped off my wet T-shirt and panties and gathered my bathrobe around me.

As soon as I was decent, Papa said, "Get my robe ready for me." I picked up the cloak, lay it over the trough's edge, and turned to leave.

"I'll be there soon," he said.

As I walked up the slight hill on that peaceful moonlit night, I pulled tightly on the ties around my robe, searching for some sort of security.

A sense of foreboding filled my heart because whatever happened next, there was nothing I could do about it.

# 24
# THE LONG EVENING FROM HELL

W hen I arrived at the Army truck, I found Jerusalem and Hosanna on the cargo bed floor, dozing in sleeping bags. Behind them was the raised platform with a foam mattress bed covered with dirty old blankets. An olive-green tarp covered the cargo bed.

I crawled past my sisters, grateful they were sound asleep. I plopped onto the foam mattress bed, gathered a blanket around me, and curled up in a fetal position. My body started shaking, really shaking. I had never been put in a situation like this before.

I kept saying to myself, *What is happening to me? What is happening?* I felt so distant from God and afraid to call out to Him. If God *had* spoken to Papa about this, that could mean only one thing: He was angry with me, and I had no favor with Him.

*Oh, Mama, Mama, if you were only here.*

My eyes were tightly shut. I took myself to another place, far, far away. I had to go there.

Within a minute, Papa arrived, wearing his robe. He lay down next to me without saying a word, opened my robe, and held my breast.

"Take comfort, my dove," he whispered. "Your heart for your family is answered. Your warmth toward me has won me over. I will love them again."

Papa scooted even closer to me. I didn't move. I kept my eyes shut tight and mentally stayed far away. I transported myself somewhere else.

He pulled my legs apart and put his fingers into my private hole. It wasn't long before the same confusing yet intense feelings returned to me—the feelings of an explosion. When it was over, he repeated what he had done, but I heard sickening, groaning sounds from him, acting like I didn't exist. Then the convulsions returned, and it felt like my body was betraying me because I had no control over what was happening. My body seemed to do whatever my father made it do.

This type of activity continued for an hour or two, but I lost track of time. One thing I knew: I felt a strong urge to go to the bathroom.

"I need to go," I said.

"Do you have to?" my father asked.

I knew why he asked. He didn't want me to leave the truck. Maybe he thought I'd wake up Uncle Billy.

"Go there," he said, pointing to a gap between the foam mattress and the wooden sidewalls. It wasn't a request; it was a demand.

What happened next was the sickest moment of the long evening from hell. Papa maneuvered me into the gap and then spread my legs. His fingers, once again, started their probing and caressing. I kept my eyes closed. I didn't want to be there.

"Start peeing!" he said, and I let it loose. I felt like an animal.

He got wet, of course, but he didn't seem to mind.

When I finished peeing all over him, he scooted me back onto the foam mattress, where he picked up where he had left off. Once again, I kept my eyes closed and took myself to that same place that was far, far away. He had his way with me for another hour or so, maybe longer, because Papa kept acting like I wanted what he was doing. I wished I could tell him that I hated what he was forcing me to do and how raw and sore I felt, but I couldn't. I was traumatized.

The entire time I felt a two-ton brick of shame on my chest. My girl's heart was devastated by a father I had desperately longed to please. Now he had proven himself to be utterly unworthy of my devotion.

Sometime during the long night, I passed out. When the first rays of sunshine crested over the horizon, I was still naked, lying next to my father. A pair of blankets covered us, but I felt as though I was submerged under a sheet of great darkness. The realization that I had lost something infinitely precious meant that my innocence was gone.

It was a new day. *Now what? Where do I go? Where can I run?*

I gathered a warm blanket around me and whispered a prayer. *Oh, God, will you even hear me now? I know You don't hear the prayers of sinners. I know I am a sinner.*

Papa was snoring in a deep sleep, and our robes were strewn about the bed. As quietly as I could, I sat up and searched for something I could put on without waking him up because I had to go to the bathroom again. As I looked around at my options, I turned toward my sleeping father. I wished more than ever that he was dead. Never before had I felt such hate in all my life.

Then he stirred. In a half-sleep, he reached out. "Elishaba, my dove. Where are you going? Come here, my beautiful. I want to hold you."

The request repulsed me. I had to come up with something. "I have to go potty and make you some coffee," I said, hoping that would appease him.

But the worst was yet to come.

I made my father coffee and cooked up a breakfast of tortillas and eggs over a campfire, something I'd done hundreds of times over the years.

But this time was different.

Of course, I had to act like nothing at all had happened around Uncle Billy and my sisters. I had to pretend that everything was okay between Papa and me, who seemed to play along. When breakfast was over and we were out of earshot of the others, he approached me.

"Elizabeth," said, using my more formal name to show that he meant business. "This is a secret between you and me. I better not learn that you have told anyone. Do I make myself clear?"

I gulped as tears formed and released down my cheeks. "Papa, please take us home. You promised that you would accept the family if I loved you."

My father stared at me with a sick look in his eyes, almost like he was in a whole different world. "Whatever you say, my dove. You are in control."

*Control?* That was a hoot. Nonetheless, I gave it a shot. "Okay, take us home."

"Then that's what we'll do," he replied. Papa turned on his heels, a cup of coffee in his hands.

*That was easy,* I thought, which made me nervous.

*Too easy.*

We packed up, loaded up the truck, and took off down the mountain. We had been driving on the bumpy dirt road for an hour or two when Papa jerked the steering wheel to the right and turned into a heavily wooded meadow.

"I'm hungry. Time for lunch," he announced.

The girls were happy to run around, and Uncle Billy took off on foot to explore. That left Papa and me alone.

As I was preparing sandwiches for lunch, Papa followed me like a puppy dog. I couldn't shake him. But then I saw his tongue was hanging out, almost as if he was panting. Very strange. Some weird stuff was happening in the middle of the day.

He was watching me prepare lunch when I turned around—and received the shock of my life. I screamed. Standing before me was my father with his zipper open, exposed and hard. I dropped the sandwich in my hands, too shocked to say anything.

"Tell me, what do you think?" he demanded coldly.

"I don't know what to say," I squeaked.

I did know what I had to do, though—run. I took off toward the woods with my father giving chase.

"I'm warning you," he yelled. "If you speak out against me, you will receive eternal damnation."

I paid him no heed and kept pumping my legs, bound by my tight skirt. I could easily outrun my father, but what slowed me down were these thoughts: *What if Papa is right? Will I be damned to hell if I say anything to anyone else?*

I wondered if I had anything to live for, but if there was a tiny thread of hope, I wasn't going to throw it away. I took refuge behind a tree, panting for breath. When my father approached, I gathered my courage.

"I really don't understand," I began, fighting for words. "I thought you believed this was wrong. You've told us never to look at each other when we're undressing. You agreed that I was to be a virgin for Jesus forever. You knew, Papa . . ."

"No," he interrupted, his voice reasonable. "I will not discipline you for loving me. In truth, I've been waiting all this time for you to finally love me for real."

"Oh, Papa," I cried, "I've always loved you! I'm your daughter." He couldn't have been talking about this type of love.

I felt betrayed. How could this new, horrible thing that he called *love* be okay when he condemned it in others?

Almost as if he could read my thoughts—something he seemed to be good at—my father said, "Elishaba, I want to warn you: listen to me very carefully because you must understand. God has given me dreams and signs that you are to be all these things for me. And if you speak against them, telling me that they are evil, you will be speaking against the Holy Spirit. As I have made clear to you before, speaking against the Holy Spirit is a sin that will never be forgiven and will send you straight to hell."

The weight of being eternally damned fell squarely on my shoulders again. It would have been easier for me if my father had held a gun to my head than use God against me. I crumpled and curled up on the ground, my tears mixed with the pine needles and sticks.

I felt him kneel beside me. "Listen, every young woman goes through this. It's part of accepting this part of your life. You've finally reached the age. When I held you in the shower as a baby, the way your little pee-pee hole stuck out filled me with all sorts of love for you. I knew then that God created you just for me. You'll get over it."

*Get over it? How could I ever feel this is right?* Oh, the sick feeling I felt in my heart. In my fetal position, I wept. I never felt so forsaken.

My father stood over the top of me and lifted my skirt, holding me down with his strong arms. I knew I could not resist. Then he reached inside my panties and probed and poked with several fingers and then with what felt like his whole hand. I experienced such excruciating pain that I was sure I was bleeding.[1]

When he finished, he turned me over onto my back and flashed his stiff private back and forth in my face.

"Hold it!" he commanded. Papa kept at it as he lowered himself onto me. His tongue was hanging out, and his eyes were bulging.

"I'm coming," he said. "I'm coming."

*What does he mean by that?* I was so naïve about all this and extremely baffled.

Before I knew what was happening, my mouth was full, and I was gagging as a warm, gross throw-up came out.

"Drink it, drink it!" he demanded.

Gasping and crying, I felt like a complete failure and a stupid creature, something less than a human, while my father's liquid ran down my dirty, tear-stained face.

---

1. I was so bruised and raw afterward that it was hard for me to even walk for several days. I thought it was wrong to look at myself, so I had no idea why I hurt so bad down there.

# 25
# AFTERMATH

In my nineteen years of life, I'd been belittled, ignored, and yelled at by my father. I'd felt the sting of his whippings countless times.

But his emotional abuse and the physical, searing pain he inflicted on me didn't compare to the consuming shame I felt after being used sexually by my father. It was as though I had died on the inside or had an incurable disease that would eventually take my life. The heart wounds were deep. Feelings of betrayal by my father and rejection by God filled my mind.

Unanswerable questions also flooded my subconscious:

*How did this happen?*

*Why did this happen?*

*Did I tempt him?*

*Should I have resisted more?*

Papa took me on a walk around the homestead after our arrival. Out of earshot of everyone else, he defended his actions. "Believe me, the Bible approves of our love for each other," he asserted. "I created you, and you were created for me."

I was starting to pick up a pattern: Papa was so concerned about being a perfect Christian that he had to turn his sin into something righteous. Hearing him excuse his behavior caused me to shake, which he noticed.

Papa stopped as we neared a creek. "Let me repeat what I said earlier: Do not tell anyone about our special secret. No one would ever understand the unique bond we have. Perhaps your mother will, but we'll cross that bridge when we come to it. For now, you have to be careful to keep this from your brothers. If you don't, you will cause them to sin, and their sin will send them to hell."

Hearing him mention my brothers reminded me of his promise to pardon Joseph and Joshua if I became his Queen Esther.

"Are you going to forgive my brothers?" I asked. "You promised me that you'd do that."

My father didn't respond, but I knew he heard me.

Then Papa surprised me when we returned to the homestead. Standing outside the cabin, he called everyone in from their chores. Mama warily stepped outside with baby Abraham gathered in her arms.

"I've decided to forgive Joseph and Joshua and move on," he announced to the family.

I fought back tears of relief, thankful beyond words that my guilt-ridden sacrifice had been accepted. But that feeling was short-lived when Papa glowered at Mama. "I need to talk to you," he muttered.

I imagined that she wanted to talk to him as well.

I had a bad feeling about this, which was confirmed within a minute of them walking into the cabin. That's when we all heard my parents get into a full-throated argument, punctuated by yelling and screaming at each other. Then they lowered their voices, no doubt to keep us from hearing their marital spat. The next thing I heard was a bloodcurdling scream from my mother.

"How could you do this?" she shrieked in a high-pitched voice.

I had a good idea what Papa said to her: *I'm getting to be an old man, and I need Elishaba to bring me delight while you have the babies.*

Nonetheless, my mother's spine-chilling scream terrified my siblings and me. We looked at each other with big eyes. We'd never heard Mama howl like this before. Even though I had a strong inkling of what was said between them, I couldn't say anything to my siblings.

Then my father's voice thundered from the cabin.

"You're a rebellious woman! Get thee behind me, Satan!"

"I knew you were going to do this!" my mother yelled back.

We heard more commotion and muffled sounds. My father must have started beating my mother because she kept yelling, "Stop it! Don't hit me!"

This went on for another few minutes until Papa exited the cabin, his hand firmly gripping Mama by her long hair. She was resisting, which only hurt her more. Baby Abraham, naturally upset, was fussing in her arms.

Papa steered Mama toward us. Her eyes were downcast in shame.

"Your mother is a rebellious woman who doesn't deserve your praise," he fervently declared. "She is not a Proverbs 31 woman worthy of your respect. You no longer have to listen to her, and you don't have to obey her either."

I felt so bad for Mama, being humiliated like this. But then Papa turned the knife.

"From now on, Elishaba will be baby Abraham's mother."

*What?*

My parents' eleventh child was three months old. Mama, in shock, clutched

Abraham closer to her breast. Birthing babies and mothering them was the only worth she found in the eyes of Papa. Her God-ordained role of mother to his children had been filled without complaint. Now even this was being denied her.

"What do you mean Elishaba is Abraham's mother?" she stormed back. "I'm his mother! I brought him into this world!"

I felt horrified for my mother, but Papa was unmoved. Without a word, he took the baby from her and walked over to me. He handed the infant boy to me, leaving my mother dejected and alone. She hung her head in defeat.

Turning to my siblings, Papa said, "Since Elishaba is the new mama in this family, you better not cross her."

I could feel their resentment and their underlying bitterness about my father's favoritism, but out of fear, they kept quiet.

My father wasn't done. "Tomorrow morning, we're leaving the mountain and going on a preaching trip. Everyone's going except Mama. She will stay behind and take care of the animals."

Once again, my world was upended. A sense of chaos filled my heart as I wondered where he was taking us, but I also knew my father wanted Queen Esther by his side during the trip.

Under my father's orders, I slept in his rocking chair that night and not in the big bed with him, Mama, and baby Abraham. Maybe Papa figured that having me in the same bed with him and Mama—which was our sleeping arrangement the last few years—would be like pouring salt into the wound.

After breakfast, I helped my brothers fill the '41 Chevy and a trailer with provisions. Along with Uncle Billy, we hit the road for the northern part of New Mexico. Our first stop was the small town of Tres Piedras, across the valley from the ski resort town of Taos. The community of Tres Piedras, with a year-round population of one thousand, was hosting the annual "Rainbow Gathering." For some reason, Papa wanted to see all his old hippie friends and perhaps evangelize a few.

"I'm calling this my 'Preaching Trip,'" he explained to my siblings.

For an entire week, we camped with ten thousand other free-spirited souls seeking to escape consumerism—and modesty, from what I could see. I spotted colorful folks living colorful alternative lifestyles in a colorful variety of tie-dyed dress and undress. All I could do was shake my head. Back at the homestead, Papa had been vigilant about us looking away whenever we changed clothes, used the portable toilet, or stepped into the communal hot tub in our underwear. But at the Rainbow Gathering, he didn't seem to be bothered by the nudity everywhere.

It turned out it was nudity for him, but not for us: he threatened me and my brothers and sisters with "correction" if we didn't look away whenever we came upon naked revelers, which was often. I watched him, though. His eyes soaked in everything. So did Uncle Billy's. I didn't see that much preaching going on.

From Tres Piedras, we drove around the state and camped where we saw fit. Throughout this time, Papa had me sleep in a tent with him and infant Abraham, who gave us cover, of course. His sexual demands intensified, and I got an education real quick on what he wanted from me. I felt like I was being sucked down a drain with no way to free myself.

My Uncle Billy was no dummy.

Sooner or later, he figured out what was happening between his twin brother and his niece.

I could tell that Uncle Billy wanted to say something to Papa, but my father kept me on an invisible chain. Papa made sure I was physically next to him at all times so my uncle couldn't ask him what the heck was going on.

One time, though, I was in the back of the truck taking care of baby Abraham. My siblings were off in the woods, having fun.

This was my uncle's chance. I saw him grab my father's elbow and steer him away from the truck. I couldn't make out their conversation, but it got heated in a hurry. Uncle Billy was challenging him, but I heard my father say something like, "I'm not speaking with you until you can show me where I'm wrong in Scripture."

After getting nowhere with my father, Uncle Billy stewed over their confrontation for days. Even my brothers gave him a hard time for having a "bad attitude." I pretended not to understand why.

As for me, I just kept saying to myself, *Why is it so hard to find this wrong in the Bible?*

Then a darker thought formed in my mind: *If Uncle Billy can't prove it wrong, then I'm doomed.*

After several weeks, we drove back toward our homestead, but instead of taking the direct route, Papa took us to the foot of the Pecos Wilderness not too far from Mora County. We camped out a couple of days, and then Uncle Billy and my brothers drove the old '41 Chevy truck back to the homestead, taking the long route around the mountains. The boys returned the following day on horseback with fresh food and supplies. They also brought along Gypsy, Papa's horse.

Then we started trekking into the wilderness. After a long, hard day of hiking higher and higher up a mountain trail, carrying Abraham on my back and helping my sisters with the milk goats, we finally made camp under the jagged mountain peaks that reached nearly thirteen thousand feet in elevation. This was where the bighorn sheep lived among the steep rocks.

As usual, I made dinner for everyone, but it was becoming more and more apparent that I had become Papa's wife with each passing minute.

That evening, when Papa and I were in the tent with Abraham, I gathered my courage to say something.

"This doesn't feel right, Papa. I'm your daughter."

My father glared at me. He didn't like being challenged. "Are you being rebellious to me like your mother? Are you resisting the authority given to me by Almighty God?" he thundered.

"No, Papa. I don't want to go against you at all! But it can't be right what we're doing. Can't we go home to Mama and you be with her?"

Furious, my father balled his fists and brutally beat me while I covered up as best I could. I wanted to scream for help, but I didn't want to scare my siblings. I had been so traumatized over the years by my mother's cries for help.

Early the next morning, battered and bruised, I knelt painfully next to a small stream and cried out to God.

"I am a wicked person," I admitted out loud. "Lord, I know I don't deserve to go to heaven, but please forgive me. It feels so wrong to do this with Papa, but I need Your help to know why. If I'm wrong for saying it's wrong, please God, I am ready to be nothing but a servant. But just stop Papa."

My father's shadow fell across me.

Uh-oh. Now I was in big trouble.

This time, instead of beating me again, he turned away, muttering to himself. I could tell he was angry and close to exploding with rage.

When I returned to the campsite, it was apparent that my father had done a 180-degree turn in how he felt about me. A few days earlier, he'd told me that I was the reincarnation of his beloved K.K. Now I was the devil to him.

"I should cast you out from this family for what I heard today," he said icily.

The thought horrified me. I didn't know how to live or survive in a world without my family. Besides, I was damaged goods. I was no longer a "virgin for Jesus." Who would want to marry me after what I had done with my father?

As I pondered my grim future, I realized that I had only one hope: to become a servant in the family I loved.

"Please let me serve you," I begged. "I promise to faithfully serve you for the rest of my life without any complaining. Don't cast me out."

My father looked right through me with a wave of cold, silent anger that chilled me to my bones. He acted like he did not hear a word I had said to him.

Which made me all the more nervous.

After our first night of camping at high altitude, Papa mounted Gypsy and rode off toward our next campsite. Our family knew these mountains well.

After we packed up and got on the trail, I was well aware that Papa could be lurking behind a tree, watching me as he had done so often when we were growing up. As my older brothers maneuvered their horses along the trail, I walked and carried baby Abraham on my back. Papa's black fury seemed to hang around like a physical presence.

I feared for my life since Papa always carried a holstered pistol on his right hip. As I trekked along the path, fright like none other I'd ever encountered gripped me. I continually cried out to God, asking Him to forgive me for whatever it was that I had done wrong.

After walking a long time in the wilderness alongside my horse-mounted brothers, we arrived at the new campsite. As the sun was setting, my brooding father finally appeared. Papa maintained his silent anger toward me while we made camp among the tall Douglas firs and Ponderosa pines in the Pecos Wilderness. I had no idea what he had in mind, but then he ordered my brothers to go home and bring Mama to the camp in the morning. I felt a small hope that Papa's rejection of me would provide an opening for Mama to get back in his good graces.

By this time, I hadn't seen Mama for more than two months. When she arrived, I was surprised by the change in her attitude. She was cheerful, even content. Perhaps she had enjoyed the alone time at home. She also seemed more submissive to Papa—like she knew her place in the pecking order, which was behind me. It was clear she accepted her new role.

At the same time, there was an undercurrent of hostility between us. I could tell Mama didn't like how I had taken her place in the marriage bed. I didn't blame her for feeling that way because *I* didn't like what was going on.

Nothing changed in our sleeping arrangements. I had been sleeping on the same foam mattress bed with my parents for several years, always to my father's left side while my mother slept on his right side. Now that I was Abraham's "mother," he slept next to me.

Now that we were back together inside the tent, Papa made me rub his feet while we waited for my exhausted mother to fall asleep, which happened pretty quickly. Then he had his way with me like he did every night since the hot tub incident. I felt like a sex slave, but if I didn't do what he wanted, he would hit me in the morning when no one was around.

The threat of physical pain trumped the emotional suffering I felt each time

I sexually served him. But I soon realized that Papa was playing a shrewd mind game, trying to make things look "normal" between us so that Mama would favorably accept her husband's incestuous relationship with her daughter. I didn't know how Papa persuaded Mama to go along, but I knew how evil his threats could be.

About this time, Papa told Mama and me that he had a new revelation from the Bible. He opened his Bible to 1 Peter, found the passage he wanted, and began reading: "For after this manner in the old time the holy women also, who trusted in God, adorned themselves, being in subjection unto their own husbands: Even as Sara obeyed Abraham, calling him lord" (1 Peter 3:5b-6a, KJV).

"See?" he said. "I'm going to follow the faith of Abraham, and two of you will be like Sarah and call me lord from now on."

*Really?* But I knew better than to ask why, and it seemed natural to address my father as "lord" because he had always behaved as my lord and master anyway.

To cover up our evil relationship, though, Papa would take great pains to take me off alone with him. Or he would act like an invalid and spend half the day in the tent, telling everyone—including Mama—to stay out while I was with him, saying he needed me as his full-time nurse. The reality was that I was there to serve his hungry sexual needs.

What he was doing reminded me of the story from the second book of Samuel in the Old Testament where Amnon, a son of King David, was obsessed with his half-sister, a beautiful young woman named Tamar.

Amnon devised a ruse in which he feigned illness and asked Tamar to prepare him food and take care of him. Once she was inside his chamber, though, he pressed her to have sex with him. When she vehemently refused, Amnon raped her against her will.

As I acquiesced to my father's insatiable demands for sex inside the tent, I felt very much like Tamar must have felt.

Raped and violated.

But I had nowhere to go.

# 26
# LOOKING FOR A SIGN

Every day my ungodly relationship with Papa seemed to deepen the hardness of my heart until I almost despaired of living. I simply existed in survival mode. My self-protection consisted of trying somehow to convince Papa that his understanding of the Bible was flawed.

Strangely, he seemed willing to listen. "Okay," he said. "I'll pray for a sign from God."

We had this conversation while we were still in the wilderness. Papa was in no hurry to go back to the homestead. He fervently believed that we were in the end times when Jesus would return for His "elect," so we were staying put.

We heard from my brothers that a couple of our donkeys had escaped. Papa told us to search until we found them, which seemed impossible in such a vast wilderness.

Just before I departed that morning, when we were alone, Papa bowed his head and prayed out loud: "Lord, please let Elishaba find an elk's antler with seven points to prove that we are holy and right before You."

My chore was to search for the lost donkeys, but now I'd been handed a second task. "While you're out there, I want you to keep an eye out for those antlers. I think God will lead you right to them," he said.

As I wandered through the woods, a weird thought came to mind: *Am I looking for something that could prove to be my undoing?*

At the same time, I knew I *had* to look for those antlers because, sure as a sunrise, my father would question me about my search. The idea of coming upon a seven-point antler revolted me as I walked, eyes scanning the ground, hoping against hope that I would find nothing.

At the same time, I was afraid of Papa's infallibility. For all I knew, he could have placed several seven-point antlers in areas he knew that I'd look for the lost donkeys. I didn't *want* to search for the antlers, but my conscience wouldn't let me say I had looked when I hadn't. Sure enough, when I returned to the cabin empty-handed, Papa asked for a detailed explanation of where I'd been.

After hearing my description, he gave me an order: "Go back out and look some more."

But it was suppertime. I was hungry. Plus, I needed to make dinner for everyone.

I knew I wasn't allowed to be hungry or even mention that I was famished. But cooking over a wilderness fire took extra time, and I needed to get started before dark.

"My lord, what about dinner for every—?"

Papa cut me off. "God told me that He would give us a sign. It's up to you to find it."

Pressure. I hated it. I could not relax for a moment. I knew my father and feared his machinations. But I never did find those antlers before it got dark.

A few days later, Joseph came riding in on his horse, holding a single elk antler shed in the wild. He had picked it up randomly because finding antlers was always thrilling—like stumbling across buried treasure. We all rushed to have a look.

"It's a six-pointer," Joseph said, prompting a sigh of relief from me. After all, six was not seven.

I watched Papa inspect the antler closely. I immediately knew what was happening: he was figuring out a way to prove that he was right. It was written all over his face.

Animals had chewed on the antler, which left a few jagged points. Papa pointed to one of the small spiked places with a sly smile. "There's your sign— the seventh point," he said.

I knew there were six points; any novice hunter could see that, but my father was insistent: God had given him the fleece he asked for in the form of a seven-point antler.

I was reminded that I could not argue with Papa. As a smooth manipulator of the truth, he could not be contradicted.

I noticed something else about my father: he barely read his Bible, preferring to spend most of his time with me, doing as he pleased.

Walled off in his self-absorbed world, he ignored Mama and my siblings, shutting them out of his heart, mind, and life. Papa even began drinking wine, which he'd never done before.

"The apostle Paul said it's good to drink wine," he said, opening to 1 Timothy

5 to prove his point. "See here? It says, 'Drink no longer water, but use a little wine for thy stomach's sake and thine often infirmities.'"

As with everything with my father, a "little wine" was open to his interpretation.[1] He forced me to drink with him so I would be more compliant with his sexual demands. I got used to the taste of wine, but I hated the feeling of being slightly intoxicated and realized that alcohol impaired my ability to resist his predatory advances. After a month or two, I made a conscious decision not to drink anymore with my father, even though he pressured me a great deal. I had to continue serving him his alcohol from bottles of wine we hauled up from the valley floor.

While he got a buzz going, Papa liked to watch a tame dove that flew freely inside our cabin. Papa named the bird Spirit and acted as though God's Holy Spirit was manifested in our pet dove.

One day, one of our cats killed Spirit, filling Papa with vehement anger, probably because he called me his "dove" and harbored a superstitious feeling that I was part of that bird.

"Elishaba, this is a curse because of your resistance toward me! God's wrath has come upon you. You must suffer even greater punishment for fighting me!"

Then he ordered me to bring all our cats to him.

I was frightened. "What are you going to do, my lord?" I asked.

"Shoot them. They have become the spirit of the devil."

I knew I couldn't protest unless I wanted the back of his hand. I had no choice but to round up the half-dozen cats who lived with us and put them in a cage.

Papa glared at Mama and the rest of us. "Go up behind the junkyard and dig a deep hole," he ordered.

We all stood there with stark confusion on our faces.

"Well, don't just stand there. Go!" Papa screamed. "And take those evil, possessed cats with you. I'll be right behind you."

A terrifying feeling of death filled my soul and threatened to devour me at any moment. The piercing look from Mama's eyes haunted me as well.

While my brothers and I dug a hole, I couldn't help from thinking, *This is all my fault. Mama must hate me.*

Several cats meowed to let them out of the cage, which nearly broke my heart. I knew they were doomed.

Sure enough, my father was on a mission when he arrived.

"Hand me a cat," he commanded. I obeyed because I had to. I pulled one feline out of the cage and handed it over.

Without missing a beat, Papa placed the tip of his pistol against the cat's forehead.

---

1. My father developed a serious addiction to wine and alcohol that would plague him for many years.

*Blam!*

Then he casually tossed the dead cat into the hole.

One after another, Papa made us watch him shoot every one of our precious kittens and throw their furry carcasses into our dump pit, pronouncing: "They are damned because they have come against the Holy Spirit, just like the devil."

The killing spree didn't end there. A problem that had been festering for years on the homestead came to a head. It seemed that our constant trespassing to graze our sheep and poach a variety of elk and deer irritated our surrounding neighbors to the point where they filed formal complaints with the county sheriff. Papa vilified them as "unsaved enemies of the Gospel."

One time, we were in Las Vegas, New Mexico, for an animal auction when Papa was recognized. Two sheriff's deputies arrested him and led him off in handcuffs, leaving my younger siblings vulnerable to Child Protective Services since Papa had to spend the night in jail.

Somehow everything got sorted out, but Papa viewed his arrest as a form of harassment. When fines came in the mail from the New Mexico Department of Game and Fish, my father saw a darker motive. "We are being persecuted for righteousness's sake," he railed. "They can rot in hell before I pay this blood money."

Since we didn't have enough pasture, the pressure kept mounting until Papa decided that we had to butcher all of our sheep and put an end to being shepherds on the mountain. Hearing this news distressed me because tending our flock was the *only* time I could be away from Papa. I had bottle-fed many of these sheep when they were mere lambs. They followed me everywhere on the homestead, and I knew their names. When I called them, they would follow me.

The day came when we had to start killing them. As I looked at each lamb with tear-filled eyes, I told them that I loved them for the last time. Then I led them to the slaughter tree, where I wept uncontrollably as Papa ordered my brothers and me to cut their throats and hang them up to bleed out.

With each slash of the knife, something inside of me died.

# 27
# BECOMING NOMADS

In 1996, a year after I became Papa's sex slave, it was clear that our life in New Mexico was falling apart. With no suitable grazing land, no lambs, and no reliable source of income, we were having problems getting enough to eat. There were only so many barn patties and homemade bean enchiladas we could choke down.

We somehow survived the winter, often only eating a bowl of mush once a day. In March 1997, Papa gathered the family around him and said, "God told me that it's time to leave Rainbow Cross."

Looks of panic came across our faces. Life on the homestead was all we'd known. If not here, then where? Mama looked like she was ready to faint. She was just a couple of weeks away from delivering her twelfth child.

"Where are we going, Papa?" asked Jerusalem.

"Where God leads us," he replied.

I didn't like the way that sounded.

Two days later, we said goodbye to the Sangre de Cristo mountains and hit the road. We packed our worldly belongings—which weren't much—aboard the '41 Chevy truck, a '51 Chevy flatbed, and the 6x6 Army truck, which Papa had named "Armageddon." Then we loaded up our seven horses onto a trailer, hitched it to the '41 Chevy, and drove nearly four hundred miles southwest to Silver City, New Mexico. Papa said we could make camp in a nearby national forest, where we would have grazing rights to feed our horses, saving us a ton of money on feed.

We set up a good-sized teepee in a remote campground, and that's where Mama gave birth to another girl on March 15, 1997. Papa always fulfilled the midwife role, but he had passed out from drinking too much. I took care of Mama and finally got Papa awake when the baby arrived. He named her Psalms.

One thing we did to pass the time was play music. Over the years, we had acquired instruments from thrift stores and pawnshops and had begun to pluck away on banjos, fiddles, guitars, and mandolins. Foot-stomping bluegrass music was what we learned. The instruments gave us joy amid an often-oppressive atmosphere. Papa would play the guitar while we all followed along, trying to play by ear to whatever song he would twang away at while singing with a nasal bluegrass tone.

The music stopped when our horses escaped our makeshift corral a couple of months after Psalms' birth. Papa exploded and ordered my younger brothers to find them. Then he turned to me. "Help me hitch up the horse trailer," he demanded.

I knew that meant standing behind the '41 Chevy truck while he backed up. At just the right moment, I'd lift the horse trailer hitch and drop it on top of the ball receiver on his heavy-duty truck.

I'd done this chore many times, but this time proved anything but routine. Papa backed up like a banshee, moving way too fast. I screamed, "Stop!" but he never heard me.

The next thing I knew, my left shoulder was pinned between the back of the truck and the horse trailer—and Papa was still gunning the engine! I screamed as I felt life being sucked right out of me. I heard a pop and felt excruciating pain in my shoulder. I thought it was all over—

—when the truck mercifully stopped.

Papa hopped out and discovered what I already knew: I was pinned between the truck and the trailer.

"What's wrong with you!" he yelled. Whatever happened was undoubtedly my fault.

I was too weak to reply.

Papa hustled to the cab and pulled forward a tad to free me. When he returned, his face darkened with rage. "You dummy!" he ranted. "Don't you know better than that? You should have stopped me."

"But you didn't hear—"

He still wasn't listening to me.

"Where's the gun?" he demanded.

Holding my busted shoulder, I could barely stand up. "Ah . . . I'm not sure."

That was a lie. I had packed his rifle underneath a bunch of stuff in the back of the truck.

Papa stepped forward, and clearly the idea of asking if I was okay was the furthest thing from his mind. "Did you hear me? Get the gun! I'm going to find those horses and shoot every one of them."

He was capable of performing this murderous act. I knew I had to pretend to search for his rifle.

With my left arm hanging listlessly, it took all my remaining strength to pull myself onto the back of the '41 Chevy with my right arm. I acted like I was doing a thorough search, and I did find our medical bag.

"What's taking so long?" my father boomed.

"I'm trying, Papa! I can't find it!" Meanwhile, my right hand was pushing the rifle further into the pile of stuff. I rustled through the medicine bag and found just what I needed: a syringe and a dosage of cortisone. I gave myself a shot, but no relief was forthcoming.[1]

Then I entertained a thought: I could take that gun and shoot myself. No more sexual torture every night. My broken shoulder would be pain-free. On the negative side, I'd go straight to hell for taking my life, which I didn't want to do. Hell was a scary, scorching-hot place filled with fire and smoke, as Papa had preached many times.

The thought of killing myself passed as my brothers arrived on the scene.

"We didn't find the horses," Joseph told Papa.

"Then what are you doing here? Don't come back until you find them."

Chastened, Joseph and David gathered up some camping gear. They knew if they didn't find our horses before the sun set over the Mogollon Mountains, they were sleeping under the stars.

With my brothers gone, I sensed our time in Silver City was rapidly coming to a close. US forest rangers had repeatedly dropped by our campsite to warn us that our horses were overstaying their welcome on federal grazing land.

"You need to be moving along," said one ranger.

Papa, who mistrusted authority figures, didn't like hearing that message.

While camping in Silver City, we had met a sweet little family in town. Steve and Abagail had a ten-year-old daughter named Ruth. Abagail, who was pregnant, seemed enthralled with Papa and our large family. It didn't take Papa long to try to convert her along with Steve and Ruth.

My father always liked putting a wedge between couples, and Steve and Abagail were no different. Somehow, he convinced Abagail to leave her husband—sound familiar?—and bring her daughter along and come live with us, even though she was expecting. I'm sure he said something about how they would be doomed to suffer horribly in hell forever unless they joined us.

On the day Papa pinned me between the truck and the trailer, Abagail showed up with Ruth in tow, saying she wanted to be part of our family. Hearing her say that made my father happy—a rare situation.

---

1. He probably broke my collarbone, which healed up wrong and left me with a disfigured left shoulder.

Papa knew that Steve wouldn't appreciate coming home to an empty house and would immediately call the cops to report a missing wife and child. My father, who had an uncanny sense about staying a step ahead of the authorities, figured a black-and-white New Mexico State Police cruiser would be dispatched to our campground to sort things out, which meant we didn't have much time.

I saw Papa pull Abagail and Mama aside. They listened and nodded in agreement. The next thing I knew, Mama packed a couple of duffel bags and rounded up the nine youngest children. I helped everyone get into Abagail's big Suburban, along with Ruth, and kissed my youngest brothers and sisters on the forehead. Then I waved goodbye as they left in a trail of dust.

"Where are they going, my lord?" I asked Papa as they sped off.

"There's an old crippled woman who lives out in the desert. Mama knows her too. I told your mother to take everyone there until things calm down."

"So, what are we going to do?" I asked.

"We're going to pack up and leave in the morning as soon as the boys find the horses. Then we'll go back to Rainbow Cross, get some supplies, and then rendezvous with Mama.[2] We'll take it from there."

I didn't think we'd be leaving before the crack of noon. Papa had never been an early riser, especially after having his way with me half the night.

With Mama gone, I figured things between us would start earlier, and they did.

The morning after I broke a bone in my shoulder—at least that's what it felt like to me—I was fast asleep in the back of the '41 Chevy with Papa[3] at daybreak. That's when I was startled to hear a police officer on a bullhorn.

"Robert Allen Hale, this is the New Mexico State Police. Come out with your hands in the air, along with anyone else with you."

Papa was naked and cuddling me with one hand. Startled by the intrusion, we both knew we had to get some clothes on. When I tried to put on my skirt, my left shoulder pulsated in pain.

"Ouch!" I cried out. There had been several "ouches" during the night, but that didn't stop my father from taking pleasure.

I managed to get decent quickly, as did Papa. When I poked my head out the side of the truck, I faced the shock of my life—we were encircled by a dozen patrol cars and probably twenty cops, some with guns drawn.

"Where is she?" the state trooper with the bullhorn demanded.

---

2. "Rendezvous" was a word that Papa Pilgrim used a lot.
3. After we left the homestead, Papa wanted to make sure that he had me for himself, so we slept many evenings in the back of the '41 Chevy.

"Who?" Papa asked.

"You know who. Abagail. And her daughter Ruth. Where are they?"

Papa thrust his chin out in defiance. "They're not here. See for yourself."

The state troopers had a look around, searching everywhere, including the teepee lodge, but they found nothing. The lead trooper returned to question Papa. "You don't know where they went?" he asked.

"I'd tell you if I knew," my father replied. He maintained a poker face, which I recognized as a sign that he was lying.

The lead cop reached into his breast pocket and pulled out a folded sheet of paper. "The U.S. Forest Service has officially asked me to serve you papers. Your grazing rights have expired. You must pack up and go immediately."

At that moment, I grimaced when a shot of pain walloped my tender shoulder.

"You okay, ma'am?" The officer showed genuine concern.

"My shoulder's hurting," I allowed. "I got pinned between the trailer and the truck yesterday afternoon."

"Do we need to take you to the ER? We can call an ambulance if you want."

Papa quickly stepped between us. "No, she'll be just fine. It's not much."

The cop looked puzzled. "Ma'am, how old are you?"

"Twenty-one." My voice was shaky.

"Listen, you are old enough to make your own decisions. We can call the paramedics to take a look at it. I'd be more than happy to do that for you."

I wanted so badly to say yes. This was a golden opportunity to get away, but it felt like magnets held my mind, heart, and soul to Papa.

"No, I'm okay."

"Just know you can change your mind at any time, ma'am."

Then, turning to my father, the lead cop said, "Our orders are to see you off and escort you out of town."

"We can't go until my sons come back with our horses. They're out there lookin' for them right now," my father said.

"That's fine," the cop said. "We're not going anywhere."

I had started a campfire to make some coffee when I looked toward the far end of a large field: Joseph and David appeared, riding a pair of horses with several other mounts in tow. They'd found them!

Their gait slowed as they came upon the ring of police cars surrounding our campsite. The lead cop ordered them to dismount for questioning. Then I was hit with a shock: a half-dozen gun-toting troopers rushed my two brothers, threw them to the ground facedown, and demanded that they tell them where this woman and child were.

"We don't know!" Joseph pleaded. "We really don't know."

They were telling the truth. Papa had purposely not told them where Mama and Abagail had gone just in case something like this happened. After ten minutes of asking the same question over and over—"Tell us where they went!"—the state cops gave up and said my brothers could go. When Joseph and David stood up, they looked like they had seen a ghost. The experience shook them up.

We told them we had to pack up and go. Within an hour, we loaded the horses onto the trailer, took down the teepee, and packed the cooking pots, pans, and dishes onto the three trucks.

I drove the 6x6 truck with the trailer and the horses and followed Papa in the '41 Chevy. Joseph, behind the wheel of the '51 Chevy flatbed, trailed us.

With a police escort following us, we caravanned north. I weaved all over the road since my left arm was nearly useless, making steering nearly impossible. When I did turn the wheel, I bit my lip from the pain.

After a half-hour of trailing us, either the police got tired of driving forty miles per hour behind our slow-moving trucks, or they decided they'd done their job, so they peeled away.

Papa was in no hurry to go anywhere. For the next few days, we drove along the back roads and camped out at night. It was clear, though, that the state police were keeping tabs on us. On several occasions, we were pulled over and subjected to searches and questioning. After each interrogation, we were let go—but each encounter with law enforcement unnerved me. I couldn't believe we had to live like this, but Papa seemed unfazed—like he was used to it.[4]

By the time we got to Ledoux, Papa felt we could make a run for it at night, and that's what we did, driving the three heavy trucks up the rutted dirt road to the homestead.

Once back at Rainbow Cross, Papa decided to sell all the horses except for Shema, Gypsy, and a filly and purchase a minibus and small camper trailer. He figured that the authorities wouldn't be on the lookout for these new vehicles, but to be sure, he had us dress in disguises—mainly wigs we purchased at a thrift store.

When he felt the coast was clear, we left the homestead and drove a circuitous route to the crippled lady's house, where Mama, Abagail, and the children were hiding.

They were overjoyed to see us, which felt good. And then we hit the road, living like vagabonds. We started in Colorado and meandered toward Montana. Each time we would camp for the night, we would back the small filly out of the camper trailer,[5] sweep up the horse manure, cook dinner, and make beds. Then a bunch of kids would sleep in the trailer.

---

4. We had no idea there was a statewide manhunt in progress for Abagail and Ruth.
5. Papa felt he had no choice but to leave Shema and Gypsy back at the homestead to fend for themselves. Neither would survive the abandonment.

Papa ordered my older brothers and me to scrounge for food in dumpsters behind supermarkets and grocery stores to feed us. My heart was filled with shame each time I reached into a dumpster or trash can and pulled out a loaf of stale bread, half-rotted fruit and vegetables, and other perishables, but we were too hungry not to do it.

To raise cash to pay for gas and incidentals, Papa taught us to beg. He had us older children put on a sad face and carry one of my younger siblings, always unwashed and wearing dirty clothes. We'd position ourselves on street corners, stretch out our free hands, and say, "Can you spare any change? We need gas money to get to the next town." Another line I used went like this: "I have thirteen brothers and sisters, and we haven't had anything to eat since yesterday."

I felt so humiliated, begging with baby Psalms on my hip, pretending to be her down-and-out mom. The scorn in people's eyes! I felt so degraded, especially when passersby yelled, "Get a job!" I hated the world and hated my dad for making me beg, which Papa picked up on.

"You are so proud!" he yelled one time in northern Colorado. "You're so worldly because you are concerned with what people think of you."

To get back in Papa's good graces, I begged with more enthusiasm and got good at separating cash from people's wallets. Papa's attitude brightened every time I handed him a fistful of bills and loose change after begging outside a supermarket or a busy downtown district.

Whenever our clothes wore out or my younger siblings outgrew their garments, my sisters and I would go into thrift stores and steal clothes. Papa justified our actions, telling us, "The clothes were given to them, so they didn't pay anything. We can take them."

Since we wore long skirts, it was easy to stuff clothes under our dresses, which we did. Papa forbid me from stealing underwear for myself, however. He made it known that he didn't want me wearing anything under my pioneer skirt. If I needed to wear leggings because of the cold, they had to have holes in certain places because my father wanted quick access with his prying fingers.

Nearly all the time, I hated the world and hated my father for making me beg. I know Abagail didn't like it either, but there was no way out. Once Papa established control over her, she was no better off than Mama or me. She had no car, no money, and no way to contact her husband, who had to be worried sick about his wife and daughter. Oh, and there was one more complicating factor: Abagail was in her last trimester of pregnancy.

Eventually, after several months of living like nomads, we made our way to a remote valley in Idaho. Papa decided to take me—of course—and Joseph and David back to the New Mexico homestead for supplies and to close things down for the coming winter.

While we were gone, Abagail saw her chance to escape. She told Mama she was leaving because she would be giving birth soon, and my mother understood. Abagail had sold the Suburban at one point, so she and Ruth started hitchhiking. They got a ride to the nearest police station, where Abagail turned herself in. After spending the night in jail, Abagail and Ruth were reunited with Steve and returned to Silver City.

When we arrived in Idaho and heard this story, as well as news that Abagail had taken the blame with the authorities, Papa was relieved. He bowed his head and didn't say a word. Maybe he knew that it was for the best since we couldn't be on the run forever.

I envied Abagail's courage and wished I could do the same. But I couldn't abandon my brothers and sisters.

They could never survive Papa without me.

# PART V

---

# THE LAST FRONTIER

# 28
# THE CALL OF ALASKA

With Abagail and Ruth gone from our midst, we had to do something. We couldn't keep bumming around the Rocky Mountain states, living off handouts and whatever leftover food we could scrounge out of dumpsters behind supermarkets. If the pickings weren't good, we'd walk into a mom-and-pop diner, hunger written all over our dirty faces, and beg for something to eat.

Sometimes my brothers and I gathered our rifles and hiked into the woods to hunt for an elk or a deer, growling stomachs propelling our steps. We were conditioned to believe that since we were doing God's work, we could take extraordinary measures to feed ourselves, including poaching wildlife without a license.

I'll never forget the time when a friendly, well-meaning couple saw us begging on a street corner and offered to buy us dinner at a nice steakhouse. We followed them into a western-themed restaurant, where the kind man approached the hostess and asked for a table that would accommodate all of us.

A couple of waitresses put together several tables, and we sat down. The nice man smiled as we were handed oversized menus by a young, perky, blonde-haired waitress.

"Order whatever you want," he said magnanimously. "Dinner's on my wife and me tonight."

I held up the menu and pretended to read, fearful that the nice couple would discover that I couldn't read very well and most of my siblings couldn't read at all. I didn't want to embarrass myself, as I had the time when I was in someone's house with my parents and the mom showed me her kitchen. "So, where do you do most of your cooking?" I asked innocently.

The woman of the house pointed to a microwave. I'd never seen one of those before, so I moved in for a closer look.

"You can open the microwave," the mom said.

She showed me how to do that, and I peered inside. "Where do you build the fire?" I asked.

I heard lots of laughter, including from my parents. I wanted to crawl in a hole and hide. Embarrassing moments like that taught me not to ask too many questions. Tonight was one of those occasions.

A few minutes later, when the waitress returned to take our orders, I looked to my father for guidance.

"I'll have one of your T-bones, medium rare, with a baked potato and all the trimmings," he said.

"What size?" the waitress asked.

My father, who loved taking advantage of other people's generosity, regarded the menu. "The sixteen-ounce will be great."

Since I was sitting next to my father, the waitress looked at me for my order. But first, I had to ask permission to do so.

"My lord, can I eat too?" I asked.

That was the most normal thing for me to say in this situation. I *always* had to ask my father for permission before I could eat anything. As for calling him "lord," not "Papa," that was second nature as well.

"Let me think about it," my father responded.

Time stood still for a moment as an awkward silence ensued. The couple and the waitress acted like they didn't hear right, which prompted an about-face from my father.

"Ma'am, for the kids here, just bring hamburgers and fries for everyone, along with root beer drinks."

I could see that our waitress, who looked my age, figured out what was going on. Tears pooled in her eyes as she finished writing down all the meal orders.

The exchange set the tone for a tense evening that should have had a celebratory air. When the first batch of meals came out, several waitresses set big plates with giant hamburgers and a mountain of fries in front of me and my siblings, which looked amazing to my hungry stomach.

But none of us dared take a bite. We were never allowed to eat until Papa started eating, and his steak dinner hadn't arrived. We waited patiently as our waitress delivered Papa's rib eye and the couple's steak dinners, but I could tell that our waitress was not happy with my father when she set his plate down.

When Papa took a forkful of baked potato, that was our signal. I immediately started in because I was so hungry.

While I was still chewing my first bite of a delicious hamburger, Papa leaned closer, his eyes looking over the top of his glasses. "You don't need to eat all that burger," he said. "Have a few bites, and then I will tell you when to stop. You have plenty of brothers who will gladly eat that for you."

At that instant, tears began flowing down my cheeks as I let my unkempt hair fall over my face to hide my expression of sadness. Aware that every bite I took could be my last, I knew better than to eat fast, or Papa would call me a pig and stop me from eating before I hardly had any food.

I had only taken a few little bites when my father pierced my soul. "You've had enough. Pass it on."

I complied and handed my plate to one of my older brothers. To help cover the embarrassment of this awkward moment, I turned and helped my little sister Hosanna, who was trying to figure out how to hold a hamburger twice the size of her hands. A lump formed in my throat, watching her eat while I couldn't.

I knew Papa was playing it carefully, making it look like I didn't want to eat my food. To add insult to injury, there were parts of Papa's steak that he couldn't chew since he didn't have any teeth. They had all rotted away. When his last tooth had to go, he had me pull it out.

"Elishaba, chew this up for me," he said, placing a quarter-sized piece of steak on my plate that he had just spit out of his mouth.

This wasn't the first time he asked me to chew his food for him. Whenever he wanted to eat peanuts, I became his teeth and chewed the nuts into smaller pieces so he could enjoy them. But—not without feeling guilty—each time I chewed and swallowed a few nuts for myself.

I noticed several waitresses gathered near the kitchen, talking as they kept glancing in our direction. Our waitress was still dabbing away tears.

What hurt more was watching my siblings enjoy their big burgers, fries with ketchup, and vanilla ice cream with chocolate sauce for dessert—mouthwatering foods we *never* got to eat. As the dishes were cleared, the couple took care of the bill, which amounted to several hundred dollars. When we got up to leave the restaurant, the kind man pulled my father aside and asked him why his daughter called him "lord."

My father's eyebrows narrowed. "Elishaba, take everyone to the van," he ordered.

*That didn't sound good.* As I led my siblings toward the parking lot, I overheard Papa sweet-talking this couple, telling him that Mama and I *wanted* to call him "lord" as a sign of respect for being the family patriarch and leader.

I was hoping that would be the end of it, but as we got in the minibus, Papa got into it with Mama regarding the issue of calling him "lord" in public. They argued up a storm.

"I don't think we should have to call you 'lord' in public," Mama stated. "People don't understand."

"You mean you want to hide your faith?" my father roared. "Is that what Sarah did with Abraham?"

I'd heard the verses from 1 Peter 3 a zillion times, how Sarah obeyed Abraham and called him lord. For the last couple of years, I called Papa "lord" because that's what he asked me to do. To use the familiar "Papa" was to invite a stern reprimand or, if he was in a foul mood, a fist to my shoulder.[1]

Upon being challenged by Papa, my mother cowered, which she usually did when she experienced my father's wrath. "No, my lord," she meekly responded.

While we were out on the road, Papa heard that the Alaska state government was *paying* people to live there. Something called the Permanent Fund Dividend. The way Papa explained it, the state of Alaska was bursting at the seams with tax money from oil exploration, enough to pay each resident between one and two thousand dollars annually. With a family our size, that would be a lot of money.

The idea of moving to the great state of Alaska—two-and-a-half times the size of Papa's Republic of Texas—took hold of my father. Sure, it got incredibly cold that close to the Arctic Circle, but living at the nine-thousand-foot level in New Mexico meant many days of frigid, below-freezing temperatures too.

When Papa told us what he was thinking, my mother and all of the older children liked the idea of making a fresh start in Alaska. We were tired of our nomadic lifestyle and hoped that our lives would improve if we moved to the 49th state. Another plus was that I'd never seen Papa this exhilarated about anything. Whenever my father got excited about something, we wanted to keep him that way.

Papa said we needed to make an exploratory trip to check out what Alaska was all about. For a family of thirteen with no money, there was only one way to get there—drive. We took the minibus, pulling a rundown travel trailer.

To earn money along the way, Papa had us play and sing our gospel hillbilly music at flea markets and street corners. People were quite generous when we passed the hat or left open the fiddle case; sometimes, we received hundreds of dollars in one day. The wads of cash were enough to make Papa happy for a week, though his cheerful attitude didn't make my secret life with him any more comfortable. I always felt a tension that threatened to bubble to the surface.

Anytime we stopped in a new town, the first thing I had to do when we got out of the minibus was kiss Papa on the lips—no matter who was looking. I found this order challenging to follow, especially as it included his insistence that I walk beside him with my hand familiarly tucked through his arm as we shopped or strolled along a sidewalk. I struggled with feelings of self-condemnation.

Papa didn't care. He wanted the world to see that his daughter loved him very

---

1. Papa had no problem nailing me in my sore left shoulder if that was the shoulder closest to him.

much. I worried that strangers thought we were a couple because of our unkempt Western clothes and cowboy hats and my lack of makeup and hairstyling.

The simmering tension between us grew. I could tell Papa had a growing grudge against me and could sense my resistance in public.

We would stop at laundromats along the way that had coin-operated public showers. Papa always found a way to make it clear that he needed my help in the shower, which was his way of getting alone time.

I could never understand why this was acceptable to the world around me.

On our long, slow route north toward Canada in our minibus and trailer during the summer of 1998, we traveled via back roads from one town to the next. After what happened with Abagail and Ruth, Papa was taking no chances with the authorities.

To reach Alaska required a long drive through Canada. Passports were not needed at the time, which saved us plenty of money.

Leaving the Lower 48 behind, I felt a tug in my heart as we slowly motored toward the beauty I imagined awaiting us: I pictured Alaska as old-fashioned, rugged, and straightforward. The endless miles[2] were made even longer because our minibus was constantly breaking down, which frustrated Papa because repairs cost us money and time. My older brothers had become quite good at troubleshooting and fixing our vehicle once they got the parts, but that could take days.

Making progress through the Northwest Territories and the Yukon Territory took forever. Our destination was Fairbanks, Alaska, which I thought was a tiny village where people gathered with CB radios to communicate with each other.

I was concerned for Mama, heavily pregnant with her thirteenth child. As we traveled toward Alaska through Canada, I was well aware that a new baby sister or brother would soon join our family. When Mama's contractions started, we found a lake where we made camp while my mother gave birth to our newest family member on August 4, 1998. My parents named her Lamb Yukon Rose Hale. We thought our "Canadian" lent an exotic flavor to our all-American family.

For several weeks, my siblings and I enjoyed fishing for grayling out of the streams that flowed into the lake. We also picked wild plants to make tea and fended off hordes of bloodsucking mosquitoes. The challenge to survive on fish, rice, and wild plants made us feel like we were well prepared for the "Last Frontier," as Alaska billed itself.

---

2. The distance from New Mexico to Fairbanks was more than 3,500 miles.

We had fun with the northerners who seem to understand bush life. One of them was a guide who lived across the lake from where we were camping. Intrigued by our family, he offered us a ride in his bush plane, a de Havilland Beaver, four at a time. This was the first time I flew in a plane, which was the most exciting thing I'd done in ages. Then he asked my older brothers to fly to a wilderness camp to help out for the day. I was so jealous that I felt sick to my stomach. I wanted to be free like they were.

The guide's father, who lived in Whitehorse, the capital of Canada's Yukon Territory, offered to let us stay for few days. Using his indoor shower was a treat—but Papa needed "help" there too. While we stayed with this family, we heard about a small herd of deer roaming the hillsides outside Whitehorse.

That gave Papa an idea. "We're going to take a drive," he announced to the family.

We all piled into the minibus. "Where are we going, Papa?" one of my younger sisters asked.

"We're going to get us a deer," he replied.

We had to drive around a bit in the country, but we found a small deer herd. We pulled over to the shoulder. "It's your turn to shoot, Elishaba," Papa said.

I reached for my 7mm bolt-action Ruger rifle that I carried around the New Mexico mountains as a shepherd. A dozen deer, a hundred yards away, munched on prairie grass, unaware of the danger they were in. I shouldered my weapon, sighted in one of the bucks, and squeezed the trigger. He dropped, and the rest of the herd scattered.

My brothers and I ran to the deer, killed instantly from a high shoulder shot. We field-dressed it and then butchered the meat into smaller pieces, placing the venison cuts into a freezer at the house we were staying at.

The next day, the guide's father told us that the locals were looking for a missing deer. Papa and my brothers and I looked at each other. We all knew instantly what that meant: we could find ourselves in jail.

Twenty minutes later, I witnessed Papa thanking the man for the hospitality but adding that we needed to hit the road for Alaska. We loaded up and got out of there right away. Once again, the feeling of being on the run threatened to overwhelm me.

Would it ever end?

Besides being the family patriarch, Papa had one other significant interest in his life—playing music. While we were still in New Mexico, there was a time when Papa wrote down a variety of instruments on pieces of paper and dropped them into his floppy hat.

"God has shown me how to choose who should play what," he announced from his big chair in the cabin. "Whatever you draw out of the hat will be the instrument God wants you to play. I better not hear any complaining, or you won't play whatever you get."

He held out his hat. "Draw one out," he directed. "Whatever instrument you draw will become your main instrument."

When it was my turn, I squealed in delight when I drew the fiddle.

Then Papa decided to have each of us draw a second instrument out of the hat. These were string instruments such as the mandolin, fiddle, banjo, acoustic guitar, bass fiddle, flute, and dulcimer.

I was trembling in my skirt. I wanted to play the guitar so badly, but Papa told me the guitar was a man's instrument, so I was to leave it alone.

Papa held out his hat. On the second go-around, I drew "acoustic guitar" out of the hat. To my shock, I got the very two instruments I wanted.

Well, Papa had told everybody that God chose our instruments, so what could he say now? He reluctantly allowed me to learn the guitar and enjoyed my strumming, but then one time, his mood switched instantly. "Put that guitar down," he said. "Your instrument is the fiddle. That is the one that God blessed you with. I'm not so sure about the second one."

I had become accustomed to Papa going back on his word. Once again, he showed me that I couldn't trust him. I took solace in playing foot-stomping bluegrass tunes that seemed to find an audience whenever we performed in campgrounds or on street corners. Papa liked it when we picked up enough spare change to fill the gas tanks and buy more flour and rice—and wine for his nightly bout of drinking.

Throughout our long trip, we stopped at a few bluegrass festivals, where we had the opportunity to ask musicians questions about how to play our instruments. I tried hard to practice the few pointers I received about the fiddle, but Papa never wanted me to go off and practice. His controlling possessiveness hadn't lessened, and nothing had changed in our personal relationship as he continued to take advantage of me.

He also seemed to have an attitude that none of his children could ever outdo him in anything. Whenever I picked up the guitar and messed around with different chords in an attempt to write a song, he would get upset and put a stop to my creativity, fearing that I might outshine him in some way.

Everyone had to know their place with Papa, and boy, we sure did.

When we finally pulled into Fairbanks, I was honestly surprised. This was no backwater town; Fairbanks felt like a major metropolis even though there were only thirty thousand year-round residents.

We found a white man with two Native wives who seemed keen on taking us in.[3] He owned a big junkyard and allowed us to park our minibus and travel trailer there if we were willing to help clean his yard.

The next day, my parents left us to check out what it took to get the Alaska Permanent Fund money. They had just gotten back when an official-looking SUV drove into the junkyard with lights flashing.

"Someone must have called child protective services," my father said. He started walking toward the SUV—a stalling measure.

I knew exactly what to do. I gathered all the younger children around me. I hunched on my knees and looked everyone in the eyes. "Children, make sure you're smiling and tell them how happy you are when they ask you how you're doing. Also, if they ask you where you go to school, say that you are homeschooled and that us older ones teach you." I had been told to say this phrase many times.

I knew I had to get into the trailer to pick up a few things and hide the braided whip. Then I went outside. Papa was still chatting up the state officers—a male and two females—from the Office of Children's Services.

I swept up Lamb, the youngest, in my arms and took her into the trailer with me. I started boiling some water on the propane stove. I was adding rice and holding Lamb in the crook of my left arm when they entered the trailer with Mama.

I trembled as they introduced themselves. Lamb smiled and wanted to be held by Mama, so I handed her over, which softened the lady OCS officer's heart. Before I knew it, Papa found his guitar and directed us older kids to get our instruments. Outside the trailer, in a middle of a junkyard littered with broken-down cars and swarming with mosquitos, we delivered an impromptu hoedown of hillbilly music. Before we knew it, the state workers were clapping along, having a good time.

When we finished playing several numbers, the lead female investigator rendered her verdict. "You are a beautiful family," she began. "When that little one of yours smiled, it was obvious she is loved. I will put in a good word for you guys."

Papa beamed. We had fooled the world again.

One of the junkyard owner's wives—I'll call her Akna—made me feel like

---

3. Alaska's indigenous people are collectively called Alaska Natives and constitute 16 percent of the state's population.

family. Something about her made me feel like we were related. Maybe it was because we both knew what hardship, hunger, and harm were all about. Akna gave us tips on surviving in Alaska and where the good dumpsters were to dig into.

One evening, we were outside a grocery store when we met a young man who loved the bush. He told us about a cabin in the middle of nowhere between Fairbanks and the town of Nenana, a distance of around sixty miles. His family didn't own the place, but they used the cabin when they wanted to.

"You should check it out," he urged.

"But how can we find it?" my father asked.

"I'll draw you a map."

That was all the impetus that Papa needed to pack up and hit the road. We found the cabin all right. It was tiny—just sixteen-by-sixteen feet with a loft, for a total of three hundred square feet. A small table and a couple of beds were pretty much it. We stacked in there like sardines and made the best of it because we had a goal: establish residency to get our share of the Alaska Permanent Fund Dividend.

Papa had made up his mind. "Alaska is the place for my family to thrive untroubled by authority," he proclaimed. "We will become Alaskans and make an indelible mark here."

I was warming up to this fantastic, untouched land and the natural beauty around me. My first exposure to the beautiful northern lights, a spectacular natural light show visible at certain times of the year, was every bit as beautiful as I thought it would be. At times I would look up and imagine what heaven was like as I watched those glorious lights. I could almost visualize all of God's angels living in that unspeakably lovely heavenly realm.

Looking to the heavens is one way I coped. I was still my father's sex slave. I couldn't refuse him if we happened to be alone.

Winter was coming on, and the temperatures were getting frigid. We went around collecting all kinds of stuff to stay warm at army surplus stores and from the trash cans we dug through. Papa was unsettled, however, and worried about the horses we left behind in New Mexico. He wanted to return to the homestead to organize the move, which would involve bringing all our things and the Army trucks.

"Mama, I think you should stay here with the younger children while I take some of the older ones back to New Mexico. I will bring the ones who can drive the trucks back."

I knew the other reason why Papa was doing this. He wanted more alone time with me. But his plan didn't make sense—and was dangerous. How could my mother and my younger brothers and sisters survive an Alaskan winter living in a tiny cabin a few miles from the nearest store without a vehicle?

I was surprised to hear Mama speak up boldly. "No, you cannot leave me here with the children," she declared. "If you do, we won't be here when you get back. We will freeze to death. I don't know how to survive these temperatures."

As much as Papa didn't like listening to Mama, he knew she was right.

We left a bunch of stuff in the little cabin that we now claimed as ours and left for New Mexico in December 1998, not understanding how ill-prepared and ill-equipped we were to survive the sub-zero temperatures during the long drive.

Somewhere on the Alaska Highway, we broke down. Since the engine quit in the minibus, we couldn't run the heater. Off to the side of the road, we draped ourselves in blankets and took turns huddling around a propane stove. Even then, we came close to freezing while my brothers did their best to fix the minibus. I'll never forget Papa's prayer: "Lord, if we are to die, then I ask that we all die together."

I didn't want to freeze to death; none of us did. Somehow, my brothers got the minibus running again, and we limped into Whitehorse on Christmas Day, wrapped up in blankets and wearing parka coats.

A large Catholic family noticed another large family—ours—parked downtown. They invited us over to their house, where they served us leftovers and filled our cold bodies with warm food, hot chocolate, and coffee.

In many ways, it was the best Christmas ever.

We got back on the road, heading south to the Lower 48 and New Mexico. I had mixed feelings about returning to the old homestead because of the memories of how my father abused me. I pinned my hopes on returning to Alaska, but I knew the decision to move wasn't up to me.

At this point in my adult life, I had no power to decide anything.

# 29
# THE 49ᵀᴴ STATE

Returning to New Mexico was not only like walking back into a nightmare, but my heart was broken when I realized that my lifelong horse Shema— who was my age— was gone.

My brothers and I searched everywhere for her until we found her bones under her favorite tree, where she would go to birth her babies. Grief overwhelmed me, thinking about how she died without us there, but I didn't cry. I *always* shed tears when we lost an animal, but something was different this time: there were no tears to cry, which scared me. *Had I become closed off inside my heart?*

We all thought we would pack up everything and head right back to Alaska when spring arrived, but Papa got cold feet when he figured out that living in the Last Frontier would take some money. Papa wasn't going to work—his "job" was being the patriarch—but my older brothers and I would have to find some employment, which meant getting involved with people. Another thing that gave him pause was the thought of enduring brutally harsh, long winters with below-zero temperatures that reached minus forty degrees and even minus sixty degrees. We'd have to have the right clothes and adequate shelter, and that cost money as well.

Upon our return to Rainbow Cross, Papa put us to work doing a major cleanup around the homestead—raking fields, repairing fences, chopping and stacking firewood, stashing things away, and fixing up the trucks we left behind.

Except for repairing our old trucks, none of this made sense to me. I thought we were leaving New Mexico for good. Since Papa had us working round the clock to make our homestead more livable, I feared that we would stay right where we were. I was hoping for a change of scenery, something different than the life I'd known, but if I expressed that to Papa, he'd tell us we were staying put, just to show us who was boss.

While Papa procrastinated, we all got really sick during the summer of '99, like a plague had hit us. It must have been some type of flu bug. All we could do was lie around the cabin, moaning and wondering when we would feel well enough to return to our regular lives. Several of my siblings came close to dying, which scared me. I walked around like a skeleton, unaware that we got so sick because we didn't have sound immune systems. We'd been separated from humanity for most of our lives.

Before we knew it, the leaves were changing, and fall was in the air. Which meant winter was right behind. Even Papa saw the wisdom of staying put another winter in New Mexico. But the prospect of depositing those Alaska Permanent Fund Dividend checks was like setting out a plate of cookies in front of my father. Although we knew he could change his mind at any time, he maintained that we were moving to Alaska once it warmed up. But he was never anxious to leave New Mexico, which made *us* anxious, wondering what would happen. But then I found out he had stopped paying rent on the Rainbow Cross property. Really, it was a matter of time.

What complicated things was that Mama was pregnant with her fourteenth child, due sometime in the middle of May. Mama had her way of being humorous while passive about the hardships of life. "We need to get on the road, or we're going to have another Canadian baby," she said.

Papa, though, didn't want to tempt fate.

"We will wait until the baby is born, and then we will leave for Alaska," he announced one evening over dinner. And then he threw in an extra comment: "Then again, I'm not sure we should go at all."

Mama and I didn't know what to make of that, except that Papa was being Papa, making decisions on a whim about where he thought God was leading him.

One time, while washing dishes with Mama, she gave me a sideways smile. "Papa is fighting God," she said, "He knows God wants us to move to Alaska, but he's afraid that the move will change things for him."

Once again, I assisted my father in helping Mama give birth to a baby girl: my fifth sister, Bethlehem, born on May 13, 2000. After Mama healed up, we resumed packing. One of the most significant ordeals was getting birth certificates for all my younger siblings, which took a whole day in Las Vegas, New Mexico. We also visited a clinic where a nurse who knew our family administered the necessary vaccination shots.[1]

Sometime in the early summer, we left the homestead for good with all of our earthly belongings lashed to two Chevy trucks, one 6x6 Army truck pulling

---

1. This nurse helped us with verifying the birthdates for the birth certificates because of the yearly shots and records she kept.

a trailer, and the minibus. They were equipped with antennas so we could communicate by CB radios. Thankfully, I drove the 6x6 Army truck—the one named Armageddon—while Papa manned the minibus, so I didn't have to be in the same vehicle as him.

Knowing our record for breaking down, I wondered how far we'd get before one of the trucks quit running. Then something happened while driving through Denver. I was motoring in the slow lane of Interstate 25 when the left front tire suffered a blowout. Armageddon immediately veered left across four lanes of traffic. I fought for control of the ten-ton truck that was twenty-seven feet long. Somehow, I didn't strike any vehicles, but I did smack the concrete wall separating northbound from southbound traffic. Fortunately, there was no further damage to the old Army truck, but with a busted tire, we weren't going anywhere.

Traffic backed up. Then we heard sirens. A fire truck, with lights flashing, arrived on the scene to rescue us and get us off the jammed freeway. The firemen towed us to a nearby park and promised they would find us a spare tire. I don't know how they did it, but they managed to scrape up a new tire within a couple of hours *and* change it. We were so delighted by their generosity that we pulled out our instruments and played a gospel hillbilly song that left those firefighters with tears and smiles in their eyes.

Pleased by the reception, we stayed in Denver a bit longer, playing our bluegrass, foot-stomping music on the 16<sup>th</sup> Street Mall, where Papa kept a close eye on the till. He loved it when people dropped coins or dollar bills into the open fiddle case, because that meant we could eat.

We eventually got back on the road, where the 6x6 Army truck broke down for good somewhere along the plains of Montana. After learning the ancient vehicle was too costly to repair, we hooked a chain to Armageddon and dragged her to the home of a kind man who offered to help. We left the vehicle parked in front of his place with Papa promising that we'd come back for it someday. Papa was always making promises like that, knowing full well he wouldn't follow through.

With no vehicle to drive, I knew where I was going next—the minibus, where Papa directed me to sit right next to him as he sat behind the wheel. Many of the younger siblings rode on bunk beds we had built inside the minibus, where they cuddled with cats, a baby goat, and a raven named Shadrach. Underneath the beds were several stinky milk goats and a pair of Great Pyrenees dogs, each weighing a hundred pounds.

Sitting up front with Papa, I felt trapped. Naturally, he noticed my disappointment, which subjected me to questions about my "fallen countenance" when we were out of earshot of the others.

"My virgin, God knew that I needed you here beside me again. I believe this is God's way of showing that you belong to me," he said with utter sincerity.

I looked straight ahead as if I didn't hear him. I thought about a baby fawn and an injured baby hawk that we had picked up along the way. I had developed a strong bond with "Song Fawn," the name I gave to the baby deer.

"You're not going to answer me?" my father demanded, his voice carrying an edge. "Do you not want to be here with me?"

I stalled again as I tried to think of a way to respond that wouldn't get me in trouble. I had to be careful.

My father filled the void. "Oh, so you would be happier driving one of the other trucks?"

"My lord, I didn't say that!"

Maybe my frustration about having to sit next to him showed. I wished I could have gone in another truck and gained some freedom from Papa, but that wasn't happening.

"Everything about you tells me you don't want to be here with me," Papa countered.

Time to give in.

"No, my lord. Of course, I want to be here with you. There's nowhere else I want to be at this moment."

Papa declaring that I didn't want to be with him cut deep, but what felt just as bothersome was trying to convince him that I did *want* to be with him. Only Mama understood what I was trying to do.

The interrogation that day was followed by the administration of painful discipline from Papa's heavy, trained hand after setting up camp for the night. Even though I was twenty-four years old, I might as well have been four years old for all the difference it made.

Papa was on a schedule. We had to be in Alaska by a specific date to qualify for Permanent Fund money that year, which would amount to a lot since we were a family of sixteen.

As we approached the Canadian border, we turned off at a rest stop to clean up and put on our best gingham clothes. Papa had Mama and all of the girls wear white head coverings so we would appear to be a demure religious family. At the border checkpoint into Canada, Papa laid on a thick story about traveling to Alaska and starting a new life as a pioneer family leaving behind a worldly civilization. To underscore his point, he had us step out of the trucks and minibus with our musical instruments and serenade the border officials with a couple of bluegrass songs.

They fell for the act and waved us through. If Border authorities had bothered to look closer, they would have found a baby deer, a raven, a few goats, and a couple of big dogs in the vehicles.

And several guns.

The main reason why Papa wanted to move to Alaska was so we would live in a place as remote as possible, committed to living pious lives without the influences of the world and with no interference from neighbors, from authorities, and from mean-spirited Christians who had not received the same "revelations" from Scripture as he had.

The fact that we qualified for generous public assistance and Permanent Fund money was the icing on the cake.

Like a modern-day Moses, Papa led us to Alaska like the Israelites making their way to the Promised Land. It didn't take forty years to get there, but it felt like it took us every bit of forty days to drive to Fairbanks, the 49th State's second-largest city.

Papa viewed Fairbanks as the best location to get our bearings while waiting for God to lead us to a particular place He set aside just for our family. The old stories about adventurers staking a claim and living wherever their fancies took them no longer applied. We would have to work and earn money somehow. To get the Alaska Permanent Fund Dividend and welfare—public assistance— meant we had to manipulate the system.

We children had been taught that the world was there to serve us. With this as a guiding principle, we went to thrift stores and stole more clothes. We surrounded the dumpsters outside grocery stores and supermarkets and pulled out day-old baked goods and rotting fruits and vegetables, hoping to find enough food to feed us for a couple of days.

Life felt more and more like bondage. My father's cruel and excessive "discipline" toward all of his children was hampered because we lived among more people in Alaska, but he still found ways to make our suffering just as severe.

For instance, when he wanted to beat me, he would take me to the back of the trailer, stuff a rag into my mouth, and hit me in the shoulders and head with his closed fists. My siblings weren't spared from beatings either. Watching my older brothers and sisters get whacked by my father hurt more than the blows I took from him. Though he whaled on us, he was careful not to hit us in the face since that could produce bruises and unwanted attention from the authorities.

"I love to give corrections," he said whenever he struck one of my siblings or me. We all lived in fear of his wrath, which had intensified since we left New Mexico for reasons I didn't understand. All I knew was that he was quick to punish any one of us as an example to the others.

Our first winter in Fairbanks was a painful learning experience. The cold was so intense that even our truck batteries blew apart. At minus forty degrees or more, being outside and trying to breathe hurt. Staying warm in our trailer was challenging because the propane stove couldn't keep up in those mind-numbing temperatures.

We stayed in the same junkyard, where the elderly owner allowed us to live among his wrecked cars and work for him in trade for the right to live there. We also earned a bit of money from him when we did extra jobs.

Papa set out to make us indispensable. After becoming half-drunk on his boxed wine when the sun went down, he would start up the generators and have us work outside in subzero temperatures, laboring under the spotlights as we took parts off cars and trucks, doing anything that would pay us money.

Papa supervised us while he sat in a warm vehicle with the motor running and the lights on, watching to make sure his crew didn't slow down. Anything we earned went straight into his pocket.

Sometimes Papa would make me sit with him in the dark cab. I felt like his scapegoat as he unloaded all of his self-imposed problems on me.

"I have the most rebellious, good-for-nothing children," he growled one time. "Every time I turn around, the boys are breaking something. Joseph and Joshua are so proud and think they can do anything. I don't know what I'm going to do with them. I don't believe they are Christians. Sometimes I wonder about you. I feel like every one of you is quickly turning to the world."

I felt uncomfortable being singled out, so I tried to help him see the bright side of things.

"Papa, we haven't been here that long. God is already doing all sorts of things for us." I wanted to convince Papa that everything would be okay and that God was not punishing us for some reason.

"What do you mean God is helping us? You're an idiot. We can't find a place to live, and there's no boat in sight."

*A boat.* Ever since we arrived in Alaska, Papa talked about acquiring a boat to navigate the Yukon River and give us access to the wilderness, where we could hide out from the world. This would provide us with the isolation he sought and keep us away from evil influences.

Papa was coming up with all kinds of ideas, like commercial fishing for salmon, but then he learned that you had to have a special permit from the state. The Alaska Department of Fish and Game wasn't issuing any more, which meant you had to buy a salmon permit on the open market. The cost was one hundred thousand dollars, and we didn't have that kind of money.

My father leaned toward me, holding out his wine glass for a fill-up. I could tell he was getting tipsy. I let him talk.

"Nothing is going right. The worst thing is we are stuck in the world," he moaned.

Then Papa abruptly changed the subject. "By the way, you better keep your eyes and hands off of other people. Do you hear me?"

*Where was he going with this?* My heart started beating faster and faster. Recently, we had been around some attractive young men—trappers—out in the Alaskan bush. Papa must have been watching their eyes.

"Oh my lord, you don't need to worry about that. Remember, I'm all yours. You know how faithful I am to you. I can even be around them, and it doesn't bother me."

*Thwack!*

Out of nowhere, a balled-up fist struck me on the head. Inside the cab, I had nowhere to go. I curled up into a ball and covered up. Papa adjusted by delivering blow after blow to my midsection and legs. He stopped when he hurt his right wrist and bruised his knuckles.

These types of frightening and painful episodes were increasing in frequency. Whenever I didn't answer Papa quickly enough, or he thought I was just telling him what he wanted to hear, he believed I was lying to him. That would merit the same discipline all over again. My older brothers thought I was a troublemaker, but they had no idea what was going on between Papa and me.

No idea at all.

# 30
# HEART OF DARKNESS

After our first winter, Fairbanks was judged too worldly by Papa to consider living there permanently. But Papa wasn't letting go of his dream of living in the wilderness.

We drove six hundred miles south to Homer, a town of four thousand on the tip of the Kenai Peninsula. Homer was also at the end of the Sterling Highway, surrounded by wilderness and ocean waters. Driving into town, I saw a large sign announcing Homer as the "Halibut Fishing Capital of the World."

Papa was still fixated on finding a place that could hide us from people. He didn't like the idea of anyone—especially someone from the government—interfering with our lives.

After checking out the dumpsters behind the local Safeway, we drove outside Homer and camped alongside a good-sized stream. We slept in the travel trailer, a tight fit.

I always had my pet deer, Song Fawn, with me unless I left her to go sleep. She always trusted that I would be back for her. Frequently, I would leave her curled up on a bed with the babies and kittens sleeping with her. Once awake, she would bounce to her feet and come running to me.

I loved taking her out in the bushes, laying her down, and speaking to her with strange little squeaking sounds that meant "Stay!" And she would remain right where she was, watching me pretending to be a mother deer eating grass. Then I would give her a different squeaking call that meant "Come!" She would immediately jump up and come bouncing straight toward me wherever I was.

Although I was a twenty-five-year-old adult, I was still a girl at heart and felt no embarrassment as I bounced up and down through the bushes with her, much as her mother would have done.

Papa, however, grew envious of the close relationship I had with my pet deer. He started giving me odd jobs that separated me from Song Fawn, who didn't like being tied to a leash all day. Our separations became more and more frequent, and my heart ached for her. She was growing to adulthood, losing her spots but still ever so beautiful when she looked up at me with speaking eyes and pawed at me lovingly with her hooves.

One morning, Papa took me away to be with him all day. I yearned to get back to my pet deer because my heart was heavy. When we returned to camp, I ran to meet Song Fawn, but her eyes were faded and cold. She stood stiff and shaking as I held her, her squeaky little sound of welcome faint. It was clear her life was waning.

I held her in my arms as she died within an hour. When we buried Song Fawn down by the river that day, I felt like I had buried the only real friend in my life.

Papa was determined to find the perfect spot for us.

A remote property on the other side of Kachemak Bay sounded promising, so Papa rented a skiff for a scouting trip. We packed up the camping gear and filled the small boat with Papa and the eight oldest children. Mama stayed behind with the youngest six kids. Once across the bay, we cruised along the coastline, looking for places to live. We stopped at a couple of wooded properties with For Sale signs, but it became apparent that no matter how cheap the land and buildings were, we would have to buy a boat to get there and bring in supplies.

After camping one night, we cruised along the coastline, checking out properties, when a large boat pulled up next to us. Black clouds were billowing on the horizon. The water was getting a lot rougher from swirling winds.

"A big storm is coming in," the skipper said. "You need to seek shelter."

"Then we'll head back to Homer," my father yelled.

"I wouldn't recommend that. You need to stay put and wait it out. You're overloaded as it is."

The boat captain had a point. Our skiff was full of Hales and packed with gear, weighing it down. But I knew that Papa wouldn't heed their advice; he never did with outsiders.

"Appreciate the concern, but we'll be just fine," Papa said. "I'm not worried about a thing."

My father turned to my brothers. "Let's fire that motor up and get across the bay."

I gathered up my little sisters Jerusalem and Hosanna and cuddled them close to me at the bow. The dark clouds hanging overhead let us know that it could start raining hard at any minute. The storm was coming in fast, causing the skiff to bob up and down in the turbulent marine waters.

My brothers did an incredible job keeping us afloat as we zigzagged across the bay, avoiding whitecaps and a large whale crossing our path. However, a grim thought weighed on my mind the entire time: none of us knew how to swim, except for my father. I looked at the gray, foaming water with dread. If the boat capsized, we were goners. We would drown within a minute in the frigid water. There were no life jackets on board.

Pelting rains arrived. We started taking on water from the small waves hitting our boat. My brothers bailed as fast as the water came in while I held shivering Jerusalem and Hosanna close to me. Crossing the marine bay turned into two hours of white-knuckle hairiness.

Interestingly, the skipper who gave us the warning was waiting for us when we pulled into Homer's harbor and tied up to a dock. He was angry with Papa for taking such a dangerous risk.

"Do you know how close you came to losing your family?" he asked. "I told you to wait out the storm. You didn't have the right boat to make that crossing. What you did was incredibly stupid."

Papa adjusted his hat and smiled. "We're all fine," he said.

I expected my father to give this skipper some guff, but he didn't want to bring too much attention to himself or our desire to find a place in Alaska's vast wilderness where we could all live away from civilization.

Surely there had to be a suitable place.

Because of the close call in Kachemak Bay, none of us felt comfortable living in a setting only accessible by boat. Besides, Papa realized that if we wanted to get a boat big enough for our family, it would take more money than we had.

What to do next? Our prayers were answered when a lumber guy living in Anchor Point, fifteen miles from Homer, wanted to hire our hardworking family. This lumber guy owned a large pile of logs and needed us to put them through a chipper. The smaller pieces would be made into pressed plywood and other wood products.

We camped on his property and worked the chipper machine for several months, but our relationship went south when the owner stopped paying us for work that we'd completed. Naturally, my brothers and I felt like we had been stiffed, but Papa saw things through a different lens: "See, I told you that the world hates you, but none of you would believe me."

The situation got tense. The logger man even pulled out a gun.[1] We packed up in a hurry—goats, dogs, cats, and all—and got out of there.

The only pet missing was Shadrach, our raven. He got left behind when we left the chipping yard in a hurry. We drove fifty miles along the Sterling Highway and camped out at a spot overlooking the ocean. All we could talk about at dinner was how much we missed Shadrach.

The following day, though, we heard Shadrach's distinctive squawk. It was him! I don't know how he followed us up the coast, but he did.

We were quite the sight, all our old trucks and animals parked at a campsite along the Sterling Highway. Word traveled fast about us, and we became a tourist attraction overnight. One time, a group of sweet retired couples dropped by to see what all the commotion was about. Like in Denver, we pulled out our instruments and played our favorite gospel bluegrass tunes for the fascinated onlookers.

Then Shadrach swooped in and landed on one of the gray-haired ladies, who immediately screamed bloody murder and set off a huge ruckus.

"Oh, it's okay," I soothed, extending my arm for Shadrach. "He's our pet."

Things calmed down, but Shadrach flew the coop several days later and never returned.

Meeting some of the locals led to us hearing about a lawyer in Kenai, another thirty miles to the north, who was looking for caretakers of a ranch property he owned in nearby Soldotna. The two-story house with four bedrooms, three bathrooms—toilets that flushed!—and a basement was easily the biggest and nicest house we'd ever lived in. But the place needed some work, and the ranch could use some upkeep. We got a great deal on renting the home and moved in.

Papa returned to his role as lord of the manor from his rocking chair. I sat on the floor, at my father's feet, every muscle in my body tense, in survival mode. His long, gray beard was flecked with splotches of red wine; I'd been serving

---

1. It's a long story, but the logger man had put up one of his excavators as collateral since he fell behind in paying us. He refused to hand over the excavator when things went south, so my older brothers tried to repossess a backhoe one night. I accompanied them with my father. The logger man heard the commotion and came out of his house, dressed in a bathrobe with a gun in his right hand. My heart raced as he walked up to my brothers. Words were exchanged, but he refrained from shooting anyone. I believe the logger man didn't want to hurt my older brothers because he had grown to love them. But he hated my father, which suited Papa just fine because he loved fights like this. Afterward, Papa had me write a letter that talked about how evil this man was and how he punched him one time and broke his nose. Then we drove all over the Kenai Peninsula posting photocopies of this letter in public places. I wanted to hide each time I tacked up a letter, knowing that the locals would read my awful accusations.

him since it got dark.

Papa was in a peculiar mood again, and I was his closest target. "Elishaba, you are a rebellious daughter. You don't obey me. You only obey when you want to, and even then, it's just because you're trying to get by."

How many times had I heard him talk like this? All my life, I'd been trapped by him.

"My lord, how can you say that? I've sacrificed everything for you. I stay by your side day and night and obey everything you tell me to do." I was desperate for my father to see how I'd sacrificed everything for him.

He rocked forward in his chair and stopped. "Really? You'd do anything I say?" he asked, locking eyes with me.

*Uh-oh. This is not going well.*

"Haven't I in the past?" I ventured.

My father stroked his beard as he considered what to say next. And then he lowered the boom: "If you really love me and obey me, then break your fiddle in two. But I know you won't do that because you care more about your fiddle than you do about me."

I hesitated in shock. Was this some sort of a test? Of course it was, which meant that another piece of my heart died for the thousandth time. Feeling numb to the world and angry at life, I got up and walked downstairs to the basement, where I opened the fiddle case and picked up the instrument.

I'll admit that I was feeling suicidal. Since I couldn't take my life at that moment, I did the next best thing: holding the fiddle by the neck, I violently whacked it over the back of a chair. Just one powerful blow was enough to destroy the instrument, leaving the top of the neck in my right hand and the rest of the fiddle a collection of wooden shards on the floor.

I stood there shaking uncontrollably, knowing the shattered fiddle was no different than my shattered heart. In this frozen moment, my heart and my music died within me and disappeared into the darkest of darkness.

One time, the four oldest brothers heard of a building contractor in Kenai who needed drywall hung on some new construction. I wanted to hang drywall, even though I'd never done it before. Not only would I escape Papa for a short time, but I could earn some great money for the family.

My father fidgeted. On the one hand, we needed the cash. On the other hand, Papa didn't want me getting used to the freedom of not being around him.

"Okay, you can work with your brothers," he said to me, "but I want you to stay close to them. If you need to talk to the contractor, you are only to approach him through your brothers. You are not to talk to him directly. Do you understand?"

"Yes, my lord."

I was a good worker and learned how to hang sheetrock quickly, even while wearing a long, heavy skirt that reached my boots. It always blew the men away when I showed up with muscles bulging out of my plaid shirts.

After a few days on the job, though, Papa realized that I was enjoying hanging sheetrock just a bit too much, so he started arriving at the job site and watching me work, which was nerve-racking and embarrassing. It was like he didn't want to leave me out of his sight after we moved onto the ranch property, where it was easier for him to take advantage of me since our family was no longer sleeping all together in the travel trailer. Once the lights were out, his lust for my body took precedence over everything.

Most of the time, in the same bed with Mama and Bethlehem, I'd fall asleep, hunched over my father's feet until he woke up and kicked me. Or I'd lie underneath his right arm, rubbing one of his hands while he slept. Then I'd fall asleep with his hand lying on top of me. If he woke up and found me sleeping, he would elbow me in the stomach or slap me in the face to wake up.

"So, you're trying to get away from me now? Now you can rub my hands."

*Not again.* I felt trapped and so dead-tired. I had to rub his hands or feet and wasn't allowed to sleep until he finally turned over. That's when he would finally give me permission to lay down and cuddle up close to his back.

"Get closer," he would demand. If I didn't snuggle very close to him, I was doomed to rub his feet for the rest of the night. He'd kick my legs every time he caught me asleep. The only time I could sleep was when I heard him snoring.

But I never got enough rest.

We knew living on the ranch in Soldotna was only for the short term, so Papa resumed his quest to find us just the right place to live in Alaska, which was a good way for my father to maintain his sexual grip on me.

He had me accompany him in the truck on overnight trips to look at various properties hither and yon throughout this immense state. Whenever we pulled over into some back alley, parking lot, or woods for the night, I knew what was going to happen: he would have his way with me. There was nothing I could do about it—unless I wanted a beating from his balled-up fists.

I hated driving in an old truck with a king cab, our latest addition.[2] The back

---

2. My brothers could fix anything, so they were always buying vehicles that didn't work, rebuilding them, and then selling them to make a buck.

bench seat was barely wide enough for one person to lie down on, so with Papa and I squeezed back in there, I barely got a wink of sleep since I was wedged in like a sardine.

One night, a bright light shone on my face.

"Put your hands in the air and come out," said a male Alaska state trooper. "We have a complaint. You shouldn't be parked here."

Papa didn't have his pants on. Come to think of it, I didn't either.

My father immediately woke up. "Oh, that's my daughter, Officer," he said.

I was so embarrassed and wondered what the trooper thought.

The next evening, I was sitting next to Papa in the front bench seat. I couldn't ride shotgun: I had to be so close to him that my legs straddled the manual gear shift.

While he kept one hand on the wheel, I suddenly heard his fly unzip. Then in one fell motion, he grabbed the scruff of my neck and pulled my head into his lap.

"Give me some love!" he demanded.

I felt caught in a trap while he squeezed my breast with his free hand and swerved around the road with the other hand on the wheel. My neck was twisted in pain as I waited for this humiliation to be over.

*Oh, God, please, if I die, will You pardon me for this sin? This is so awful and so hard to bear. Please, Lord, remember that I have obeyed my father, and if he has made me do what is evil, then I ask that You set me free of this and take me to heaven.*

These frightening times happened on multiple occasions inside the truck. If I weren't as energetic as Papa wanted, he'd pound on my back, yelling, "Why are you stopping?"

When I went back to work on him, I cried and wondered what I had done to deserve such a cruel fate as this.

One day a contractor we were working for told us about an excellent place to go hunting. Hunting always excited Papa since bagging a moose, or an elk, meant meat on the table, so he decided to allow us to participate in our first legal Alaska hunt. We purchased the necessary license and tags.

His decision posed a dilemma. The hunting spot was only reachable by hiking in a few miles, something Papa couldn't do because of his knee problems.

I wanted to go badly, but I also knew Papa would never let me go. I believe he was terrified that I'd tell my older brothers about what was going on during the hunt.

My two little sisters, Jerusalem and Hosanna, really wanted to be part of this hunting trip, even though they were relatively young. Papa thought hard about that since he knew that if my two little sisters went, I would have to go along to take care of them. I knew well the battle in his mind and wondered how he would play this game.

One night after dinner, he called me over.

"About this hunt," he said. "I haven't made up my mind yet, but if I do let you go, it's only to take care of your sisters."

"So you're saying there's a chance, my lord?"

"Yes, there's a chance."

For several days, I treated him nicely and smiled demurely at his every request. I gave him everything he wanted. I was well aware, however, that my hopes could be dashed in an instant. He surprised me when he said I could go with my sisters as long as I did not talk to the contractor. I readily agreed to his request.

On the appointed day, Papa took eight of us older children to the trailhead with our backpacks and rifles. When we started on the trek, he joined us on the trail for a while, saying he would turn around when the going got steep. About midway there, my father came alongside me and sighed emotionally.

"I'm surprised that you would prefer to go on this hunt instead of staying behind with me," he began.

I knew what he was doing. He was stirring the pot and seeing how I would react.

"No, it's not that, my lord. Please—"

"Since you're leaving me all alone," he continued, "I'm asking myself why you are no longer faithful to me."

I kept my head down as we continued to walk. I was torn up inside and didn't know what to say. But I had learned from the master how to play the manipulative game, so I acted as though I wanted to stay when actually I desperately wanted to go on the hunting trip.

"You know I really want to stay with you, but Jerusalem and Hosanna need me to take care of them," I said. "Mama has her hands full with Job, Noah, Abraham, Psalms, Lamb, and Bethlehem, so this will give her a break."

Which was all true, especially with Psalms and Lamb, who were demanding preschoolers. Bethlehem, a toddler, had started walking.

Papa played along, the manipulator that he was. "This must be your decision, Elishaba," he said, which sounded more like a challenge than an option.

I was thrown into a quandary.

*Why is he saying it's my decision? He makes it sound that way, but he'll hate me if I decide to continue on the hike. If I choose to go back with him, he'll hurt me. What should I do?*

Deep down inside, I knew the right answer. I didn't want to stay behind for even a moment. The joy of going on a hunting excursion with my siblings would be well worth all of the suffering I would receive on my return.

"I've . . . I've decided to go, Papa," I stammered. "I will not stop thinking about you the entire time. I promise."

He stopped in his tracks, but we had arrived at the steep part. He remained silent, brooding and thinking what to say next. Before he could open his mouth, I hurriedly gave him a quick kiss and then turned and ran so I could catch up with my siblings.

I glanced back at Papa. His face was wooden as he turned away from me. As the darts of his silent rejection pierced my heart, I tried to ignore them and hurried up the trail to catch up with the rest of our group.

And then I smiled. At least for the next twenty-four hours, I would be free from my father.

# 31

# THE WRANGELL MOUNTAINS

In early 2002, while living on the ranch in Soldotna, we heard about a town *beyond* the middle of nowhere—McCarthy, Alaska, a hamlet populated by a couple of dozen hardy souls three hundred miles east of Anchorage.

McCarthy was a semi-ghost town that had its heyday a hundred years earlier when copper and gold mining brought hundreds of fortune-seeking frontiersmen and their families to the area. When the bottom dropped out of the copper prices in the 1930s, so did the town's fortunes. McCarthy was so isolated that it was sixty miles from the nearest paved road.

To get there, you had to drive the last sixty miles from the town of Chitina on a dirt-and-gravel road littered with potholes in the summertime and covered with snow and ice in winter. The dangerous road across the Alaskan wilderness traveled through swampland, permafrost zones, and mountainous areas prone to rockslides.

Papa decided that we had to check out McCarthy, even during a frigid winter. An unusual joy lit his eyes when he heard McCarthy was about as far away from civilization as one could get in North America.

We loaded up the crew-cab pickup truck and a Suburban for the long drive from the Kenai Peninsula. Mama stayed behind with several of the youngest children. The fact that the journey was more than five hundred miles long, in the middle of winter, with bone-chilling temperatures below minus forty degrees and minus fifty degrees and a series of severe snowstorms in the forecast, didn't deter my father. God would protect us, he said, because we were pilgrims seeking a place far away from the evil, wicked culture of mankind and its alluring temptations.

We needed the two vehicles to fit everyone and our stuff: blankets, warm clothes, food, musical instruments, a chainsaw, shovels, chains, and extra gas.

We wanted to push hard and get there in a day, but three feet of snow fell during the trip, slowing progress since the unplowed roads were nearly impassable. Whenever our truck or Suburban veered into a snowbank, the other vehicle would pull it out with its winch.

We found a wide spot in the road the first night and stopped there. We kept the engines running so we had heat and slept for several hours. We resumed driving on the snow-clogged roads at dawn and got stuck more times than we could count. Each time that happened, we knew the drill: grab the shovels, shovel snow away from the wheels, and winch up the vehicle in distress.

On the second night, we made it to a footbridge over the frozen Kennicott River just outside of McCarthy. We could see a path where locals were driving across the very wide frozen river, but it was too late—midnight—to go into town, so we pulled under the bridge and parked there since blizzard-like conditions had dropped visibility down to several feet. There was nothing we could do but keep the vehicles running and grab a few hours of rest.

In the morning, while driving into McCarthy, we got stuck in the heavy snow. We were shoveling out when we heard a snow machine coming in our direction. A bundled-up man drove up, pulling a wide trail groomer behind his snow machine.

Turning off the engine, the good-looking man with a salt-and-pepper beard and a tumble of gray hair underneath a gray hat greeted us.

"Hi, there. Need some help?" the man asked with a warm smile.

"I think we can manage, but thanks," my father said. "How far to McCarthy?"

"Well, you're almost there. Howdy. My name is Gary Green."

The gentleman couldn't have been friendlier. He was our kind of people. My father introduced himself as Papa Pilgrim and said we had come to check out McCarthy. "If we like it, we want to move here," he said.

Mr. Green beamed. "Well, if you like it quiet, then you've come to the right place. I've been here thirty years myself. I'm a bush pilot. Got a little company called McCarthy Air. I do a lot of tourist flights in the summer."

Well, I didn't know we were meeting a local celebrity. My brothers and I grinned at each other. The day was getting better already.

When we finally freed ourselves and drove into the small village of McCarthy, we found a handful of one- and two-story weather-beaten wooden buildings dating back to the early 1900s. Most were abandoned and barely standing, but some had been fixed up or were at least habitable. We parked and started walking around.

We saw someone shoveling the roof of McCarthy Lodge. He stopped what he was doing to gawk at the family of twelve walking up Main Street in the middle of winter.

The man climbed down a ladder and introduced himself. Said he was Neil

Darish and was the owner of the only commercial establishment open year-round in McCarthy.

Mr. Darish invited us into the lodge's dining room, where Papa introduced himself and our clan. I'm sure we were quite the sight clad in our rough flannel shirts, thick jackets, wide-brimmed leather hats, and—for the girls—our long, flowing skirts. We certainly looked the part of a pioneering family.

The lodge owner explained that McCarthy rarely had visitors in the winter, but during the long summer days, the town drew a sizable number of outdoorsy people interested in hiking in nearby Wrangell-St. Elias National Park, the nation's largest at thirteen million acres. He told us that McCarthy had been founded in 1906 when the Kennecott Copper Mine was going gangbusters a good five miles away. Back then, hundreds of miners shopped for food and provisions in several general stores, bunked in clapboard boarding houses, frequented dance halls, and looked to saloon girls for entertainment.

Papa didn't have much patience for the history lesson, but he showed enough interest not to appear rude. Then again, my father needed something from the lodge owner, which was information.

"We're thinking of moving here," he casually said to Mr. Darish.

The lodge owner responded warmly to hearing that the town might receive a nearly 50 percent increase in population sometime soon. He had to figure we were serious. Who would make their way to McCarthy in the middle of an Alaskan winter unless they were sincere about moving there?

As Mr. Darish probed for more information, Papa adopted a homespun, aw-shucks manner and painted a picture of a simple mountain family that had spent nearly twenty years living off the land in the Sangre de Cristos in New Mexico. Now God was calling us to pick up stakes and live pious lives in one of the last frontiers left for Americans.

When Papa finished, Mr. Darish said, "That's wonderful to hear. Would you mind if I let some other townspeople know? I'm sure they'd love to come over and meet you."

Papa looked at me, and I knew what he was thinking: *Short of knocking on people's doors, how does that happen?* Besides, my father wasn't big on us being around people he didn't know. For as long as I could remember, we weren't allowed to make eye contact with strangers and could only speak to others after our father gave us permission to do so.

"I suppose that would be all right," Papa allowed.

Mr. Darish walked over to a desk, where a CB radio sat. I listened to him call several nearby families. Within twenty minutes, a steady stream of locals dropped by the McCarthy Lodge to check out this pioneer family from New Mexico looking to move in and live among them, including Gary Green.

Then Papa had an idea for us older kids. "Go get your instruments. Let's show them what godly bluegrass music sounds like."

I loved hearing that idea, so Joseph, Joshua, and I hustled and brought back a fiddle, a mandolin, and two guitars. Then we joined Papa and sang several toe-tapping numbers, which got the folks clapping along. The lively music left good vibrations in the air.

Papa was trying to make an impression on these people, and he succeeded.

Knowing my father's tendency for deceitfulness, I hoped he would be wise in these early attempts to build good relations locally. I'll admit that the attention the McCarthy townspeople lavished on us felt good and reassuring to my insecure heart. I hoped that Papa would choose to have us live in such a friendly and welcoming village with every fiber of my being.

We headed back to Kenai, eager to tell Mama about the trip. Papa seemed to have a fire lit underneath him and moved us into action. Quickly, we purchased seven Ski-Doo Tundra snow machines for cheap; nearly all were run down or not running. No problem. My brothers could fix them.

The snow machines all fit on a flatbed trailer we owned. When Papa said we needed to make another scouting trip to find a place where we could live, we loaded up the crew-cab truck and Suburban and said goodbye to Mama, who was staying behind with the younger children again. This would have been sometime in early March 2002, or the "Third Month," as my father would say.

Once we returned to McCarthy, Papa was beside himself with excitement, eager to get on his new "roaring steed" and zoom off into the snowy wilderness of Alaska in the search for a new home.

I also had a lot of fun driving my snow machine. I had grown up on horses, not snow machines, but it felt wonderfully natural to tear through the forest on steel rather than horseflesh. In a unique sense, I felt free . . . to be me! To a girl bound tightly to her demanding father, this was a rare and precious sensation.

I sometimes wondered what the locals felt about this huge Pilgrim family nosing around in search of property. *Did they feel harassed? Put upon?* Whatever they felt, it looked like they would be stuck with us because Papa was certain that God led us to McCarthy.

"I know He has a place ready for us," Papa said.

During our exploration trip, we found an old trapper's cabin and squatted there. Winter was still in full fury: a heavy blanket of snow and ice covered the Alaska bush. Our biggest challenge was staying warm as the temperature dipped to minus twenty degrees. Somehow, we managed to make it through each night without getting frostbite.

Our property search took us miles from the town of McCarthy. At times we lifted our snow machines over fallen logs, working together to get where we wanted to go. Papa couldn't help; his body had weakened considerably from diabetes since his sugars dropped precipitously because of all the exercise he was getting. My brothers and I picked up the slack; we didn't know how to give up, no matter how wet, cold, hungry, or frozen we were.

Sometimes Papa couldn't go on, so it fell on me to stay behind with him. The hard part was noticing how he was using his fatigue as an excuse to send the others ahead so that he could be alone with me.

We ran into another pilot during our search for a suitable place to live. Kelly Bay, the owner of Wrangell Mountain Air, with his wife, Natalie, told us to check out a property outside of town, alongside McCarthy Creek, up the McCarthy Valley.

"It's every bit of four hundred acres, fourteen miles up McCarthy Creek and near the end of the McCarthy glacier," he said. "What makes this private property unique is that it's located *inside* Wrangell-St. Elias National Park, which is public land."

Papa's eye lit up. "Can you live there?"

"Sure, you can. It's part of the old Mother Lode copper mine. There are around two hundred miles of tunnels underground and a hundred and twenty acres of livable land down by the river. It's called the Marvelous Mill site. There are still some old ruins from the miners' bunkhouses. The owner, an old prospector, started to put a house up. Name is Walt Wigger. The house isn't much to look at, though. He never finished it."

"How do you get there?"

"Well, you could fly there," the Wrangell Mountain Air pilot said. "I've flown over the property many times and even landed on a small airstrip near the main house, but it wasn't a smooth landing. The airstrip could use some work. The trouble with the place is that you can't drive there. There's no road."

"So, how do we find it?" my father asked.

"Just follow McCarthy Creek on your snow machines. You'll have to cross it a bunch of times, but you'll eventually find it. Walt abandoned the place a few years ago. I think he's in Fairbanks," Mr. Bay said.

We had to check out this abandoned property. The next day, seven Tundras—all topped off with gas—left McCarthy to find this plot of land.

The trip up the creek valley was quite an adventure. We ran our noisy snow machines up one side of the creek and then would hit a roadblock and have to cross the river. Fortunately, it was a big snow year, and McCarthy Creek was still frozen. After a dozen or so creek crossings, we found the property—our

Hillbilly Heaven. The homestead was situated in a picturesque valley with steep walls of mountains on each side. A stunning glacier glistened in the distance, and the silent, majestic beauty of the valley was inspirational. Still, fear rose in my throat, wondering if this place would become another Rainbow Cross, with its inevitable burden of awful memories.

By this time, I was doing a pretty good job blocking out reminders of my New Mexico life. I cried out to God again and again. *Lord, will Alaska be the haven for which I long? Can you change my father so he can leave me in peace?*

Eventually, we returned to Mama and the little ones in Soldotna, where we listened to Papa tell my mother about this Mother Lode mine property we'd found. Papa was pretty animated, saying that he was sure God was leading us to the Wrangells.

I was excited that we might have found a home in Alaska. I was hopeful that we would be happy again. If Papa was happy, then we would all be happy.

Now it was a matter of finding Walt Wigger. Mama, who had a pretty good nose for finding out information like this, went into Kenai and found a Fairbanks phone book.

There was a listing for a Michael Wigger. When Mama came back, we all gathered around while she called the number.

"I would like to speak with Walt Wigger," my mother said into the phone.

"This is his son Michael," a voice said. "Why do you want to talk to him?"

Mama explained that our family was interested in buying the property outside McCarthy, the one next to the Mother Lode—

Michael Wigger cut her off. "My dad won't sell."

My mother didn't give up. She made her pitch on why our family wanted to live in such a remote place. "Can you please give me his number?" she asked.

Her persistence paid off because suddenly, Mama was waving her hands, motioning for a pen and paper.

She wrote down the number, thanked Michael for his time, and quickly dialed the new number.

We all waited in anticipation and listened in. Walt Wigger wasn't interested in selling, just as his son said.

"Wait, wait!" Mama said in a panicky voice. "We'll give you thirty thousand dollars right now as a down payment. In cash."[1]

Suddenly, Mr. Wigger was quite interested in selling. He and Mama spoke a bit more, and then he told her to meet him at a certain coffee shop in Fairbanks the following day.

When Mama hung up, she said, "He wants to make a deal."

---

1. I didn't know this at the time, but no bank would have loaned money on this property. The fact that Mama offered a cash down payment told Mr. Wigger that we were serious.

Our entire family drove to Fairbanks, squeezed into two vehicles. We swarmed into the coffee shop, where Mr. Wigger was waiting for us. He was alone.

He looked to be getting on in years. The old prospector had to be in his eighties.

Even Papa knew he had to soften up Mr. Wigger to get him to sell. He asked the old miner a few questions about how long he'd been in Alaska and how he got into mining.

"Came here in '38, at the urging of my uncle who lived here. Got into logging, building, lots of different things. I taught myself to fly and became a bush pilot. Raised a family with five kids. Wife is gone now . . ."

Lost in his memories, his voice faded.

Papa filled the void by describing our journey of faith from New Mexico to Alaska and how he felt God was leading us right to his land, as remote as it was.

Mr. Wigger looked at us warily with a slanted smile, almost as if he questioned Papa's integrity. "That's all very interesting," he allowed.

Papa turned to my sister Jerusalem. "Give me the box," he said.

Jerusalem, thirteen, was responsible for carrying around our money in a special little box, which she handed to Papa.

My father flipped open the lid. Inside was a bulging white envelope. Papa reached for the bundle and placed it in front of Mr. Wigger.

"Go ahead and count it," Papa said. "It's thirty thousand dollars in cash."

Inside the fat envelope were three hundred $100 bills—our nest egg from the Alaska Permanent Fund checks and money my brothers and I earned from construction projects.

Mr. Wigger's expressionless smile was hard to read. He sighed as if thinking about what to do. Then he shrugged his shoulders. "Okay," he said, reaching for a paper napkin.

Just before signing the napkin, he looked up. "Oh, I have a bulldozer up there. It's parked in the bushes next to the house. I want that bulldozer and plan to get it sometime."

My brother Joseph spoke up. "How do you plan to get it out of there?"

"Well, I just might drive it out," he replied with a smirk on his face. "There's an old mining road that goes up that valley, but the Park doesn't want anyone using it. Let's just say it will start quite a fuss."

I could see the wheels turning in my father's head.

Right there in the restaurant, he and Papa forged a deal: we would pay $450,000, payable in annual payments of $30,000, interest-free, which was a little more than we were receiving from Alaska's Permanent Fund Dividends. Since I had no experience with money, I had no idea if we could afford this or not, but I figured Papa knew what he was doing.

I watched Mr. Wigger sign the napkin and shake hands with Papa, who was beside himself with excitement. I got the impression that Mr. Wigger was mesmerized by such a determined clan, but I'm sure he had no idea what he was getting into.

In due course, we would discover the same thing.

# 32
# THE MOVE TO MCCARTHY

While the paperwork was being completed to purchase the big homestead outside McCarthy, Papa cracked the whip, saying we had to be ready to take possession of our new home before the start of "breakup season" in late April.

Otherwise, the ice bridges across McCarthy Creek would turn to mush, and there would be no way to get our worldly possessions and supplies to our new home until the following winter. There used to be an old mining road up the valley, but years of mudslides, fallen trees, and loose dirt made the muddy route impassable in summer. The only other way to get supplies out there was to have provisions and necessities flown in by bush plane, which was expensive.

The homestead wasn't officially ours until late April, which cut things close. We faced quite the challenge with seven snow machines pulling sleds full of supplies and children. It felt like we were doing things the hard way, which we *were*. We were returning to the rigors of wilderness life. Only this time, it was much colder.

We ran into problems right from the beginning. Papa was crossing McCarthy Creek on his snow machine when the ice broke loose, dunking Papa in the freezing water.

We stopped to help but dared not laugh, even though he looked funny as he crawled out of the waist-deep water wet and bedraggled. Uh-oh—he looked like a volcano ready to explode. Since Papa was proud of his ability to ride a snow machine, I knew losing control was a blow to his self-esteem.

I rushed to his side to help him out of the river and pull off his wet boots and socks. One of my brothers fetched him dry socks and new boots.

I suddenly heard the sound of another snow machine coming up the creek.

"You all need some help?" asked the driver. He was a bearded man in his fifties, bundled up against the cold.

"Who's asking?" Papa answered sharply, which caused me to wince. The man was just trying to be friendly.

"John Adams. I met you in McCarthy back in March. I saw you packing up for the move-in today. I thought I'd check up on you guys and see if you needed any help. It's a long trip for these snow machines. They can break down."

Mr. Adam's concern touched me. McCarthy struck me as a place where everyone looked out for each other, which made sense for a town this remote. Locals had to call on each other first if there was any type of emergency.

"Thanks for checking on us, but we'll be okay," Papa said.

Riding fourteen miles up the mountain valley on our snow machines loaded down with supplies took nearly an afternoon. When we finally settled into our new home for the night, I discovered nothing had changed between Papa and me. He still wanted me at his side when we slept, and he still wanted his rubdowns.

My heart ached within me. *When will I ever be free from Papa?*

The next day we had a visitor: Keith Rowland, a general contractor and family man with five kids that we met in McCarthy. He had driven his snow machine over the mountain pass, which was dangerous and crazy. Perhaps my father thought Mr. Rowland was making a point that we weren't the only wilderness family out there. For Papa, his arrival was the perfect time to send a message.

"What do you think you're doing, barging in like this on our family's privacy? We haven't been here twenty-four hours, and we have to be bothered by intruders like you! I want you to get off my property and don't ever come back!"

Mr. Rowland turned off his snow machine and stood up. "Hold on here. I just came up to greet you and congratulate you and your family for moving into the area. There is no need to get into a kerfuffle over this. We have been coming to this creek valley for years on our snow machines. I came all this way to welcome you and make sure everything was okay."

Papa wasn't swayed. "Well, you are no longer allowed to come across our property without my permission." Papa was hot and unwilling to relent.

Mr. Rowland returned to his snow machine, chastened. "Have a good day," he said curtly just before he and his snowmobile roared down the valley.

Technically, Mr. Rowland was trespassing since the private property's lower hundred acres ran along the creek. Anyone wanting to get to the McCarthy glacier would have to cross our property.

But that was not the issue. I think Papa was happy to realize he had control over something that other people wanted, which frightened my heart.

I could see the beginning of new battles—battles that would isolate us even more.

Over the next couple of days, we hauled more supplies up the valley, worried that the ice would break loose at any moment. Not wanting to push our luck any further, Mama and my older brothers made one last trip down the valley to return to Soldotna to conclude any unfinished business and collect the rest of our belongings.

Anytime my older brothers were away, I felt like I was in great danger. Papa tried to hide his ungodly behavior from my brothers, but with them gone, I felt entirely alone in the world.

Now I was the mother of nine of my little siblings and a "wife" to my papa, meeting his demands late into the night. During the day, my siblings and I chopped wood, gathered water from Diamond Creek, and hunted the agile wild goats that climbed the rock faces on the tall mountains surrounding us. We needed the meat.

My sisters Jerusalem and Hosanna, thirteen and eleven, respectively, became pretty good at cooking goat stew and other dinners. They certainly made my life easier.

One day we were excited to see a silver bush plane flying low overhead. We ran out into the yard and looked up with anticipation. It was Gary Green's plane! We spotted Joseph and Joshua, harnessed and sitting with their legs hanging out the side door. They reached behind them and tossed food and provisions to us, boxed to survive the fall of a couple of hundred feet.

There was no way for them to get to us. Snow still covered the runway we heard about, and it was too dangerous to walk in from McCarthy on snowshoes because avalanches were sliding down the mountains in roaring waves almost every day.

While my brothers were gone, Papa didn't do anything to help out. Instead, he commanded us to do this and do that. The rest of the time, he sat around strumming his guitar and writing down a long list of more things we needed to do. His enthusiasm and excitement about our new home started to give him all sorts of visions and ideas. The game changer was that he had the right machine to make that happen—a bulldozer that came with the purchase of the property.

Had he ever operated a bulldozer before? No, but a little detail like that wouldn't deter him. One afternoon, when enough snow had melted, Papa decided to take the massive yellow machine with a heavy, broad steel blade mounted to the front for a spin. What a disaster!

Papa started knocking down every tree he could find. There was no rhyme or reason for what he was doing. Then he ordered my siblings and me to limb the fallen trees and pile up brush.

After tearing up our yard, he drove the bulldozer toward a grove of alder trees that I was pretty sure was on national parkland. I followed, wondering what he was up to. With the blade lowered, he started pushing over one alder after another.

"Papa, are you sure this is okay? I think we're on parkland."

My father didn't like the question. "Why does it matter to you? Once I clear these trees, it will be too late for them to say anything."

I shrugged my shoulders, but I didn't have a good feeling about what he was doing. After clearing a plot of alders, he turned his attention to the landing strip, plowing snow and dirt off the runway. He intended to make the landing strip operational so the next time we hired a bush pilot, he could safely land on the runway.

"Elishaba, get some help out here!" he yelled over the din of the 'dozer.

I gathered up some of the kids and walked out to what looked like a long rectangular strip of mud. The next thing we knew, we were throwing rocks and stones off the runway while Papa drove back and forth, smoothing the surface with his blade. With each pass, more rocks and stones would magically appear, and we'd have to start all over.

This was hard work!

Then I saw a noticeable hump in the dirt in the middle of the runway—a knoll the length of a 6x6 Army truck. I didn't know much about airplanes, but I knew enough that a landing would be dangerous, if not impossible.

"Papa, there's a hump! See?"

I pointed to the rise in the middle of the runway, which seemed clear as day.

Papa peered straight ahead. "What hump?"

"Over there."

Papa's eyesight had been going downhill. "I don't see anything," he declared, relatively sure of himself.

"Maybe if you get out of the bulldozer, you can see what I see," I suggested.

Papa's nostrils flared. "You better be right."

My father turned off the bulldozer and hopped off. I know why he agreed to have a look: he wanted to prove that I was wrong.

But I wasn't. From ground level, my father nodded. There was a considerable mound of dirt in the middle of the runway right in front of him.

He didn't say a word, but I could tell he hated being shown up. Instead of conceding that I was right, he stormed back onto the bulldozer, his pride stung. The heavy piece of equipment instantly changed into an angry beast bent on destruction. With Papa behind the controls, the bulldozer charged to the center of the strip, where my father lowered the blade and pushed dirt around. Each pass unearthed large boulders and even more rocks.

Instead of leveling out the landing strip, Papa created more of a mess. Within fifteen minutes, there were so many boulders and rocks strewn about that the runway looked impossible to fix.

Once Papa saw he was digging himself into a deeper hole with each pass, he exploded.

"Elishaba, send everyone back to the house and get over here!"

I shooed away my younger siblings in the direction of the Main House and turned my attention back to Papa, who had just turned off the bulldozer.

"What is it, my lord?" I was still panting from the exertion.

My father leaned closer from his seat behind the controls. "You will stay here and move all of these boulders that are in the way—now. Don't you come home until you're finished. Do you hear me, you rebellious daughter?"

My bitterness toward Papa rose in me. I wanted to shriek, *No! What you are asking is impossible!*

Then Papa started up the bulldozer and headed back to the Main House, his tread spraying mud everywhere. I stood mute, watching as the source of all this devastation roared away. Then I looked at the unmanageable upheaval on the runway, which seemed to be a metaphor for my life. For a moment, I despaired.

"No, Papa will never change," I whispered to myself. "I might as well bury myself right now."

All these years, I felt like Papa kept a record of all my wrongdoings. Whenever his hot anger flared, my past misdeeds would be brought up and held against me. I knew the runway fiasco would be added to his long list of grievances.

As I tried to move several of the more enormous boulders on the runway, it was almost as if I took on Papa's anger while I struggled vainly to obey his unjust order. The rage within was so hot that it blocked out any connection I had with God or even the desire to cry out to Him at that time. I felt so lost and forgotten that I became unjust myself—to the point of accusing God of forsaking me.

Then, the responsibilities of an elder sister pressed upon me once again, and I determined to move these impossible boulders. Still, even with maximum effort, I had to give up. The task was simply too great for me in my hunger, weakness, and depression.

Such was my new life in Alaska, which was turning out to be just like my old life in New Mexico. My heart sank when I realized Papa was building a bathhouse—my black hole and my prison cell.

Physical work like pushing boulders and throwing rocks off the runway stopped when my brothers returned. Papa said my job was to stay at his feet. This restriction made me feel guilty as I watched my siblings work hard on their chores while I sat around wanting to do something, anything. Papa's favoritism toward me was designed to make my siblings jealous of my position yet keep me under his control.

"You don't even know how to work," he explained one time while I sat at his feet, rubbing them while he rocked in his chair. "Your sisters can out-cook you any day. You can't even empty a slop bucket without sloshing it."

His derisive words hit home until I reminded myself that I *did* know how to work hard. How could he deny me this self-respect when he knew how hard I'd worked as his servant all my life?

If I defended myself, he would go out of his way to provoke me. "So, are you trying to tell me that you would rather be like your sisters and not take care of me?"

Oh, my. I knew this was an old, loaded question designed to pit me against my siblings. Maybe my reading ability wasn't that great, but I did recall Proverbs 29:22 (KJV), which could have been written of him:

> An angry man stirreth up strife, and a furious man aboundeth in transgression.

So much discord in our home!

His awful comments tore me down all through the day. If I could have found a way to die naturally, I would have leaped at it many times. I even thought that committing suicide would be a godsend, but I had been taught that a vengeful God would be waiting for me if I ended my own life. I could rest assured that I would be sent to the hell I so deeply feared.

So I endured hell on earth.

# 33
# SETTLING IN

If I thought that living at the nine thousand-foot level in the Sangre de Cristo Mountains was the definition of isolation, I changed my mind once we settled into Hillbilly Heaven, Papa's name for our new homestead.

At least we could drive off the mountain in New Mexico. Here in Alaska, fourteen miles up the McCarthy Valley and surrounded by Wrangell-St. Elias National Park, we didn't even have a passable road between us and civilization. If Papa's goal was to remove us from the outside world, he succeeded beyond his wildest dreams.

My siblings worked every day of the week because there was always a project, always something, that needed to be done at Hillbilly Heaven. Once we pretty much leveled the runway, Papa hired a pilot to bring in goats, dogs, and rabbits that we could breed and sell. However, in the coming months, we would learn that raising animals in Alaska's challenging climate wouldn't be successful. We had so much to learn.

Then my brothers made a portable sawmill to produce lumber from the numerous trees on the property—lumber we could use to repair our buildings and construct new ones. Again, the Arctic-like climate worked against us.

Just having enough food on hand to feed seventeen souls daily was a job in itself. We hauled sacks of flour, cornmeal, and canned goods to the homestead with snow machines and sleds until the breakup season. Anything we needed in the summer was delivered by a packtrain of horses that we'd purchased.

Gas, tools, and construction supplies were stored in McCarthy in a ten-by-ten-foot *wanigan*, an Alaskan word for shed, that belonged to Walt Wigger. He said we could use it, even though he didn't own the land underneath the wanigan.[1]

---

1. Walt Wigger had left the shed but warned us that if we stayed there, we would be squatting on someone else's property.

One spring day, Papa directed me to shoot a mountain goat because there was no meat to eat. There was an incredible lack of protein in our diets. The fact that it was illegal to hunt inside a national park was never a consideration of his.[2]

I took sixteen-year-old Israel with me, and we began climbing a nearby peak with rifles slung over our shoulders. Six hours later, we got lucky: several goats were ahead of us, foraging on mountain grass. A single shot from my big-game rifle dropped one. Israel helped me drag the dressed goat back to Hillbilly Heaven, where the family rejoiced with a warm stew.

To make some money that first summer, Joseph, Joshua, and David stayed in McCarthy and offered seasonal tourists guided horseback rides to historical sites around McCarthy and the Kennecott Mines five miles away. The boys remained in the *wanigan*, which was where we also parked our old vehicles. The town gossip was that we were opening a junkyard.

One morning, we were camping out in the middle of McCarthy in this ten-by-ten-foot box of a home. A friendly neighbor dropped by on a sunny day to introduce himself. He was kind and polite, dressed in blue jeans and a regular shirt and jacket. He wanted us to know that he was going to be our near neighbor now. We had a friendly chat about his cute cabin on the hill and how close we were.

"What do you do around here?" Papa asked.

"I'm with the Park Service. I'm a ranger."

I saw Papa stiffen. He had never liked being around people in authority—state police, local cops, child protective services agents, pastors, teachers, etc. Ever since we had moved to an "in-holding" private piece of property surrounded by federal land controlled by the National Park Service, rangers had been added to his list.

After a quick handshake and the neighbor's departure, Papa was seething as he gathered us around himself in the tiny place.

"That man just lied to us." Papa spoke through clenched teeth, clearly outraged.

I felt confused. What was Papa getting at? I couldn't understand what he meant. How did this nice man lie to us?

---

2. This was the only time I poached game in Alaska. Not long after this hunting trip, I got a "subsistence hunting license" from the State of Alaska, which made me feel a lot better about what I did to feed the family. In the future, I would go hunting often for moose, Dall sheep (mountain sheep), and mountain goats.

I stood there, cooking breakfast at the stove and trying to pretend I was busy. Papa walked right up behind me. I could feel his hot angry breath as he challenged me.

"I have to go back and call this man's shot. I have to tell him he's a liar. What do you think?" he asked.

I fumbled for appropriate words, knowing full well that nothing I could say would calm him down. So, I tried to weasel out of it.

"I really don't understand what you mean. How did he lie?"

"You knucklehead," he roared. "Do you mean to tell me you can't even see it? Are you that blind? This man is a park ranger, and he tried to deceive us by acting like he was some kind of nice neighbor. He's a Trojan horse in disguise, someone who came here to spy on us. Now, are you coming with me?"

I had been put into this position too many times to be caught by his manipulation again. I didn't want to go. With growing confidence and feeling quite justified, I said, "My lord, you talk about loving our neighbors as ourselves and how we are supposed to even love our enemies and do good to them. Is not this our opportunity?"

I knew down deep this would be a lost effort, yet I had to try. Papa whirled me around to face him.

"All right then," he huffed. "You will pay for this one. If you're not going to stand up with me, I will go alone. You are an unfaithful good-for-nothing."

For the first time in all my life, I stood my ground and stayed behind. I don't even know what kept me back other than my conscience telling me that I should reject Papa's hypocrisy.

My father chased the man down. It was awful to hear him yelling, "You're a wicked liar!" and see him pointing a finger at his chest.

From then on, I never heard the end of it from Papa about my faithless inaction. He made it clear that he would prove that the world hated us and that his children were becoming worldly through my actions and resistance toward him.

Papa's rage gave him an idea to get back at the Park Service and me: he would show us who was boss by taking the bulldozer and clearing the old miners' road between Hillbilly Heaven and the town of McCarthy, which was overgrown and covered with mudslides and rocks.

"I am surrounded by children who are fearful and worried about pleasing people," he declared that evening. "This is my business, and this is why I must take this bulldozer down the mountain."

From the mess he had made with the runway, I knew that he wasn't very good at operating that heavy piece of equipment, but he was a Hale, and nothing daunted him. As my father started scraping dirt and knocking down trees and overgrowth on the old miners' road, my brothers and I worked alongside him, clearing limbs and brush and pushing away boulders and stones.

Papa's decision to demolish trees and move tons of dirt along nearly fourteen long miles of wilderness road, much of it on public land inside the Wrangell-St. Elias National Forest, set off a legal firestorm that would consume our family. But my father didn't care about the consequences of taking the law into his own hands.

He had decided long ago that he would determine what he could and would do.

Before our first whole winter, Mama gave birth to Jonathan, making me the oldest of fifteen children.[3] I felt no joy because of the deeply ingrained bitterness I had toward my father. Papa made my life so full of misery that I hardly cared about his punishments anymore. I could never do anything right in his eyes anyway.

Neither could my siblings. One time my brother Noah, nine at the time, was hungry. I can't say I blame him. There was never much to eat, but Papa caught him taking a chewy oatmeal cookie out of the cookie jar. Mama always had a couple of dozen homemade treats on hand in case Papa asked for a couple.

"Noah is a thief!" my father announced as judge and jury. "If he is going to steal food, then he will stay here right under the table and only eat the crumbs that fall from the table."

This meant that Noah was grounded—forced to stay under the table except for the times he needed to use the camp toilet. The only thing he was allowed to eat twice a day was a small portion of rice and a piece of bread, washed down by a glass of water. His punishment ended after three weeks on this starvation diet.

Other times there was so little to eat that my younger brothers ate the dog food and hay, which broke my heart. But I was hungry too. We all were. At considerable risk, I snuck slabs of cornbread to my brothers when they were doing their chores, but there were so many mouths to feed. Life was stringent and unbearable, but it's all we knew.

Papa's decision to tear up National Park land with a bulldozer would take on a life of its own in the spring of 2003 when park rangers discovered what had been done. Suddenly, the Hale family was all over the news, and our days of

---

3. I had no idea at the time that Jonathan would be the last child and the Pilgrim family would be complete.

living quietly ended.

A significant "land rights" battle ensued, drawing national attention from the media in the Lower 48 and major newspapers in Alaska. Reporters and film crews from the BBC and CNN made the long pilgrimage to McCarthy and Hillbilly Heaven to interview Papa, who could be counted on to call park rangers "wicked liars" and "unfaithful good-for-nothings." Instead of living peacefully and unmolested in the Alaskan wilderness, we became famous—which was a two-edged sword.[4]

If you were a land-rights activist, then you believed we were getting railroaded by heavy-handed park service bureaucrats. If you were an environmentalist, you were infuriated at what Papa did to the pristine wilderness land.

Papa saw a chance to turn the controversy to our advantage. A couple of months earlier at Hillbilly Heaven, the little cabin we were staying in—since the Main House needed some work—caught on fire and burned down.[5] My father had us gather around the burnt pile of wood and make sad faces for a picture. He enclosed the photo with a letter to the local newspaper, saying, "If we hadn't been gone trying to find horses to make it up the mountain, then we wouldn't have lost our home. We would have been there." He also went on the radio and described a harrowing escape from a fire that destroyed "everything we owned."

Word of the tragic fire circulated among the land rights people, who decided they had to do something for this courageous family. An airlift was organized. Suddenly, we had bush pilots landing on our runway in planes loaded with boxes of food, clothes, towels, blankets, and supplies, bringing great joy to a bunch of unkempt mountain kids. The Main House was filled with boxes and buckets of goodies.

For a bunch of children who never received gifts, this was spectacular. For me, who'd been taught to be distrustful of others, it felt good to know that some people actually loved us.

---

4. This "land rights" aspect of our family's story was covered in depth in Tom Kizzia's book, *Pilgrim's Wilderness*.
5. At the time of the fire, Papa had taken the older brothers, my little sister Jerusalem, and me into town to find some horses. Mama and the younger siblings stayed behind in a tiny cabin we had insulated to survive the harsh winter. Their only heat was a small wood-fired stove. High-powered winds swept over the mountains, not allowing the smoke to escape the stove pipe. They started choking as dense smoke filled the cabin. Mama escaped with the family to the unfinished Main House. Before they knew it, the cabin was engulfed in flames. We lost all our personal belongings, but none of us really had much anyway.

# 34
# MORE CHUNKS OF MY HEART

When my sister Jerusalem turned fifteen in the fall of 2003, she was very skinny and very beautiful.

She could also play the mandolin like a champ, which had Papa praising her as his "prodigy child." I didn't know what that meant, but I knew she meant something special to Papa. Hearing him praise her made me jealous, so I decided to get back at my younger sister.

One time, I caught her saying mean things about Papa and me with Israel, so I tattled on both of them. Papa demanded that they see him immediately.

"Is it true that you were talking bad about Elishaba and me behind our backs?" he asked.

"Sure," they said in unison, nodding. They weren't even ashamed of what they did.

Papa sent them both out of the house to work. "You will not eat until I forgive you," he said. "Meanwhile, you will haul water and do the chores. I want to see you here every day for a whipping, which Elishaba will do."

What? I had to strike my sister and brother with the whip?

That's what I did, and it was horrible. I hated hitting my siblings with a whip and grew to dread waking up each day. To keep my sanity, I told myself it was better that I disciplined them because I was beating them less severely than Papa did, but my father figured that out. "If you don't administer correction properly, I will beat them until they are black and blue," he announced.

I believed him, so I put more effort into hurting them, which took another chunk of my heart. Still, I held back, and it must have shown because when Papa saw how difficult it was for me to beat my siblings, he thought up different ways to punish them. He especially had it out for Abraham, who had been in my special care since he was a baby. Every time Abraham did something displeasing to Papa, another rock went into the backpack that my father made him wear. He had to walk around carrying these rocks until Papa deemed that he had atoned for his sins. Then Abraham was allowed to dump the stones over a nearby cliff as a symbolic demonstration that he was forgiven . . . until the next time.

And then there was poor Jonathan, the youngest sibling. Every time he whined, Papa would attack him by placing his hand over his mouth until he turned blue in the face and fainted from a lack of oxygen. On another occasion, Jonathan kept fussing, as toddlers do. Papa got so angry that he threw him outside the Main House and kicked him across the snowy yard. My youngest brother cried out in disbelief.

I ran after Papa and tried to block him. "Stop! You can't do that!" I screamed.

So Papa started beating me instead, which traumatized Jonathan even more. I picked up Jonathan and rushed him back into the house, where I held him next to the big barrel stove to warm him. He reached out and touched the hot stove, which burned his hand.

More screams! His cries pierced my heart as I rushed to dip his hand in water at the kitchen sink.

I spent days nursing his scorched hand while listening to Papa say over and over, "That's what you get for being careless. You can't even keep your little brother from getting burnt."

The cruelty I had to endure from him never ended. Like the time he shocked me when I thought I could no longer be surprised. It happened one evening when we were soaking together in the bathtub. I noticed a faraway look in Papa's eye.

"Elishaba, let me ask you something. Are you concerned about Jerusalem taking the same place you have with me?"

His comment paralyzed me. I didn't know what to say, and then I steadied myself. I needed to protect Jerusalem and my other sisters from the harm my father inflicted upon me nearly every day.

"Papa, you better not ever do to her what you have done to me," I said, surprising myself. "If you do, I will take Jerusalem and run."

I couldn't believe I had stood up to him. I waited for my father to choke me, right there in the bathtub.

Instead, he adopted a conciliatory tone. "Oh, my dove, you need to hear this," he said in his sickly tone of voice. "I would never touch your sister like I touch you. She is not the same as you. God made it clear to me long ago that you are the one for me, and I just want to comfort your heart in that."

My heart wasn't comforted, nor did I believe him. I let the matter drop but not before vowing to myself that I would keep a close eye on my father and Jerusalem. If he ever crossed the same line with her as he did with me, we would find a way to escape Hillbilly Heaven.

After a year of living at Hillbilly Heaven, the next installment was due for the property.

We didn't have the thirty thousand dollars. Maybe half that.

Papa had me drive him to Fairbanks to visit Walt Wigger and ask for more time, which he granted. What else was he going to do?

We knew a young man in Fairbanks that we had met at the junkyard we lived in when we first came to Alaska. He was a godly young man who made his living trapping out in the wilderness and on rivers with his father. For some reason, he was intrigued by my father's challenges in Scripture and liked engaging him on various issues. He told us that we had an open invitation to stay at his place any time we needed to be in Fairbanks.

This was one of those times. While we sat in his living room, Papa had me prepare coffees for the two of them as they started debating the Scriptures. There wasn't much for me to do but sit on the couch and watch them go back and forth—in a spirited but friendly manner—on what God was telling us in certain verses in the Bible. The man was handsome and single and in his early thirties—attributes that I couldn't fail to notice. I had just turned twenty-seven.

Papa caught me looking at him, an absolute no-no in his book. I wasn't allowed to "look" at anyone. Nor were my sisters. This is why strangers felt we were so weird. We weren't allowed to look at anybody that we didn't know well or who hadn't been screened by Papa.

Papa interrupted himself. "Go to the car," he said.

I knew better than to ask why. I had never felt so embarrassed as when I put on my coat and gloves and left the warmth of that young man's home for the cold of the Suburban. The temperatures were below zero.

I crawled into the back seat and wrapped myself in a thin blanket. Hours passed by as I shook uncontrollably from the cold and cried out to God to save me.

Just when I thought I would freeze to death, Papa came outside and got behind the wheel. "Come sit with me," he said.

He turned on the motor and started driving around the neighborhood. "Why did you look at that young man?" he asked.

"My lord, I couldn't help it." I wondered if this would be the end of me.

"What do you mean, you couldn't help it? Can you be more clear?"

"Papa, when you were talking to him about marriage and the type of woman he should marry, you were describing somebody just like me. Thoughts went through my mind."

"Thoughts? Don't play games with me. What thoughts did you have?"

"I like him, and I thought about what it would be like to be with him."

That was it, as far as my father was concerned. "So now you have committed adultery. You've left me in your own heart and mind for another person."

That was the start of a long night that ended at a laundromat. Once we drove up, I knew we weren't there to wash our dirty clothes. We were there to use the public shower—together.

He got some tokens from the lady working the night shift. Papa told me to get in the shower and wait for him.

The showers were located in the back of the laundromat, away from public view. No one else was there at that time of night, not that it would have mattered to my father.

I had just finished undressing inside the shower when my father opened the door, his face furious and both hands balled into fists. He immediately started pounding me like a prizefighter. My brain was rattled by blow after blow until I started feeling dizzy and nauseous, falling to the floor of the shower.

I saw stars, and everything was spinning around, but my father didn't relent one bit. Sudden darkness came over me, and I was sure I was leaving this earth. I curled up in a fetal position, completely naked, unable to block the booted kicks. Terrible groans came out of my mouth while stuff came out of both ends of my body.

Before I passed out, I felt like I left my body in the shower and looked down on a dying girl.

The next thing I remember is the lady standing at the shower door with my father, handing him a pair of towels and asking him if he needed help.

"No, I can take care of my daughter," he said.

In the haze of the moment, I wished I were dead.

He helped me get dressed and back into the Suburban. My father looked to be worried, which puzzled me. Was he worried that he would get caught beating me? Or was he genuinely concerned about my welfare?

We got in the car and started driving. I had no idea where we were headed.

"Where are we going, Papa?"

"To the hospital. We will sleep there tonight, in the parking lot."

*Hospital? We never went to the hospital unless it was an emergency, and even then . . .*

"Why are we going there?"

"I'm in a lot of pain. I need to be close by so that you can take me to the ER if nothing changes."[1]

---

1. Yes, it's highly ironic that I went to the hospital for my father when it was me who probably needed medical attention following a beating, but that's the way things were.

We parked and tried to sleep, but my father's moaning didn't allow me any rest.

When the sun came up, my father wasn't any better. I was worried, which felt weird to me. This was a man I wished were dead, but since I didn't know anything else and he was my lord and master, I was scared to death I'd lose him—and it would be my fault.

I left Papa in the car and walked into the ER. I told the admittance nurse my father was in bad shape and needed a wheelchair to transport him. Once we were checked in, we were taken to a partitioned ER room where Papa was placed on a bed. Tests were done, and blood work was drawn.

An hour later, a doctor in a white lab coat stepped into our area, pulling the drawn curtain tight.

The doctor consulted his clipboard and then stared at my father, boring a hole through his forehead with his eyes. "Robert Hale, have you been drinking?" he asked.

My father stumbled for words. "No, I don't drink," he blurted.

Which was an out-and-out lie. His deceit shocked me. But what the doctor said next was even a greater surprise.

"Robert Hale, don't lie to me. Do you want our help or not? Your stomach looks like you're pregnant because you're dying of a pancreatitis attack. I need you to cooperate and tell me what's going on."

With a sheepish look on his face, my father admitted that he did drink some wine on occasions. "But it's for medicinal purposes," he added with as much conviction as he could muster. There was no mention of the boxed wine or how much he drank on a regular basis.

The doctor listened, made a notation, and then turned on his heels and left, disgust written on his face. In a later visit, the doctor informed my father in no uncertain terms that he would be a dead man if he took another drink of alcohol.[2]

It also became clear that we weren't going anywhere quickly. My father was checked into a hospital room, where I was impressed with the care he received from the nursing staff. I stayed with him, sleeping on a hard and uncomfortable day couch. Several times, a nurse dropped in and asked, "Is there anything we can do for you? Get some rest. We'll take care of your dad."

Each time I said thanks but no thanks.

One time I fell asleep on the day bed only to wake up hearing the bleating of my father's voice. "Wake up, you sleepyhead. You should take lessons from the nurses taking care of me. They love what they do and do a great job—a way better job than you do."

---

2. Surprisingly, my father stayed away from wine and alcohol for the rest of his life.

Another kick in the teeth. This from someone who tried to get me to take care of his sexual needs whenever the door was closed.

At one point, the handsome young trapper came by to visit. He sat on one side of Papa's bed while I sat on the other side, careful not to make eye contact with our visitor by looking straight down to the linoleum floor.[3]

When he left, I hated myself with a loathing that seemed to deepen in situations like this.

And then something good happened in my unhappy life.

In the winter of 2004, Mama and my four oldest brothers, Joseph, Joshua, David, and Moses, drove to Palmer, Alaska, to get some hay for our horses, which wintered in McCarthy with a nice man who said he'd watch them.

Like all of us who lived at Hillbilly Heaven, the chance to get out from underneath my father's thumb was a draw. Papa was acting more erratically than ever, which could be traced to his declining health. He was horrible to be around, especially after the sun went down.

I stayed behind to take care of the rest of the kids while Mama and my brothers made the trip west. Palmer wasn't around the corner. The small city of 6,500 was more than 250 miles to the west, nearly an all-day drive due to the poorly maintained section of dirt road from McCarthy to Chitina as well as spots of mountainous terrain.

While there, my brothers wanted to visit a home church in the area. We'd stopped going to church years ago; Papa never found a pastor or Bible teacher who matched up eye-to-eye theologically with him. My father had the corner on truth, and he didn't want any other voice influencing us.

My four brothers *wanting* to go to a church was a bit dangerous since my father would never approve of that. But my four brothers, all in their twenties, were willing to take the risk. I have to believe that the chance they'd meet a girl or two swayed their decision as well.

That night, my brothers did meet some cute girls—Sharia and Lolly Buckingham. They were the two oldest of *nine* children belonging to Jim and Martha Buckingham, who lived in Palmer. Nine wasn't quite fifteen, but we had big families in common. And they loved the Lord.

When Mama and my brothers came home from their supply run, they looked surprisingly cheerful and hopeful about something. We soon learned what had happened when we all sat around the big room in the Main House, listening to them tell us that they had met this special family named the Buckinghams.

---

3. I was forbidden to make eye contact with any male close to my age.

"They asked us all kinds of questions and really wanted to know all about our family," Joseph explained. "They're really nice. Just like us."

A hopeful little song began to form in my heart as I listened. More than anything, I longed to meet these older girls that my brothers talked so glowingly about.

Maybe we could become friends with this Buckingham family.

But that all depended on Papa.

He always had the final word.

# 35
# OUT FOR HIRE

When fall came around, my brothers became guides for a big-game hunting company that organized expeditions for Yukon moose and grizzly bear. I could tell that my brothers loved being away as much as the adventure. A bush pilot flew them to a remote hunting camp, where they proved to be very good at tracking wild game for clients.

I took advantage of the fall hunting season as well. I never enjoyed killing animals, but providing meat for my family was a way I could please Papa and not be around him—a win-win. I loved walking day or night alongside horses loaded down with field-dressed moose, joined by my younger brothers. Something about those times in the wilderness fed my spirit, especially the sense of danger since the mountains were infested with grizzly and black bear. We carried .454 Casull pistols on our hips in case of an unexpected encounter.[1]

In the town of McCarthy, it was getting more evident by the day that we were not welcome. The wanigan that Walt Wigger had left behind created a controversy among the townspeople, who didn't appreciate all the junk and old cars we kept on property that wasn't his—or ours. The overrun lot had become an eyesore.

One time, Papa, some of my brothers, and I stayed at the wanigan for a few days. Suddenly, we were surrounded by a dozen or so McCarthyites who gathered around us, eyes glaring. One announced that they had given us plenty of warning, and now it was time to get out.

We already knew we were no longer welcome. We presented this image of

---

1. One time I was walking around Fairbanks, hidden under my cowgirl hat, wearing cowboy clothes with a .454-caliber Casull in a leather holster strapped to my waist. A local woman passed me. "Well, it's Annie Oakley herself," she declared. Naturally, I had no idea that Annie Oakley was a legendary frontier woman and sharpshooter who starred in Buffalo Bill's Wild West Show in the 1880s.

being a poor, needy Christian pioneering family that needed kind, neighborly help, but it was becoming more evident that the way we conducted our lives wasn't very Christian. They also thought Papa was self-righteous and judgmental, and they hadn't forgotten that he had declared that some of them—like the park ranger—were agents of the devil himself.

When the McCarthy townspeople approached the wanigan, Papa had already acquired a piece of property a mile or two outside of McCarthy, on the other side of the footbridge. We could move the ten-by-ten-foot wanigan there easily, but—typical Papa—he took his time doing anything.

Surrounded by a crowd, Papa relished one more opportunity to antagonize and provoke the ungodly.

"Elishaba, get your fiddle.[2] I want you to play and leap for joy for the persecution we are now enduring," he said. As far as Papa was concerned, his prophecy had come true: we were just like Noah's family, standing alone in front of our ark while the world mocked us.

My heart wasn't in it. I did what Papa asked for by playing a song, hopping a bit and scratching the dirt with my shoes, but I couldn't "leap for joy." I felt embarrassed and humiliated in front of these townspeople, who took pity on me.

The wanigan stayed put, at least for the time being. Then Papa had to take an overnight trip for some reason. This was my chance to fix the wanigan mess. I rushed into McCarthy and hired a couple of Christian men, infidels in Papa's eyes, to load the small shed onto a trailer and take it across the private bridge just outside of town. The junk that didn't get thrown away was moved as well.

Papa was quite shocked when he got back, but it was my turn to tell a manipulative story. "My lord," I flattered him, "I had to stand up and protect you from the persecution of the neighbors. This was the only solution I could find. Plus, we already had the property."

I don't think he believed me. Papa chose not to punish me physically, but he banned me from any more contact or activity with the townspeople. "I don't know what's gotten into you," he complained. "You have become a man-pleaser, polluted with worldliness. You and your sisters will henceforth be hidden from the world. You can no longer communicate with any of the locals in McCarthy, and you are to stay out of sight anytime we pass through."

This type of talk went on for weeks. Papa was clearly nervous about the growing independence of my four oldest brothers who had grown into strong, young men, fully capable of handling themselves. He was losing control of them.

"Elishaba, I have a big burden for your brothers," he said one evening at the Main House. "I'm afraid their hearts are being drawn away by the people of

---

2. After Papa goaded me into destroying my fiddle in Soldotna, we found another used one for me to play.

McCarthy. I intend to do something about it. Having our horses in McCarthy is giving them an excuse to keep worldly relationships. We should sell them."

How on earth were we going to resupply our food stores after the breakup season? Or even during winter? We all heard Papa say we should get rid of the snow machines at one time, but I couldn't believe he'd actually go through with such a stupid decision. I'd learned to expect the unexpected from him, however.

Fortunately, he let the thought go, but his crazy ideas and indecisiveness put everyone on edge.

All of us had learned to pick our battles.

When the summer of 2004 came around, the battle we wanted to win was to stay in contact with the Buckinghams. At Hillbilly Heaven, we had a wireless phone system that enabled us to make calls via an antenna located on Sourdough Mountain. We loved calling the Buckinghams. With the phone on speaker, we'd crowd around and talk about what was happening in our lives.[3]

None of this escaped Papa's attention. He threatened me on many occasions that he would stop the phone calls and break off our budding relationship if I let it become more important to me than he was.

"Elishaba, don't forget where your place is," he said. "It's beside me."

Fortunately, there were no young men in the Buckingham family near me in age—just older girls and younger boys. The oldest son was Jim Jr., twelve years younger than me. Otherwise, Papa would have cut all contact immediately.

My four oldest brothers suddenly found reasons to go back and forth to Anchorage on business. When they passed through Palmer—which was on the way—they would stop and visit the Buckinghams. I envied their freedom.

Papa was in a quandary, torn between losing control of my brothers but needing our new friends to keep our horses for the coming winter, which the Buckinghams had graciously agreed to do.

One time, the brothers came home telling us of a conversation they had had with the Buckinghams concerning the Scriptures. I could tell they were being persuaded to see God's Word differently from the way Papa had always taught us. This scared me because I was afraid that our feisty father would do what it took to prove to the brothers they were wrong. Worse, this would give him another opportunity to end our relationship.

We talked on the phone about the two families going on a caribou hunt together. When Papa agreed, the excitement was intense! With Mama staying behind with several of the younger ones, the rest of us met Mr. Buckingham and

---

3. Remember, we had no TV, no radio, no iPods, and no Internet.

the older children in Glennallen, a town of four hundred roughly halfway for both families. When the vanload of Buckinghams arrived, they jumped out and embraced us with hugs and loving acceptance. Then we led them to a rundown cabin where we had squatted before. The cabin was just south of Glennallen near the Tazlina River.

While everyone huddled inside the old cabin, I cooked tortillas and chicken soup for everyone, all the time thinking: *We'll probably be friends for only a little while because this nice family won't be able to stand us after they get to know who we are. Papa will make sure of that.*

Everyone seemed to love dinner, which surprised me since the soup was full of bones and whatever leftovers we had scraped off our plates the day before. After cleaning up, we pulled out our instruments to show the Buckinghams how musically talented we were. Instead of looking down on our hillbilly, out-of-tune bluegrass music, they grabbed their instruments and tried to join in.

The night ended very late. The girls slept outside in a tent and while the guys took over the cabin. I dared not look in Papa's direction as I went with the flow. Crawling into a tent with a bunch of laughing, singing girls was more fun than I had ever known. I had no idea what Papa was thinking, nor did I care. This was a first for me.

A light snowstorm greeted us in the morning, but that wasn't going to stop us from hunting for caribou in the subzero temperatures. Everyone wanted to go, so we hopped into a pair of big vehicles. Papa made me sit up front with him, but my quaking heart was in the back of the passenger van with my newfound friends and siblings.

On the drive north on the Richardson Highway, I noticed Papa looking quite depressed. His black mood shook my soul. He glumly stayed in our eleven-passenger van[4] while I led the older Buckingham girls and my brothers into the woods. To be honest, I didn't care about finding a caribou. I just wanted to experience this little bit of heaven on earth and make it last forever.

Winds swirled clouds of snow around us, turning the landscape into a white canvas. I led everyone, paying attention to where we had come from, but it didn't take long before we got lost. We decided that we better try to make it back to the road. I told everyone not to worry about a thing. "I know my direction in the woods very well, so I will get everyone back," I said.

Lolly, the second oldest Buckingham, was in my corner. "Elishaba, I'm so glad we're with you. We'd really be lost if we didn't have you."

I wasn't so sure. I thought I knew where we were and could find our tracks, but maybe we were lost. But part of me didn't care how lost we were because I

---

4. The Hoffman family, who lived in Glennallen, gave us the passenger van after hearing that one of our cabins burned down at Hillbilly Heaven.

was having so much fun with these Buckingham girls. I did my best to retrace our steps, but it took us a good three hours before we made our way back to the road. Neither van was there, however.

We walked along the two-lane highway. Eventually, Papa appeared in the passenger van. He didn't seem to be very happy. "How come you're so late? Did you get lost?" he asked.

I didn't have a good answer. It just happened. But a desperate thought nagged me: *Now you've ruined everything.*

This was confirmed when we got back to the cabin. Papa started to question Mr. Buckingham about his testimony, but I knew exactly what he was doing. I'd seen it happen dozens of times before: Papa creating disagreement so that he could justify severing our budding friendship.

Mr. Buckingham wasn't flustered at all. He graciously answered my father's questions, but the way my father continually pressed him, it was apparent that he was trying to make mountains out of theological molehills. After a while, I think Mr. Buckingham figured out what was going on.

"Tell you what," he said. "I'll take the kids into town and bring back some lunch. How does that sound?"

Taking a break sounded great. At least the Buckinghams were coming back. No sooner were they on their way than Papa declared that we were dealing with another infidel in our midst. "Mr. Buckingham may seem like a nice man, but it's clear to me that he's a pretend Christian and a deceiver. I have grave doubts about that man and the rest of his family since he's deceived them as well."

Jerusalem spoke in his defense. "No, Papa! They believe in Jesus just like we do!"

Papa was unmoved. When the Buckinghams returned, the tension was thick enough to cut with a Buck knife. We did our best to ignore what had transpired, and "girl time" in the tent was fantastic. When our three-day hunting trip came to a close, it was time to say goodbye to the Buckinghams.

We girls were crying as we parted with long, embracing hugs. I wondered why these kind people loved us ragamuffins so dearly. When Sharia squeezed me tight, I could feel her communicating that she hurt for me. "I'm praying for you," she whispered. "We'll be waiting for all of you at our house."

That's right. Before trekking for caribou, we had already made plans to go to their house after the hunt—all the Papa Pilgrim family. Some things needed to be worked out, but the idea was that we'd drive back to McCarthy and pick up Mama and the rest of the children and then caravan to Palmer, where Mr. Buckingham assured us that they had plenty of room and open hearts.

Would Papa call it off?

Standing outside the cabin, I waved as the Buckinghams drove away, tears building in my eyes. Then I ran to the outhouse and sobbed.

"Oh, God, please help me now," I pleaded. "I know Papa's mad and that I have it coming. Please don't let me lose the Buckinghams!"

As soon as I walked back into the cabin, Papa got out of his chair to address all of us.

"So what do you all think about Jim Buckingham. Is he saved or not?"

This was a classic no-win question. If we said, "Yes," Papa would condemn us and denounce us as being deceived. If we said, "No," he would condemn us for associating with an infidel. Looking around the room, I could tell my brothers felt the same way I did.

When Joseph came to Mr. Buckingham's defense, Papa's response was predictable: "Jim Buckingham is such a deceiver that he even deceived my own children. Can you see what a danger this man is to my family?"

My father's face flushed with anger as he recounted a conversation in which one of my younger brothers described shooting a caribou even though he was too young and didn't have a license. Papa jumped in and said *he* had shot the beast, but the looks on my brother's face and the rest of our faces said he was lying. An awkward moment ensued in front of the Buckinghams. Papa was embarrassed that he'd been caught in a lie.

His rant continued, condemning us for quickly turning and listening to another man speak about God's truth, which struck me as hollow. For the last five to seven years, I hadn't seen Papa reading his Bible very much, let alone teaching us out of the Good Book like he used to do when we older kids were old enough to listen.

"I will speak up for Mr. Buckingham," I said. "I thought what he had to say about grace was excellent. Grace is something we don't earn because it's a free gift from God, given to all who believe in His Son, Jesus Christ."

My knees knocked as I waited for my father to explode. This wasn't happening because of a theological disagreement between him and Mr. Buckingham. This was happening because my siblings and I were having fun with the Buckingham kids and ignoring him. He was jealous.

Suddenly, Papa grabbed a piece of two-by-four lumber next to the fireplace. He immediately started beating one of my younger brothers, who held up his arms to block the blows.

I stepped between them. "No, Papa. I'm the one you need to hit. I'm the one you're angry with."

He raised the two-by-four and was about to strike me—

—when Joshua grabbed his arm.

A struggle ensued, but my twenty-five-year-old brother was too strong for him. He wrestled the stick of lumber to the ground and kicked it away.

Papa, after catching his breath, looked at me, eyes blazing. He pointed to the door.

"Get out! Now!"

Sockless, I slipped on my boots, grabbed a coat, stepped out into the bitter cold, and started walking. I was woefully underdressed for the subzero temperatures.

*Papa said go, so this time I will keep going.*

Nearby was the Tazlina River. The ice-covered river was too wide and fast to be completely frozen in the middle.

*Perfect*, I thought. *I can walk toward the middle, crack through the ice, fall in, and drown in the freezing water. Since I would be trying to cross the river, I wouldn't be taking my own life. God will forgive me.*

Each time I got close to the edge where I might break through the ice, leading to an icy death, I couldn't take that last step. But then the contours of a new plan came into mind: I would make it look like I fell into the freezing river. Then I would head toward McCarthy, walking through the wilderness and covering my tracks. Before the night was over, I'd surely freeze to death. But I didn't care. Papa had commanded me to go, and his order resulted in my death.

I really wanted to die and be done with this crummy life. What did I have to live for? More sexual abuse from my father? More beatings, more verbal lashings? I barely ate or got enough food to eat as it was. I'd eaten only one meal in the last eighteen days. I hadn't consumed any of the chicken soup or tortillas that I prepared for the Buckinghams after our arrival.

I don't know how far I walked on this cold trail of dark despair. All I knew was that my sockless feet felt frozen. Every now and then, I'd sit down in a pillow of snow and rub my feet to increase circulation. Then I'd start moving again.

The next time I sat down, I was too exhausted to move any further. I was freezing to death and knew it. I closed my eyes. I was ready to let Death come to me. I lay down in a fetal position, my teeth chattering.

Then I heard voices in the distance—the voices of my younger brothers. When they found me, they told me how stupid I'd been, that I could have died in the extreme cold, exposed to the elements.

I was too mentally out of it to argue. My brothers dragged me to the highway, where Papa was waiting in the heated van.

Not much was said on the drive back to the cabin, where Joseph and Joshua were waiting.

Later, they would tell me that Papa had not permitted them to go looking for me. They believed he forbid them to go because he knew they would have never allowed me to go back to Papa if they had found me.

Which was probably true. But like me, my brothers were trapped as well.

We all were.

# 36
# THE MEMORY CARD

After my near-death experience in the snow, there was a change of plans. No, Papa didn't cancel our trip. Thank goodness that was still on. But he directed my younger brothers to drive back to McCarthy and pick up Mama and the rest of the children. Then they would caravan back to this cabin south of Glennallen. From there, we'd drive on to Palmer, where the Buckinghams lived.

Which meant Papa and I would be alone in the cabin for a couple of days, and that wouldn't be good for me.

I approached my older brothers. "Please, just ask Papa if one of you can stay here with us. I can't explain why. It's too hard. But I know Papa will treat me nicer if someone else is here."

Joseph, Joshua, and David looked at each other knowingly. "Elishaba, you know we can't do that," Joseph said. "First of all, Papa would never agree, but we don't want to even ask 'cause if we did, he would call off this trip to the Buckinghams. You know how important this is to us."

I groaned, but I understood their predicament.

My father waited an hour or so after their departure, and then he started beating me ferociously.

"So, you're willing to forsake me for a bunch of unbelieving girls?"

*Thwack.*

"How come you're ignoring me? Aren't I important to you?"

*Thwack.*

"You have willingly disobeyed me with a rebellious spirit that God hates with a vengeance."

*Thwack.*

I'd been battered before, but this assault was at a much higher level in intensity and fury. It was like all of Papa's frustrations at seeing my older brothers seek and gain more and more independence—and keep their hard-earned money in their own pockets—were coming to a head.

I moaned from the pain and wished I could die for the second time in twenty-four hours. There were purple bruises from my shoulders on down. I curled up on the floor and wept. The bitterness I felt was genuine.

Then I heard his voice.

"Take off your clothes. I want you to dance for me."

*What?*

I saw an object in his hand. It was one of those new cameras I'd heard my brothers talking about—something about being digital and not needing film.

"What are you worried about?" my father continued. "There's no one around. Come on. I want to see you."

I straightened up. "But I don't know how to dance," I mumbled, which was true.

"Oh, yes, you do. You just don't want to, but I'm commanding you to do this for me."

This back-and-forth went on for a while until I realized that resistance was futile. I started stripping off my clothes—and noticed Papa doing the same.

He sat down on the edge of the bunk bed and held up the camera at me. He was fully aroused, which repulsed me.

"Come on, move. Make it go. If you can't, then get me the whip. That'll make you move."

My head was spinning—from what Papa asked me to do and from a lack of food.

"Papa, I can't stand anymore," I said with a faint voice. I began to sink to the floor. My body was shutting down.

Papa quickly got up and helped me into the bottom bunk bed. Then he handed me the camera and told me to film the vilest acts that can happen between a father and a daughter. This went on into the night until he fell asleep.

When I woke up in the morning, I dressed for a visit to the outhouse. When I returned, Papa was stirring, but he was too lazy to go outside to relieve himself.

"Help me," he said. "I need the pee cup."

I thought of the many times at the homestead when I would be half-asleep only to wake up with his pee all over me. No wonder our bed smelled like urine.

He always had me hold his private when he needed to use the pee cup, and this occasion was no different. So gross!

Then he had something else for me to do.

"When we get back to the homestead, I want you to sew a little leather pocket onto the side of my Bible case."

"How come?"

"So I can put this special card there."

Papa reached for the camera and pressed a button, which released a wafer-thin memory card.

My heart sank. This would be one of the dirtiest jobs my father asked me to do, which was saying something. Attaching images of the evil things we did next to the Word of God didn't feel right.

Not at all.

When the family arrived, there was lots of exciting talk about going to the Buckinghams' place. Not wanting to put a damper on things, I did my best to assume a happy face even though there was no hint of a smile inside of me.

While cleaning up the cabin and packing up, I decided to change my shirt into something cleaner while everyone was outside. Only Jerusalem was inside with me.

"Elishaba, what happened?"

My sister was staring at my upper arms and shoulders, which were black-and-blue from the beating.

"Oh, it's nothing," I managed as I finished buttoning up the new shirt. I thought of what Papa had said when he saw the bruises during his filming. "That's what I love about you, Elishaba. You're courageous and willing to lay down your life for me. Even your brothers are cowards and shrink at my punishments."

A suspicious look came over Jerusalem's face. "You're lying," she declared.

I ignored her. I was not about to make a scene and give Papa an excuse to cancel our trip to the Buckinghams' home.

Spirits were high as we took off for Palmer. I sat on the floor between Papa and Mama's bucket seats in the front of the passenger van, feeling like a bag of wheat. Papa demanded that I keep my hand on his leg and "care" for him the entire way. I couldn't see out from the floor, leaving me feeling demeaned and miserable. Mama never said a thing; she was used to her husband's ungodly behavior.

Relief came when we found our way to the Buckinghams' log cabin in a snowy neighborhood known as Lazy Mountain. The family of eleven surrounded us with hugs and even a few tears as Mr. Buckingham introduced his wife, Martha. Before we knew it, all twenty-eight of us were standing in a huge circle, holding hands and singing a hymn, followed by a prayer from Mr. Buckingham thanking God for bringing our families together again.

Lurking in the back of my mind was this all-important question: *Where am I going to sleep?*

When we stepped inside their home, I saw that the Buckingham girls had prepared beds and places for all of the Hale girls in their bedrooms, which sounded great to me. My brothers would stay with their brothers. My parents would sleep in their unfinished basement, where curtained-off beds were set up for them.

I knew this arrangement wasn't going to work for Papa, but even my father knew that having me stay with him the entire night would invite questions that he didn't want to hear.

So he came up with a plan. At our first dinner, he boasted about how I faithfully cared for him, making it sound like he was a medical basket case who needed me to massage his hurting knees and rub his arthritic feet so he could fall asleep. I also administered his insulin shots since he had diabetes. But when I was done, I'd be free to join the girls in their bedroom.

So that's what I did the first night—finding myself in the basement with Papa and Mama. Finally, when Papa was finished with me, I went upstairs and crawled into my bed next to Sharia, the oldest. She was still awake and flashed a warm smile.

"I've been waiting for you," she said. "Are you okay?"

She must have had the spiritual gift of discernment because her question unnerved me. I was afraid she might draw the truth out of me.

"Oh, yes, everything's fine," I babbled. "Papa just needed me to rub his knees a little longer tonight."

Telling the lie hurt, especially because Sharia and her sisters had been so open and welcoming to me and my family, who'd been told that we could stay as long as we wanted.

In the morning, Mr. Buckingham, a lieutenant colonel in the U.S. Army, drove to Anchorage, where he worked at the Alaska Command. Mrs. Buckingham was homeschooling the Buckingham children, so my younger siblings joined them even though they had far less education than I had and couldn't read or write very well.

I noticed that Mrs. Buckingham had the children highly organized, and their chores never seemed like work. Their family closeness was an eye-opener to me, especially at dinnertime when Mr. and Mrs. Buckingham went around the family room—they didn't have a dinner table big enough to seat so many—and thanked each person for what they did that day. How the parents went out of their way to recognize the children's hard work and accomplishments, including any Hales, was something I'd never experienced.

After several dinners of hearing commendations and "atta-boys," Papa was becoming unglued at how the Buckingham family seemed to have it all together. When we retired to the basement for the evening, he expressed his pent-up exasperation.

"These people are going against the Word of God," he said, which made no sense to me. "They think they can mix God with the world by the way they dress to fit in and look nice to everyone. Jim is leading his family astray. Why, he doesn't even believe in God's predestination of mankind, that He chooses who He wants to be with Him in heaven. He's a wolf in sheep's clothing preaching that we have free wills to choose God. And I'll tell you one more thing: it's ludicrous that he thinks that once saved you're always saved. If a man turns away from God, he is cast out forever, and that's all there is to it."

But my father was just getting warmed up.

"On top of that, they have idols in this house. I need to start purging this house. I really don't know why it's taking me so long."

Uh-oh. My father was going to make a scene.

"Oh, Papa, can't you give us some time to talk to them? I'm sure when they see how wrong it is to have idols, they will change."[1]

My controlling father ignored me. He walked upstairs to the dining room table, where some decorative artificial burgundy grapes sat in a bowl. He grabbed them and threw the plastic grapes into the kitchen trash can. I was afraid he was going to throw their mirrors and dolls in the trash as well. It's a good thing they didn't have a TV, the ultimate idol in Papa's eyes.

James Jr., a teenager, happened to watch everything unfold. "What are you doing?" he asked after Papa unceremoniously threw away the fake grapes.

"These are evil idols, and I have a responsibility to purge your home," my father replied.

If the Buckinghams thought this was bizarre behavior, they didn't say anything. Fortunately, Papa must have felt like he made his point because he didn't search for dolls in the girls' rooms.

Another thing I noticed was how disciplined Mr. Buckingham was regarding meal times. When he said dinner was at 6:30, then every Buckingham had to be ready to eat.

This presented a problem because our family was not permitted to eat until Papa appeared and took the first bite, but who knew when that would be? Papa had never been punctual about anything in his life.

During our three-week stay with the Buckinghams, there would be many times when the Buckinghams would finish eating their meal while we were still waiting for Papa to appear. Our stomachs would be growling from the delicious smells and sights of bacon, scrambled eggs, coffee cake, casseroles, hamburgers, and hot dogs.

And then it happened. One evening, while we were having fun playing music and talking, it was nearing midnight. Mr. Buckingham said it was time

---

1. I had been careful not to call my father "my lord" when around the Buckinghams. That would have really stirred the pot.

for everyone to go to bed.

A switch flipped in Papa's mind.

"Who are you to tell us when to go to bed? I can tell that you're not a man who is following the Spirit. Instead, you're led by your fleshly desires and full of vanity that's not pleasing to God," he exploded.

Mr. Buckingham did not respond in kind. "Thank you for sharing what's on your heart," he said. "But it's a weeknight, and we get up early around here. Okay, everyone. It's bedtime!"

My father made no move to stand up. To make a point, he kept us playing music for a while longer even though the Buckinghams all went to bed.

One evening, I stood in the kitchen helping the girls wash the dishes and noticed Mr. Buckingham walk over to my father and sit down next to him. Something told me that something interesting was about to happen.

Then Lolly said we should all go for a walk when we finished drying the dishes.

*Papa will never let me leave him to have fun with the girls, so I can't say yes. But I want to go so bad.*

I glanced sideways and noticed Mr. Buckingham, appearing grave, talking in a low voice to my father.

"Don't you want to take a walk with us girls?" Lolly asked.

"Yeah, I do, but I have to make sure it's okay with Papa first," I replied.

Papa must have heard me say this because he turned away from Mr. Buckingham and said I could go on the walk, but he wanted me to see him when I returned. For once, I had played my cards right to win a bit of freedom.

I didn't waste any time since I knew Papa could change his mind. We quickly gathered our jackets and gloves and were out the door. It felt like a dream as we girls walked down the road, laughing and throwing snowballs at each other. Even though I was twenty-eight years old, I almost felt like a child again, acting a little bit out of control, with excitement propelling each step.

When we returned, there was a strange tension in the air. I realized Papa was down in the basement and was probably quite angry that I'd been away so long.

Just before I headed down the stairs, Mrs. Buckingham stopped me. "Don't go down there right now, Elishaba. Jim is talking to your Papa, and he needs some time."

Immediately, my heart began racing. *What on earth should I do? If I tell Papa that Mrs. Buckingham told me not to go down there and he finds out that I obeyed her over him—*

Disconcerted, I responded rudely to Mrs. Buckingham. "I *have* to go down there! You can't stop me. Papa wants me down there right now."

She nodded, but her voice took on a stern tone. "Oh, yes, I can. You're not going down there right now. I want to see you go upstairs to where the girls are. You can visit there."

This was indeed a big step for me—obeying someone else's orders over what I knew Papa wanted me to do. In one of the bedrooms, I found the girls sitting around talking and having a good time. I did my best to join in, but my chaotic thoughts persisted.

*What could Mr. Buckingham be talking to Papa about?* It had to be serious. Maybe they were having a discussion about me, which filled my heart with fear. If the Buckinghams found out about my relationship with Papa, I knew this would be our last day here.

One of the girls had gotten out her Bible to share something she learned. A thought came to mind: I would convince these girls that marriage was wrong and that we should be thinking about being unmarried virgins dedicated to God and our fathers for the rest of our lives.

There was one chapter in the Bible that I knew practically by heart: 1 Corinthians 7. I reached for another Bible and read them the pertinent verses about how the one who stands firm in his heart, has authority over his own will, and has decided in his own heart to keep his own virgin will do well in this present life.

I felt sure I was convincing as they graciously listened. Then Sharia opened her Bible and asked us to look at 1 Timothy 4, which described how in later times some would abandon the faith and forbid people to marry, but everything that God created is good, including marriage. Then she boldly shared from the first book of Genesis that God designed marriage to meet our need for companionship and provide an illustration of our relationship with Him.

I'll admit that the scales were coming off my eyes. For the first time, I felt like someone else might be backing up my suspicions that Papa was deceiving me about what God wanted.

Feeling quite discombobulated, I mustered up enough courage to take a stand, knowing Papa would settle for nothing less. If I didn't, I'd have to confess to my father that I didn't confront this onslaught or do my best to convince these girls that they were wrong.

We were having a lively discussion when someone brought word that Papa was done talking with Mr. Buckingham and had called for me. Any time in my life Papa called for me, my heart sank to my boots. This occasion was no different.

When I arrived in the basement, I hoped to hear how it went with Mr. Buckingham, but Papa didn't want to talk about that. Instead, he questioned me closely, checking why I hadn't come down earlier.

"I needed you to stand up for me," he said pathetically, like he had been on the losing end of an argument. "Where were you? Why didn't you come to be with me?"

"Please forgive me, Papa," I said. Then, I tried to reassure him by adding, "I heard you two were talking, so I took the opportunity to try to convince the Buckingham girls of what we believe about marriage." For once, he seemed satisfied with my response and nodded approvingly.

I would later learn that Mr. Buckingham had gone to my papa specifically to ask him if he had a sexual relationship with me, his daughter. Papa lied, not only denying it outright, but he volunteered to Mr. Buckingham that he had never lusted after another woman other than his wife.

The next day, I fixed my father a cup of coffee and was walking down to the basement when I heard my parents having a heated discussion behind the curtains.

I stopped and listened. They hadn't heard me come down the steps.

"It sounds like they let the mother go, even though she knew about it." Mama sounded a bit desperate.

*Oh, my heart. Who are my parents talking about?*

Then I heard my father's voice, strained. "Well, Jim is a danger to us. I believe he is trying to catch me in the wrong. Sounds like he turned that man in for having sex with his daughter. She was underage, so that's how they got him."

*Underage? What does underage mean?* I wondered.

Mama spoke next. "Not really. She was only seventeen, but it sounds like she was already eighteen when they caught the guy and put him in jail for raping his daughter."

And then I heard the most disturbing thing ever from my father.

"That's why I don't have to worry about anything. Elishaba was nineteen, and she wanted it."

*Oh, my word. That is enough.*

I carefully tiptoed back upstairs and heated Papa's coffee while their conversation spun in my mind. So that's what Mr. Buckingham must have been talking to Papa about.[2]

Just then, I heard Papa calling for me and asking me where his coffee was.

---

2. When Mr. Buckingham spoke with my father, he told him how he had gone to the authorities and told them about a father raping his seventeen-year-old daughter. The man was arrested, tried, and convicted of incest and rape and was serving his sentence in an Alaskan prison. What Mr. Buckingham was doing was sending my father a message that he could be next, which is why my parents were having an intense conversation while I eavesdropped.

When I arrived in the basement, Papa peppered me with questions.

"What took you so long? Where have you been?"

I had to come up with an excuse quickly. "I was making your coffee and going to the bathroom," I lied.

My answer got him off my back. A part of me felt encouraged, however.

Now someone else knew what I was going through.

# 37

# MORE UPHEAVAL

On a difficult night, Papa kept me up late in the Buckinghams' basement. When he finally said I could go, I trudged up the basement stairs, feeling used by a horrible deceiver, but also feeling that I couldn't go to the girls' room because I was such an awful hypocrite.

I grabbed my coat and snuck outside, where I crawled into a bench seat in our passenger van. I pulled my coat over me and wept for a long time.

"Oh, God, I cannot live a two-faced life like this anymore. I feel so degraded. So miserable. Where are You, Lord? Why do the Buckinghams' daughters get to be free? I don't see their papa angry with them or making them stay close to him."

I don't know when my tumbling words ended because I fell asleep within moments.

I awoke to the sound of someone calling my name. Sunlight filled the vehicle. I stirred, then swung open the side door. When the three older Buckingham girls saw me, they ran in my direction. They helped me out of the van with teary hugs.

"What's wrong?" Sharia asked. "Why are you out here?"

While their love and concern lifted my spirits, I tried to push them away.

"Please, let me go. I have to see Papa. Otherwise, he will be mad at me."

They tried to convince me otherwise, but I had to leave them. I hustled inside their log cabin home and took the stairs to their basement, where I found Papa. He was upset with me for causing such an upheaval among everyone.

"What are you doing, Elizabeth?" he asked, purposely using my old first name to let me know that I had done something stupid. "And what do you plan to say to them now?"

I made up some plausible story that calmed Papa's nerves. With a nod, he sent me upstairs to survive another day on my wits.

The following morning, before breakfast, I was in the girls' room getting ready for the day when Mrs. Buckingham asked if she could come in and have a word with me. I didn't know what to say because Papa always wanted me to see him upon waking up each morning, but Mrs. Buckingham was insistent.

"I'm concerned for you, Elishaba," she said. "Is there anything wrong? You seem so attached to your papa."

I struggled to find an answer. Sharia and Lolly shared looks of concern.

"It's hard to explain," I began. "You see, Papa needs me all the time. You've seen the insulin shots I give him. If I'm not there for him, he gets discouraged."

One of the younger girls came inside the room and whispered conspiratorially to Mrs. Buckingham. "Papa Pilgrim is right outside the door," she said.

*What was he doing up here?*

Mrs. Buckingham pulled me deeper into the room and whispered, "Elishaba, do you have a sexual relationship with your papa?"

I nearly fainted in shock. I knew what she was asking, even though I wasn't sure what *sexual* meant. No one had ever asked me this question before. I was too frightened to answer, but I also knew I could not lie. Instead, I chose to sidestep her question.

"It's been hard having people accusing me of having a relationship with Papa like I'm his wife."

My brave front dissolved. I buckled over in tears as Mrs. Buckingham wrapped her loving arms around me.

"Don't worry," she said. "I have to ask because there are people in this world who don't treat their daughters right and have a wrong relationship with them. We just went through this with another family. The dad went to jail because he was sexually abusing his daughter."

I couldn't believe my ears. I had never heard or thought that any other daughter in the whole world had suffered what I'd gone through.

"If you ever need someone to talk to, I'm here for you. There's nothing to be afraid about," Mrs. Buckingham tenderly added.

I bit my lip. Her comforting words traveled deep into my heart, but I knew I had to act like we never had this conversation because Papa would question me.

Then I heard my name being called from the hallway. It was Papa.

"I have to go."

I quickly wiped away my tears and found Papa sitting outside the door. The controlling look in his eyes spelled trouble. For a moment, I contemplated running back into the consoling arms of Mrs. Buckingham.

Instead, I grimly followed Papa into the basement where he questioned me—for hours. I did all I could to reassure him that I stood my ground with Mrs. Buckingham and didn't say a thing about our relationship. I also made it clear how important it was to me that I remain faithful to him.

Then he ordered me to stay in the basement, even though Christina Buckingham had promised to take me for a dogsled ride. She loved animals and had a dog team. Now I was stuck in this prison and feared what the Buckingham family might think of me. What was Papa telling them? Would they feel sorry for me?

My dark world seemed so gloomy compared to this family. The Buckingham home was filled with life, joy, and love. Though Papa tried to convince me our life was righteous and right, it certainly looked evil when I compared it to theirs. How could their way of life be wrong when all they did was continue to love us as if we were a part of their own dear family? My tortured thoughts went round and round while I remained in my dungeon all alone after my father left me to contemplate my sins.

I cried out to the only power I knew. God was deeply connected with my papa in my mind, yet there was something different about the God I increasingly encountered in Palmer. I knew He heard my cries, even when Papa wasn't around. However, I still had a hard time believing in Him and trusting that He felt my pain.

Nonetheless, I felt compelled to cry out as I lay my face on the bed.

"Oh God, even though Papa says what we're doing is right, I feel like such a sinner. I feel like You have turned Your head away from me because I'm such a wretch. If what we're doing is wrong, Jesus, please show Papa and please help the Buckinghams tell him. Please, make our family like their family because I can't go on like this."

Suddenly, I heard a faint call from a distance. I immediately stopped crying and held my breath.

"Elishaba . . . Elishaba . . . Elishaba . . ."

I wanted to answer badly, but Papa had commanded me not to say a word.

Lydia Buckingham, just eight years old, kept calling, "Elishaba, Elishaba, where are you? We want you to play with us."

She seemed to be running all through the house calling, but her voice faded. I was left alone once again.

*Wait a minute. I'm not alone! God sent a little voice to tell me that someone is thinking about me.*

And that was enough to keep me going for one more day.

I don't know how the Buckinghams put up with us as we entered our third week with them.

And I don't know why Papa didn't say it was time to pack up and go.

Then Moses, our quiet brother, approached the Buckinghams on behalf of all the Pilgrim children and begged them to never forsake us. He explained how we had been rejected and abandoned by others our entire lives. To be rejected by them would be devastating.

In a quiet moment, I found Mrs. Buckingham alone in the kitchen. There was something I had to say from my heart.

"I don't know how to explain this, but you are probably going to suffer a lot of hardships through our family," I said. "Please, please don't ever turn away from us. If something does happen, just know that we children really do love you and want to be a part of your family."

Mrs. Buckingham was touched. "Let me reassure you that we will never stop loving you."

That evening, though, Papa picked another fight over the meaning of some piece of Scripture.

Mr. Buckingham refused to be drawn into the conversation. "You know, I love to talk about the Word of God, but I don't believe it would be beneficial for our relationship, or wise, to put the family through a discussion about scriptural differences that only promote contention."

I leaned back behind Papa so he could not see me giving Mr. Buckingham a thumbs-up, which left me feeling guilty.

For the first time, Papa chose not to fight back. But that didn't mean he had been defeated.

The next time we were in the basement, he fumed. "I told you Jim would fail the test," he complained. "He couldn't even answer the question I asked him. Instead of being a man about it, he was a coward right there in front of his children. Everything I've been telling you is true about him being a deceiver."

The following evening, when we gathered for dinner, Mr. Buckingham clinked his glass with his knife. "I'm asking that while the Hales are in our home that we do not discuss scriptural doctrines," he announced. "I feel it will not be edifying to the Lord, nor will it build our relationship together as two families."

Papa picked at his food, stewing. He waited until dessert was served, and then he ordered my siblings and me to meet him in the basement.

Once there, his outrage bubbled to the surface. "We're living in a hypocrite's house, like sheep surrounded by wolves," he began. "I hope you children can see the hypocrisy of the Buckinghams. They won't even allow us to talk about Jesus in their own home. What kind of people are these that you claim to love?"

We hung our heads and dared not say a thing.

"These people are full of vanity mirrors all over their house and don't even go to church in everyday clothes. They iron their nice new clothing and dress up to act godly one day a week."

Papa was referring to the one time they took us to their church and wore their "Sunday best."

He wasn't finished laying down the law. Papa said we could no longer sleep in the same rooms with their children, and the boys would sleep in the horse trailer outside.

"Oh, and one more thing. I better not hear that you guys have stopped talking about Jesus. Now go."

I started to join my siblings, but Papa quickly called me back.

"Elizabeth, you will not go with them. Since you have defended the Buckinghams, you will not leave my side."

That night, I had to sleep in the basement with my father. But this was not the worst thing that happened. When we went upstairs in the morning, we found my brothers with sad looks on their faces. The house was quiet. I didn't see any Buckinghams or hear Mrs. Buckingham in the kitchen, cooking breakfast.

With a sad voice, Joshua said, "The Buckinghams are gone. Mr. Buckingham took his whole family to work with him this morning. He woke up my brothers and me before they left and reassured us that they loved us, but they could not be around us anymore."

I was crestfallen. My younger sisters began weeping and crying, but Papa didn't have time for that. "Pack up. We're leaving," he said.

Before we departed, the whole family—except for Papa and me—hung messages of love and gratitude for their hospitality on their walls.

And then we hit the road. Instead of heading back to Hillbilly Heaven, Papa led us in the direction of the Kenai Peninsula, where we had piles of logs that we could turn into lumber and hard cash.

Cutting timber on the Kenai Peninsula was a great antidote to the pain we felt losing the Buckinghams. Working hard helped us forget how sad we felt. Papa gave us no time to grieve our loss anyway. He became even more grossly demanding toward me, and his unwelcome attention gave me no peace, even in front of the family.

We stayed in an old bus we had set up near the Kenai River. Papa would lie on the bed inside, watching me through the dirty window as I helped my brothers saw lumber. His eyes searched for me like a laser beam, focused and burning.

Anytime Papa was out of earshot, we couldn't stop talking about the Buckinghams. We complained about Papa and how his combative behavior ruined relationships for all of us.

Though I joined in, a heavy weight of guilt fell upon me. I knew how displeased Papa would be if he knew what we were saying about him. Not only were we going against Papa's wishes by talking about the Buckinghams, but the brothers were becoming more and more outspoken about a father whose whims ruled their lives.

Whenever Papa wanted to be alone with me, he would drive me to a little laundromat where there were showers. Along the way, he questioned me about all the things my brothers and I were talking about. I repeatedly lied to him about our conversations to deflect his wrath away from us. I didn't want Papa to know we questioned him in any way, but he was not convinced.

Once again, my father tried hard to use biblical examples to prove that his sexual relationship with me was good and right before God. The more he tried, the more stubborn I became against him and his self-serving use of God's Word, but that only fueled his anger. In my heart, I was becoming more convinced of his wickedness. I believe God's Spirit was strengthening that conviction.

During one of our laundromat outings, Papa gave it another try.

"My dove, God has revealed to me an even greater place of understanding about your relationship with me."

He acted as if I was on his side in this sin, which only served to increase my sense of disgust.

Undeterred, he rattled on. "God has given me a new name for you. It's Abishag."

He explained that Abishag was the beautiful young Shunammite woman who served King David in his old age. One of her duties was to lie in his bosom and keep him warm.

"David was no longer spending time with Bathsheba, his wife," he reminded us fervently. "When David was long dead, no one could ever have Abishag because she was committed to being his for the rest of her life. This meant he also went all the way with her. In other words, he called her his virgin even though he went in unto her."

*What?*

I knew what my father was asking for: he wanted to get me pregnant. The idea terrified me. There was something else he was saying: he no longer needed Mama to have children.

A deep sense of foreboding came over me because it was becoming quite obvious where his jealous mind was taking him. Nothing good could come out of this. He wanted me to accept that nothing could ever change between us, and even if he died, I would be bound to him for the rest of my life.

The horror of that thought dismayed and depressed me. Would there never be a way for me to escape Papa Pilgrim, even after he was dead?

As if reading my mind, my father's full intention became shockingly clear.

"My number one prayer has always been that our family would either live or die together," he said. "But God has changed that prayer in my heart. My number one prayer now is that you would accept me all the way, with nothing holding you back."

I stood as cold as stone. There was no way in the world I would agree to become pregnant by my father voluntarily. The very idea sickened me in its sheer wickedness.

*Jesus, NO!* I cried out.

The issue hung between us, rancid as rotten meat. Each time the subject came up, I fought against him furiously.

Then he tried a different approach. "The Bible says a father can marry his daughter, but the only reason why we haven't already is because the world today wouldn't understand it," he said.

Then he tried to justify his position by saying Lot married his daughters after the destruction of Sodom and Gomorrah. "If you read the story properly, you would see that God eventually blessed Lot with descendants through his daughters."

Everything in me wanted to scream. I couldn't believe that a holy and just God would support such a relationship between a father and a daughter when everything in my tortured, God-given conscience cried out that it was wrong, wrong, wrong!

But I didn't know enough to argue, so my tongue was silent. But Papa gave me an idea: I could read the story of Lot and see for myself. Though I could only read slowly and with difficulty, I decided to find out the truth about Lot and his daughters.

When Papa wasn't around, I found the story of Lot in Genesis 19 and read how Lot and his family fled Sodom after angels warned them of the impending destruction of the city and neighboring Gomorrah. Then Lot's wife turned back to gaze at the destruction, despite being warned not to, and turned into a pillar of salt.

Lot and his two daughters escaped and lived in a cave away from any civilization. The daughters were worried that no other men were available to help them conceive children, so they got their father drunk and had sex with him. They never "married" their father. They just conceived children with him.[1]

Before I could say anything to Papa, he caught wind of my secret search while we were still in Kenai.

"Elishaba, you don't need to read the Bible. You're a woman, and women

---

1. I also discovered that Scripture was quite clear that Abishag did not have sexual relations with David in 1 Kings 1:1-4.

learn from their head, the man. I am that man for you."

"But I was reading about Lot and his daughters, and the Bible doesn't say anything about them getting mar—"

My father balled his fist.

"By the way, I want to start hearing you call me 'lord' a lot more than you do. You've gotten away from that habit, and I want to hear it again. Do you understand?"

"Yes," I managed.

Then, seeing his angry face, I quickly added, "Lord."

But I wasn't about to give up. One time when Papa wasn't around, I approached my mother.

"Mama, Papa once told me that you knew the Bible well. Is my relationship with him wrong? Have you found anything in the Bible?"

Mama shook her head. A look of sympathy came over her face. "It's true that I know the Bible well, but nothing I bring to your father works. He turns it all around and twists Scripture to fit whatever he wants to be true. I'm sorry, but I gave up on that a long time ago."

One day, sometime after noon, we looked up from sawing logs and saw a familiar fifteen-passenger van driving toward us, kicking up mud on the dirt road. In a few moments, the entire Buckingham family swarmed out and embraced us with holy hugs that felt like they came from heaven.

They visited for a few hours and shared a picnic lunch they had brought with them. But then they said they had to drive back to their home in Palmer, which astounded me. They would drive four hundred miles that day just to tell us that they loved us.

I wished they could have stayed for several days instead of a few hours. Before they left, Jim and Martha Buckingham said we were welcome to join them for Christmas, a couple of weeks away.

My younger siblings jumped for joy. I clutched my chest in delight. Such love!

But then we all looked to Papa to see what he had to say. We had never celebrated Christmas, exchanged presents, or had a special Christmas meal because Christmas was a pagan holiday, my father said. Christmas was just another day for us.

But we did have good feelings about the Christmas season because back in the Lower 48, playing hillbilly Christmas music on street corners and in farmer's markets earned us a lot of money. Folks were generous during the holidays.

I don't know why Papa said yes to the invitation. Perhaps it was because the

Buckinghams were still taking care of our horses for the winter, and he feared that saying no would put us in a bind.

Or maybe he thought that saying yes would please my older brothers, who were becoming bolder and bolder in letting Papa know that they didn't *have to* stick around.

Whatever the reason, I was just glad to have something to look forward to.

This was going to be the best Christmas ever!

# 38
# CHRISTMAS DAY

On the frigid morning of a snowy Christmas Day, 2004, the Pilgrim family parked their vehicles and walked up the Buckinghams' driveway to the friendly log cabin they called home.

The door flung open, and we were embraced with a flurry of hugs, tears, and greetings of "Merry Christmas!" The Buckinghams' gracious hearts made us feel welcome, especially after the awkward way our last visit to their home on Lazy Mountain ended. I spotted an empty corner in the family room; that must have been where their Christmas tree and presents had been, but the family removed the tree and their gifts to not offend Papa.

For the next few days, my brothers helped the family build new fences to be neighborly since they were keeping our eight horses there during the harsh winter months. There were runs to the local feed store to buy hay, which was stored under tarps.

After the fifth day, Papa had enough. We were downstairs in the basement late one afternoon when he told me bluntly that he wanted to end our relationship with the Buckinghams.

"Why?" I asked, even though I knew the answer.

"Because you and your brothers and sisters are too influenced by them."

"How can you say that Papa? I've been sacrificing all my time with the girls just to be here for you."

Papa pounced on my words like a lion. "So it's a sacrifice, is it? That means you don't really want to be with me, right? You would rather be running around doing things with those Buckingham girls instead of being here for me."

"Oh, Papa, it's not that at all . . ."

"Don't talk back to me, you idiot!" he shouted, nostrils flaring.

Then Papa slapped me in the face and punched me in the stomach. I doubled over in pain and started to cry out, but he warned me quickly, "Don't you dare make a sound."

I clenched my teeth and whimpered. Just then, someone upstairs started calling, saying it was time for dinner.

"Wipe those tears off, and don't cry in front of them if you know what's good for you," he ordered.

I sniffled for several more minutes until I calmed down. Then I followed him upstairs to the family to find everyone standing around, waiting to gather in a circle to lift a prayer of thanksgiving for the food we were about to eat. Instantly, I felt embarrassed and looked away, unable to meet their compassionate, inquiring eyes.

Mr. Buckingham, the family patriarch, bowed his head. "Heavenly Father, I thank You for Your love that You show to every one of us. Your mercies are great, and Your compassion is overwhelming. Despite our sin, you show grace. Thank You that You're ready to forgive and lift us out of the mire we get ourselves into. Thank You for bringing the Pilgrims into our lives so that iron can sharpen iron. May You bless this food tonight as we partake of Your generous provision for us."

As a chorus of amens rang around the room, my heart melted. I began to cry. So many tears streamed down my flushed, pink cheeks that I couldn't hide them and didn't even try. Inside, I hoped someone would see me and understand my broken spirit. Since I had to pretend everything was okay or risk Papa's wrath, I whirled around and hustled to the basement, pretending that I needed to get something for Papa.

I burst through the curtain walls and looked around for something—anything—that I could legitimately pretend my father needed. Nothing popped up to me. The bleakness of the moment led me to fall to my knees on the concrete floor. I cried my heart out, sobbing and feeling sorry for myself, but I knew my time was short. In desperation, I struggled back to my feet before Papa would come after me, and turned around.

There stood nineteen-year-old Christina Buckingham, tears glistening on her cheeks as she looked at me with heartfelt compassion. "Oh, Elishaba," she murmured brokenly.

I'm not sure if I ever felt more loved in all my life than at that moment.

Christina wrapped her arms around my shoulders and drew me close. Oh, how I wanted to stay and be consoled by her, but I quickly pulled back.

"I have to go, Christina. If Papa catches me down here with you . . .'"

Then her older sisters, Sharia and Lolly, arrived. Each took one of my hands, begging me to share with them what was wrong.

I couldn't tell them the truth, even though I wanted to. I ripped their arms from me and cried out, "Let me go! I must get back to Papa, or he will be really mad."

Too late. There he was, stroking his beard at the top of the stairs with a scowl.

"You can go," he said to the Buckingham girls. "Let me deal with this rebellious daughter."

He waited until they left the basement. The first thing he did was command me not to cry out.

"I warned you not to let on when you were upset, but you wanted the others to feel sorry for you."

"Please forgive me, Papa. I'm truly sorry. I just couldn't hold back the tears."

I bowed my head. I never saw his fist, which he swung hard, catching me flush on the side of my face. The stunning blow knocked me to the floor.

"Please have mercy on me," I moaned.

"Get up off that floor, you coward," he raged. "Don't you dare talk to me about mercy. You don't deserve mercy, and you won't get any."

I stood up once again, feeling dizzy and grasping a couch for support. My world was spinning in circles. With a sob, I fell back onto the sofa. Papa came at me, fist raised. "I told you to stand up, you disobedient daughter!"

Once more, his fist caught me, this time on my jaw. I blacked out for a moment and crumpled into a wretched heap on the floor. His wrath undiminished, he again commanded me to stand up. I staggered to my feet, no longer caring what happened to me.

My jaw felt broken, but worst of all, the whole side of my face was badly bruised. Suddenly, Papa realized he had a problem. There was no hiding what he'd done to me. All the Buckinghams would see the physical violence done to the side of my red face, which pulsated with pain.

Papa walked me over to an external door from the basement. "Here's what we're going to do. You're going to go out to the car and wait for me there. Put some snow on it. If anyone asks you what happened, you'd better tell them that you fell on the ice."

I put on a coat. My body shook all over from shock as I stumbled out into the dark, cold night and crawled into the chilly passenger van alone. As I sat there in my misery, I fantasized about someone coming out to save me from my tormentor.

My head ached with piercing, darting pains. No one came to rescue me. I don't know how my father explained my sudden departure, but he appeared after a while, carrying our clothes and toiletries in backpacks.

"The others are staying here and will take the other vehicle in the morning," he announced as he started up the car.

I didn't say a word. I was in an emotional daze. Besides, I generally didn't speak unless my father demanded me to.

The snowy and ice-covered road unraveled before me as we drove east toward Glennallen. I was feeling really sleepy, in pain, and unable to think. Over the weary miles, Papa thundered on relentlessly, questioning me, demanding to know why I was so rebellious and wouldn't listen to him. My spirit felt numb, my heart was broken, and my body ached.

One time when I fell asleep, he slapped me across the face and pulled over to the side of the road.

"Get out and put your head in the snow—right there in my headlights," he demanded.

My body felt like a box of lead as I slowly pulled myself from the passenger seat. I did what he ordered—and dipped my head into soft, fresh snow. Then I stumbled back to the passenger van, my body temperature low from shock and exposure to the subzero temperatures. I felt like I was freezing to death, but my father didn't care.

Somehow, half dead with cold, fatigue, and emptiness, we arrived at the Glennallen cabin we regularly squatted at. My nightmare was not over, however. Being totally alone with Papa meant that he could have his way with my body again.

The next day, New Year's Eve, the rest of the family joined us at the Glennallen cabin. I was still experiencing deep pain because of the horrendous beating that left black-and-blue splotches on my face, but no one wanted to acknowledge that I had been whacked by an angry, out-of-control father who ruled the family with an iron fist. My siblings were upset with me for causing them to leave the Buckinghams. I felt so alone!

After the rest of my family arrived at the Glennallen cabin, my father decided to move on to McCarthy, a trip of 125 miles on snow-slick roads. And then the following day, we'd return to Hillbilly Heaven before people saw me in my battered condition.

All of us couldn't fit in the little wanigan, but John Adams, a longtime McCarthy local, was always willing to have our company, so everyone else would stay in his warm cabin for the night.

Not Papa and me. We would stay in the freezing wanigan, where John couldn't see me.

Mama and my siblings went on ahead to McCarthy while Papa and I rode in the Suburban. Instead of driving in the direction of McCarthy, we drove aimlessly around Glennallen. At the same time, Papa had me hold a Bible in my lap and read him 1 Corinthians 7, in yet another vain attempt to prove to me that a father could "keep his own virgin."

When I read the beginning of verse 38, about how the man who marries his own virgin does well, he pounced on that as justification for how he treated me.

I continued reading verse 38, which also said the one who does not marry his own virgin does better, but Papa didn't want to talk about that.

Suddenly, our vehicle was lit up with red-and-white lights. We were pulled over on New Year's Eve!

My heart thumped as I waited for the Alaska state trooper to walk up to Papa's window.

"I'm a little bit concerned," the trooper said. "I've seen you drive around and around. I thought I'd check to make sure everything is okay."

I kept my head down so that my long brown hair covered my bruises. But a thought came to mind: *Here's your chance to get rescued. Show him your bruises.*

But I couldn't. Then I heard Papa spin a pretty good story.

"I'm just seeing in the New Year like any good Christian should by caring for my daughter and listening to her read God's Word," he said.

We had never celebrated New Year's Eve in our lives—another pagan tradition, my father said. I felt the trooper's eyes fall on me, but I didn't turn to make eye contact. The Bible remained on my lap.

"I see," the state trooper said. "Well, everything appears in order. Happy New Year, sir."

"Happy New Year to you too," my father replied, but I could tell he didn't mean it.

After the trooper left, Papa decided to press on to McCarthy, even though it was the middle of the night.

As the miles slowly passed by, I wondered what 2005 would bring.

One thing was sure: I didn't think I could survive one more year with my father.

Little did I know how soon he would prove me right.

# 39
# THE SHACK

The next day in McCarthy, my brothers, Papa, and I hopped on our Ski-Doo Tundras. We hitched them to sleds filled with food and supplies for Hillbilly Heaven.

We left Mama and the children at John Adams's bed-and-breakfast house in McCarthy while we powered up the frozen trail with its seventeen river crossings. Many of the crossings had ice bridges requiring work before we could bring Mama and the children back home. The resupply trip took all day.

When we awoke at the homestead the following morning, Papa ordered my brothers to complete our work on the ice bridges. I jumped at the opportunity.

"Please, Papa, can I go with them? I'm sure they need my help." I knew all too well what he had in mind when I'd be alone with him.

"No, I need you to stay with me and rest. It's been a long, hard trip."

My heart sank at his words. I tried to convince Papa that the brothers needed my help, but my request was made in vain.

"What you're asking for is nonsense. Staying here with me is much more important than anything you can do outside."

I noticed expressions of disgust from my brothers. Their dirty looks encouraged me, though. Perhaps my relationship with Papa repulsed them. But what could any of us do, especially me?

The more I thought about my options, the deeper my prison became. The foul life I was forced to live was utterly abhorrent to me.

I hated it.

Really hated it.

Once the snow bridges were repaired, the plan was for all of us to go down to McCarthy, where we'd bring Mama and the rest of my siblings to the homestead as well as another load of supplies.

I sat behind Papa, bundled up from the very low temperatures. The roar of the snow machine covered my whimpering. Occasionally, I'd cry. Any tears that were released quickly froze on my flushed cheeks.

And then, on a straight stretch, Papa did it again. He stretched out his left hand and reached under my skirt to poke his finger into a hole in my snow pants.

Papa had ordered me to cut the pants' seam and not wear any underwear to provide easy access for his probing fingers. I couldn't figure out which was worse: the sick feeling in my gut each time he did this humiliating act out in the open or the sexual abuse and beatings behind closed doors.

When we arrived in McCarthy, I climbed off Papa's snow machine, hoping for a flash of warmth from the house my family was staying in.

"Keep your scarf around your cheeks," Papa said. "I don't want to make anyone suspicious."

Mama gave us some hot soup while John Adams looked on, a trustworthy neighbor who was glad to help. Then Papa announced a change in plans: he said the two of us would spend the night at our wanigan while everyone else rode snow machines up the valley to Hillbilly Heaven. I panicked at the thought of being alone with my master so quickly again.

While Papa went to the bathroom, I begged my brothers, asking if one of them would stay behind with me.

"It's not safe," I explained. "Papa has been beating me so much. If one of you is there, he won't hit me. Please, someone stay with us."

"Sure, I'll stay."

My brother Joshua spoke up. His reassuring words gave me a sense of safety.

He was smart about it and didn't say anything to Papa. Once we left for the wanigan, my brother waited a few minutes and then followed us. When Joshua came through the small door, my father looked up in surprise.

"What are you doing here?" Papa asked.

"I came to spend the night with you. I thought I could help with the fire since it's so cold."

We all knew how to manipulate my father and had a secret language of survival. My father, tired and weary, didn't even argue.

Joshua's presence cost me, however. Since my brother was sleeping close by on a small bunk, Papa made me sit up and rub his feet until Joshua was sound asleep. As I sat up, leaning over my father's feet in the middle of a stormy night, my mind spun with awful thoughts as I tried my best to stay awake and do my duty. With my twenty-ninth birthday rapidly approaching, I wondered:

*Why am I stuck here with my father?*
*What if all this is evil?*
*How can I get away?*

I thought about what Papa had taught me from 1 Corinthians 7, the chapter that he regularly referred to in order to justify our relationship and the foundation for why I was to stay an unmarried girl and to serve the Lord through serving my father.

I felt angry that God would make such a law. The more I thought about it, though, the more I realized it didn't make sense. The apostle Paul was clearly talking to both the unmarried *and* the married. He made the commonsense point that the unmarried were better able to devote their undivided attention to God because they didn't have a family to look after.

I woke up to Papa prodding me. I quickly realized I was alone again with him because Joshua was already up and gone, riding a Tundra back to the homestead. The world spun around in my dizziness, and my body ached all over. I was thankful my brother had started a fire and warmed up the shack. We were in the midst of a major cold snap. The temperatures outside were a frigid minus fifty below.

I made Papa some coffee and wondered if we were going back to the homestead as well.

"Going home? You and I are not going home," he replied.

This sounded scary, so I kept to my duties by making him breakfast. While I watched him dive into his scrambled eggs—my stomach was growling, but I was not allowed to eat unless he permitted me—I gathered my courage to ask him something about 1 Corinthians 7. I had been reading from the New International Version (NIV), which had easier English to understand.

"Papa, what I don't understand is how you tell me that I am to serve the Lord without distraction as an unmarried woman does. But I don't have time to serve the Lord. Instead, I serve you like a married woman."

"What? Are you questioning me? If you are serving me, you are serving the Lord."

"Papa, the verse says, 'her aim is to be devoted to the Lord in both body and spirit.' But I'm not really serving the Lord. I don't even have time to read my Bible."

My father reacted furiously when I dared question his interpretation of Scripture.

"I want to know who you have been talking to," he demanded. "Are you so quickly persuaded by some wayward goats in sheep's clothing?"

He took a step toward me. This wasn't going well.

"Papa, my body belongs to you. I can't even look at myself without seeing you. I will never get married. I only want to be free to serve the Lord as you have taught me to do."

My response failed to win over my father, whose eyes filled with wrath. "So, you've been reading the Bible. What else is in the Bible that you want to prove me wrong about?"

"Papa, there are things you taught me in the Bible that have got me all mixed up. Some of it doesn't make sense anymore."

My father considered what I said for a moment. "Are you going to stand there like a proud, strange woman trying to prove her father wrong?"

I stuttered for an answer because my brain was confused. Just then, Papa whacked me on the side of my head, just above my left ear, surprising me in more ways than one. In the past, Papa was careful never to hit us in the head or face since visible bruises could cause trouble with outsiders. This time, he smacked me so hard that the shack spun in circles.

"Answer me, wise woman. Come on. Give me an answer."

I kept trying to get something out, but my mouth wouldn't work. Blow after blow, my father struck me with his powerful fist on my head and shoulders and into my stomach.

I hit the floor as my world turned black. I heard my father's words in the distance.

"Get up, you yellow-bellied coward."

I knew I was fighting for my life with every breath I took. When I grabbed the corner of the small counter to pull myself up, I received an uppercut to my stomach that knocked the wind out of me.

"Papa, please have mercy on me," I gasped. "I will do whatever you want."

And then I fell to the floor again and curled up in a fetal position to protect myself from the monster who stood over me.

"Papa, please," I moaned.

"Why have you stopped calling me lord, huh? Is it because you are becoming polluted by the world?"

"No," I managed through the pain.

More punches. More kicks.

"Don't call me Papa anymore. I want you to call me lord."

"Yes, my lord."

He continued to mock me with each jab. The more I defended myself, the more hell I caught. This went on for another hour or two. After so many punches, my body felt like hamburger meat. I leaned up against the counter, trying to stand as my father commanded me to, but my knees kept giving out.

Falling to the floor, I sought mercy. "Please forgive me, my lord. I was afraid of what others would think if I called you lord."

"So now you admit it. You were concerned about what others think, right?"

I didn't answer. I held my hands over my head while he kicked me again and again. Most of his blows landed on my sore legs.

When Papa tired of striking me, he left to get some more wood. I had to go to the bathroom. While Papa was outside, I pulled up my skirt and sat down on our small camper toilet. My legs were all black and blue as far up as I could see, and my flesh was almost bleeding.

I abruptly threw my dress down when Papa came through the door with an armload of wood.

"What are you doing? I didn't give you permission to go potty."

"I'm sorry," I mumbled as I stood up. He dropped the wood onto the floor and reached for the belt holding up his pants.

"You think I'm finished with you, but I haven't even started yet!" he roared.

Then he lashed me several times across the back, leaving welts. I had to do something to save myself from the excruciating pain that burned my body.

Papa was lifting his belt for another round when suddenly there was a loud knock. John Adams was opening the front door—

Papa leaped and slammed the door in his face. I heard John's voice saying, "I've come to check on you. It has to be sixty below. Would you like to come over for a hot bath?"

"We're fine, John," Papa assured him. "I would appreciate you leaving us be."

Inwardly, I groaned. Our friendly neighbor could have rescued me.

After a minute or two, Papa stepped outside to make sure John wasn't still around. I noticed he left the belt on the counter.

When I looked at that black leather belt, a thought came to mind. An idea that I'd never considered before, but I was desperate. Without a second thought, I quickly tossed the belt into the wood-burning stove—at the exact moment Papa walked back in.

Even my father was shocked.

"Who have you become?" he demanded. "You adulterous beast. You have turned your back on God and me."

His right-handed punch landed on my left cheekbone once, twice, three times . . . Papa was directing all his fury to my face.

I decided to make a run for it—without boots or warm clothes. In weather this cold, this was equivalent to a death wish since I couldn't survive these icy, frigid temperatures for more than a few minutes.

Fortunately, when I opened the door to escape, Papa pounced upon me like a wildcat. He grabbed me by my hair and yanked, slamming me into the door. I tried to escape, but his firm grip on my hair pulled me back into the shack.

Then, when Papa was using the camper toilet and distracted, I reached for the little phone sitting on the counter. Eager for help, I dialed the family number for Hillbilly Heaven and left the phone off the hook, hoping they would hear the distress I was in.

Papa caught on quickly. He grabbed the phone and pulled the plug from the wall.

"So now you think you can call the police? Is that what you were doing?" my father asked.

"No, my lord. It's not that at—"

My father walloped me with a wicked fist to the back of my neck, sending a jolt of electricity down my spine that left my body limp. I fell to the ground, unable to move. I was paralyzed. Through a fainting voice, I said, "I'm dying, Papa. You have killed me."

This was it. I was ready to breathe my last when I heard God speak to me: *I will never leave you or forsake you.*

That encouragement was the last thing I remember until Papa lifted me off the floor and set me on a small bench. My body was tingling all over. To my surprise, I was getting my feeling back.

I cautiously pressed my hand against my swollen face. Seeing my movement, Papa laughed cruelly.

"Oh, now you're worried about what your face looks like, eh? Here, I'll make the other side look just as even."

The words were barely out of his mouth when a series of left jabs nailed the right side of my face like a punching bag. I tried to deflect the blows with my arms, but my reflexes were dulled. My lips were so swollen and bruised that blood dripped down onto my tattered blouse.

Then he inflicted a new round of verbal wounds. "You have nowhere to go," he taunted me. "No one out there will love you. You know too well what I'm talking about. Now that you've given yourself to me, I'm the only one for you, whether you like it or not."

What I did know was that I could barely see out of my eyes. Finally and thankfully, I lost consciousness altogether.

When I awoke, I was naked, lying on the bed with my father on top of me. He was carrying on with his customary, predatory invasions of my body, acting as if nothing had happened. When he was done, he gloated over my bleeding bruises. "Get up," he demanded. "I want to see."

I didn't make a move—until he yanked on my breast to get me moving. "Come on, my dove, my only one. Stand up straight and dance for me."

In a daze, I halfheartedly complied, but I couldn't understand how my father could enjoy the ugly, messed-up body I had become.

And then he filmed me.

Each time I moved my hips for the camera, I felt like the scum of the earth.

# 40
# LIFE BEHIND A MASK

After thirty-six hours in a house of horrors known as the McCarthy wanigan, Papa allowed me to go outside to get firewood. The bitter cold that froze my eyelashes felt better than being inside the terrifying shack.

Papa ordered me to wear a ski mask in case someone was out and about. After stepping outside the wanigan, I saw a parked truck. I had to see what I looked like in the driver-side mirror. I looked both ways to make sure no one was watching.

When I pulled off my mask, I gasped in shock.

*Is that really me?*

I looked hideous, unhuman, and dead. I gazed at a pair of lifeless eyes, open and beady, and tried not to shudder. The face surrounding those eyes was puffed up like bread dough, and my skin was a collage of different colors: purple, red, and black. My lips were cracked and filled with lines of dried blood.

Instead of giving in to the death I saw, another thought came to mind: *You can survive this.*

I wasn't educated growing up, but I had learned the most important skill in life: how to survive. I always found a way to take one more step, see things through, and make it to the next day, even when I wondered if that was possible. Someday things would get better.

I just had to make it to "someday."

Pulling the ski mask back down over my wounded face gave me great comfort. I could heal. And I would heal because I knew God was watching over me. This was a time to trust Him with my life; He was all I had and my only hope.

I walked into the shack with an armload of firewood.

"What took you so long?" Papa asked.

I looked up. Papa was lying naked on the bed, watching movies he'd taken on the camera. He was fully aroused.

I pretended I didn't see him as I busied myself with the fire.

That's what I needed to do: pretend he wasn't there, and that's the world I entered into.

Papa proposed the idea of taking me somewhere else to give me time to heal up, saying we could have a good time together.

Thank God that's as far as his idea went because I told him repeatedly that I wanted to return to Hillbilly Heaven and be with our family.

"What is it that makes you want to go home so bad, huh?" he asked one time.

"Umm . . . it feels like the right time. Also, I know you don't want anyone in the town of McCarthy to see me."

I thought I would play on his fears a bit.

"What are you going to tell your brothers or the little children about what happened to you?"

I knew he was referring to my lumpy, bruised face. I had an answer prepared for him.

"I know exactly what I'll say: 'In case you're wondering, what happened to me is a good example of what happens when you disobey Papa.'"

Papa smiled. For him, it was the perfect answer.

That's when my father agreed that we could go back to Hillbilly Heaven. It did feel like home when we arrived to the sight of yellowish light coming from the Main House, nestled among deep piles of snow. When we pulled into the compound, the family poured out to greet us. I quickly got off my snow machine while Papa took his Tundra for a spin around the cabin to turn it around. He always had his perfect way of doing certain things.

This gave me a few free moments with my brothers.

"Elishaba, are you okay?" Joseph asked.

I quickly tore off my ski mask. He and my brothers were beyond shocked by my appearance. My misshapen face was filled with purplish bruises and raspberry-colored patches of skin, and my eyes looked like slits through my swollen cheeks.

"It's been horrible," I allowed.

Five brothers surrounded me. Joseph was flanked by Joshua, David, Moses, and Israel.

"Elishaba," Joseph said, "we've been praying for you. We want you to know that we are on your side. We understand, and we disagree with Papa's actions."

My heart lifted. I wasn't alone.

My brothers had my back.

When we went to bed that night, I was exhausted and dropped off to sleep quickly, but not for long. Papa woke me up with an elbow in my chest, saying, "Wake up! You have no business sleeping. You haven't taken care of me like you should."

For the next couple of hours, I sat weeping, brain-dead in the darkness while rubbing Papa's legs, knees, hands, and feet and listening to him snore.

At some point, I fell sound asleep only to be awakened in the morning light with Papa's elbow in my chest again.

"Sit up," he said. "I want you to explain to me right now what you're thinking and why you are so resistant to me."

My head cleared at that moment. Suddenly, all my fears of Papa melted away as truth reigned in my heart. I felt a new boldness I had never felt before.

"Papa, I'm going to tell you the truth. I've lied to you for so long now. All the times I've told you that I accept you and your relationship with me, all the times I've told you I loved you and told you how much I believed you, I lied. It wasn't the truth."

*There, I said what I was really feeling.* It was like the Lord gave me the perfect words to say. What I said felt right and good to confess to Papa. My spirit soared.

I wasn't finished. "And Papa, I would like you to give me a week away from you for prayer and fasting. I need time to talk to God about everything that's happened between us."

Papa's face nearly turned white with shock.

"Get the whip!" he ordered.

I almost had a smile on my face for the joy I felt inside of me. All the beatings or whippings Papa could give me now couldn't take that feeling away. I ducked under the curtains and fetched the braided leather whip.

Mama and all my brothers and sisters were sitting around on the couches, so they saw everything. Even the pity on their faces did not make me pause as Papa thrashed me soundly, but he did allow me to go off on my own to fast and pray.

The following morning, I bundled up in cold-weather gear with my Bible in hand and trekked to Diamond Creek to find a quiet place with God.

I called out, "Oh, God, are You there? I don't know if You can hear me, but if You can, please show me what is right. I need a Bible verse that says something like, 'It is a wicked thing for a father to lay with his daughter and come in to her.' I can't find it anywhere."

Part of my problem was that the Bible verses that talk about unlawful sexual relations—found in the Book of Leviticus in the Old Testament—were hard to understand in the King James Version. In the eighteenth chapter, I read that "None of you shall approach to any that is near of kin to him, to uncover their nakedness: I am the Lord" (Leviticus 18:6, KJV). I wasn't sure what it all meant.[1]

When I reluctantly returned in the late afternoon, Papa was silent and gave me a look of cold rejection that made my heart pound like an army of horses. That night, I crawled into a bed in another room with my sisters. I couldn't believe Papa allowed me to do this, but he did.

Before I fell asleep, I heard Jerusalem whisper, "I know what is going on with you and Papa."

Shame hit me like a two-ton rock. I wanted to die right there on the spot.

"You know?"

"Pretty much. One time, I was on the other side of Papa when he was moving in a strange way with you. I asked Papa what he was doing, and he told me that whatever I saw, he didn't want me to tell anyone. While you were stuck in McCarthy with Papa, I told the brothers. We've been talking and knew something was wrong when Papa beat you up in the wanigan. This is not the first time I've seen you bruised up. Even the Buckinghams know."

I begged her not to talk about it anymore. I was afraid Papa would hear us talking and wanted to sleep.

The next day at Diamond Creek, by myself, I realized that I had shown more love to Papa than to God. I had worshipped him, if I was honest. Furthermore, the idea of keeping my family together was so important that I had barricaded my mind against the truth of what was happening to me, who I was, or what my convictions were.

On the third morning of my separation from my father, Papa had enough. "Your time is over," he began. "This is your rebellious spirit, and it ends now."

I complied with reluctance, but the break from my father confirmed I was on the right track.

I celebrated my twenty-ninth birthday on January 23, 2005, which was a reminder that I'd turn thirty in a year—a depressing thought, for sure. Where

---

1. It would have helped if I knew that "uncover their nakedness" was translated as "have sexual relations" in more modern English versions like the New International Version. While Leviticus 18 decreed that sexual relations were forbidden between a man and his mother, father's wife, sister, granddaughter, etc., the verses never specifically mentioned a father and daughter, although verse 6 in the NIV does say, "No one is to approach any close relative to have sexual relations."

were the years going? In my mind, there was nothing to "celebrate."

Papa didn't acknowledge my birthday. His mind was set on taking a trip to McCarthy that day for some reason. He loved his snow machine and looked for any opportunity to use it. I loved driving one, too, but I knew he wouldn't let me go along. Because his beatings disfigured me, he didn't want to expose me to anyone in town who might see me.

He left me behind with strict instructions: I was to stay in the back room—where Jerusalem and my sisters slept—and not come out until he got back. He was afraid that someone might show up unexpectedly, like John Adams.

My body still hurt from the beatings at the wanigan. I needed rest, so I crawled into the lower bunk bed and saw my sister's Bible on the blanket.

*Maybe God will speak to me.*

I'd seen my father open his Bible many times, saying God had a specific verse waiting for him to read. Maybe this was one of those occasions.

I flipped open to the Book of Psalms, where my eyes flashed onto a verse underlined in red pen. It came from Psalm 27:10 (KJV):

> When my father and my mother forsake me, then the Lord will take me up.

The Scripture hit me like a thunderbolt. There was no doubt God was telling me, *I'm here, Elishaba. I will pick you up and hold you. I have not forsaken you.*

I knew my parents had forsaken me. Papa mistreating me was a given, but Mama was helpless. She could do nothing for me, and I was left alone to suffer in this world.

This verse turned out to be the best birthday gift ever—a gift of love, a gift of knowing that even if I wasn't worth anything to anyone, I was worth enough to be taken up by God.

I found a pencil and a piece of paper and wrote out the Bible verse from Psalm 27:10 as best I could. Then I slipped out of the room, found some adhesive tape, and stuck the verse on a pole in the middle of the main room.

Going back into my sisters' room and shutting the door behind me, I knew I was making a bold statement that would cost me a lot, but I didn't care anymore.

Hungry and tired, I passed out and fell asleep. A couple of hours later, in the afternoon, I woke up to a man's voice calling my name—John Adams.

"Elishaba, I know you are here," he said. "I came to wish you a happy birthday."

I wanted to leave the room and thank him—but I remembered that Papa ordered me not to move or speak to anyone.

My younger siblings tried to cover for me. "She can't come out," one said. "Papa gave her a project to work on."

I had never been so close to running out of my prison and letting someone from the outside world see the truth for himself, but my fears of ruining the lives of my little siblings held me frozen in one spot.

After what happened in the McCarthy wanigan, I knew my father had entered a new phase—a violent one filled with unpredictability.

If he was capable of doing *that* to me, he was capable of anything, including murder.

This is why I needed to be thinking about escaping—before it was too late.

# PART VI

---

# THE ESCAPE: PART II

# 41
# TWO SISTERS

Bundled up in snow pants, coat, and boots, I lay in my sleeping bag, shivering uncontrollably.

Jerusalem, the little sister I had long prayed for, sat beside me, full of encouragement.

"We're going to be all right, Elishaba. Just wait and see."

"I don't know," I replied. "I can't stop shaking, and my head hurts. I can't get warm for anything." Winter still maintained a firm grip on this April morning, with temperatures hovering at twenty below zero. The severe cold penetrated all our layers.

The narrow escape by snow machine from Hillbilly Heaven had more of an impact on me than I thought. I was drained emotionally and physically from the harrowing experience, knowing my life hung in the balance. The next time I saw Papa, he wouldn't beat me. He'd shoot me.

We were free from Papa Pilgrim—but were we? Doubts formed in my mind. Would he find me? Had I done the right thing? It was as though Papa had an invisible chain around my neck, even as I hid underneath a tall spruce tree, shaking in my sleeping bag and listening for the sound of snow machines. I knew Papa would come looking for me sooner or later, which left my spirit unsettled.

Jerusalem broke up my wandering thoughts. With a funny smile on her face, she pulled out a bunch of papers from her coat pocket.

"These are some notes the Buckinghams mailed us after Christmas," she said. "Remember how Papa made us throw them in the trash? I saved them."

"What do they say?"

"I didn't understand everything, but they seemed nice."

Jerusalem had taught herself to read some, like I had. She opened the first note, and while we couldn't make heads or tails of some of the words, we got the gist—the Buckinghams said they loved us and were encouraging us to keep our eyes on Jesus. While it was nice to hear of their love and concern for my family, it seemed like we should have bigger things on our minds.

"We are in a fight for our survival," I said. "This is about getting away from Papa, even if we have to live in the woods the rest of our lives."

I was fully prepared to do that. We were on our fourth day of hiding underneath the spruce tree, nibbling on cheese and raisins, and eating snow as our source of water. The only times we left our hiding spot was to go to the bathroom or stretch a bit. We would occasionally hear the high-pitched sound of a snow machine that sounded like Papa's, but eventually, the distinctive whine would become less and less.

However, we never relaxed our guard and were extra careful not to do anything that would betray our whereabouts.

We needed to contact the five brothers who'd escaped a few weeks earlier: Joseph, Joshua, David, Moses, and Israel. They were working in Glennallen, 125 miles away, doing odd jobs. I had a phone number of where they were staying written on a piece of paper in my snow pants.

It would be too risky to walk a half mile into town and find a phone. The townspeople knew us, and word would get back to Papa. The only way I could think of to contact my brothers was to call from the phone in the wanigan, which wasn't that far from where we were.

But what if Papa was there? We would be taking a real risk. I was well aware of Papa's clever ways.

On the fifth day, we could wait no longer to contact our brothers. Jerusalem and I decided to get up in the middle of the night and call from the wanigan.

"We are going to have to be really quiet, Jerusalem," I said. "Papa could have hidden his snow machine back in the woods to make it look like he's not there."

As we neared the shack, we took off our boots and hung them over our shoulders, creeping forward in our socks. Even then, the crispy ice crackled in the bitterly cold night, scaring us. My heart was racing as we rounded a corner and saw the dark features of that little box of hell.

"Jerusalem, stop! Look. Over there . . . in the trees. It's Papa's snow machine. He's here."

We carefully eased out of there and left in a hurry, hoping Papa didn't hear us approach the wanigan.

On the way back to our camping spot, we found a small jug of frozen water. I picked it up and put it inside my coat, where it melted slowly. A half hour later, we each had enough for a small drink of water. That's when I realized how completely dehydrated we were.

We needed more water, plain and simple. We started a small fire and melted snow in a little pot we had, keeping the flame low.

The welcome water revived us. Then we talked about calling our brothers from John Adams's house, which wasn't far from the wanigan. That was a risk we had to take.

At daybreak, we sneaked up to John's house, careful not to reveal our presence. No one was home, so we burst inside and used his phone to contact our brothers.[1] They were delighted to hear that we had escaped. I explained where we were and made arrangements for them to pick us up at 10 p.m.

We stuck close to the woods and made it back to our hideout to await their arrival. As the ten o'clock hour neared, we watched the road for headlights that would come from the truck my brothers were driving. The truck had a snowplow on the front, so the vehicle would be easy to notice.

"There they are!" we said simultaneously.

But the truck passed us!

"They don't know where we are!" I exclaimed.

"Calm down," Jerusalem said. "They won't leave us here. Let's go to the road. We have to risk it."

We leaped over logs, stepping in and out of deep snow—and then we saw my brothers' truck pass us in the other direction—back toward Glennallen.

*Oh, no!*

We hustled as fast as we could to McCarthy Road. Once there, we took off running after our brothers' truck in the moonlight.

The vehicle never slowed.

We stopped running, disappointment filling our lungs as we took deep breaths in the subzero cold. I couldn't believe it. I knew they were looking for us—

—when suddenly the truck came to a stop and began turning around.

They were coming back!

"How do we know it's them?" Jerusalem asked.

She had a point. "Let's hide until we know for sure," I replied.

We took cover behind a tree beside the road and waited. When I got a better look at the truck with a snowplow coming over the hill, I immediately recognized my brothers' vehicle.

"It's them!" we both said simultaneously.

We jumped onto the road, waving our arms.

The truck skidded to a stop. Joseph and David jumped out and hugged us with relief. Everything I'd imagined an escape to be was happening before my eyes.

It felt like heaven to be safe with our siblings, but I told the brothers that I

---

1. McCarthy is the type of place where many residents don't lock their doors.

could not be anywhere Papa could find me.

Joseph reasoned with me. "Elishaba, you will be just fine with us. We will take care of you."

What I couldn't fully explain to my brothers, which made me ashamed, was this feeling that if Papa found me, I would cower and fall into his arms again, even if it was entirely against my wishes.

We discussed what to do and where to go. I knew where I wanted them to take us.

"There's a little fishing cabin along the Copper River to the north of Chitina. Papa will never find us there."[2]

Joseph nodded. "You got it. Just show me where to go."

Upon our arrival, Jerusalem and I made the six-by-six plywood shed—which smelled from the fish that the Natives harvested and dried there—into our new home. We spent our days going on long walks talking about our futures.

My brothers brought us food and checked up on us every couple of days. At first, our time at the tiny cabin was fun, as I felt the freedom to be me and talk without fear to my sister. But I was surprised when feelings of depression came over me. I wondered if life going forward meant living alone in a world unknown to me.

With each passing day, my sister begged me to think about going to the Buckinghams' place in Palmer. She said we had an open invitation, and that's where she wanted to go.

*It'll be fine with them.*

*They would love to take us in.*

*All we have to do is let them know we're coming.*

I remained stubborn, resistant. How could I face those beautiful people? Especially after what happened at Christmastime? I felt too ashamed.

A small airstrip located near us had a pay phone that stood out among several trees. We would go there once in a while to call the brothers. But one time, Jerusalem insisted on calling the Buckinghams.

"Jerusalem, no. Please don't call them."

She wouldn't listen, however.

After she dialed their number, I quietly said, "Okay, but I'm not going to talk to them."

I walked a short distance away and watched Jerusalem laugh and chat

---

2. The small town of Chitina was the same distance from McCarthy (around sixty miles) as it was from Glennallen.

animatedly with the Buckinghams.

*Look how free she is, so able to be herself. But the Buckingham sisters could never like me as they like her. I'm a ruined mess and a wicked person. I'm sure they won't even want to talk to me.*

My thoughts were interrupted when Jerusalem called out, "Elishaba, the Buckinghams want to talk to you."

My first reflex was to say no, but something compelled me to take the phone.

I cupped the black handset to my ear and heard Martha Buckingham's inviting voice on the other end.

"Elishaba! How are you? Jim and I are just so excited to hear your voice."

I couldn't believe that they had stopped everything they were doing to talk with me—as if I was important to them. Instantly, a river of self-loathing poured out of me.

"I had to leave my papa because my relationship with him was wrong," I stammered. "I'm sorry for lying to you about that. I really am."

Martha responded for both of them. "That's all in the past, Elishaba. Your father sinned against God's law and against you. It wasn't your fault."

I took a deep breath and exhaled. "Thank you," I said. "That's good to hear."

"We're proud of you, Elishaba. Taking the step to leave your father couldn't have been easy. We have been praying for you and will continue to do so. You have done the right thing. Don't let the devil make you doubt."

We talked a bit longer, and then Mr. Buckingham closed with an invitation. "Come visit us. Let us love on you. You've been through a lot."

I told them I would think about it and thanked them for their kind words.

When our conversation was over, Jerusalem and I walked back to the cabin, our feet feeling light. She was overflowing with joy about how the Buckinghams wanted us to visit, but I also felt a heaviness of spirit. While our conversation reassured me that I had done the right thing leaving Papa, it was also clear that others knew about my dark, secret sins, which was why I felt unclean.

I began making mental plans to live in the woods by myself. I could find trees to sleep under or a trapper's cabin. Following the escape, I seemed to be like a restless animal, unable to be tamed. I felt terrible for my sister, who realized my inner battle and kept a close watch on me.

It's good she did because one afternoon, I was tempted strongly to take my life.

Sitting along the banks of the Copper River, I saw gaps of surface water on the ice-covered waterway. I envisioned jumping up and down where the ice was thin and disappearing for good, thus ending any problems that I gave my family.

A fierce contradiction raged in my heart. On the one hand, I wanted sympathy from those who knew me and could understand my pain, but on the other hand, I hated myself. I didn't know how to find victory.

But I knew how to survive, and this was not how I wanted to end things.

After many days of inner turmoil, I finally agreed with Jerusalem and my brothers to visit the Buckinghams. My brothers then talked about going back to the homestead and picking up my other sister, Hosanna, so that the eight of us older children could go together to Palmer and stay with the family.

My brothers dropped by on their way to McCarthy and Hillbilly Heaven. I took Joseph and Joshua aside.

"I need your help with something," I said to both of them.

"Just ask," Joseph said. "What can we do?"

"Papa took pictures and videos of my naked body and stored them on a camera card tucked away in the leather case around his Bible. I can't go on knowing that he can still look at me that way. Can I trust you to get that card back from Papa and bring it to me?"

The look on my brothers' faces was the look of two soldiers who would not fail the mission given to them, no matter what they had to do.

When my brothers arrived at Hillbilly Heaven, my father raged futilely as he learned of their plans to take fourteen-year-old Hosanna with them, but even he realized that he was unable to do anything about it. Then they confronted Papa about the memory card.

My father acted like he didn't know what they were talking about. He even turned on the camera and showed them a bunch of scenic photos.

"Elishaba said it's in a secret pocket inside your leather-bound Bible," Joshua said.

Joseph found the Bible and opened it up. His fingers checked for a memory card inside the leather case, but nothing was inside the slot I sewed.

"Where is it?" Joseph demanded.

"I don't have it."

This went on for twenty minutes—my brothers saying the card existed and my father insisting he didn't have it.

Joseph and Joshua's persistence won the day. My father threw up his hands and retrieved the memory card from another secret spot. Before he handed it over, he took a pair of scissors and cut it in two.[3]

When my brothers returned to the cabin near the Copper River, our sister

---

3. I've wondered why Papa would voluntarily give up the memory card and make sure it was cut in two before he handed it over. I think it's because he realized there was a lot of incriminating evidence on that camera card.

Hosanna accompanied them. They also handed me a plastic baggie containing a memory card cut into two pieces.

"You got it," I said. "Amazing."

"It took a little doing, but Papa didn't have a choice," Joseph said.

Seeing the two halves of the memory card gave me a sense of relief. I still boiled with hatred toward my father for making me take part in such horrible videos.

"So, what are you going to do?" Joshua asked.

"This," I said.

I opened the stove door and tossed the baggie into the flames.

Watching the two pieces of camera card melt in the heat gave me a great sense of relief.

Now it was the pieces of my heart that had to be put back together.

# 42
# ON TO THE BUCKINGHAMS

Three weeks after my dramatic escape, the eight oldest Hale siblings pulled into the large property belonging to Jim and Martha Buckingham, several miles outside of Palmer.

The sight of their beautiful log home took my breath away, as if I were in a dream. The Buckingham daughters were the first to rush out the front door, screaming with delight and quick to give us hugs and squeeze our shoulders. The freedom I felt walking into their loving home was breathtaking.

There was so much to catch up on. When the evening meal was announced, Mr. Buckingham declared, "Girls first," causing my heart to sink. I hesitated and tried to melt into the background because Papa and the boys always ate first. This didn't feel right.

The Buckingham girls pushed me to the front of the line. "You're first," Lolly said. "You're the oldest."

I had *never* eaten first in the Pilgrim family—and sometimes I never got to eat at all because all the food was gone or Papa decided that I didn't need to eat. But the Buckinghams, with smiles, insisted that I serve myself before anyone else.

Feeling self-conscious, I reached for a white plate. I took a square of lasagna and some salad, sat down on a living room sofa, and waited for the others to arrive. Once we started eating, I felt like everyone was watching me chew my food. I wanted to hide under the cushions!

After dinner, the Buckinghams took my sisters and me downstairs to the basement—but nothing looked the same. I associated the basement with Papa's abuse of me, but all that faded as they ushered us into a room attractively decorated for the Hale girls. I noticed three beautiful dresses hanging on hooks, made with love for us by the Buckingham girls. Sharia, twenty-one years old at the time, told me she made my outfit. I felt like a princess when I put the print dress on. I never felt so pretty before.

When I drifted off to sleep that night, I repeated over and over, *Please, Lord Jesus, please let me stay here.*

In the morning, I took the Buckingham parents aside after a delicious breakfast. I hadn't eaten this much food in weeks, but more than that, I knew this was where God wanted me to be. Even though I had no idea what the future would bring—and I'm sure they didn't either—it felt right being under their roof.

"I'm scared to say this," I began, "but I need a home where I can be safe. I feel protected with you. Can I stay here with you for a while?"

Mr. Buckingham's eyes teared up. "Elishaba, we were hoping and praying you'd ask us. Our home is your home, and our family is your family."

Mrs. Buckingham gave me a big hug that filled a void in my longing heart. I knew she fully accepted me.

I asked if there was anything I could do; I was used to doing chores. Good news: the Buckinghams needed some help building a greenhouse. All the Hales pitched in for the next few days, but then my brothers had to return to Glennallen, where their summer guiding business was heating up.

They felt responsible for Jerusalem and Hosanna, so they wanted my two younger sisters to join them in Glennallen. But they were all for me staying behind with the Buckinghams and were grateful that "Papa Jim" and "Mama Martha," as we began calling them, were willing to take me in.

This would be the first time since I was a toddler that I wouldn't be around any of my siblings. Instead of feeling sad, I convinced myself that I was embarking on an adventure.

My first exciting experience was accompanying the Buckingham family on a missions trip to remote Kako, accessible only by bush planes since the nearest road was four hundred miles away. The Kako Retreat Center provided Christ-centered youth camps and workshops to benefit Native people living in the remote Yukon-Kuskokwim Delta region. We were going there to help out.

Papa Jim and Mama Martha stayed in a cabin with their younger children while their older children were assigned to other cabins as camp counselors. Lolly and I were placed in the same cabin for girls ages five to seven, which was an eye-opener. I quickly discovered that these young children were unloved and suffering the same kinds of abuse that I had been through.

Light bulbs of recognition went off in my head. The more I found out about how much these innocent girls had been abused, the blacker the darkness felt. Gazing at the reflection they provided, I began to realize I hadn't fully accepted the awful ugliness of life with my father.

One night, I was tucking the girls into bed. One started to cry. "I miss my mommy," she sniffled.

I sat down next to her and held her hand. "I'm sure your mommy misses you too," I offered, hoping to encourage her wounded heart.

"No, I won't see my mommy. I live with my grandma. I hope my little sister is okay."

"Why won't your little sister be okay? Do you want to tell me about it?"

She wiped away her tears and sat up beside me. I put my arms around her and stroked her straight black hair. She seemed to feel safe with me, so I asked if anyone had hurt her.

"Yes, a big boy pulled down my pants and hurt me. He does it all the time. I'm scared to go back."

"Do you have a daddy?"

"He died. My grandma said he drank too much."

I sensed it was the right moment to open up my bruised heart. "I am so sad for you," I said. "I know what it is like because someone hurt me too, and I will keep anyone from hurting you while you are here."

Then I kissed her on the forehead with the reminder that she wasn't alone in this world.

During our ten-day stay, Lolly and I loved our free time together. We'd find a place in the nearby woods and have a talkfest. Lolly had such a way of drawing me out that it wasn't long before I revealed the emotional turmoil I felt.

Yes, it was amazing to be "free," I told her, but I didn't feel free. "I don't know how to talk to people or act around others, especially those older than me," I confided. "There are times when I feel like a wild horse that hasn't been tamed yet."

Lolly reminded me to be patient. "You've gone through a lot—stuff that no one should have to deal with."

But Lolly and her family didn't know that much because I was holding back. They were willing to be patient, however.

Papa Jim was leading the daily worship services with the camp kids in the main log building. When he caught a summertime cold, I made a beeline for the camp kitchen and prepared him a cup of hot tea with lots of lemon and honey in it. I carried the steaming mug to his cabin, doing my part to nurse him back to health.

"Here, Papa Jim," I said with a tinge of pride. "I made you a special tea that should help your throat."

He accepted the tea with thanks, but Papa Jim saw a teachable moment.

"Elishaba, I appreciate your concern for me, but I want to make something really clear here: I don't need you to take care of me. Martha does a good job of that."

I knew he meant well, but his response cut hard through my bleeding heart. *I must be evil in Papa Jim's eyes. He sees me as a harlot, just like my father did.*

I ran to a nearby pond and hid behind a grove of bushes, where I let out a horrifying cry. The moment brought forth an attitude of revenge against my father, who led me to harbor thoughts of self-hatred, times when I wished I was never born and felt so unworthy of anyone's love, especially a parent's.

And then I thought of the Native girl with the coal-black hair. She probably wished she had never been born, but God had a plan for her, just as He did for me.

I wanted to find out what that plan was.

Living with the Buckinghams meant a lot of new experiences, like glancing into a mirror whenever I wanted to. Suddenly, I worried about what I looked like. Too many times, I felt so ugly that I worked overtime to make my appearance pretty. Using shampoo and hair conditioner helped my tattered hair feel soft and manageable.

Going to the bathroom and sitting on a clean potty and using toilet paper was incredible. And the ability to flush! I was also fascinated by the seemingly endless rolls of toilet paper underneath the bathroom sink. I loved taking a shower so much—with hot water!—that I washed my hair five times one day, just because I could.

Having fresh, clean clothes furnished by the Buckinghams was perhaps the biggest adjustment. Sometimes I'd change my clothes three times a day because everything was so new and I wanted to look my best.

Sleeping in my own bed for the first time was a revelation as well, but I often felt weird and lonely when I got under the covers by myself. There were nights when I woke up the Buckingham sisters because I was screaming from nightmares about my past.

Overall, though, I was incredibly happy and enjoying my new life. I did my best to be funny and hardworking and make myself useful around the Buckingham home.

One of my chores was helping Christina clean the bathrooms. One day, we got into a water fight with the shower attachment. There was so much laughter and screams that it wasn't long before we had a sizable audience watching us spray each other and get our clothes all wet. We giggled like schoolgirls the entire time.

When my brothers came by for a visit, Joseph—my childhood playmate and sibling rival—noticed a big difference in me in just a few weeks. "Elishaba, it's encouraging to see you be yourself again, my determined, excited big sister. It saddened me to see that die in you."

I thanked Joseph for sharing those thoughts with me. Seeds of hope sprouted in my parched soul because there were times I needed encouragement, especially when I saw how the Buckingham girls were teaching music lessons and working part-time jobs, while I could barely read my Bible and certainly couldn't read a note of music.

Even though she had nine children of her own, Mama Martha kept an eye on me and sensed when I needed an encouraging word, a warm hug, or a listening ear. Whenever I looked her way, she gave me a reassuring look and a smile.

From the time I came into their home, the Buckingham children were eager to know more about wilderness life in the Wrangell Mountains. I told them exciting stories about riding snow machines over ice bridges and falling into the freezing river when the bridges gave way from the weight. I described the tortillas I made and how we didn't eat meat unless one of the brothers or myself bagged a deer or moose. They couldn't believe how primitive our lives were. I was happy to satisfy their curiosity and enjoyed their appreciation of our old-fashioned pioneering lifestyle.

At the same time, I felt there were large parts of my tragic past that could never be spoken. I wasn't ready to reveal the entire truth about Papa to any of the Buckinghams because I feared they would call the police. If that happened, the authorities would take away my younger siblings, and I would never see them again. I didn't want to be responsible for that happening.

One evening, we gathered around the living room after dinner. The younger children were off to bed. Suddenly, things got quiet when Mama Martha said she wanted to have a family talk. This form of open communication was something they regularly did, but this time I sensed they wanted to talk about me.

I was right.

Mrs. Buckingham began with another reassuring smile. "We have some questions for you, Elishaba. You don't need to be scared about anything because we love you, and you're not in trouble."

Then Mr. Buckingham stepped in. "Something Mom and I have been wanting to ask you is if you have considered talking about the things that your father has done to you and your family."

I felt numb. I searched my mind for the best way to answer them. "You wouldn't want to know," I said. "Things were pretty bad, and I wouldn't want to put you in a situation where you would have to do something about it."

Mrs. Buckingham spoke. "You don't need to worry about us because we're here to stand beside you. It's important for you to be honest with us about what went on at the homestead. The Bible says that the truth will set you free, but you will never be free until you're able to be completely truthful."

I felt the ground crumbling underneath me.

"Well, I'm afraid to say anything because my brothers warned me that if I did—"

I had already said too much. I buried my head in my lap and didn't know what to say.

Sharia, sitting beside me, wrapped an arm around my shoulder. "Elishaba, don't forget we love you. Maybe it's time you stand up for what you know is right, not what your father or brothers think."

Hearing their oldest daughter talk like this helped me muster some courage. "You guys don't understand," I blurted. "If I told you what really happened, I would be doing something that could turn the rest of my family against me. And if I tell you something, doesn't that mean you have to tell the authorities?"

Again, I felt I was saying too much.

I saw Mr. Buckingham turn and look at Mama Martha, as if there was some unspoken communication between the two. Then he addressed me.

"We understand your fears," he said. "We don't want you to think that you have to share with us. It's just that with my job in the Army, I have to report any abuse or lawbreakers if I learn about it, or I could get into trouble. What I would like you to think about is that you have been taught that it is a sin to tell what goes on in your family. But when there is evil and abuse, God will give you strength to help you do the right thing. Sure, the Bible tells you to honor your parents in the Lord, but if your father asked you to do evil, who should you obey—him or God?"

"God," I said.

I couldn't open up that evening—I wasn't ready—but what Papa Jim and the other Buckinghams had to say gave me a lot to think about.

Another thing on my mind was whether I should join the Buckingham family for church on Sunday morning. They attended Palmer Christian Fellowship Church, where Papa Jim was the teaching pastor, so obviously, this church was important to them as well as the fellowship they enjoyed with other believers.

The Hales had never been a churchgoing family because Papa didn't like hearing teaching from the Word of God that didn't match up with how he viewed Scripture. Pastors in the pulpit were "nothing more than wolves in sheep's clothing," he said, a phrase he used a great deal to describe anyone who didn't interpret Scripture as he did.

Papa Jim told me that I was free to do as I wished on Sunday morning, but they would love for me to join the family.

After a couple of weeks, I felt like I was ready to go. I enjoyed the music and hymns, though I found it hard to sit still. I liked Mr. Buckingham's preaching, which seemed to be straight out of the Bible. That was good for me because I was hungry for a new way of understanding God's Word.

What I found most challenging about church was interacting with others, especially men. For as long as I could remember, I was not allowed to look at or talk to a man, so it was awkward whenever the Buckinghams—who knew everybody, of course—wanted to introduce me to their friends.

Then in the fellowship hall after the service, I went into the kitchen to refill my glass from a refrigerator water dispenser. A young man about my age had the same idea. We both extended our hands at the same time, but he quickly pulled his hand back.

"Ladies first," he said.

I froze. I looked down at the floor and mumbled, "No, it's okay. You go first."

The young man didn't budge. "Really, you can go first."

"No, you go."

This repeated a few more times until I could see he wasn't going to budge, so I filled my glass and got out of there.

The Buckinghams were a hospitable family, always having people over for Bible studies. I watched how Sharia and Lolly interacted with young men as if it was normal. That was definitely out of my comfort zone. I felt self-conscious and awkward in mixed settings and kept my head down.

A week later, I noticed the young man who insisted I go first to get water at church enter the Buckingham home. He had dark brown hair, wire-rimmed glasses, a medium build, and a thick Bible in his hand.

And that's how I was introduced to Matthew Doerksen.

# 43
# A TURN IN THE ROAD

L ife was packed in those early months with the Buckinghams. As Alaska turned into the Land of the Midnight Sun, Papa Jim and Mama Martha said Jerusalem and Hosanna were welcome to move in since they needed schooling. My brothers were leaving for extended stays at hunting camps, where they would be big-game guides.

I reacted poorly to Jerusalem and Hosanna's arrival because I suddenly had to share the spotlight with beautiful sisters closer in age to Sharia and Lolly than I was. A gloomy attitude followed me everywhere like a black cloud.

"Eba, smile," said James Buckingham, sixteen years old and the oldest son.[1] We were working out in the yard on a warm afternoon.

"If I don't feel like smiling, I'm not going to smile," I huffed as I loosened earth with a spade.

James stopped shoveling. "If you smile, your heart will follow later."

I didn't crack a grin that day, but James gave me something to think about. Over time, my attitude improved as I saw how the Buckingham parents treated the three Hale daughters equally, without favoritism.

But why was life so hard to understand? Sure, I was free from Papa's vise-like grip on my life, but everything seemed so mixed up. I wasn't used to making my own decisions, voicing my opinion, or eating three square meals a day. I was afraid of messing up, like when I dropped a plate that shattered on the kitchen floor.

I swiftly opened the nearest closet for a broom and dustpan, begging Lolly, "Please don't tell your dad." Breaking a plate back at Hillbilly Heaven would

---

1. The Buckingham family's nickname for me was Eba, pronounced *Eee-bah*. I was given this name by the Buckinghams' youngest son, Joshua, who was one year old and couldn't say my name. When he called me "Eba," this became my new special name.

have resulted in a significant punishment, like several good whacks across the back or no food for the rest of the day.

Lolly began laughing. "It's okay. What do you think Dad would do to you? Lock you up?"

*Well, yes.*

Just then, Papa Jim entered the kitchen as I was on my hands and knees, sweeping up the last of the broken pieces.

"Eba, what have you done?" His slightly raised voice and arched eyebrows told me that he was irritated with me. I understood why: breaking a plate was serious business.

"I'm sorry. I didn't mean to," I managed. Then I stood up, holding a dustpan filled with shattered pieces of white porcelain, feeling trapped and ready to receive the punishment due to me.

Papa Jim recognized what was happening. I saw his eyes turn moist. "You don't have to be afraid of me." He spoke softly. "I'm not going to hurt you. I couldn't care less about a broken plate."

Papa Jim showed me grace and mercy. This way of living was so different, which was taking some getting used to.

The first Arctic frosts caused the birch tree leaves in Palmer's high country to turn bright yellow and burnt orange. Fall—the shortest season of the year in Alaska—was upon us.

My sisters and I worried about Mama and the younger children and how they were faring without eight Hales helping out around the homestead. And how was Papa reacting? Everything was a mystery.

The big project at the Buckinghams was a small log cabin that we were building for my brothers to move into once hunting season was over. It was clear that my brothers had been welcomed with open arms by the Buckinghams, and the families had grown closer together.

Love was also in the air: romance was brewing between Joseph and Lolly *and* Joshua and Sharia, which resulted in a lot of good-natured teasing. When my brothers were around, it was pretty cute how they made goo-goo eyes with the elder Buckingham daughters. After several months of courtship, the two couples were talking marriage, which made for exciting times on Lazy Mountain.

I was thrilled for Joseph and Joshua, who'd never been happier. Sharia and Lolly, in their excitement, were encouraging me to be open to the idea that I could get married and have a family someday. They were saying things like, "I'm sure God has somebody out there for you" or "You'd make a great wife for some lucky guy."

I think they talked that way because Matthew Doerksen had a way of making himself part of the woodwork around the Buckingham home. He was always in the background: he never approached me to have a conversation, and I certainly wasn't going to chat him up.

I avoided all men because I didn't see how being married would be a good thing, and I could never see myself raising children. Since marriage was off-limits to me, I was reconciled to being lonely for the rest of my life. Besides, Matthew, a college-educated draftsman a couple of years older than me, didn't seem like my kind of guy. He looked like the super serious type, and I was, well, Elishaba, the Alaskan Mountain Girl.

I had other things on my mind, like getting that cabin built. I showed the Buckinghams that I knew how to saw logs precisely and correctly with their portable sawmill. Thirteen-year-old Daniel Buckingham was my little helper.

While working a log through the sawmill one afternoon, I noticed Papa Jim and Mama Martha, several Buckingham children, and Jerusalem and Hosanna coming toward me. From the solemn looks I saw, I knew something had happened.

A terrible feeling rose in my throat.

What I didn't know at the time was that Papa Jim had a friend of a friend who knew an investigator with the Alaska State Troopers. When Jim Buckingham spoke with the investigator during this preliminary call, he told him what he knew about my story, which wasn't a whole lot but enough to share the big picture. The investigator took notes but said that until I was ready to come forward and provide more details about the sexual abuse, state police couldn't act.

At the same time, my eighteen-year-old brother Israel was living in McCarthy, where he was shoeing horses for the summer tourist trade. He was the oldest Hale child remaining in the McCarthy area; the seven younger children—all minors—were with my parents at Hillbilly Heaven, where life had to be a pressure cooker.

Then Papa blew his lid at the homestead, beating two-year-old Jonathan within inches of his life. Mama, showing some backbone, ordered Papa to leave—get out. Papa grabbed Job and Noah, thirteen and eleven at the time, and headed to Anchorage.

When the three of them returned to McCarthy for reasons unknown, they ran into Israel at the wanigan. Israel said he'd talked to Mama, and he would take the boys back to the homestead.

Papa jutted his chin. "No, you're not. They're my sons, minors under my care. You can't do a thing about it."

A shouting argument quickly turned into violence when my father swung and landed blows to Israel's face, shoulders, and stomach. One of his lips bled from a punch.

In the past, whenever Papa got physically violent with us, we would cover up, protect ourselves, or yell at my father to stop, but we never fought back. Something about crossing that line—a child hitting a parent—kept us from physically defending ourselves.

Not so for Israel that day. For the first time ever, someone stood up to my father. Israel not only fought back, but he pummeled my sixty-four-year-old father with a fury of fists, dropping him to the ground. And then my brother ran to the McCarthy-Kennicott Community Church, where he knew there was a phone in the basement. He called the only person he knew for a situation like this: Jim Buckingham.

Papa Jim listened to Israel's description of what happened. Papa Jim's advice was straightforward: "You need to call the police. And you need to tell them everything you know."

Since McCarthy was a "lawless" town and among the seventy communities in Alaska with no police presence, Israel had to call the Alaska State Troopers' office in Glennallen. After reporting the brawl between him and Papa Pilgrim, Israel told a police detective about the sexual and physical abuse my father had inflicted upon me for many years, adding that I had escaped and was living with the Buckingham family outside of Palmer.

Papa Jim spoke first as he and the others formed a half-circle around me.

"Your father got into a fight with Israel in McCarthy," he said. "Israel called the State Troopers and told them about everything that's happened between you with your Papa. Now the police want to talk to you."

I gasped. Not for what could happen to Papa but because my new family might find out all the awful details about my past. I was afraid I would mess things up for Joseph and Joshua and the Buckingham daughters and my other siblings living with the Buckinghams. What would we do without this lovely and gracious family? Where would we live? How could we support ourselves? How could we learn to be normal?

"I encouraged Israel to call the State Troopers because I want to see our family protected," Papa Jim said. The way he said *our family* told me that he included my siblings and me. "God has ordained the authorities to be there for us. That is why I am encouraging you to talk to the police, to bring justice."

This was all way too much. Everything was happening way too quickly.

"Can I think about it?" I asked, standing near the cabin under construction in the backyard. "And can I pray about it?"

"Of course. We're all here for you," Mama Buckingham said as the others nodded.

The rest of that afternoon, I felt a growing desire to tell Mama Martha *everything*. I had grown to trust her and felt safe around her. I had dreamed of having someone that I could tell my deep, dark secrets to all my life. But if I shared everything, would I be fully loved? To me, this was taking a considerable risk.

Trembling and feeling unsteady, I made my way through the big house to the front porch, where Mama Buckingham sat contently in her rocking chair, reading her Bible. She greeted me with a warm smile.

"Come have a seat, Eba," she said. "Sit here on this rocking chair."

From her welcoming and calm manner, it was evident that she had been waiting for me to talk with her.

I took in a deep breath. "I need to talk about some hard stuff," I began, afraid that I was about to pop my family's bubble of newfound happiness and cause the Buckinghams not to have anything to do with me or the rest of my siblings.

"Take your time. You are a special young woman," she affirmed. "I've been praying that you would come talk with me."

I sat there, my long, straight brown hair hanging forward over my face, unable to look at her for all the accumulated years of guilt and shame but knowing that there was to be no more hiding. This was the moment of truth.

I had no idea how to begin. I chewed on my bitten fingernails and waited, sensing her eyes seeking mine, my thoughts racing about the secret life I had hidden from her and the Buckinghams.

It took more than an hour of back-and-forth discussion before I opened up honestly to Mama Martha. After many years of practiced deceit that I learned from Papa, I hadn't had much practice telling the truth wholly and fully. Mama Martha didn't mind; she was patient and kind. Eventually, after several false starts, my sordid story began to emerge.

For the next couple of hours, I sat on the porch dumping out my guilt-ridden past. I didn't speak English very well, and my vocabulary was limited; I'm sure all the terms I used to describe my past sounded like gibberish. Trying to tell Mama Martha that my father touched me in my private places was the hardest thing to explain. I felt naked and fidgeted around for a throw blanket or a pillow to cover myself.

Mama Martha was attentive. "Let me get you something," she said. I watched her get up and walk into the house.

These few moments gave me one last chance to escape and never be seen again. Before I knew it, she was back, handing me a pillow and a blanket, which embarrassed me. It has always been hard for me to accept kindness from others.

"You didn't need to do that." I was trying to make myself feel better.

"Well, I got to take good care of my girl. So where were we?"

Mama Martha had this easygoing way about her that drew me in and made me feel like spilling all the details. Not even the worst of my horrible tale shocked her as she nodded, sympathy written all over her face.

At last, when there was nothing more to say, I looked at her and said, "By now, I'm sure you won't want me to live with you anymore. I would be a bad influence around your family, especially your daughters. I know you couldn't trust me."

Instead, she stretched her hand out and placed it on mine.

"Oh, honey. I love you so much more now that you've been open with me and allowed me to look into your life and your heart. It doesn't make me think less of you. I admire you even more. You are a brave person. None of this is your fault. We all have choices to make in life, but you are making a good choice right now in speaking the truth. The truth is going to set you free."

I couldn't believe her forgiving attitude and love toward me. What she said made it much easier for me to look her in the eyes without fear, though it was hard to see through all my tears.

I still had some doubts, though. "How can I talk and speak against my papa to the police? Papa always told me that I was to lie to the authorities to protect my family, just like Rahab did in the Bible."[2]

Mama Martha shook her head. "Eba, even those people in the Bible who lied still had to endure the consequences of their actions for the rest of their lives. When Jacob lied to his father to steal the birthright that belonged to Esau, he suffered the consequences of his lies. His father-in-law lied to him and gave him Leah instead of Rachel in marriage. His sons lied to him and caused Jacob to spend many years mourning the loss of Joseph. We can never go wrong speaking the truth."

Hearing her say this gave me great comfort and confidence. I felt a huge weight falling from my shoulders.

When we finished our talk, Mama Martha asked if her husband could join us.

---

2. Rahab was a prostitute in Jericho who lied to searchers that she didn't know where two Israelite spies were—even though she'd hidden the spies in her own home. After being spared in battle, she married into the nation of Israel, putting her into the lineage of Jesus.

"Of course," I said.

Papa Jim settled into a chair while his wife summed up the conversation of the last couple of hours.

After hearing out Mama Martha, Papa Jim turned to me, somber and severe.

"Elishaba, these things should have never happened to you. I want you to know that a husband should cherish his wife and never touch his daughter inappropriately. Mom and I love each other. Our marriage is a wonderful thing and something that God intends even for you too."

Then he asked me a tricky question. "Would you be willing to tell a police officer what you just told us?"

I stumbled for words while looking to the floor. "I don't know. I have to think about it. I'm pretty sure my siblings wouldn't be happy with me at all."

Papa Jim regarded me. "Can you honestly say that your mother and siblings will be safe if you don't say anything?"

He made a good point. The thought of saving my family was the only reason I would consider talking to the police.

"I'll do it," I said.

# 44

# THE INVESTIGATION

A few days later, I gripped Mama Buckingham's hand tightly as I walked into the Palmer office of the Alaska State Troopers feeling like a scared little girl. Papa Jim trailed a step behind to support me and help me feel safe.

The sight of several police officers in crisp black uniforms with Glock 22 pistols on their duty belts sent shivers down my spine. These men were The Law, representing the people I spent my life running and hiding from.

Mama Martha kept reassuring me. "You are amazing, Elishaba. You're doing a very hard thing, and God is using you to save others from evil bondage. If you can't do it for yourself, do it for your family."

I begged the officers to allow Mrs. Buckingham to accompany me so that I wouldn't be alone. They were kind and fatherly, clearly understanding how nervous I was.

I took a seat at a wooden table in a small, box-like room in front of a male policeman, feeling cornered and trapped. My hands shook ever so slightly. The only comfort I had was Mom Buckingham sitting quietly in the far corner.

The investigating officer smiled and assured me that I was a brave individual to come forward. He only needed to ask a few questions before I just dumped it all out. Two hours of testimony passed quickly. When I arrived at the end, I wondered what I had done. My head was spinning, and my fingers were tingly.

When the officer nodded that we were finished, I dove into Mom Buckingham's arms. "I'm very proud of my girl," she whispered into my ear.

Papa Jim had been waiting patiently outside. He greeted me warmly, saying, "I'm sure you did well, Eba."

I felt like I had broken through a brick wall. But when we got home, a veil of depression came upon me. I eased away from everyone's presence and crawled into bed. My pillow became wet with tears as bitter thoughts about my father whirled in my head.

*Papa, I hate you, I hate you. How could you have done this to me? You've ruined me. I loved you, I served you, but you betrayed me. Now, what am I? I'm nothing but a dirty old rag with no hope. Oh, I want to die . . .*

I heard footsteps coming down the stairs into the basement. I looked up and saw every Buckingham and every Hale gathering around my bedside. Then they started singing an old-time hymn that I loved:

> When peace like a river attendeth my way
> When sorrows like sea billows roll
> Whatever my lot, Thou hast taught me to say
> It is well, it is well with my soul

My troubled soul was filled with hope and love. A resolve to see this through spread throughout my heart.

My next traumatic experience was facing the Palmer grand jury and explaining the horrible things that happened to me all over again. I sat in a chair in front of a couple of dozen people while Palmer Assistant District Attorney Richard Payne questioned me. I found it hard to look up as I tearfully retold my awful story.

At one point in the hearing, Mr. Payne asked me, "How come you never got pregnant?"

When I hesitated to answer, the assistant DA asked the same question in a different way, utilizing language I had used in an earlier meeting with him: "Did your father put his private inside your private?"

I looked around, scared of my surroundings. I saw male and female police officers, investigators, and grand jury members, all with eyes glued to me. I felt so dirty and ugly that I wanted to run away to a place where no one would ever find me again.

I took a deep breath, torn as to whether I felt trapped or safe.

"Elishaba, you are a beautiful young woman," Mr. Payne continued. "You need to understand that it doesn't matter how far in or where on your body your father tried to go into you. Your father still raped you."

Somehow his words helped me to speak up.

"Truth to be told, I really don't know how far my father went into me," I began, my shaky voice barely a whisper. "Anytime he was trying to do it, I resisted him so much that I ended up black and blue from the blows of his fist. There were times when I didn't know what he was sticking inside of me. I just know it felt big, and it hurt. He promised me he wouldn't get me pregnant if I did what he said, which was, 'When I am ready to come, just stick it into your mouth.' Performing this act was sickening to do and made me feel something less than an animal. But I figured out that if I didn't do that, I would end up pregnant."[1]

The grand jury room was silent for a long time as they digested what I said. Then Mr. Payne cleared his throat and spoke again.

"If your father pushed his private anywhere into your body, even a little bit, he molested you," he stated. "Elishaba, you have been molested and raped by a man that was supposed to be your father."

I forced myself to look up from the floor and saw compassionate, tearful faces of the grand jury. As humiliating as it was to speak of those evil things done in secret, I felt comforted and supported.

On Thursday, September 22, 2005, the Palmer grand jury indicted my father, Robert Allan Hale, on thirty felony charges, including first-degree sexual assault, one count of kidnapping, and eight counts of incest. A judge issued an arrest warrant. Authorities did not release my name because of the state's victim's rights law.

The following day, Alaska State Troopers flew to McCarthy in a helicopter to arrest Papa, but they didn't find him at the wanigan. A search of the surrounding area netted nothing. Police believed that when my father saw the incoming helicopter, he took off in the direction of Chitina in a navy blue 1990 Dodge Ram camper van.

If the Buckinghams had a TV, we would have seen the statewide news programs leading with the story of the manhunt for Papa Pilgrim, the patriarch of a pioneering Christian family accused of sexually abusing one of his fifteen children. The public's help was sought to find him.

Papa Pilgrim was a wanted man in a sparsely populated state with more

---

1. I didn't know this at the time, but it *is* possible to get pregnant from pre-ejaculate fluid that enters the vagina. In fact, the Centers for Disease Control and Prevention says the "pull-out" method has a failure rate of around 22 percent, which meant I was quite fortunate to never get pregnant during ten years of frequent sexual abuse from my father. I can still remember the times when Papa told me that God wanted him to get me pregnant. If that happened, "I would have to hide you out in such a way that the world forgets about you," he said. "No one will be able to understand the kind of God-given bond between us." When I said I didn't want to have a baby by him, he got mad at me. "The only reason you're fighting me on this is because your heart is evil and turned toward Sodom," he declared. "If you're not careful, you will become like Lot's wife, who looked back and was turned into a pillar of salt. I will know that you're ready to fully give yourself over for the Kingdom of God as soon as you are ready for me to go all the way. This is my number one prayer."

than a half-million square miles of wilderness. Alaska's mountains, ravines, and forests provided an endless supply of hiding places. If there was one person who knew how to survive off the land, it had been my father—but not any longer. I knew Papa was in poor health and couldn't remain on the lam forever. At least, that was my thinking after friends called the Buckingham home to tell us that he had avoided arrest.

I knew Papa was a smart man and wasn't about to let the law catch up with him easily. He had always stayed one step ahead of the authorities, so it didn't surprise me that he went underground when the State Troopers came to arrest him.

As news of his escape became widely known, it was hard for me to grasp that my testimony had made Papa the subject of a statewide manhunt.

*Maybe I'm a betrayer. Perhaps I'm the one who turned against my family and brought all this grief and fear.*

Every time I heard the latest news bulletin about my father, I was thoroughly ashamed and wished it would all end quickly.

My thoughts ran wild when I'd fall asleep. Nightmares of my papa beating me and sexually abusing me revisited my mind. I'd wake up screaming and crying, feeling defiled all over again.

I had to get away and clear my head. To do that, Sharia and I camped out in the mountains overlooking the Buckinghams' homestead. Being in the great outdoors felt like home, made even better by the company of a girlfriend who'd become a sister to me.

I enjoyed showing off my knowledge of how to live and survive in the woods. We laughed and talked and prayed together. Every time I heard a helicopter or a plane overhead, I was sure they were looking for Papa. Still my past weighed heavily on me, leaving me feeling helpless.

One night, inside our two-person tent, I woke up convinced that someone was on top of me, smothering me, and I was about to take my last breath. I wanted to cry out for help and tell Sharia goodbye, but then I heard a sinister voice in my head tell me, *Don't say anything. She won't believe you. Just give up. This is your opportunity to die in peace.*

I cried out, "No!"

Then I shook my sleeping sister. "Sharia, I . . . I need your help. Something's wrong." She quickly recognized that I was having a serious panic attack and immediately prayed for me.

It took a while to calm down, but the alarming incident shook me up.

After a few days of camping, we returned home and learned that Papa was still a fugitive. I struggled that something might happen to my father when the police found him. He might draw a gun, and he'd be shot dead in an instant. I wanted him in jail, where he would be safe and my family would be safe from him.

Nearly two weeks after an all-points bulletin for his arrest, Alaska State Troopers hadn't gotten their man. Papa Pilgrim had disappeared into the wilderness. The state's largest police departments were backing off their search.

On Wednesday, October 5, 2005, an Alaska Railroad special agent named John Waychoff returned to work following a two-week moose-hunting trip. His boss handed him a flier with my father's picture and a description, which he placed on the dashboard of his Alaska Railroad vehicle, a Ford pickup. As a joke, Waychoff said to his supervisor, "I'll catch this guy today."

Waychoff next conducted a routine check of railroad property in Eagle River, a few miles northeast of Anchorage. When he finished his rounds, Waychoff was leaving the area when he saw a navy blue camper van coming in his direction, driving slowly.

The grizzled old hippie behind the wheel looked familiar. He glanced at the flier and then at the driver coming his way.

*It's him!*

Waychoff rolled down his window and motioned for the driver to stop.

The driver's eyes got big. The camper van slammed to a halt and started to make a U-turn. Waychoff blocked his path with his pickup, hopped out, and ordered the driver out of the vehicle.

Instead of a spit of anger, Papa Pilgrim meekly complied. He was unarmed, and his long white beard was tucked into a scarf.

Waychoff asked him if he was Robert Hale. When he nodded, Waychoff ordered him to turn around so he could handcuff him.

Papa Pilgrim complied. As soon as the handcuffs were slapped around his wrists, my father said, "I'm cold. Can you close my jacket?" Then he was directed to sit on the pickup's tailgate until police arrived to take him into custody. Waychoff would later tell reporters that he thought my father had given up, like he was "ready to be done with it."

Anchorage Police Department patrolman James Conley arrived on the scene within minutes. The old man who'd sat on the tailgate looked tired and defeated as the Anchorage cop walked Papa Pilgrim to his squad car for the trip to the downtown police precinct.[2]

My father had done all he could to escape and hide out in his vehicle, but he was unable to escape the eye of our all-seeing God. News of his arrest came as a great relief because just about anything could have happened. My father had driven past Palmer on his way to Anchorage, and he knew where the

---

2. The description of Papa's arrest comes from reporting by Tom Kizzia for the *Anchorage Daily News.*

Buckinghams lived.

What could have happened if he had stopped at the Buckinghams' log cabin home, looking for me? I shuddered after considering the possibilities. Though the police said he was unarmed at his arrest, he did have a gun in the camper—his trusty .454 Casull revolver.

I believed God protected us all.

My father's arrest was front-page news. People seemed fascinated with Papa Pilgrim and his family, most likely because of our story's uniqueness. As things settled down, I struggled with the thought that I would have to face him in court and testify against him one day.

The prosecuting attorneys talked with me multiple times and with others in my family, seeking to build a rock-solid case against my father. Each round of questioning opened the healing wound in my heart again. I don't know what I would have done if it hadn't been for the comfort my Heavenly Father gave me and the love I received from the Buckinghams.

One morning, I was sweeping the living room floor with tears dripping down my cheeks when Mom and Dad Buckingham asked me what was wrong.

"How can I forgive my father?" I sniffled. "He has taken everything away from me. I'm nearly thirty years old and should be getting started in life." These words came out with loud cries from deep in my throat.

Dad Buckingham spoke up. "Eba, do you think if a man shoots you in the shoulder, leaving a gaping wound, that he can turn around and ask forgiveness as if nothing happened? The man can be so sorry that he takes you to the hospital and sits by your side, but it won't change the fact that you now have a hole in your shoulder for the rest of your life. Your father has wounded you, and your pain is so great that it can't disappear quickly, even if he is truly sorry."

I resented all the guilt and garbage of my past. I was jealous of the older Buckingham girls. Most of them had already graduated from high school. Not only were they teaching their younger siblings, but now they were teaching us Hales. What a humiliating experience for me, sitting with the younger children and doing first- and second-grade lessons, learning the three Rs—writing, reading, and 'rithmetic.

Nevertheless, I had to face the fact that the older Buckingham children had life skills I didn't have. *Who am I compared with them?* I asked myself.

I worked hard to make up for my glaring lack of education, doing extra homework. Around the house, I pitched in wherever I could—doing dishes (try cleaning up for twenty after dinner), tackling the laundry, cleaning bathrooms, and working in the backyard, trying to be useful. Proving myself worthy of love and appreciation was all I knew.

Many evenings, Dad and Mom Buckingham would sit late into the night talking things through with me, working through my turmoil. They reassured me time and again, but they were realistic, too.

"Eba, our love for you isn't based on what you do or how hard you work around here," Papa Jim said. "God accepts and loves us even when we don't think we're worthy of Him. We want to see you happy and a part of the family. You have been through a lot, and it's going to take time to see life in a new way."

I took Papa Jim's godly wisdom to heart.

But I'd never been the most patient person in the world.

# 45
# LOVE IS IN THE AIR

No sooner was my father in custody than a helicopter was dispatched to Hillbilly Heaven with Palmer Assistant District Attorney Richard Payne and several social workers with Alaska's Child Protective Services on board.

For my younger siblings, the sight of a helicopter landing at the homestead was like Martians arriving from outer space. When Mr. Payne and the social workers interviewed my mother, Mama confirmed my testimony and agreed to come out of the mountains with my younger siblings. The Buckinghams arranged for them to move to Lazy Mountain and into a cabin that belonged to a gentleman attending the church Papa Jim pastored.

My older brothers also moved into a cabin at this time—the one that I helped build on the Buckingham property. Matthew Doerksen, the stray who loved hanging out with the Buckingham family, was invited to move in with my brothers. The more the merrier, right?

Matthew, who worked for a construction company in the area, was an interesting guy, quiet and unassuming. His parents lived near Fairbanks on a hay farm his stepfather owned. Bales of their hay ended up at the Buckinghams' place, under a tarp.

One evening, I had a dream that left me so troubled that I got up in the middle of the night and paced the upstairs hallway, trying to shake off the vivid experience. In the dream, I was walking down a muddy road, feeling depressed. The rain kept falling, creating wide ruts that caused me to slip with every step. Then Matthew walked up and asked to take my hand, but I shrunk away in fear.

He didn't give up. He kept extending his hand, saying, "Here, take it."

I relented and took his hand into mine. His hand felt so strong, yet there was a softness to it.

And then I woke up. The strangest feeling came over me: *I think I'm falling in love with Matthew.*

When I told Mom Buckingham about the dream—and how I was developing feelings for Matthew—she almost went through the roof with excitement.

But I didn't tell Matthew a word. I couldn't. I wasn't ready yet.

My eyes still averted from his when we were in the same room, and I couldn't bring myself to approach him and start a conversation. He was shy around me as well, but out of the corner of my eye, I saw him looking at me.

But what did I know about this boy/girl thing? I had been told all my life that the reason I was put on this earth was to serve Papa—in every way possible—and that I was not to look at, talk to, or engage another man.

All this was so strange to me.

At my father's arraignment in Palmer—thank goodness I didn't have to appear—bail was set at fifty thousand dollars, which meant my father needed to come up with ten percent of that amount to be released from jail until his court date. He didn't have five thousand dollars to buy a bail bond. Let's just say the rest of his family was in no mood to pass the hat.

Fortunately, there was some happy family news to take my mind off the looming trial. On Christmas Day, in front of more than two dozen Hales and Buckinghams, Joshua got everyone's attention away from the food and presents. Then he got down on one knee and asked Sharia to marry him, setting off an explosion of happiness.

We were all absorbing this breathtaking moment when Joseph announced that he had something important to share. To Lolly's tearful surprise, he too got down on one knee and asked for her hand in marriage as well!

There was a chorus of affirmation and unleashed joy all around. As we enjoyed the moment, Dad Buckingham told anyone who would listen that when the Hales first stayed with the family, he teased his oldest daughters, saying, "You might just marry one of those wild boys someday."

To which a smiling Mom Buckingham repeated what she said at the time: "Over my dead body!"

Joshua and Sharia weren't wasting any time: they set a date to get married at the Buckingham home on Saturday, March 11, 2006.

Think about it: I was thirty years old and had never seen a wedding before. On a frozen winter day, I got pretty emotional when Joshua, dressed in his riding clothes, came out of the woods atop his great steed. He jumped off the horse to greet Sharia, clad in a beautiful white wedding dress she had sewn herself. A couple of hundred witnesses were bundled up against the cold.

After Papa Jim read their vows and pronounced them husband and wife, Joshua hopped back on his mount and reached down to pull Sharia onto the back of his horse. Off they went as the entire wedding party threw snowballs at them.

There was no snow on the ground when Joseph married Lolly on a grassy meadow not far from the Buckingham home on Saturday, July 2, 2006, with the stately Talkeetna Mountains as a backdrop. Around a hundred guests sat on outdoor log benches while the unmarried Hale and Buckingham children planted themselves on the grass. Like my sisters, I wore a summery gingham dress in cornflower blue.

Following in the footsteps of Joshua and Sharia, Joseph and Lolly made a dramatic entrance as well. Joseph, dressed in brown pants and vest, a long-sleeved white shirt, and wearing a Stetson hat and boots, carried a flower as he walked in from the meadow's left side at the same time Lolly approached from the right. She looked like an angel in a full-length crepe dress in white with a wreath of pale rose and blue gentians in her hair.

They met in the middle, where Joseph doffed his hat, politely handed her the flower, and embraced her—setting off oohs and aahs because all of us knew the couple had never clinched or cuddled each other before this day.

As Papa Jim explained during the ceremony, Joseph and Lolly were committed to each other for life. To express their desire to be clean and pure before God and man, they chose not to have physical contact before marriage. I grinned as I remembered the times when I'd been asked to chaperone them during their courting days. I didn't know what the word "chaperone" meant, but I sure learned in a hurry!

After exchanging vows, Papa Jim could barely contain his excitement as he looked to Joseph and said, "You may kiss your bride."

The oohs and aahs were replaced by thunderous applause for their first kiss.

After a potluck buffet, Joseph and Lolly cut the cake. Then the guests were handed a blue or white balloon and asked to form a giant circle in the meadow. Once again from the left, Joseph entered the meadow atop a horse-drawn carriage led by Reuben, his grey Percheron stallion. Lolly was waiting for him in the middle of our circle.

Once Joseph brought her on board, he snapped the reins, and they were off on their honeymoon. That was our signal to release all our balloons into the brilliant sky.

As I watched my white balloon sail high into the heavens, I wondered if such a magical afternoon was in my future.

I also wondered what Matthew was thinking.

Throughout 2006, I'd be informed of a court date and that I needed to be prepared to testify against my father. Then I'd learn of yet another postponement, and it turned my world upside down every time.

Dad Buckingham had warned me that the wheels of justice turn slowly. That was a good thing because I needed time and space at a moment when strange feelings of silent love were growing for Matthew. For someone who went out of her way not to make eye contact with him, I couldn't help noticing almost everything he did, like when he'd get up early each morning to get ready for work and leave a note for everyone hanging on a beam by the kitchen. The messages contained a Scripture verse and an encouraging thought for the day. I felt like those notes were just for me. I liked practicing my reading when no one was looking during breakfast time.

That was the heartening side of life, the rays of sunlight. However, too many storm clouds swept through whenever I thought about what my father took from me, especially my innocence. Whenever those convictions consumed me, I became angry to the point of seeking revenge. My emotions would tumble like a waterfall, and I'd fall into a deep pool of despair.

Each time that happened—when things got really dark for me—I'd grab a pup tent, throw some food and a few things in a backpack, and take off for the mountains. The wilderness environment was a place I could control, whereas life in community with others was one I couldn't. To keep disaster from happening, I was determined to go my own way.

Each time I set up camp, I asked myself questions like:

*What are you running from?*

*Why do you keep running?*

I didn't have good answers, which explained why I was an emotional basket case too many times when I was around the Buckingham family. Dad and Mom Buckingham remained loving and told me they were willing to listen, but I shut them out every time. And off to the mountains I'd go.

One time when I came back, none of my clothes, shoes, schoolbooks, etc., were in the upstairs bedroom I shared with the older girls. Everything was gone.

"Where's my stuff?" I asked Mom Buckingham.

"We put it all in the cabin in the back."[1]

When I asked her why, she replied evenly that now wasn't the right time to

---

1. This gets a little complicated, but my mother and the rest of the Hale children moved to the Buckingham property and my unmarried brothers and Matthew moved into the main house basement. Mom Buckingham's parents, who were living in Georgia, moved into an addition to the main house that had a basement and an apartment. Grandmother Mary, as we called her, was a schoolteacher and helped teach me and my siblings.

discuss why she moved me out of the main house and into the little cabin. We could have that discussion later, she said.

I walked into the cute log cabin, alone, and saw my stuff packed into totes sitting by a bed. I fell onto the mattress, heaving, and cried so hard. The stinging rejection of Mom Buckingham cut to my wounded heart. I decided I wasn't leaving that bed until I was dead and in my grave. I wouldn't eat or drink. I'd let my body waste away.

Whenever the girls would bring me a meal, I'd refuse to consume any food. After two days of starving myself, Mom Buckingham came to my bedside.

"Eba," she said firmly but with no hint of anger, "you need to get up and eat. You are harming yourself. This is a sin. God would have you take care of yourself."

I listened, but I didn't reply. *Just let me die in peace.*

After a moment, Mom Buckingham had something else to add. "When people act like you're doing, they take them to a crazy home. Is this what you want us to do? If you're not careful, you could force us to do something like that."

Now *that* sounded scary to me. I didn't want to be locked up like my father.

"I'll let you think about it." Mom Buckingham got up and left.

That afternoon, one of my sisters brought me a cassette tape to listen to. The speaker was an older woman who shared her story about being sexually abused by her father. The presentation was painful to listen to, but then she said something that hit me like a lightning bolt:

> I was fifty years old and carried this heavy secret for many years, even from my husband. After messing up so many relationships, after feeling worthless, rotten, and lonely, I finally shared my story with a group of women. That's when I first felt freedom.

I did not want to wait until I was fifty before overcoming what my father had done to me. I didn't want life to pass me by. I got up and entered the main house, where I joined everyone for dinner. My family greeted me warmly, saying they were glad to see me as I filled a plate with food.

I was weak and weary, but I was also determined to overcome my painful past. I took a tentative step toward recovery, unsure what lay ahead.

The rest of 2006 can be characterized in this way:

1. Papa's trial kept being postponed, but he remained behind bars.
2. I still had a runaway attitude in my heart.
3. I couldn't get Matthew out of my mind.

Things came to a head after I went into the mountains *again* because I couldn't handle everyday life. I spent my days reading through the entire New Testament and scribbling thoughts in a journal. A story in the Gospel of Mark, the fifth chapter, came alive to me. A woman who suffered for twelve years from constant bleeding spent everything she had on treatments, but she had gotten no better. The passage continued with this:

> When she heard about Jesus, she came up behind him in the crowd and touched his cloak, because she thought, "If I just touch his clothes, I will be healed." Immediately her bleeding stopped and she felt in her body that she was freed from her suffering.
>
> At once Jesus realized that power had gone out from him. He turned around in the crowd and asked, "Who touched my clothes?"
>
> "You see the people crowding against you," his disciples answered, "and yet you can ask, 'Who touched me?' "
>
> But Jesus kept looking around to see who had done it. Then the woman, knowing what had happened to her, came and fell at his feet and, trembling with fear, told him the whole truth. He said to her, "Daughter, your faith has healed you. Go in peace and be freed from your suffering."
> —Mark 5:27-34 (NIV)

I was that woman who was trembling with fear before the Lord. I was the one who needed healing. Tears came to my eyes when I realized how personal Jesus was when He called her "daughter."

I realized I was His daughter as well. He loved me and wanted me to call him Father—and be the father I never had.

After eight days in the wilderness, a couple of my brothers arrived with some food—and a letter from Dad and Mom Buckingham. My heart sank: I knew they weren't afraid to call me out.

I opened the letter, which contained this paragraph:

> We love you, Elishaba, but we ask if you come back home, then you need to repent and say you're sorry for leaving. We would also have you know that things won't be the same for you here. We realize that you have a lot to work through, but we can't let you affect the younger children, who are also in great need as you are. Thus, we would ask that you keep your distance from the children so as not to impact them as you have been doing.

The letter fell from my hands. All I could do was cry. I couldn't even speak out loud to God as life passed through my head in waves. I saw myself alone, traveling down a road that ended in destruction. Like the woman in the Bible, I had lost everything and was considered too unstable to be around the children.

This was rock bottom. There was no further down I could go. But the rock I found at the bottom was Jesus Himself. I pictured myself as a box of nasty dirty rags with nothing to offer my Lord and Savior. I forced myself to lift my shameful eyes that were cast down and look up to Jesus' face. At that moment, I chose to ask Him to forgive me for the way I'd been acting and open my heart to a new relationship with Him that I had never known before. It was time to stop blaming my father for my actions and let Him take complete control of my past, present, and future.

With an attitude that I had nothing to lose and a new relationship with God I had never known before, I packed up camp and headed home. At dinner that night, with everyone gathered around, including Matthew, I asked for their forgiveness for the way I'd been behaving toward them.

"I'm done blaming everyone else for my behavior," I said. "I have met Jesus and know God loves me. I'm willing to receive whatever the consequences are, but I need my family, and that's you."

I looked across the living room and noticed Matthew sitting on a stool next to my brother David. He regarded me with a wide, warm smile that spoke of love and showed me that I was worth waiting for.

On January 22, 2007, the night before my thirty-first birthday, I knelt beside my bed and poured out my heart to God.

I was single and lonely, but I was in love with Matthew. That much I knew deep within me. But would he choose me to be his bride? Would he consider me worthy with my evil past?

Kneeling there, I cried out, "Lord, please allow me to become Matthew's bride within the year." Then, with tears dripping down my cheeks, I slipped under the covers with thoughts of a smiling Matthew bouncing in my mind. I knew he was thinking about marriage because he told me so in a note, but Matthew also said he needed to hear from God about His direction for us.

When I woke up, I headed to breakfast. *Everyone* was there waiting for my arrival, including the two newlywed couples, the Buckingham grandparents, and both sets of families—probably thirty in all.

No sooner had I taken a seat on the couch when someone flipped off the lights.[2] A chorus of "Happy Birthday, dear Eba" rang out. I wondered where

---

2. Remember, this was January in Alaska, when days are short. Sunrise was at 9:39 a.m. that morning.

Matthew was. When I found him sitting on the carpet, I realized he was being careful to keep his distance.

Lolly placed a warm pan of coffee cake in my lap, dotted with lighted candles that I blew out.

"Does anyone have a gift for Eba?" Dad Buckingham called out.

As I handed the pan back to Lolly, I looked up. Matthew got up off the floor and approached me with a bouquet of three red roses in his hand. A sly grin creased his lips.

Right there, in front of everyone, he knelt before me. "Elishaba, will you marry me?" he asked expectantly.

As if a mountain blew its top inside of me, I burst out in tears. "Yes!" I nearly shrieked. "Yes!"

Being engaged was wonderful. My heart skipped a beat every time I saw my love after his workday was over. If we didn't get enough time to see each other after dinner, we'd each write notes about our futures and share them the following morning. I'd never felt this much excitement in my life.

From the start, Matthew was keen on having a "no-touch" engagement, a decision that helped me build trust in him. There was something special knowing Matthew loved me for who I was, without the physical contact. We did our best to be completely open and honest with each other about our pasts. When I told him my legal name was Butterfly Sunstar but that I hated it, he helped me get a hearing before a judge to legally change my name to Elishaba Trust Hale.[3]

One evening, we were both sitting at a table when I shared a deep fear I had. "I want to know what you believe about a woman's place in the home," I said. "My father always told me that God made me the weaker vessel. Since I'm a woman, he said I have no say or voice."

Matthew reached for an old-fashioned oil lamp that decorated the table. "I see it like this," he began. "The woman is much like this lamp—delicate, beautiful, and yet so important. The man's job is to cherish her much like this oil lamp so she can shine."

Our love grew stronger with each passing day. We didn't want to wait too long to marry, so we settled on Saturday, May 12, 2007. I immediately began sewing my wedding dress—a white wedding dress.

I knew white was the color of purity, and I wasn't pure. That quality had been

---

3. Trust was the middle name given to me by my father. I decided to keep it as a reminder to place my trust in God despite all I've been through.

snatched from me. Mom Buckingham knew precisely what I was thinking: *I'm damaged goods. How can I have a normal marital relationship with Matthew, including the physical part?*

One time, Mom Buckingham and I went on a walk and had a deep discussion about the most intimate aspect of being married—the sexual relationship. "Marriage, dearest Eba, is holy and right before God. A man and his wife are supposed to have pleasure in each other, and there is no limit. Sex is supposed to be fun and exciting, something God created in beauty."

"But . . . but I'm not sure I can handle this." The thought consumed my heart.

Mom Buckingham stopped and took my hands into hers. "Your father was full of selfish, lustful desires that weren't normal. When a man and a woman are in love and God has brought them together in marriage, then the physical love between them is right and good and never a cause for shame. It's a holy mystery and a powerful bonding agent that will affect your relationship with Matthew as nothing else can. You are pure, Eba. Jesus' blood cleansed you from all your sins. You are now free to represent yourself as a pure princess of God to your Matthew."

Her words were just what I needed to hear.

There were so many things to learn about getting married. When Matthew's grandmother asked me if I planned to wear a veil, I had no idea what she was talking about. Then I realized that it was customary for the father to walk his daughter up the aisle and give her away.

Well, that wasn't going to happen. Dad Buckingham was the natural stand-in. But even though he'd become a father to me in such a short time, that didn't feel right for some reason.

At two o'clock in the afternoon of May 12 at Lazy Mountain Bible Church, I waited in a small room for my cue. I stood up and looked at a mirror hanging on the wall. When I saw myself, tears of joy ran down my face. Taking a deep breath, I uttered out loud, "How did this happen? You look so beautiful. Are you ready for this? You're about to become a wife to the love of your life."

I gathered myself and stepped outside the room and into the church foyer, where Matthew was waiting for me with a bridal bouquet. His face registered surprise since he had not seen me in my wedding dress before this moment.

We had decided that Matthew would walk me down the aisle. I took his hand—we hadn't held hands before this moment—as we passed more than two hundred friends and family members filling the pews.

After Dad Buckingham led us through our marriage vows, our first kiss seemed easy and natural. When the reception was over, Matthew had a special "get-away" vehicle waiting for us—a dump truck—with "Just Married" written in shaving cream across the side of the dump bed and tin cans tied to the rear axle. We drove off with waves and air kisses to where Matthew's silver Toyota was stashed away. Then it was off to the Highland Glen Lodge Bed and Breakfast in downtown Anchorage, both of us knowing what was supposed to happen next.

As Matthew carried me over the threshold—another custom I knew nothing about—he laid me down on the bed and said, "I'm willing to hold you all night. We don't need to do anything else."

My love grew when he gave me the freedom to make this choice—from a husband who entered the marriage bed as a virgin.

"No, I want to do this for you," I replied.

I'll admit this: I did not feel any sexual desire at that moment. I took my mind elsewhere. Matthew sensed this and was patient and kind.[4]

For our honeymoon, Matthew wanted to show me off to all his family and friends in Alaska and the Lower 48, so we spent two months driving around thirteen states. Each time we entered a city or town that I'd been to before, I experienced cultural shock as well as condemning voices in my head from my father.

Along the way, Matthew and I talked openly about my past, even though it was rough at times. He wanted to know everything about me, including more details about how I grew up. When we talked about including the Sangre de Cristo mountains of New Mexico as part of our trip, we decided together that returning to the old homestead would be a good thing for our marriage. That way, Matthew could get a sense of what life was like before we moved to Alaska.

We parked at the bottom of the mountain. After a couple of hours of steady uphill walking, we arrived at Rainbow Cross.

Matthew was shocked by the sight of our old family cabin, which was leaning precariously and looking even more rundown. We both had to duck our heads through the narrow two-foot-wide doorway into the living area, which reeked of dust and odd smells.

"You guys lived here?"

---

4. Whenever I meet women who have heard my story, they all want to know the same thing: *What happened on your wedding night? What was it like to make love with your husband?* In the beginning, my mind always left the room, but that has changed thanks to Matthew, who gently took the time to show me that sexually I was not an object to him. Our sexual intimacy stems from a sacred and mutual desire to invite each other in, giving to each other and receiving from each other. After getting counseling from my marriage and family therapist Larry Severson, I have come to understand that sex is more than just physical pleasure: it is a God-given gift of connecting, expressing, and experiencing oneness with the one you love.

"Yup. Can you believe it?"

I found myself staring at the memories:

*That's where Papa's Chair was.*

*That's where I sat on the ground and listened to him read* Pilgrim's Progress.

*That's where the poo bucket was.*

*That's where I slept.*

I couldn't spend much time inside the cabin, which felt like a dungeon. We left the dilapidated building and were walking around when we stumbled upon something I never wanted to see again: the metal bathtub.

We stopped as Matthew put an arm around my waist. "I'm sorry, my love."

We had brought our camping gear with us.

When Matthew suggested a flat spot in front of the cabin, I recoiled. "We can't camp here," I said.

Matthew didn't catch on to *why* I felt this way because at the time, I was having great difficulty forming the proper sentences to explain my complicated feelings. I told him I would feel safer if we made camp up on a hill overlooking the front of the cabin.

As I led him there, Matthew sensed something was amiss. "We don't have to do this," he said.

"No, I need to see this through," I replied. "I'm going to overcome this with you by my side." We were in this together now. I realized that God had given me a husband in Matthew, and I could push away that gift or choose to allow God to work a new life in me. At that moment, surrounded by decaying buildings and a barn, I decided to take back what was stolen from me and press forward with the love of my life.

We spent three days hiking all over the mountains. I think I wore Matthew out by showing him all the spots where I grazed sheep and rode my horses. Before we left Rainbow Cross, though, Matthew got an idea that sounded great to me. I watched as he tore away the Scriptures that my father had carved onto wood plaques that were attached to walls near the cabin and bathtub area. Then he made a small fire and tossed the plaques into the flames.

"These plaques are an abomination to the Lord," he said. "They were used by your father to get his evil ways with you and your siblings."

When we got home from our honeymoon, Matthew and I agreed that we knew each other better and more profoundly than we did two months earlier on our wedding day.

That made me feel good because I would need Matthew totally in my corner when we walked into an Alaskan courtroom hand in hand, where I would be confronted with my past.

I was scared of testifying against my father as he watched me from the defense table.

I figured he still had a hold on me, but with a husband by my side and a renewed faith in God, I would be ready to face Papa Pilgrim.

# 46
# FACING PAPA PILGRIM

Settling into married life was . . . different.

We moved into a one-bedroom home in Palmer at the same time Matthew got a new job working as a draftsman for a telecommunications company.[1] For the first time, I wasn't around *anyone* during the day, which took some getting used to.

Even something as simple as grocery shopping threw me for a loop. I'd push a shopping cart through the store, scared to spend too much money since I didn't know what I was doing. Matthew went food shopping with me a couple of times to show me how to figure out what the better deal was or where stuff was located, but my mind went blank each time I toured the aisles alone.

With no one to talk to unless I made a phone call, I struggled with my emotions as I waited for Matthew to come home from work. Then I'd dump everything into his lap, including the anger that boiled to the surface whenever I dwelled on what my father did to me. Thoughts of revenge filled my mind, but I was also apprehensive about what would happen when I faced him in a courtroom.

And then a legal bombshell: a few weeks before Thanksgiving in 2007, we received news that the Palmer district attorney's office and my father had come to a plea deal agreement. In exchange for not going to a jury trial, Papa Pilgrim consented to a fourteen-year sentence for sexually assaulting me and pleading guilty to charges that included rape, incest, and coercion.

The assistant district attorney, Richard Payne, told the news media that initially he was against making any kind of plea bargain with my father because of all the loathsome things he did to me, but two things changed his mind:

---

1. Matthew sold some property that he owned before we got married to buy this starter home for us.

- My father's health was rapidly deteriorating. Diabetes was ravaging his body. Doctors found severe blood clots in his legs and said he only had months to live.
- Mr. Payne wanted to protect me from testifying, knowing how traumatic that would be on my family and me.

I breathed a sigh of relief, but looming in my future was a different day in court. Even though there would be no trial, the Hale family had the right to face the perpetrator—in this case, my father—and share our victim impact statements, which would describe the emotional and physical wounds we suffered.

But could I hold up under pressure? I wasn't sure, and I confided in Matthew about my doubts.

"I know when I get into my father's presence that it will only take one look from his eyes to tell me what he's thinking," I said to my husband over dinner one night. "I'm afraid I'll get confused and terrified."

Matthew reached across the table and placed his hand on mine. "Type out what you want to say and then read it to him. He can do nothing to stop you."

My husband had a good idea. I had been working hard to learn how to type. The next day, I started clacking away on the keyboard. I would fill nine pages with thoughts straight from my pierced heart.

And then I started practicing what I would say. It would be the first time I'd ever get to talk to my father without the danger of him interrupting me—either with his angry words, or, worse yet, with a fist to my face.

On November 26, 2007, the Monday after Thanksgiving, fourteen of the fifteen Hale children,[2] Mama Rose, several Buckinghams, and our spouses, including Matthew, arrived at Superior Court in Anchorage.

My family, along with news reporters and TV camera crews, somehow squeezed into the small courtroom, which had three rows for spectators. Seated next to Matthew, I knew I would be speaking last, which ratcheted up the pressure on me.

I stopped breathing when a side door opened: there was Papa in a wheelchair, clad in a loose-fitting canary yellow prison jumpsuit, being pushed by a court bailiff. He looked like he had aged ten years. His silver-white hair still reached his shoulders, and his straggly beard still drooped from his chin to his chest. His beady eyes, behind a pair of black-rimmed glasses, searched the courtroom as if he was surveying a hostile environment. When his gaze came in my direction,

---

2. The youngest child, Jonathan, was four years old, too young for such a proceeding.

I averted my eyes.

I squeezed Matthew's hand. "This is worse than I thought it was going to be," I whispered.

"You're going to be fine," my husband soothed. "He will never get out of prison."

We stood as Judge Donald Hopwood, a middle-aged man dressed in a traditional black silk gown, walked in and took his place at a raised wooden podium.

He looked at his notes and got right down to business, announcing why we were all there on this November morning—to hear from the victims of crimes committed by the defendant Robert Hale. He glanced at a list. "I see that the defendant's wife will be first. Kurina Rose Hale, are you ready?"

My mother led off by saying her husband insisted that only he had a perfect understanding of the Bible and spiritual matters. "This is how he justified all his immoral activity," she said. "Our family lived two different lives. On the outside, we looked quaint and could be quite charming when it suited us. But behind closed doors, the battle was always raging."

And then Mama said something that caused my ears to perk up. "Pilgrim brainwashed my daughter and convinced her to have sex with him," she said.

*Wait a minute. That's not what happened. Papa tried to brainwash me, but I was never convinced to have sex with him. He certainly did his best to justify and rationalize what he did. Papa knew what he was doing.*

Her husband took advantage of a naïve, immature, and uneducated daughter and chipped away at her natural-born defenses until he satisfied his sexual urges. When I grew older and became more resistant to his sexual slavery, he beat me with his fists and with a rod.

Mama meant well, and I knew she was on my side, but her remarks reminded me that this was going to be a rough day.

Next was my youngest sister, Bethlehem. "Papa, do you know that I am seven now?" she asked in an angelic voice that faded off into tears. Her words cut me to the heart. *It is my fault that she has lost her father. If only I had never been born.*

Lamb, nine years old, was next. Reading from her letter, she said matter-of-factly:

> Dear Father, I have lots of things I want to say to you. It has been over two years since I have seen you. I hope you will listen to what I say and not think I'm saying something that I don't think. I remember how you used to read letters and mark all over them about what you thought the person was trying to say. Please, please don't do that to my letter. Please listen to what I say because I love you and want to share my heart with you.

> I am not a little girl anymore. I am nine years old. I am doing third-grade work in some of my books. I wish things had been different when I was a little girl so that I would not have so many bad things on my mind all the time. Sometimes I have bad nightmares at night. One of my saddest memories is when you beat up baby Jonathan. He was just a little baby and playing with rocks. He threw a rock over my head accidentally and never even hurt me. You got very mad and started beating him. He fell over on the rocks, and you kept beating him until I thought he would die.

Lamb stopped. Choked up, she couldn't read anymore. After regaining her composure, she soldiered on.

> Mama tried to stop you, but you kept on beating him with a rod. I tried to stop you too, and you swat at me too. This would not have hurt me so badly if I had been one of the bigger children. I knew inside that it could not be right for a big man to be beating such a little baby.

Tears of anguish fell from my eyes. I looked for something to wipe my nose. I felt for Abraham when it was his turn. He was the baby brother I raised.

Reading from his letter, Abraham said, "The main thing I remember is when I saw you beat up Elishaba. I saw her on the bed lying down, and then she sat up. I saw you punch her in the chest. I went away and cried."

It was scary every time I heard my name mixed with Papa's. The shame I felt as one family member after another expressed the hurt, confusion, and fear they felt after witnessing what my father did to me took my breath away. How could Papa think his children would never notice what he did to me and the others?

Each testimony was gut-wrenching and painful to hear. My siblings reminded me of things that I had blocked from my memory, like the time when Jerusalem said, "Papa, you tied me to my brother and made us sleep on the floor for a week without food because we were talking behind your back about you and Elishaba."

Israel said, "It's hard to call you a father. I was beaten and treated like a slave."

Joshua caused me to grab another tissue when he addressed his brothers and sisters. "I want to ask forgiveness that I ever let things go on like that in our house. I don't know what possessed me. I beat my chest and wept. There is so much to undo; there is so much that can't be undone."

I was careful not to catch Papa looking at me, but I couldn't help myself from sneaking a peek at his pitiful state. If there was a second when I felt the slightest sympathy for him, I'd remind myself that his meanness, brutality, and manipulative nature were why we were in the courtroom that day.

There was a common theme from my siblings' testimony: they asked Judge Hopwood to send our father to prison for a long time because they feared what would happen to us if he was released.

I felt exactly the same way.

We were running out of time when it was finally my turn. At 4:18 p.m., Assistant District Attorney Richard Payne approached the bench. "We have twelve minutes left," he said to Judge Hopwood, "and we still have one more victim statement."

I didn't know that courtrooms were so punctual. Even though it'd been a long, emotionally tough day, I figured we'd go until everyone finished. I definitely didn't want to have this hanging over me for another night. I had lost enough sleep as it was.

Up at the bench, Mr. Payne spoke to the judge in a whisper. "It's obvious that we're going to have to go into tomorrow morning, and I would like us to break now. I know we have twelve minutes to use, but in the big picture, I don't see it making sense trying to rush her."

The judge asked how long I was expecting to speak.

"Thirty minutes," replied the assistant DA.

"If it's going to take a half hour, can we do it today?" Judge Hopwood asked.

Mr. Payne was resistant, saying that I was a slow reader and had many pages to go through. "It's going to be difficult for her to get through it," he said.

Judge Hopwood considered the request, but he didn't want to make me wait until the morning. I believe he understood that I had emotionally prepared myself for this moment—today—and if I didn't get to share my victim impact statement that afternoon, then I might back out in the morning.

"I'm inclined to go now because we have some time, so we'll just go to the end," the judge said, adding that he preferred that I deliver my statement from the witness stand instead of from the prosecution's table, where some of my younger siblings had shared their statements. I believe Judge Hopwood said this because he wanted me to be directly in Papa's line of sight from the defense table.

My heart was booming in my chest as I was motioned to the witness stand next to the judge. Matthew was allowed to accompany me. My clammy hand gripped his as we took seats side-by-side and settled in, my nine-page letter in my shaking hand.

"Can you tell me your name?" the judge asked.

"My name is Elishaba Speckels."[3]

Even answering a simple question like this was hard. My hands shook as I looked at my printed-out pages and began reading, my voice quivering and tears *this close* to falling. I started with this:

> Dear Father, I'm grateful for the chance to speak to you today. I have so much that I feel I need to say to you. This is the opportunity for me to speak what is on my mind in the presence of others. I have tried so many times to tell you the deepest concerns in my heart about the things done in secret—things that I felt were wrong, but things you insisted were right before God.
>
> I did not know the truth because you were very careful to be sure to teach me to believe exactly what you wanted me to believe. I now speak with an understanding that I did not have two-and-a-half years ago. My eyes have been opened, just like Eve in the Garden when she bit into the apple and her eyes were open to her nakedness.
>
> When my eyes were open to the truth of my relationship with you, I found myself naked and unclean before God and before man. As you knew it would, this truth devastated me, but in God, I am forgiven, and I have found forgiveness and cleansing. He has set my heart free so that I no longer sit in condemnation of myself.
>
> I'm going to try to sum up here today, in as few words as I can, my past life with being betrayed with the pain, sorrow, and hurt to the little girl who loved and trusted her father as much as I did with a pure heart. Words cannot express how my trusting heart was broken over and over again as you took advantage of my ignorance to pursue your own selfish pleasures.
>
> I was just a little girl who wanted to please her Papa. I was willing to do anything to please you, and you used my pure love to work yourself into an unholy physical relationship with me.

I then described much of the sexual and physical abuse that happened to me that I have shared in this book—as well as the physical abuse to my brothers—minus the graphic details but in a way that no one misunderstood what I was

---

3. My husband was born Matthew Doerksen, but his father died tragically at the of age of thirty-three when he was trying to help someone out of a ditch. Matthew was just seven years old. His mother, Deborah, remarried a year later to Randy Speckels. He eventually adopted Matthew and his sisters Bethany and Mary and gave them the last name Speckels, which is why we were legally married as Matthew and Elishaba Speckels. When we visited Matthew's paternal grandfather, Ben Doerksen, after our wedding, he told Matthew that he was his only grandson and the last living Doerksen on his family tree. Matthew wanted to carry on the family name, so after the victim impact statements, we went to court and had our names legally changed to Matthew and Elishaba Doerksen.

talking about. About ten minutes in, I couldn't hold back the tears any longer. Each sentence was difficult to get through, like when I recounted how Papa had my brothers lay across a barrel and whipped them with a braided leather whip, drawing blood. Or after we bathed together in the wilderness and he told me not to get dressed but to put on a robe and wait for him on the bed in the back of the truck. With each account of his hideous abusive behavior, the courtroom gasped. Many times I had to stop, compose myself, and blow my nose before I could continue:

> As young children, we were taught to trust everything that you said. You always had the latest word from God, and it seemed like you helped God make the judgments on whether we had done something bad enough to go to hell.
>
> My brothers and I lived with a terrible fear of dying and spending our lives in eternal hellfire. We would do just about anything to get your approval, hoping that with that approval you would indicate that we were among the saved ones. I can hardly believe how I could have been simple-minded enough to swallow the things that you said, like the number one prayer you prayed—that we would all live or die together.
>
> Or the time you told me if we don't all die together, then at least your hope was that I would die with you. According to you, without my help, you could not get Mama pregnant, and therefore I would be a murderer, killing babies that God wanted you to have. I definitely didn't want to kill babies.
>
> You told me that it was in the Bible that even God condoned a father having a sexual relationship with his daughter. You had purposed that your children would not be able to read and write so that they would never find out whether what you were saying was true or not.
>
> Somehow, I learned to read a bit, and I would try to search the Scriptures when you were not looking. Whenever you would catch me, you'd become very angry, and often I would get a harsh beating for being rebellious, trying to prove you were wrong. All my life, I watched you twist the truth of things to make yourself be the one in the right. If you could manage to shift the blame onto someone else, you would feel you had won great victory.
>
> You carefully made up signs and visions that you used on me. Whenever I would show the least bit of resistance to your physical advances, you would remind me that God was the one that approved of our relationship. And yet to me, it often seemed like you would just make up a vision with the forethought of needing to use it later, to get your own way.

Of course, I would never have dared to speak of my doubts openly because you said to question you would be the same as blaspheming the Holy Spirit of God. And that would be a sin that could never be forgiven. I'm glad now that I can stand and speak with confidence that all those visions were lies.

You convinced us that life being separated from others, even from Christians or a church family, was the way God intended us to live. You told us that marriage was wrong for us to think about or even believe in.

Then I described how Papa ordered me to beat the other children on his behalf, but I had to stop for a minute because I was so choked up by the terror I caused. When I composed myself, I told him that like Romans 1, he had turned the truth of God into a lie:

You were purposed to give the picture of what a loving, godly family we were, when behind the scenes life was a living hell for our family. We didn't even know how bad it was until we could live outside our home and see that other families did not live under the same terror. To this day, many of us children suffer almost nightly with horrible nightmares about the way you treated us. Most nights, my dear husband wakes to my terrifying cries and has to hold me close and pray for me before I can feel calm again. This is not the way it should be.

I have heard that you continue to say to this day that you did nothing wrong. How can you say this with a good conscience when so many people witnessed your behavior over and over again? You did force me into doing what you wanted me to do, and you forced me to give up the purest intents of my heart for the sake of trying to make you happy.

Whenever I tried to question what you were making me do or question the reason you gave to make it sound like it was okay to have a sexual relationship with your daughter, you would get so angry at my resistance. At those moments, I would find myself seeing stars from your heavy hand, beating me.

There was no end to the ways you could think of to punish me for not meeting your physical demands. It seemed like you would do anything to find an excuse to beat me up. In my weakest state, I would always end up giving in to the pressure to once again meet your sexual desires. You got a sick delight in looking at all my bruises you had put on me when I resisted you.

You would boast at what you had done as if there was some secret delight in being able to overcome my resistance. All this you did in the name of God and love. I can remember you trying to convince me time and time again that I just didn't know how blessed I was, that every woman would just love to have a man who knew how to love like you did. I now know differently. My husband, Matthew, has shown me what real love is, which is totally gentle, unselfish, and full of caring for my physical needs.

I then spoke of the specifics: the time Papa beat me up in the Buckinghams' basement, leaving a bruised lump on my jaw, and how he didn't want the Buckinghams to see me in that condition and banished me to sleeping outside in the van. And then the three days of horror at the wanigan in McCarthy:

> After beating me severely, I made a desperate dash for the door. You grabbed me by the hair and half-slammed me into the door, dragging me back in, and started punching me with those trained fists that you yourself boasted about—your own great abilities in the boxing arena. I can testify to how skillful those hands were in delivering the punch.

When I got back to Hillbilly Heaven, I said I felt the support of my family. They could see that I had suffered greatly. But that beating in the wanigan was a turning point for me. Even if it meant dying and going to hell, I could not live that way any longer. When my older brothers confronted my father, Papa hauled off and punched Joshua in the face, knocking him to the floor and breaking his nose.

Then I escaped on a snow machine with Jerusalem, which led me into my final words:

> I did leave you because I hated you. But I can declare before God that I have no bitterness toward you anymore, for I have learned that bitterness is the only way I can allow you to destroy the beautiful work that God has done in setting me free from the horrors of the past.
>
> I go on in the joy of the Lord with a husband, brothers, sisters, mothers, fathers, and children, all around me. I pray that someday you will also have the joy of being united with your family in your heart because you have been willing to admit who you have been and what you have done, and through the humility of admitting these things, find forgiveness from God.
>
> Elishaba Trust Speckels. It is well with my soul.

And that's how I finished—with this challenge to my father to acknowledge and confess his despicable actions to my family and me because an apology was in order. A big apology.

It was a relief not to have to come back and finish up in the morning, but I didn't sleep well that night. I knew that Papa would have the final say in the morning after having an entire evening to think about how he wanted to respond to me and everyone who delivered a victim impact statement.

Would he admit before God and man that what a dozen-and-a-half people had spoken was true and genuinely apologize for the harm he inflicted on us? Or would he maintain that he had done nothing wrong and was being persecuted by his family?

Maybe an apology was too much to ask for, but he'd had more than two years behind bars to think about how he found himself in this predicament.

On Tuesday morning, my father took the witness stand.

Once again, my hands grew moist as I hung on to Matthew for support. In his familiar Texas twang, my father spoke slowly—v-e-r-y s-l-o-w-l-y—with a distinctive drawl that made words sound longer than they were. My first thought was, *We're going to be here for a while.* My second thought was, *Oh, no. This is not going to be good.* I could tell by the sound of his voice that he hadn't changed.

My father took his time, knowing that he was in control once again. He began by talking about his father, I.B. Hale, and what a great man he was and how he drove a horse-drawn milk wagon through high school and became a famous football player who was offered more money to play in the NFL than anyone had been offered up to that time.[4] He talked of his father's FBI work and how I.B. trained FBI agents in martial arts and shooting. "He was a beautiful man, a legend," my father stated.

But Papa lost everyone when he said some people thought his father killed President John F. Kennedy. He spoke of his "father-in-law, Mr. Connally," and how I.B. Hale was in a car behind the President and John Connally during the fatal motorcade through downtown Dallas. After the assassination, he and his father wept together over Mr. Kennedy's death on that fateful day in November 1963.

Referring to his father, Papa said, "His persecution after he was dead is just like the persecution I'm experiencing here because I'm considered dead. They can persecute me and say whatever they want to say."

---

4. I.B. Hale, a tackle out of Texas Christian University, was the first-round draft choice of the Washington Redskins in the 1939 Draft, the No. 8 pick, so it's highly doubtful that he was offered more money to sign than quarterbacks Sid Luckman or Davey O'Brien, both drafted ahead of him.

*Okay. I see where this is going. He's going to air his grievances while he takes his sweet time telling us his life story.*

Then he spoke of K.K., never mentioning her by name but recalling how she died in a gun accident. "She was precious. I lost her," he choked, overcome by a memory that led him to start crying.

"Nobody had answers, so I became a pilgrim the rest of my life, trying to figure out what happened. Went down a lot of alleys, went to a lot of places, been around the world, looking for God. Then God found me."

He spoke of going to a church in Texas after I was born and hearing Jesus speak to him before answering the altar call and walking up the aisle. Then he abruptly shifted gears and said he wasn't running from the law when he got arrested. "I was in McCarthy the whole time. I called my wife."[5]

That led him right into his altercation with Israel. "I said to myself, 'This boy is going to kill me.' I set myself, and I hit him. That's the only time I ever hit anyone with my fists since I've known the Lord," he said.

It took every fiber of my being not to scream out, "You're lying!" I began to wonder why I ever chose to face my father in this court hearing. If only I could question him in a way that let everyone see the truth. Instead, he was being allowed to say whatever he wanted, and I was forced to hear his tormenting and controlling words.

He said Mr. Buckingham should have told Israel to call Mama or one of the boys, not the police. As for the accusations thrown against him, "I can hardly believe the lips of my children, using words like 'beat unmercifully.' They don't know what it's like to be hit. Israel found out that day."

He said the only time he ever lied to the family was when he said Mama was a virgin when they got married. And then, as if in a trance, he said, "I call sexual intercourse 'communion' between a man and wife. We married, the commitment was there, but we never had communion together. When she was thirteen, she used her body to get love, and when she was fourteen, she went to Hawaii and came back with a venereal disease—"

Richard Payne jumped out of his chair and spoke to Judge Hopwood. "This would be a good time for a break," the assistant DA said. "It's 10:30, and people are trying to get to the restroom. I would like a break. An hour and a half is a lot."

But the defense lawyer wanted to continue, noting that people were entering and exiting the courtroom, no doubt to use the facilities.

Judge Hopwood banged his gavel. "Let's take a ten-minute break."

Mentally, I was ready for a pause as well.

---

5. Papa was arrested in Eagle River, a suburb of Anchorage.

When we returned, Papa continued trashing my mother, saying that on their Hawaiian honeymoon, when she was a couple of months pregnant with me, he found her at another campsite in the arms of another man. "She committed adultery on our honeymoon. The point is that I was faithful. My own family didn't want me to be married to Kurina. They saw something I didn't see."

Then he turned to the New Mexico years and his "corrections."

"I never spanked my children on the buttocks. I grew up in fraternities and knew how dangerous that was. I just would not do that."

He said he sent the children to an aspen tree to get a twig, and they'd come back, and he'd talk to them about what they did wrong. "When the correction was over, I would take the child in my arms and embrace him and wait until those little sobs went away. There was a healing process. 'Papa, forgive me. Papa, thank you for the correction.'"

He told of a time when he was taking a bath, and several of us children had done something wrong, and one of us said, "Papa, you got to correct us. You don't love us."

I think I would have remembered that.

"I had never heard the word abuse before," he droned on. "It wasn't part of our terminology. My children turning these things into 'unmerciful beatings' is not true. They are lies. They were done in love and care."

And then he talked about me, which caused the blood to drain from my face.

"I was careful. I never touched her. I scratched her back one time. I had no desire whatsoever toward Elishaba. Her love was special. My love for her was special. My love for Jerusalem was really special."

And then he broke down: "I declare here in front of my Father in heaven this day that I never lusted after my little girls."

I wanted to throw up. I fought my upset stomach and wished I could stand up and call him out.

He spoke in a monotone, hopping from one grievance to another until Judge Hopwood stopped him just before noon. He'd been talking for the better part of two and a half hours. Everyone shifted in their seats because they were uncomfortable.

"There are limits to these things," the judge said. "We don't have all the time in the world."

Judge Hopwood suggested that when we returned from the noontime recess, my father focus on what the court needed to know before sentencing. Then the judge banged his gavel.

When we returned at one o'clock, Papa did focus—on his family. He said he was concerned about us "bearing false witness" and that our statements "signed my death warrant."

"I will never be around other prisoners," he moaned. "I'm a dead man if I go into open population."

After three hours on the stand, he finally addressed the core issue:

"It's impossible for me to have raped my daughter for ten years in the same room with fifteen, sixteen other people, and no one knew anything about it," he drawled. "It's a shame they lied so much."

Regarding the beatings in the wanigan, he said he noticed his belt in the stove—the one I'd thrown into the fire so that he couldn't whip me again with it.

"I was trying to get the belt out. She came to close the oven door. I pushed her away. I wasn't meaning to slap her. Sometimes you hit the wrong place on the eye, and the whole face goes black. But that was it, in total. There was nothing about sex. Nothing about rape or any of these things. God commands me to answer these charges. That's what I've tried to do, Your Honor."

He further stated that I had committed serious perjury and needed to repent before God.

I listened, hardly believing my ears. *Have I gone crazy? How could he deny this?* I almost got up and ran out the back door.

Fortunately, the judge was unmoved. He told my father that it was time to wrap things up.

Papa's final words: "I can't change anyone's mind. The damage has been done. I know this is the last time I will be with them, and they know it too. So, Lord Jesus, thank you for being with me today, be with the judge and attorneys and my family. Each tear has its reward."

I was devastated when Papa ended his words. I had tried so hard to open up my heart to him. What more could I do? Nothing, except to hold back my tears. I was terrified that if I cried at this moment, someone might try to make something out of my sorrow for my father.

Then another thought came to mind: knowing this would be his last opportunity, he made sure he abused me one more time.

The final statements from Richard Payne and Papa's court-appointed attorney went by in a blur. As reality set in regarding my father, I was numb: there would be no apology, no saying "I'm sorry," no acknowledgment of the pain he inflicted on my siblings and me.

He had his story, and he was sticking to it.

Judge Hopwood wasn't buying. "The denials don't make any sense," he said. "I have to consider that each and every allegation is true. The other thing I'm considering is the consistency of Elishaba's statement and also the family members here in court, and all the testimonies are consistent. All of them spoke in earnest, and they were all very direct. They are telling the truth."

I wanted to hear those words—*They are telling the truth*—five times over. And then Judge Hopwood said this:

> One thing that is remarkable here is the courage of the family to speak up after suffering from the bondage that they were in so long. That they have spoken from the heart in front of a camera is a first huge step. These kinds of wounds, especially sexually, take a long time to heal, and most times, they don't. The harm here, especially to Elishaba, is enormous. The physical harm at the time of the beating and the sexual assaults was substantial. And the psychological harm then and now from all those things continues.
>
> It is apparent to me that Mr. Hale still believes that he is omnipotent. He thinks he is the final authority. I don't think that has changed. He still uses religion for all the wrong purposes. I believe that the family is sincere in what they believe, but Mr. Hale uses religion for very bad purposes.

And then Judge Hopwood formally sentenced my father to fourteen years in prison for sexually assaulting me, among other charges, calling what happened to me "one of the worst cases of domestic abuse I've seen. . . . just about as bad as it gets."

I exhaled. Our long ordeal was over. I watched as a bailiff wheeled my weeping father out of the courtroom, head bowed. He tried one more time to glance over his shoulder, realizing this was the end, but handcuffs prevented a final look.

He was gone. This part of my ordeal was over. As people stood up to leave, I knew news cameras and reporters were waiting in the hallway. Matthew took my hand and led me out, running interference as loud questions were shouted at me.

My husband hustled us to the parking lot, where he opened the passenger door to our "honeymoon wagon," being the gentleman that he was. Then Matthew hopped behind the wheel, but before he turned on the engine, he reached over and hugged me, sensing I needed to cry and let my emotions go. Matthew didn't say anything, but he didn't need to either.

"Okay, we can go now," I said, blowing my nose. As we exited the parking lot, I realized that I would never see my father again.

# 47

# PAPA PILGRIM'S FINAL DAYS

On Memorial Weekend in 2008, I got word that Papa was on his deathbed. It was looking like the prison doctors were right: my father really had only had six months to live.

I had not seen him since the sentencing; I couldn't bring myself to do it. There were extenuating circumstances as well: I had miscarried a month after I read my victim impact statement but had quickly gotten pregnant again. Now I was two months along and wanted this baby desperately. I deeply desired to be the mother of my *own* child. I knew how to care for babies. If the need arose, I could even change a baby's diaper on the back of a horse.

Then Joseph called and said Papa was nearing the end. My brother, along with my mother, Joshua, David, Moses, and Israel, had visited him in prison that spring, begging him to repent, but he stood firm and didn't want to talk about it.

Knowing the end was drawing near, I felt compelled to see him one last time. I asked Matthew what he thought.

"Honey, if this is what you need to do to find closure, then I will see if I can get you in."

"I'm not talking about closure," I said. "I want to do something to save my father so that he will make it to heaven."

The "duty" my father had given me most of my life to "save him" was kicking in.

The following day—Memorial Day, a Monday and a holiday—I paced the floor, eager to hear any news about my father. Matthew was reading the news on his phone when he took a call from my brother David. Matthew listened intently and then thanked David for sharing the news.

Then my grim-faced husband put his arms around me. "Your father just died."

I cried in his arms. A peace that surpassed all my understanding came over me. I knew without a doubt that God had spared me from seeing my father again.

It wasn't up to me to save Papa or to convince him of his sin.

One of my father's dying wishes was to be buried next to K.K. back in Texas. That wasn't going to happen.

At Aurora Cemetery in Wasilla,[1] our family gathered around my father's casket to give him an honorable burial since he was our father. I will admit that it felt creepy being near my father's decaying body.

As we gathered around the grave plot, my mother, all fifteen of us siblings, Linda, one of my father's past wives, and his oldest son, Alan Hale, did our best to remember the sixty-seven years of life for Robert Allen Hale.

None of us had anything good to say, and that alone was something to be enormously sad about. My older brothers explained that they were with Papa at the end, trying to convince him that he could be forgiven and walk as a new man into Jesus' arms, that it wasn't too late.

But he refused to listen, stubborn as a mule right to the end.

The first step toward repentance is admitting that what you did was wrong or that you wronged someone. My father wasn't willing to take that step.

Joshua then said a few words.

"Our father has chosen to walk in what he knew was evil, and yet he called evil good. May God have mercy on him. We now bury years of pain, abuse, and evil and choose to walk on with the hope we have in Jesus to be forgiven. May we teach our children the evil of our past and the hope that they have in being a people who can grow and flourish together in God's love."

I felt dark and unable to put my thoughts together as they lowered Papa's casket into the earth. Tears of grief came down my cheeks, and I wanted out of there as soon as I could. One thought comforted me:

*Papa Pilgrim can never hurt us again.*

---

1. Wasilla is around twelve miles west of Palmer, a twenty-minute drive.

# 48
# FORGIVENESS FROM THE HEART

The summer solstice arrived on June 21, 2015, a Sunday, the longest day of the year with nineteen-and-a-half hours of daylight. In Palmer, Alaska, the sun would set at 11:44 p.m. on this Father's Day.

Standing in my kitchen and looking out the window, grief filled my heart. A "father wound" left me with a deep ache inside my heart. Papa's abuse was in my past, but I still had plenty of scar tissue.

Seven years had passed since Papa Pilgrim left the confines of this earth. I had been on a journey every single day—a journey of healing and forgiveness.

I felt like I started making steady progress when my sister Hosanna invited me to a Hearts Going Towards Wellness (HGTW) conference a couple of years earlier, in April 2013, held in Palmer. Organizers billed the four-day event as a "safe place for the wounded to look at the damage done to them and begin moving toward wellness." Matthew was supportive and said I could go.

I signed up for the HGTW conference with the mindset that I could help someone who might be hurting, but as I listened to the leaders speak about deep topics such as childhood trauma, shame, and family dynamics, I was reminded that I still had plenty of hurt and trauma to deal with before I could come to a place of forgiving my father.

I was assigned to a small group with a couple of leaders where we could vulnerably open up in a confidential and safe setting. Up until then, I had only shared my most profound thoughts with my husband and Mrs. Buckingham. I had built a bubble around my life and was afraid to puncture that illusion.

At our first small group meeting, one of our participants was missing. Right away, I volunteered to find her.

One of the leaders put her hand on my shoulder. "No, Eba, you are not to take care of anyone else but yourself while you are here."

I was offended. I hadn't done anything wrong, had I?

But my leader's simple correction was interpreted in my mind as this: *Oh, no. I'm in so much trouble. I'm going to be humiliated and kicked out of this conference.* It was as if my father was standing over me, poised to deliver a sting from the lashes of his whip and his words.

To counter these troubling thoughts, I had to say over and over again in my mind, *This is a safe group. This is a safe group.*

Chastened, I reminded myself that I was just as broken as others attending the conference—and that was okay.

On the conference's final day, Dr. Larry Severson, a longtime professional counselor and marriage and family therapist from Anchorage, was the featured speaker. His topic was forgiveness, which was something I needed to hear. I thought I had forgiven my father and moved on, but I was coming to the realization that I was still raw and vulnerable. Desires for revenge on the one who sexually and physically abused me until I was twenty-nine years old still filled my heart.

"Receiving God's forgiveness is powerful," Dr. Severson declared as I took notes. "Understanding what it means to receive God's forgiveness opens the door to understanding what it means when God's Word says that we are to 'forgive as the Lord forgave you' in Colossians 3:13."

Dr. Severson explained that there were two sides to forgiveness: receiving forgiveness and offering forgiveness.

"We need to receive forgiveness when we have wronged another person," he explained. "We need to offer forgiveness when we have been wronged. As we walk through life, we will find ourselves on both sides many times. We wrong others, and others wrong us. No matter which side of forgiveness you might find yourself on at any given time, there is a deep work that must take place in your heart for true forgiveness to be experienced."

*Deep work?* That sounded ominous as I continued to listen. Then he asked another penetrating question: "What has to happen in your heart before you can come to the place where you desire to offer forgiveness to those who have wronged you?"

Dr. Severson paused a moment so everyone in the room could contemplate an answer.

"First, you must be honest about the wall of unforgiveness in your heart," he continued. "When you have been wronged, many things happen inside of you, including a hardened heart toward those who have wronged you."

Sure, my heart felt like a wall that no one could penetrate. The unforgiveness in my heart was leaving me bitter, resentful, full of rage, and callous toward others. In other words, my unforgiving heart was eating me up.

"Bitterness isn't just personal; it's public and impacts others," Dr. Severson said. "Hebrews 12:15[1] says, 'See to it that no one falls short of the grace of God and that no bitter root grows up to cause trouble and defile many.' Not only does bitterness eat away at your heart, but it also impacts others negatively. That is why we read in Ephesians 4:31-32:

> Get rid of all bitterness, rage and anger, brawling and slander, along with every form of malice. Be kind and compassionate to one another, forgiving each other, just as in Christ God forgave you.

"It's human nature to seek justice; we want the wrongdoer to be punished for wronging us," Dr. Severson continued. "But we want more than justice; we want revenge. We want payback! And we want to take things into our own hands, but Jesus gave us an example to follow in 1 Peter 2:23: 'When they hurled their insults at him, he did not retaliate; when he suffered, he made no threats. Instead, he entrusted himself to him who judges justly.'"

A light went off in my mind: I needed to trust Jesus, who would judge my father justly.[2]

The more Dr. Severson spoke, the more I began to face the truth about my own heart. I had determined to just get past this whole nightmare as soon as I could. I didn't want to look deeply at what I had experienced because it was painful. I didn't want to face the impact that my broken heart was having on others. I wanted to "forgive" and move on, but now I was seeing that there was more to it.

I was beginning to see that I needed to both forgive *and* receive forgiveness. But that left me with an unsettling dilemma. To move toward forgiveness meant that I would have to face the depth of the wrongs against me honestly. That would be very painful, and I didn't want to hurt anymore. Additionally, facing the wrongs against me would also expose the wrong directions I'd taken to deal with those wrongs. On the other hand, not forgiving would leave me stuck with a hard and hurting heart that could wound others. I began to realize that I had much more to face in my own heart.

I felt my emotions bubbling to the surface. Then I heard Dr. Severson say,

---

1. All these Bible verses are from the New International Version (NIV).
2. 2 Corinthians 5:10 (NIV) states: "For we must all appear before the judgment seat of Christ, so that each of us may receive what is due us for the things done while in the body, whether good or bad." That judgment happens before God destroys the old heaven and the old earth. One more thought: Judgment is not my job but God's because He alone is just and perfect, which means He is a perfect judge. I can rest in that.

"True forgiveness walks into the situation to freely forgive without any demand or expectation placed on the one who has hurt you to face and own his wrong. If you walked away from the situation devastated, you probably went in with expectations instead of forgiveness."

I had to get up from my seat and run to the bathroom. The tears didn't stop flowing as I cried my heart out. I thought of how devastated I was the day I walked out of the courtroom having expected—even depended upon—my father to say he was sorry, but his denial of any wrongdoing left me shattered and bitter.

That day, I realized that forgiveness wasn't some magical thing that would happen in one moment. I was on a journey—and one I had to be willing to take.

Since my father was in the grave, I realized that my enemy was not a mere man rotting in the ground. My faith teaches me that there is an ancient enemy who has always wanted to destroy everything real and good, and who influences humanity to do the same. My enemy tried to destroy the dignity that God granted me when I was formed in my mother's womb.[3]

At the end of the conference, a Sunday morning, I stood up before all the attendees and shared my story honestly, holding a yellow rose. I then said these words:

"This yellow rose represents me right now because the petals are open to God's amazing grace. The thorns on the stem represent the years of hardship and abuse, yet they are a big part of who I am today. For so long, I felt less-than and worked hard to be better-than, but pain is a gift because now I can offer hope to others. I am coming alive to my true longings, and that starts with believing that God loves me.

"The closer I get to God, the more in touch I am with who I am. For me, forgiveness has been a journey. Attending this conference has helped me understand how it takes courage to forgive. I have asked God to reveal the layers and depth of my unforgiving heart so that I can forgive my father for what he did to me."

That Sunday morning, the change process in my heart began with honesty and a desire to not live as a victim any longer. Yes, I was a victim of tremendous evil and harm against me, but to remain living in a victim mode was keeping me from becoming the woman God wanted me to be.

---

3. I think it is clear to most people that evil is real, but Christians call the ancient and most evil enemy Satan, or the devil.

That process continued after the HGTW conference was over when Matthew and I decided to invest in private counseling sessions with Dr. Severson, who had a way of helping me go deeper into my broken heart.

"You have to know how big the debt is before you can forgive it," he said one time.

For me, it was shocking to understand that I would never know the joy of forgiving unless I had someone to forgive. My father had wounded me, but he had also allowed me to become like Christ, who was wounded for all but still offered to forgive everyone. Yet, everyone does not receive the forgiveness offered. That depends on fully facing our wrongs and seeing our needs.

Each layer of moving toward forgiveness took a lot of journaling, where I worked out my feelings of anger for the evil done to my family and me. Each time, though, I moved forward by claiming the truth that I was beautiful in the sight of God and others.

By Father's Day in 2015, I had faced the wrongs of my past more profoundly than ever before. I also invited Jesus into the darkest parts of my heart. The healing process felt like I was climbing a mountain. There were times when my muscles would grow weary, leaving me discouraged and wondering how I could take any more, but with the faithful love of my heavenly Father and the wisdom of Dr. Severson, I was ready to reach what felt like the summit. I wanted to express heartfelt forgiveness to my father.

It was time to find a new level of healing. Time for me to take forgiveness further. Time to visit my father's grave for the first time since his burial. Without hesitation, I got in the car for the short drive to Aurora Cemetery in Wasilla with my Bible and a yellow rose.

On the longest day of the year in 2015, Father's Day, I stood before a gray headstone with Papa's full name inscribed on the marble, along with the years he lived (1941-2008), a cross, and a Bible. An epitaph said:

### Also known as "Pilgrim"

I knew he was no longer there, but I wanted to talk to him as though he was still alive because I had feelings and emotions ready to be expressed.

I knelt on the ground on top of my father's grave. For a moment, I stared at the headstone as my thoughts raced to remember my father. At first, my mind went numb, but since I had done so much work to open up and allow my heart to feel pain again, everything hit me at once. I wept out loud like I had never wept before. And then a torrent of thoughts released like a flood:

> Papa, I come today because I wish to express my forgiveness for all my losses as your daughter. I can only hope that before you left this

earth, you cried out to God and accepted His forgiveness.

At times, I have looked out my kitchen window, and the tears just fell as I pondered the unmet longings I had as your daughter.

At one time, I was a tender rose blooming up beside you.

At one time, I had a deep longing as your little girl to feel safe with you.

I needed you to teach me safe boundaries that would give me stability throughout my tender years.

I was a normal, sensitive girl who needed a wall of protection—a fortress around me. I wanted that fortress to be you!

I needed you to be a fun daddy who did not suddenly change from happy to mad.

Your anger filled my soul with so much fear—fear of you, fear of others, fear of myself, fear of man, and a wrong fear of God.

I wanted so badly to run and hide from your wrathful presence, but instead, I froze. I was dead on the inside, while on the outside, I performed what I knew as the "good girl."

I craved your gentleness and safe touch, but every time you touched me, something happened. I felt an obligation to give to you what you demanded of me. What I was reaching for became the very tool used against my needy heart.

I needed you, Papa. I needed you.

I needed you to make me safe, show me love, and forever be my father, to model to me what a good man should be.

I needed you to be there on my wedding day. Oh, if only I could have put my pure arm into yours as a Daddy's girl walking up the aisle for you to give me away.

Why, why? Oh, Papa, why? How could you? This has been the cry of your girl's heart for many tormenting years.

My heart breaks to realize that you could not give what you did not have.

You did not have a purity to give; therefore, you lived in the torment of sin.

You could not accept God's unconditional love for you; therefore, you did not have love to give.

You gave torment because you lived in torment.

Though I grieve the loss of my earthly dad today, I can tell you that my Heavenly Father is ENOUGH. What you could not give me, my Father in heaven has filled me up with.

Today, I leave a gift for you.

It is the most profound gift a daughter can give to an earthly father who greatly abused her.

I give you my deepest heart of forgiveness.

I FORGIVE YOU, PAPA!

Do you deserve forgiveness? No, but none of us do.

That makes you no different than anyone else.

Today, I lay a yellow rose on your grave as a token of my forgiveness. The thorns on the stem express the years of pain and hardships. The petals open up to God and show His amazing grace and remind me that He has never forsaken me.

I stopped and opened my Bible to read Psalm 23.

The Lord is my shepherd, I lack nothing.

He makes me lie down in green pastures,

he leads me beside quiet waters,

he refreshes my soul.

It started raining, which felt like God was crying with me. Even though the clouds were dark and the rain fell, I felt free and clean inside.

I walked down the path back to my car, looking to the cloudy heavens, knowing that God was not a God of evil and destruction, but a God of restoration.

A warm sense of forgiveness filled my soul.

I knew I was truly free from an evil past with Papa Pilgrim.

After everything he had taken from me, that was something he could not touch.

**On Father's Day in 2015, I laid this yellow rose and note on my father's gravestone in Wasilla, Alaska.**

# EPILOGUE

When I visited my father's gravesite on Father's Day in 2015, I was the mother of two children.

My first child arrived seven months after my father's death, on November 20, 2008, when I gave birth to a precious daughter that Matthew and I named Esther.

Why that name, especially because my father used to call me his "Queen Esther"?

Before her birth, we didn't know if we were going to have a son or daughter. One evening in a restaurant, Matthew and I wrote down names that came to mind on a napkin.

"Grace sounds nice," I said.

"Yeah, but how about Esther?" Matthew replied.

Everything stood still for a moment. I thought, *Oh, no. Esther can't be her name since my father used it for evil with me.*

But something about the way Matthew's eyes lit up and the way he said her name touched me.

Quickly, I decided that I wasn't going to let my father steal our joy. With a confident smile, I said, "You know, Esther Grace sounds good together."

Matthew's eyes brightened again. "It sure does," he said.

"And what do you want your child to call you?"

Matthew thought a moment.

"Papa."

Another *oh, no.*

When Matthew noticed my reaction, he explained with hesitancy in his voice how he always liked the thought of being called "Papa," but since he knew my story well, he didn't want to hurt me.

I relaxed. "Matthew, it's okay. You can still have your dream. I'm fine with our child calling you Papa."

That night, I was reminded of the amazing transformation that had taken place within me when I opened the door for new memories to build, even if they reminded me of the past.

Believe me, I was happy to get pregnant in the first place. My greatest fear from years of sexual abuse was that I couldn't conceive a child, but God was gracious and opened my womb.

I wondered if becoming a mother was going to be any different from raising my siblings. I really didn't like going there, but when our baby girl was born, there was no question that she was an Esther Grace. I could hardly believe the difference between cradling my very own child and holding one of my siblings when they were newborns.

These days, Esther has my spunk and playfulness and Matthew's bent for perfection, but most of all, she loves to sit with Mama and share her heart. She's thirteen years old, and I'm taking the time to talk to my daughter about her growing body and encourage her to ask me any question she has.

She's such a special girl. I'll never forget one time when she was four or five years old, and I was tucking her into bed. During our bedtime prayers, she said this: "Thank you, Lord, that You made me a part of our family. I don't know which side I'm on or which side is which, but thank you that I'm part Mama and part Papa!"

At the same time Esther thanked God for our family, our little family of three desired more children and was also praying hard for another boy or girl. Our sweet Esther hardly missed a night asking Jesus for a baby sibling.

I did become pregnant, but we were heartbroken when I had a miscarriage. I knelt beside my bed and asked God in faith that He would give us a son since I knew this was a desire of Matthew's heart.

Then I became pregnant again in 2012. During an ultrasound, the baby not only looked fine, but he was a boy. Many tears of joy came from the thanksgiving in my heart.

When Michael was born on February 5, 2013, doctors quickly informed us that he had something called Down's Syndrome. Shock filled our hearts as we learned that Michael would likely have physical and possibly mental disabilities all his life.

*Will my little man suffer?* This was my greatest fear as a mom.

One day a mentor told me, "Elishaba, you cannot keep your children from pain, but what counts is how you walk with them in their pain."

I have taken this advice seriously as I've watched Michael experience immense struggles, challenging setbacks, and even life-threatening moments that left us crying out to God.

In February 2020, just a month before the start of the pandemic, Michael suffered a massive stroke that paralyzed the right side of his body. He had to undergo emergency brain surgery to save his life, leaving him a big scar on his head. We would learn that he had been stricken with moyamoya disease, a rare progressive disorder that affects the blood vessels in the brain. That is why he suffered a stroke at seven years of age.

Over two hundred people visited us at Providence Hospital in Anchorage. At one point, my sweet sister, Psalms, said, "Eba, I can tell them they have to go. You need a break."

I understood what my sister was trying to do, but these dear friends and family members were lifelines.

Today, eight-year-old Michael is walking and is back to being that amazing perfect child. He is still a bit handicapped on his right side, but he does not let that setback stop him or discourage him. It's been a beautiful thing watching the bond between Esther and Michael.

We got Michael a Goldendoodle service dog that he named Doodle Dog or "DeeDee" for short. She sleeps with him and helps him when he has seizures and medical needs. With DeeDee beside him, he is comforted through so much.

Through it all, Michael has touched people in ways that none of us can. Here's an example:

We were on an out-of-town trip one Sunday when we walked into a church. As we sat in the back row, Michael started begging me to let him stand with the greeter at the front of the church. Knowing how my little man touches hearts, I said, "Sure."

The greeter was touched by the love Michael showed him and each person entering the church. At the end of the service, the greeter came over and told us, "Your little boy has shown me Jesus by the way he looked into my eyes with so much love."

Our full, busy lives also revolve around Lazy Mountain Bible Church, where Matthew and I married.

My husband and I look forward each week to working with youth and life groups in our home. I love connecting with people on a deeper level. Relationship takes priority over anything else in this world.

I spend much of my time sitting with others and listening to them share their painful stories. I treat each visit as if they have handed me a treasure. I know what a gift it is for someone to be vulnerable. Meaningful relationships come with pain and joy.

My husband, Matthew, works hard to provide for our family. We are a tight-knit bunch, so we sure miss him when he's gone running a fruit company started by his late father, Ben. From May until September, Matthew hauls truckloads of fruit from Central California to our customers in Alaska.

The rest of the year, he's a busy draftsman, so he has a lot going on. But despite the long stretches on the road, Matthew does all he can to be there for his children.

My mother, Kurina, lives in Wasilla and remarried in 2020 to Larry.[1] After Papa Pilgrim died, she supported herself as a caregiver for the elderly, which she continues to do and enjoys.

For years, we had a strained relationship. I had the hardest time being around Mama. Whenever I talked to her, my whole body would shake for hours. I couldn't get myself to hug her since even her touch brought me back to the impact of being sexually abused since she was there when some of it happened. I didn't know how to say no or tell Mama my true feelings. It was hard to separate the responsibility I felt for her and my longing to be recognized as her daughter. What I wanted most was to hear her say that I was innocent and what happened with my father wasn't my fault.

After I did a lot of sorting out—shame from innocence and resentment from true longings—I was ready to show Mama my true heart by letting her see into me without shame. I badly wanted her to see how I had been hurt, and I was willing to offer her the opportunity to face the damage done in my heart as her daughter.

She finally agreed to get counseling with me. I'll never forget how quickly my heart was beating as I sat down next to her.

The counselor skillfully guided us into what felt like safe communication, and then we got to the nitty-gritty. When the counselor asked my mother if she was sorry for what happened to me, she said yes, but my mother also added this: "It wasn't Elishaba's fault that she wanted sex with Papa."

At that moment, I wanted to scream at the top of my lungs, "NO!" The only reason I held back was that my children were outside in the waiting room.

After a deep breath to catch myself, I told Mama firmly, "I never wanted my dad to touch me in that way."

This prompted a long discussion with the counselor in which we were both

---

1. My mother asked me not to put her new last name in the book.

able to go deeper. At the right moment, the counselor asked my mother if she could tell me that she believed me. A painful moment passed, but then she came through with the words I wanted to hear: "Yes, I believe you now."

"Can you say that again?" the counselor interjected.

"Sure. I want you to know that I do believe you never, ever wanted your father to touch you sexually. Up until today, I have always believed that you did want it. I thought you were a threat to me, and I fought against you. Fact is, I didn't even love you."

My heart wanted to stop at the sound of these words. I immediately burst into tears.

"I knew you were my daughter, but to be honest, I didn't like you. I'm so sorry I felt that way. But now I want to love you. You didn't deserve this, and it was not your fault."

That day, we experienced a breakthrough. There were still more tears and things to work through, but when we stood up at the end of the session, I looked at her and burst out, "I need a mama hug."

She reached for me, wrapped her arms around my shoulders, and did her best to comfort me.

Our relationship has gotten better and better since then. Even though she wishes our lives turned out far differently, we both know that we were abused victims of a tyrant and have that in common.

As for my brothers and sisters, they have sought to move on from the incredible darkness they have endured. Each has had their own unique journey to walk. Despite their horrific pasts, my siblings have overcome many obstacles and accomplished many things. Most are married and raising lots of wonderful children, which gladdens my heart.

I don't believe anyone has lived at Rainbow Cross in the Sangre de Cristo mountains since we departed nearly twenty-five years ago. Neighbors purchased the property and have allowed our family to visit. We've made three trips to the old homestead since our honeymoon, and several of my siblings have returned as well.

As for Hillbilly Heaven, Ray and Lee Ann Kreig of Anchorage purchased the property and love it when we make the long trip to the Wrangell Mountains, which we've done several times, but we haven't been to McCarthy or Hillbilly Heaven since Michael was born in 2013.

We'll have to go back someday.

Maybe in the winter on a snow machine.

# PHOTO GALLERY

My father, Robert Hale, grew up as the son of an All-American football star, I.B. Hale, co-captain of the Texas Christian University team voted as the national collegiate champion in 1938. There was little money in professional football in those days, so I.B. became a special agent with the FBI and caught the eye of FBI chief J. Edgar Hoover. I.B. and his wife, Virginia, settled in a nice upper-class neighborhood in Fort Worth, Texas, where they raised twin boys, Robert and William.

My parents were living in a hippie commune in the California high desert when I was born on January 23, 1976. My parents' legal names at the time were Firefly and Sunlight Sunstar, and I was named Butterfly Sunstar on my birth certificate. I'm sitting in my mother's lap (above) with my stepsister Alia. I was a towhead growing up, but I wasn't allowed to have toys after Papa became a Christian because my father said that toys were graven images, and graven images were very wicked. I played with sticks to have fun.

Robert Hale

Robert Hale

Papa wanted us to live a simple pioneer life without the distractions of modern—and pagan—society. We ended up settling on land owned by actor Jack Nicholson high in the Sangre de Cristo Mountains of New Mexico. Papa built this log cabin around a lean-to shack by himself. With no running water or electricity, every day was a challenge. Below, Papa always told everyone that I was a "Daddy's girl" and loved taking me into the shower with him in my early years.

Daniel Bresler

John Bartley

Kurina Hale

Robert Hale

We lived at the 9,000-foot level in the mountains of New Mexico on property called "Rainbow Cross." When I was seven, I asked Papa if I could be baptized since he preached so often about being "born again." I put on my best dress, and my father dunked me into a little creek. I was very conflicted because Papa hammered the point that I must now be perfect—and my eternal future was at stake. As I grew up, my days were spent doing chores like sweeping up in the kitchen. I didn't go to school growing up, and neither did my siblings. We didn't celebrate holidays like Christmas and Easter because Papa said they were pagan, but we went all out for a special meal every January when we celebrated Papa and Mama's conversion, using my grandmother's special silverware and china.

This was one of the rare times I sat in "Papa's Chair," situated in the middle of our small living space. Right behind the chair is our portable camping toilet, where all of us did our business, right out in the open. When one of us sat down, we were told to look away. One of the chores I loathed was dumping the contents of the camping toilet into our latrine pit. Another chore we did a lot was chopping wood since that is how we heated our cabin.

Robert Hale

We needed animals to survive our isolated lives in the wilderness. They provided food, wool, transportation, and emotional friendship to us kids. Our home was always full of animals, from a chicken roosting on an old Singer sewing machine to a baby horse roaming around. I'm pictured (bottom left) with a beautiful red Arabian named Shema, one of my favorite horses growing up. I started shepherding when I was six. Over the years, our flocks grew.

Robert Hale

Robert Hale

Robert Hale

One year, Papa said God was telling us to leave the homestead and confront the wicked world, so he purchased an old school bus that he turned into a motor home. He painted inscriptions that said "Prepare ye the way" and "Jesus Christ." We motored throughout the western part of the United States and fed ourselves from supermarket dumpsters. We didn't find people receptive to Papa's preaching or him saying they needed to "turn or burn." We eventually returned to the New Mexico homestead where—after five brothers—I finally had sisters: Jerusalem and Hosanna.

John Bartley

Robert Hale

Elishaba Doerksen

When I was seventeen in the fall of 1993, my Uncle Billy (right) had a major conversion experience and came to live with us in New Mexico, leaving behind a successful veterinary practice in Fort Worth and a wife and children. My father told his twin brother that God was calling him away from the "City of Destruction," which didn't sit well with his family back home.

Elishaba Doerksen

Physical abuse was part of my life for as long as I can remember. Notice the scar across my right cheek. We could receive the back of Papa's hand, a full fist, or a crack of a whip if we were deemed "rebellious," which covered anything we did that displeased him. Two of my brothers each have one of Papa's self-made leather whips around their shoulders in the picture of me spinning wool. He called them "slings" and would pull the leather whip off our necks and beat the living daylights out of us whenever we angered him.

John Bartley

In the late 1990s, the idea of moving the family to Alaska took hold of my father. Life on the homestead in New Mexico was proving to be more and more difficult. We packed up our belongings and said goodbye to the old homestead, which had seen new structures added over the years. In the summer of 1999, we drove a caravan of trucks and vehicles more than 3,000 miles to the Last Frontier.

Elishaba Doerksen

Our old vehicles—held together by baling wire and duct tape—broke down multiple times along the way to Alaska. We fished in lakes to feed ourselves and stopped in cities to play our gospel hillbilly music on the streets. We sometimes collected hundreds of dollars a day, which made Papa happy.

We taught ourselves to play our instruments; I learned to play the fiddle and the guitar, although Papa said the guitar is something only a man should play since he leads his family in singing. What a difficult life I had, which was primarily spent in servitude to my father, always at his beck and call. I befriended a baby fawn I named "Song Fawn" and was heartbroken when she died in my arms (below). When I buried her, I felt like I had lost the only real friend in my life.

We tried out several places to live in Alaska, including Fairbanks and Homer, but nothing was a good fit. Then we heard about a property inside the Wrangell-St. Elias National Park. Fourteen miles up the McCarthy Valley (top left), we found a private landholding of 420 acres. There was no passable road to "Hillbilly Heaven," as Papa called the property, so we had to bring in supplies by horse during the summer, crossing McCarthy Creek multiple times, or by snow machine in the winter, traversing ice bridges that we built.

Elishaba Doerksen

This is the Main House at Hillbilly Heaven, where seventeen of us lived in a twelve-hundred square foot home constructed in bits and pieces by the previous owner, an old pioneer named Walt Wigger. A gas generator in a nearby shed provided light in the evenings and electrified our kitchen appliances, but my mother—called Country Rose—did most of her cooking on a wood-fired stove.

Elishaba Doerksen

Elishaba Doerksen

Just like in New Mexico, Papa loved to preach from the Bible at Hillbilly Heaven. His sermons could go on for hours, but woe to those who weren't paying attention. He'd rap us on the head with his knuckles if he thought we weren't hanging on to every word he said. I loved the opportunity to get away from my father, so I hiked into the mountains to hunt as often as I could. Even though taking an animal's life bothered me, I wanted to bring home much-needed meat for the family. This is a full-curl Dall sheep that I shot. Dall sheep were distinguished by their massive curling horns.

Robert Hale

Elishaba Doerksen

Dick Anderson

These pictures disturb me to this day. The first is the bathhouse at Hillbilly Heaven, where my father took liberties with me. In the middle photo, we either had guests or someone coming that Papa wanted to impress because food spreads like this were rare. (Notice how the paneling inside the Main House was pulled off the wall, exposing the insulation.) I could only eat when my father permitted me to eat, and he determined how much food I was allowed to put on my plate. I went hungry most of my life. The last picture is my parents' bed off the living room—the bed I shared with Papa, my mother, and the youngest child when I lived at Hillbilly Heaven. My father would take advantage of me after everyone was asleep.

Elishaba Doerksen

Living in such a remote area meant that we had no friends. My older brothers—Joseph, Joshua, David, and Moses—drove to Palmer, Alaska, in early 2004 to buy hay for our horses. While there, they attended a local church where they met a family a lot like ours—the Buckinghams. Jim and Martha Buckingham were parents of nine children, and Jim (pictured above with my father) was the teaching pastor at Palmer Christian Fellowship Church. My two oldest brothers, keen on the older daughters, said we had to meet the Buckinghams, so we traveled to Palmer and stayed at the family's log cabin home. We all got along great at first, but things started to go south when my father complained that their home was full of "vanity mirrors" and the family dressed up in nice clothes to go to church instead of everyday clothes. My father forced me to spend the first part of the night with him to satisfy himself sexually, and then I would be free to tiptoe into the Buckingham daughters' bedroom. I felt like an awful hypocrite, so I went outside and slept in our passenger van instead. In the last picture, taken of me inside our van, I was not feeling right about what was happening to me.

Elishaba Doerksen

Winters were always long and hard at Hillbilly Heaven, where we had to haul water from nearby Diamond Creek—either by hand or by snow machine. We relied on a fleet of a half-dozen snow machines to periodically haul supplies up McCarthy Valley, including 55-gallon fuel drums filled with gasoline to keep our snow machines going.

Elishaba Doerksen

Elishaba Doerksen

After my father beat me up badly in early 2005, I had to wear a ski mask over my swollen face. When my brothers discovered what my father had done, they confronted him. In a flash, Papa nailed Joshua with a right hook, breaking his nose. Several weeks later, my five older brothers hopped on snow machines and escaped in the middle of the night. Even though my brothers had been brave enough to flee my father, it still took weeks for my heart and mind to decide that I, too, had to make a run for it on a snow machine. My sister Jerusalem said she was coming with me, so we escaped together, speeding down the valley toward the town of McCarthy. These pictures were not taken the day we attempted to escape.

Elishaba Doerksen

Martha Buckingham

After the harrowing escape, I was taken in by the Buckingham family. Since I hadn't had any schooling and could barely read or write, I joined the youngest Buckingham children in their homeschool lessons, starting with first-grade material, even though I was twenty-nine years old. For my thirtieth birthday, the Buckingham girls made me this wonderful birthday cake.

Martha Buckingham

Joshua Scilzo

The Buckingham family, led by Jim and Martha Buckingham (center), welcomed us Hales after we escaped Hillbilly Heaven. They took in most of us, for which we will be eternally grateful. I am especially appreciative of the love and support I received from "Mama Martha" Buckingham, who demonstrated what unconditional love is all about. She freely gave of herself and listened to me describe—for the very first time—what really happened between me and my father. I will never forget the investment she made in me when I didn't know who to turn to.

Matthew Doerksen

I married the love of my life, Matthew Doerksen, on May 12, 2007, in Palmer, Alaska. Jim Buckingham led us through our marriage vows. Matthew had a special "get-away" vehicle waiting for us—a dump truck with "Just Married" written in shaving cream and tons of balloons tied to the vehicle. We spent our wedding night at a bed and breakfast in downtown Anchorage, where Matthew told me he was willing to hold me all night and that we didn't have to do anything else. I loved him for saying that, and while I will admit that I didn't feel sexual desire at the time, I still wanted us to be intimate. Matthew sensed this and was patient and kind.

After my brother Israel was physically attacked by Papa following my escape, he called the Alaska State Troopers to tell them everything he knew about what my father had done to me. A warrant for his arrest resulted in a manhunt for my father, who took off into the Alaskan wilderness. After two weeks, he was arrested on October 5, 2005, in Eagle River, a few miles outside of Anchorage. He remained behind bars until he accepted a plea deal agreement in late 2007. Instead of a jury trial, Papa consented to a fourteen-year sentence for sexually assaulting me. My father was very ill at the time; doctors gave him months to live. They were right: my unrepentant father died alone in a prison hospital on Memorial Day in 2008.

These days, I love being with my children, Esther and Michael. My mother, Kurina, and I have made significant strides after going to counseling together.

Matthew Doerksen

Today, I am no longer a victim. I am free to be the person that God intended for me to be. The journey to forgive my father, who wounded me, and letting go of the past has helped me move forward to receive love—love from God, love from others, and the love of my husband, Matthew. Keeping the hunger open in my heart to forgive and be forgiven is an ongoing journey that also leaves my heart open for a true relationship with God and others.

# ACKNOWLEDGMENTS

For years, I heard well-meaning friends say that I needed to write a book and share my story to give hope to others, especially victims of sexual abuse. The more I heard them say this, the more I resisted. There were many times when I had enough of people telling me to write a book or wanting to make my life into a movie.

To be honest, it hurt to even share my story with a small group of women or meet with victims of sexual abuse or incest. I would be transported back to memories of what my father did to me and the emotional and physical pain he inflicted on me, his daughter.

At the same time, though, God was making it clear to me that there would be a right moment to tell my story in a book. When that happened, my attitude would change because I would better understand how and why God rescued me from hell on earth.

Meanwhile, I needed time to heal—as I mentioned in my description of my first visit to my father's gravesite.

Not long after that, I met a wonderful Australian missionary named Geoff Richards. He had come to Alaska to record a series of evangelistic radio programs with Larry DeVilbiss, executive director of Global Recordings Network. Geoff needed a place to stay, so guess who volunteered to take him in? Right . . . the Buckinghams.

Papa Jim and Mama Martha invited other family members, and Matthew and me, to come over to the house to meet Geoff and enjoy a dessert. I felt drawn to this humble man who spoke with tears in his eyes about recently losing his wife to breast cancer as well as his own fight with metastatic bone cancer. He also described the pain of losing his father and twenty-one-year-old son on the same day when his father died of an illness and his son Timothy suffered a massive seizure in the middle of the night.

After hearing him speak, Matthew and I invited Geoff over to our humble abode, where he listened to my story as well. He said I had to write a book, but I told him I didn't feel up to the task. Geoff replied that he'd authored several books and could help me. He had all the connections, he said.

I felt conflicted, however. On the one hand, I wondered if this open door was God's timing, but I also knew that Geoff was fighting Stage 4 cancer. Should I let him give me what time he had left to write my book if he didn't have that long to live?

Geoff insisted that this was something he wanted to do, if possible. He returned to Australia for treatment. When he called a month or two later, he told me his cancer was in remission, and he wanted to come back to Alaska to help me write my book.

What could I say except yes?

For three months in early 2016, Geoff and I worked together. I would either type out thoughts or dictate my story into my iPhone; we got some good laughs from Siri's misunderstanding. When we finished the 144,000-word manuscript, which we called *Unforsaken*, things didn't feel right for some reason. I didn't know exactly what it was, but I felt the manuscript was not quite the story I wanted to tell. On top of that, opening up all the wounds of my heart also opened up the need for more healing and forgiving the past.

I asked Geoff if we could take a step back. He was disappointed because he was sure God wanted *Unforsaken* to be his last mission on earth. I'd seen how Geoff was getting weaker.

"I think God wants you to know that you are enough for Him, and you don't need to do anything more for Him," I said. "This is the time to go home and be with your family."

As for what would happen with the manuscript, I encouraged him with what the apostle Paul said in 1 Corinthians 3:5–9: one does the planting, another does the watering, but only God can make it grow.

Geoff said he understood. "I have done my part, and I need to give this over to God to do with your story what He wants," he said.

This was a moment of freedom for me; we continued to stay in contact. In the fall of 2016, he invited our family to visit him and his extended family in Nowra, Australia, around one hundred miles south of Sydney.

We found wounded hearts Down Under because Geoff's cancer had come back with a vengeance. His family had suffered so much loss, and now they were facing the prospect of losing a father.

While we were in Australia, I felt comfortable enough to share my story in several churches. Matthew and I also volunteered to help out at Capernwray Bible School north of Nowra. While there, we received a call from Geoff's daughter, Fiona, saying her father had taken a turn for the worse, and it looked like he was on his deathbed. We rushed to his bedside, where Matthew held his hand and reassured him that he was a child of God and could let go and be with Jesus. With a peaceful heart, he died, leaving everyone with sadness.

I loved his immediate family and had grown closest to Fiona. His family naturally wondered if his work on my book was in vain, but I assured them that Geoff's work would be a valuable resource moving forward.

Several years passed, but I remained patient for the leading from the Lord. Then in 2019, I met an author, Leslie Leyland Fields, at a Hearts Growing Toward Wellness conference in Palmer, where she spoke on the topic, "Why Your Story Matters."

Afterward, I asked her if I could have a private meeting with her. After telling her a bit about my story and how I didn't feel the *Unforsaken* manuscript was quite where it needed to be, she offered to help by putting me in touch with her literary agent, Greg Johnson of WordServe Literary in Denver.

Greg looked at the original manuscript. While he admired the effort, he said *Unforsaken* was not up to the level that publishing companies were expecting. Greg suggested that we bring in a new collaborator to work with me. That person turned out to be Mike Yorkey.

Mike was a veteran author or co-author of more than 110 books, many of them in the Christian marketplace. He took a look at Geoff's manuscript and was excited about my story, but he felt the original manuscript didn't fully reveal the odd relationship between my father and me as well as the level of sexual and physical abuse I suffered. While parts of *Unforsaken* were useful, Mike felt he had to start all over, which meant I had to start all over, retelling my story in phone interview after phone interview and in blocks of writings that I shared with him.

We formed a great team. Mike said he hated asking me to relive the first thirty years of my life, but as we went back and forth on new chapters a half-dozen times, frequently more, and I saw the results, I became glad we put so much work into it.

Mike showed me over countless hours of working together that I mattered through his kindness and sensitivity to my story. His professional writing skill has been phenomenal, but his heart and willingness to believe in me became a trust builder. It took faith on Mike's part because he was willing to take a big risk with me to get this book written. We faced some huge, unexpected obstacles along the way, but we didn't let that stop us.

But it wasn't just Mike who helped me get over the finish line. I had tons of other help and support along the way.

I start by acknowledging the loving support from my husband, Matthew. I don't know where I'd be without him. The fact that he chose to fall in love with me when I thought I was nothing more than a bunch of dirty rags is a constant reminder to me of God's love and amazing grace.

Matthew has supported me all the way. He has not only been forgiving of my past but willing to take back what was stolen from him as my husband. Together, we have a family with two of the most precious children ever, Esther and Michael. A special thanks to my Esther girl, who trusts me to share my story with her as she grows. She has said, "Mama, I believe you are supposed to tell your story to help other people who need to know that they can do it."

Esther has been a continual reminder of my little girl's heart as I watch her grow. I believe in allowing my children to become who they are and in feeding the gifts God has given them without pushing for them to become my lost dream. Their dreams and gifts might be completely different than mine, but that's what makes them unique. Esther, a budding photographer, also took the *Out of the Wilderness* photo on the cover.

And, of course, my little man Michael, who has been a daily reminder to me that we are all beautiful and wonderfully made in the sight of our Creator. My special-needs son is perfect in the sight of his mommy and family.

On the family side, I want to thank my aunt, Patsy Dorris Hale, for her forgiveness and loving acceptance of me. She wrote a book on my father and his twin brother entitled *He Heard His Brother Call His Name*.

I owe a heart of thanks to Mrs. Buckingham, who was the first to sit and hear my story. She prepared a safe place for me to come clean. To this day, she loves me as her daughter and is ready to listen to me at any given moment. My children call her "Grandma" for a good reason. Also, I want to thank the entire Buckingham family, who gave up their lives for ours when they took us in and made us their own family.

There were readers of the manuscript who were incredibly helpful with their comments and suggestions: Suzanne Weatherly, Janice Chiu-Kitka, Gerry Gacek, Don Sargent, Don and Terese Moser, and Debbie Rowland, a neighbor of mine in Palmer. Jessica Snell, who grew up in a missionary family in Canada's Northwest Territories and is now a married mom in Southern California, was an excellent editor and proofreader. I also have to thank Nicole Yorkey, who was the first to read chapters that her husband, Mike, had written. Her comments and suggestions showed me that she was behind me the entire time. Nicole, who is from Switzerland, also sent us special boxes filled with amazingly delicious chocolate treats—handmade by her—as an encouragement to keep going.

Then there are my "heart friends" who walked with me every step of the way: Lydia Wood, Debbie Kenny, Diana Whipple, Laura McHenry, Carolyn Kuch, and Linda Moyer. All the leaders at Hearts Going Toward Wellness have been behind me: Alan and Linda Ross, Barbie Williams, Greta E. Clark, and Teresa Carlson.

My thanks to Teacon Simeonoff, a man who gave me a Native name, Kunutarpet, which means *loves all*. My pastor, Jason Daughtry, his wife, Chelsie, Mike and Emilka Clark, and our Life Group friends and countless others at our church, Lazy Mountain Bible Church, have been there for me in incredible ways.

Don and Edna Shugak, leaders of Anchorage New Life Fellowship, a ministry that takes the gospel to rural Alaska, have been so supportive of me. Don and Edna reminded me to play my violin for Jesus and not to worry about what labels others might put on me.

Also, some friends were willing to speak truth in love to me, like my friend Lindsay Jensen, who came to me in tears and told me that I needed to receive more help from others. "I came to your house to lend you a hand when you were in the middle of a miscarriage, but you wouldn't let me help you. Instead, you wouldn't stop working and serving," she said.

This life-changing exchange helped me realize that I was still serving out of duty and fear of rejection or punishment. Receiving is still hard for me, but I am learning that when I receive from others, I am actually giving something to them as well.

I dedicate this book to those who have gifted me with their stories and allowed me to journey with them, such as Olivia Storz, whom we call our "German daughter," Anna Zymurgy, my cousin Bella Wimberly, Kassandra Davis, Anna Misko, Keziah Whipple, Hope Swanson, and many others. Also, to any of you who are holding in your heart a painful, broken story that you are afraid to share, I remind you that your story matters.

A big thank you to the author of *Pilgrim's Wilderness*, Tom Kizzia, who wrote the foreword to *Out of the Wilderness*. Tom has been a dear friend throughout the entire process.

Outside of my family, it's Tom who best understands the Alaska side of my story. He not only did a ton of research when writing *Pilgrim's Wilderness*, but he spent personal time with our family before I escaped in 2005. I haven't forgotten when my brothers and I brought Tom up the McCarthy Valley on horseback to Hillbilly Heaven, back when he was working for the *Anchorage Daily News*. I remember hoping to relay a secret message to Tom that life wasn't good on the homestead. I believe he did catch on since Papa was infuriated when Tom's newspaper article revealed a dark side of Papa Pilgrim and our family. I appreciate how Tom has shown me respect for who I am and how he encouraged me to write my story.

I must salute my publishing team, The Core Media Group, who showed such great sensitivity and offered me their full editorial support. They deserve great credit for how *Out of the Wilderness* looks.

Finally, there are several other people I want to mention, including Dr. Larry

Severson, who became my professional therapist after I heard him speak on sexual abuse at the Hearts Going Towards Wellness conference in 2013. Each time we met, his words and insights resonated deep within my soul. I knew that there was a lot of stuff inside of me that I needed to face, and I knew I needed help tackling many tough things.

Dr. Severson retired from professional counseling in 2016. Tragically, two months into his retirement, Karen Severson, his wife of forty-five years, was killed in a car accident when a young man ran a stop sign and T-boned their car. This tragedy was all the more devastating for my heart because I had grown to love Karen.

As I witnessed Larry go through so much grief, I watched him put into practice the things he taught me as he took the necessary time to mourn Karen while staying connected with the meaningful relationships in his life. I, along with many others, have been deeply touched by how he came to forgive the man who killed his wife.

Gratefully, after retirement and tragedy, Larry has continued to walk with me. I still call him my counselor, but he corrects me and says, "Elishaba, I am no longer your professional counselor. I am just a friend who continues to walk with you through life."

I don't know where I would be emotionally, mentally, and spiritually without him. Our conversations have helped me unravel the confusion, anger, and frustration I felt from years of sexual abuse at the hands of my father. Larry has had a way of reaching deep into my heart and putting powerful and succinct words to things that I had no words for as well as things that I had no understanding of. He has provided me with many "ah-ha" moments.

Larry also spent time counseling me through each chapter of this book, and I appreciate how he, Mike, and I worked together on the more difficult places of my story. Finally, Larry wrote a beautiful Afterword. Make sure you read it.

In terms of therapy, I also want to thank Doug and Shawnmarie Carpenter with Alaska Marriage and Family Therapy for working with Matthew and me to understand how we respond to each other out of the wounds from our past.

Of course, last but not least, I thank my Father in Heaven for always being there for me even when I was in doubt. My Jesus showed up in the darkest of times and never left me forsaken.

I didn't understand who God was, but I knew He was there and always cried out to Him as I grew up under my father's thumb. Now I know that God is a God of relationship, not a religion of dos and don'ts. He is my shepherd who will be close to my side for the rest of my life, even as I show my scars while praising God for His mercy on me.

# AFTERWORD
## by Dr. Larry Severson

That was quite a story, wasn't it? I can assure you that it wasn't easy for Elishaba to write this book with her collaborator, Mike Yorkey. Like in our counseling times together, she had to dredge up memories and recall conversations from long ago. She did so because she has long desired that her story help and encourage readers who've experienced some type of abuse. The problem of sexual abuse is more widespread than we would like to believe.

The healing and growth in Elishaba's heart have been amazing and transformational. Here are a few takeaways we can grasp from her story:

• **Elishaba was committed to truth.** As I was counseling with her, one of the things that impressed me early on was when she said, "I know that for me to heal, I have to be completely honest, no matter how it makes me look."

Elishaba had and continues to have a heart that wants to see "truth in her innermost being" (Psalm 51:6). That's not easy to do because there is something inside us that wants to see ourselves in a better light than we really are. And we certainly want others to see us as better than we really are. We constantly fight deep exposure.

Throughout my time with Elishaba, I have witnessed her commitment to truth in her innermost being. On many occasions, Mike would try to capture a part of Elishaba's story, but something was off or not quite right. She would gently but firmly correct him. She would say things like, "Well, actually, that's not completely accurate" or "Something's not quite right here." And then, Elishaba would explain things in greater detail. Mike would go back and re-write those sections—sometimes several times—until Elishaba said, "You got it, Mike. That's the way things happened."

Truth goes beyond trying to capture a story accurately. It also includes being honest about the wrongs committed against us. The damage of those wrongs affects every aspect of our being, including the relational, spiritual, psychological, sexual, and physical areas of our lives. All these elements can become a tangled-up mess that's confusing and frustrating to untangle.

It's easier to minimize than to face the truth honestly. We would like to convince ourselves that it wasn't as big of a deal as it really was by saying, "At least it wasn't . . . ." Yet several studies have shown that those who recognize what was done to them was a crime are those who suffer the least amount of emotional and psychological damage.

Furthermore, until you face the extent of the wrongs against you, you will never see the extent to which our responses contribute further damage to our hearts and to the ways that we wrong others.

• **Elishaba invited relationship.** Abuse always happens in the context of relationship, a place where broken trust, shame, powerlessness, and betrayal happen. Paradoxically, the deepest healing always occurs in the context of relationship, a place where trust and safety occur and where you are deeply known and cared for. Elishaba opened her heart in relationship to a few trusted people who walked this journey with her. I am honored to be one of those individuals. As she has grown and changed, she has also opened her arms and lent her ears to hurting individuals and shown them what a safe relationship can look like.

• **Elishaba has shown purpose.** I've witnessed how Elishaba has devoted much time to coming alongside the hurting and wounded. She has always wanted *Out of the Wilderness* to be more than an intriguing book that captures a reader's attention. Her desire is for this book to benefit someone who might have experienced or is experiencing some kind of sexual or physical abuse. Beyond abusive relationships, all of us should seek to understand the unhealthy relational dynamics that show up and impact our relationships. There is room for growth in all of us. *Out of the Wilderness* displays many of those unhealthy relational dynamics.

• **Elishaba has committed to ongoing growth and change.** We all want to think that we are further along than we really are. We love hearing "success stories" that imply that complete healing has occurred. But there is always more to see and face. The apostle Paul recognized this when he said, "My conscience is clear, but that doesn't make me innocent" (1 Corinthians 4:4). Even when he didn't recognize anything amiss within him, Paul knew there was more. He went on to say that the Lord would bring more exposure—down to the very motives of the heart.

As we grow and change, we become a more accurate reflection of what God is like. We are all image-bearers, but we are image-bearers stained with sin that mars the image. As we change and grow, our reflection of Him becomes progressively more accurate. We reflect more accurately what He is like.

In 2 Corinthians 3:18, Paul states that as we see Christ accurately, "we are being transformed into his likeness with ever-increasing glory." Seeing Christ accurately includes seeing ourselves accurately. That's why Scripture places such an emphasis on coming out of darkness and into the light (1 Peter 2), walking in the light (1 John 1), exposing the motives of our hearts (1 Corinthians 4), living by the truth (John 3), and inviting God to search our hearts and show us anything amiss (Psalm 139).

Sadly, we can also choose not to heal and grow. When that happens, the damage in our hearts will continue to show up in our relationships. We can often be totally unaware of the damage that we do to our hearts or the damage we do to others. Our wrongs are what we need forgiveness for, and that is what God has provided for us. But we can't face what we don't see.

When we allow the deeper exposure of our hearts, God meets us with mercy and grace to help us in our time of need (Hebrews 4:16). It is then that we begin to change—not by trying harder or out of a sense of duty or obligation—but rather because we want to. When we see more accurately, we want to love better than we currently do. We don't want to relate in damaging ways. And we are so thankful for the forgiveness that God provides when we face and we own our wrongs.

For those who want more in life, start by following Elishaba's example of seeking truth in your innermost being. Pursue safe relationships with trusted people. Know that you have a significant purpose, no matter what you have experienced. You can grow in loving others well!

There is no greater purpose in life than to heed God's invitation to join with Him in loving others out of gratitude for what He has done for us. Commit yourself to ongoing growth and change. Remember, you are in process. You can continue to grow, but none of us will fully arrive until we see Him face to face. Then "we shall be like him" (1 John 3:2), all of us relating to each other with deep, unfailing love. That sounds like heaven to me!

Yes, there is much to learn in the process. You can easily find numerous books written on sexual abuse, but some take you deeper to the core of your heart than others. This is why I highly recommend *The Wounded Heart* by Dr. Dan Allender, a pioneering teacher, speaker, and writer on the reality of harm, the impact of shame, and the hope of redemption. His organization, the Allender Center, also puts on Healing the Wounded Heart conferences.

Another resource is the book *Mending the Soul* by Dr. Steven Tracy. He founded Mending the Soul Ministries with his wife, Celestia, as a way to equip community and church leaders in responding to those affected by abuse.

Dr. Allender and Dr. Tracy have also prepared companion workbooks to help guide individuals and groups, and they periodically make available seminars and workshops for those who want to attend. There are also many other high-quality resources available locally, nationally, and internationally that provide much-needed information. Ask trusted people and get recommendations.

The most important thing you can do is follow Elishaba's example and begin your personal growth journey. You, and all the people who love you, will benefit.

Love well.

*Dr. Severson has retired as president, clinical director, and counselor with Severson & DePalatis Christian Counseling in Anchorage, Alaska. He held licenses as a Licensed Professional Counselor (LPC) and as a Licensed Marriage and Family Therapist (LMFT).*

Elishaba Doerksen and her counselor, Dr. Larry Severson, met at a Hearts Going Towards Wellness (HGTW) conference in 2013, and she credits him with helping her overcome her painful past.

# ABOUT THE AUTHORS

**Elishaba Doerksen** is the oldest of fifteen children born to ex-hippies Robert and Kurina Hale, otherwise known as Papa Pilgrim and Country Rose.

She grew up in a dilapidated 341-square-foot log cabin in the mountains of New Mexico, isolated from civilization by a fundamentalist father intent on keeping his large family isolated from a godless world. When she was nineteen, her father began molesting her in unimaginable ways as well as hitting, beating, and whipping her—and her siblings—when they were judged by him to be "rebellious."

The horrific sexual and physical abuse continued after the family moved to an isolated valley in the Alaska wilderness. Ever the dutiful daughter, but confused between what she read in the Bible and the reality of her abusive relationship with her father, it wasn't until Elishaba attempted a daring escape on a snowmobile that she was able to free herself from her ruthless and controlling father.

Today, her faith in God and love for Jesus sustains her. She has been married to Matt Doerksen for nearly fifteen years, and together they are raising two children, Esther and Michael. The Doerksens make their home outside of Palmer, Alaska.

Her website is elishaba.com.

**Mike Yorkey**, an experienced author and co-author for thirty years, is Elishaba's collaborator. In the past, he has worked with:
- Ron Archer, an African-American speaker who was sexually abused as a child in *What Belief Can Do*
- Casey Diaz, a Latino gangbanger, in *The Shot Caller*
- ex-NFL wife Cyndy Feasel in *After the Cheering Stops*
- paralyzed Rutgers defensive tackle Eric LeGrand in *Believe: My Faith and the Tackle That Changed My Life*
- Walt Larimore, who shares the heroic story of his father fighting in World War II in *At First Light*

Mike is also the co-author of the best-selling *Every Man's Battle* series and two World War II novels, *The Swiss Courier* and *Chasing Mona Lisa*. His website is mikeyorkey.com.

# ASK ELISHABA TO SPEAK AT YOUR COMMUNITY EVENT OR CHURCH CONFERENCE

Elishaba Doerksen is a gifted communicator who loves sharing her life experiences and helping others overcome horrific events in their lives. She is available to speak at community events, men's and women's weekend conferences as well as seminars for those wounded by abusers, such as Hearts Going Towards Wellness conferences, as well as fund-raising events for charitable causes.

If you would like to contact Elishaba about speaking, call or text Matthew Doerksen at 907-315-1321 or contact her through her website at elishaba.com.